J MALCOLM

INDIA
SURVIVAL
● AT COST ●

A TRAVELLER'S GUIDE

Edi Schwager

LITTLE HILLS PRESS

PANTA RHEI–all is flux, all things change–according to the ancient Greeks. And that's how it is with travel books. Tips and trips which are 'in' this year can be decidedly 'out' a couple of years later (best example: Afghanistan). We do try to keep our books up to date but even so, panta rhei, especially prices.

Edi Schwager

Photographs by Alistair Nicholas
Production by Vantage Graphics
Typeset by Midland Typesetters
Printed in Singapore

© translation, Little Hills Press, 1988
© Regenbogen-Verlag, Zurich, Switzerland

ISBN 0-949773-44-1

Little Hills Press Pty. Ltd.,
Tavistock House,
34 Bromham Road, Bedford MK40 2QD,
United Kingdom

Regent House, 37-43 Alexander St.,
Crows Nest NSW 2065 Australia

All rights reserved. No part of this publication may be reproduced, stored in a retrieval system, or transmitted in any form or by any means, electronic, mechanical, photocopying, recording or otherwise, without the prior permission in writing of the publishers.

DISCLAIMER
Whilst all care has been taken by the publisher and author to ensure that the information is accurate and up to date, the publisher does not take responsibility for the information published herein. The recommendations are those of the Author, and as things get better or worse, places close and others open up some elements in the book may be inaccurate when you get there. Please write and tell us about it so we can update in subsequent editions.

CONTENTS

INTRODUCTION

WHAT YOU HAVE TO KNOW BEFORE THE TRIP

What to take

Passport (ideally valid to the end of the trip); cash, travellers cheques and definitely your vaccination certificate. It is advisable to always carry these things on your person (money belt or leather pouch around your neck). You should know your passport number by heart and it is also advisable to carry a copy of your personal documents in your luggage.

Sleeping bag: Buy a good quality, lightweight and if possible washable sleeping bag which can be converted into a blanket by opening the zippers. In this way you can also sleep well on benches (the train) or in dirty hotels. However, if you only intend to visit the permanently hot southern India (with the exception of some mountain holiday objectives) it's not worth your while taking a sleeping bag at all. A sheet is quite sufficient. An absorbent linen bag is also advisable for use as a lining for synthetic sleeping bags.

Backpack, kit bag or travelling bag?-Many backpackers ask that question. For the traveller with a lot of luggage one of the new waterproof, lightweight backpacks (aluminium frame) is the ideal solution. An ever-increasing number of travellers prefer using a travelling bag to move away from the hippie backpacker image which can become a hassle when crossing borders. Whether you have a travelling bag or a backpack, either should be secured with a closing devise (e.g. a lock) and should if possible contain your home address written in waterproof ink.

Clothes: Jeans are the best, but not if it gets really hot. Make yourself a pair of wide, lightweight trousers or wear Lungi like the locals provided that you don't feel too self-conscious in them. Synthetics can be washed easily, however they are most unhygienic in tropical conditions.

Toiletries are very expensive and of poor quality in India and neighbouring countries. It can be advantageous to take a small supply of sunscreen and hair shampoo in lightweight, unbreakable plastic bottles. For girls: Tampax are available practically everywhere.

Other small but useful travel companions: International drivers' licence, youth hostel pass, pocket knife, plastic bags (unavailable when travelling), alarm clock, transistor radio (the small 1.5V batteries are readily available); people who wear glasses should carry a spare pair or carry the prescription with them. Biros, pocket matches (little known in Asia), disposable lighters and coins or stamps from your home country are suitable as presents or Bakshish.

Money

Carry cash in a money belt and travellers cheques (together with your passport) in a pouch or similar on your body.

Carry the larger amount in travellers cheques, the smaller in cash. Eurocheques can only be cashed at a few banks outside Europe. Credit cards are something for globetrotters with money and won't be accepted in fifth or sixth class hotels anyway. Remember to keep several US$1 notes on you when you only have to change a small amount (at the border, airports, etc.).

Cash

The US dollar is still the most popular. However it is not advisable to take large sums in cash. You're not insured against loss and you'll only find a good black market during your trip if you travel to Nepal. Of course it is illegal to exchange money on the black market in any country, and you run the risk of being cheated. Apart from dollars you can exchange £ and DM at the banks with little trouble. Damaged notes are sometimes rejected. Notes of large denominations are also not readily accepted.

Travellers cheques

Safer than cash since the bank will reimburse you for stolen cheques, however this can entail some trouble (police report, waiting time of several weeks, etc.). Take travellers cheques from an international bank (American Express, First City National), others are not accepted everywhere.

The bank charges 1% of the cheque as bank charges. To make up for that travellers cheques achieve a slightly higher rate of exchange than cash in most Asian countries.

You can buy travellers cheques in US, Australian or Canadian Dollars or English Pounds. Large cheques can be changed into smaller cheques at the appropriate bank and you can obtain ten 100-cheques for one 1000-cheques, etc.

Always write down the cheque numbers and carry this separate from the cheques (e.g. in a money belt). This is most important in the case of theft or other loss.

Money Transfers

These are not possible through Post Offices, only from one bank to another, i.e. from the bank in your home country to its partner bank in Asia where the money order and transferral are best done by telex. This is the quickest way. One would think that one should not have to wait more than two or three days, however, unfortunately the rule is that you have to wait a very long time (sometimes several weeks) with transfers. The transfer will be conducted in local currency. You can obtain hard currencies in cash in some countries, but only at a great loss. You will find further information on money transfers under 'Money' for some other countries.

Earning money while travelling

Due to the high unemployment rate in the relevant countries jobs are practically out of the question. It is also not advisable to deal in precious stones: if you are not an expert you will be sure to get ripped off. You can sell some Western goods at a profit or at least at purchase price. These include cameras, pocket calculators, radios, tape recorders, etc. Cheap goods are the most sought after.

Living Costs

Living costs, of course, depend on your own lifestyle. Middle class backpackers and/or fanatical souvenir hunters usually require double (or more) than do backpackers travelling on a low budget. Overland travellers should calculate approximately US$65 for transport for the route Istanbul–Delhi. In addition approximately $15 per day should be allocated for food and lodging (Iran is the most expensive country). It is no longer worth it to buy Turkish Currency in Western Europe, as previously, because the exchange rate is better in Turkey.

Carry enough money. Don't think that your National Embassy will automatically help you out of a dilemma. You will probably get your return ticket paid for, but only after much trouble. It goes without saying that you have to repay the money after your return.

Health

You do not need to take out a special health and accident insurance for the trip when your existing insurance covers Asian countries, or can be extended for a limited period to cover the duration of your trip. Otherwise take out a limited travel insurance for sickness or accidents. You can combine this with a luggage insurance–enquire at travel agencies because they often have special offers.

Get your teeth checked before the trip.

Vaccinations

At the time of printing no vaccinations are required for the Indian sub-continent or surrounding countries (Turkey, Iran, Pakistan)–unless you arrive from an epidemic area. Since these requirements frequently change, however, take advice from your GP or from a vaccination centre prior to your trip. Whether required or not you should not miss out on the Chol-TAB-vaccination (see below) and vaccination against polio and tetanus. It is advisable to have all your vaccinations entered in the yellow International Vaccination Pass and to carry this with you. This is the only way that you can prove on request that a suddenly required vaccination is current.

Malaria

A Malaria vaccine has been developed by Hoffman-La Roche called Lariam and the effective ingredient is Mefloquin, which is used for therapeutic as well as preventive purposes. A weekly 250mg tablet should protect travellers in Malaria-infected areas from all forms of malaria, and especially against p. falciparum which is resistant to other Malaria treatments.

There is of course a further preventative available in Malaria infested areas: the prevention of being bitten by a malaria mosquito. Popular methods are mosquito nets, insect repellent creams or mosquito coils.

The various vaccinations

Smallpox: Little necessity, since Smallpox has officially been eradicated. This vaccination can lead to fever or worse illnesses and is not without risk.

Polio: Harmless oral vaccination.

Tetanus: Injections without painful side-effects, effective 3 to 4 years.

Typhoid and Paratyphoid: Combined with Cholera injections as Chol-TAB or as oral vaccination with Taboral which offers shorter protection.

Hepatitis: Expensive Gammaglobulin injections profess to offer a certain immunity however effectiveness is debatable–Yellow fever does not occur in Asia.

Establish a vaccination programme with your GP, local hospital or government vaccination centre since not all vaccinations can be carried out at the same time. Start vaccinations at least 4 to 5 weeks prior to departure. Cholera injections can be very painful and can cause fever. Small pox can result in extremely itchy skin infections. Neither are very pleasant when you must commence the trip under their influence. Vaccination regulations can be changed at short notice depending on epidemic conditions.

First-Aid Kit

Don't take too much. Most medication is available in Asian countries and is much cheaper, and prescription free. Apart from that, if you really feel ill, it is much better to visit a doctor. The Embassy physicians usually have the best reputation. Treatment is usually free in the government hospitals in Asia, however you have to pay for medication.

In the following are some helpful hints, but do remember that careless self-medication can be dangerous.

Medication against severe diarrhoea: intestinal disinfectants combined with coal tablets or Lomotil or a small opium pill. Caution: opium guarantees to stop any diarrhoea (paralyses peristalsis of the intestine) but has no therapeutic value (healing property).

Cough: It can be an advantage to take cough preparations since few suitable preparations are available along the way against bad coughs. Sulfonamides against mild infections and fevers–for severe cases Bactrim, but do consult a doctor first: it can, but not necessarily, be the right thing.

Ointment for itchy insect bites (antihistamine cream, etc. Sandosten-Calcium); also useful for sunburn and skin allergies. Such antihistamine preparations are also available in tablet form (e.g. Avril). They can however cause unpleasant delirium-like states in some cases.

Valium and related products have replaced the previously popular barbiturate family not only in Europe but also in Asia. Valium is suitable for sleeping disorders due to cramps. The local medication (such as Calmpose) is cheaper, although the same (inc. Diazem combinations). Marzine or Dramamine are useful against travel sickness or nausea. Use Alcacyl or Treupel (both rarely available in Asia) or Aspirin as pain relievers, against colds, rheumatism or to reduce fever.

Disinfectant solutions (Merfen, Mercurochrome, Iodine). Iodine is also suitable as a water disinfectant, see 'Drinking'.

Pests: Carry insect powder, or better still a spray (e.g. Baygon) against bugs and fleas. Even with massive spray actions you'll have little chance in badly bug-ridden rooms. You can safe-guard yourself against bugs in restaurants by placing a newspaper as a buffer zone between the chair seat and your posterior. It is easier to combat mosquitoes: buy coils or Odomos, an ointment smelling of lemons; both repel mosquitoes.

Intestinal worms: Undergo a 3 day cure with Vormex anti-worm tablets when there is a concrete indication or even only a suspicion.

Oblas or Tiger Balm, the Chinese wonder cures that remedy anything and everything: flu, cold, cough, sore throat, sprains, rheumatism, neuralgia, aching feet, muscle ache, headache, joint aches, sciatica, twisted neck, insect bites; it is also used as a massage aid and bath substance. It is a mixture of camphor, menthol and eucalyptus oils as well as other essential oils.

Further hints for your pocket First Aid Kit: Bandaid strips (Dermaplast), bandages (compressed in small packages), styptic cotton wool, mini-thermometer, vitamin pills (Supradyn), Condys Crystals (see 'Food').

Toilets

You will usually find squat toilets in Asia (you get used to them). It must also be said: Asians do not use toilet paper but wash with hands and water. That is why the squat toilets are equipped with knee-high water taps. We suggest you carry toilet paper with you if you don't wish to change your personal toilet habits.

What to do against diarrhoea

Diarrhoea often accompanied by nausea, vomiting and weakness hits every traveller. What can you do? Wait and drink tea. Have a day when you take it easy, stay in bed and drink only tea (without sugar), take toast and medication. Drink a lot of tea to replace the lost body fluids. Give your stomach and intestinal tract a rest on the second day as well, and eat only dry rice and no fatty or cold foods. The alimentary canal needs to recover.

Don't drink any cold drinks when you have diarrhoea, don't walk around with naked torso and keep the stomach area warm. Daily intake of Yoghurt and vitamins (B) is recommended after the medication to restore gastric flow.

It is better to consult a doctor when the diarrhoea is accompanied by high fever, bleeding bowels, stomach aches and headaches. He will treat you with antibiotics and sulfonamides. This is also the case when diarrhoea does not cease after 4 days.

Snake Bites

More travellers than admit to the fact are worried about snake bites. The chance of you seeing snakes in nature, much less being bitten by one is minimal on this trip.

Important hints against snake bites:
There are two preventative measures: high shoes and long trousers. Walk heavily and poke a stick in front of you or into the shrub. The vibrations deter snakes.
If you do get bitten: Kill the snake for later identification and injection of the appropriate serum.
Wipe bite area and tournique the bitten limb above the bite (towards the heart) to decrease circulation.
If you do not have snake serum: Completely disinfect snake bite area (with Merfen, iodine or alcohol).
Cut into the snake bite with a disinfected or heated knife and make small incisions into the skin at a circumference of some millimetres. Caution: Don't touch aorta! Press blood out to get rid of the poison. Wipe off blood.
It can be dangerous for the helper to suck out the wound; he can poison himself. Only suck with uninjured lips and mucous membrane. Spit out repeatedly.
To burn the wound is senseless and only leaves even greater scars than the incising.
Do not give the wounded person any alcohol or coffee so as not to activate the circulatory system even more.
Visit the next doctor or hospital. Take the dead snake with you–at least its description (size, colour, pattern).
Most important: Keep calm. Tough natures have been known to survive even deadly snake bites. Maybe it was not even a poisonous snake. Or it had bitten prey in the previous two days and the poison fangs were nearly empty.

The greatest danger of snakes is in the early morning, early evening and during monsoon periods.

Scorpion bites are not deadly, but are very painful.

More likely are dog bites–this means the threat of rabies. Immediately see your doctor after dog, monkey or other animal bites.

Further Health Tips

You need more sleep in the tropics. Try and sleep during the midday hours when it is hot and there is nothing much happening.

Your embassy will furnish you with addresses of doctors that speak your language. Do not swim in the ocean with open wounds or injuries. You can get infections from that. Try and avoid handshakes when greeting people (it is unhygienic)–you can get infected with hook worms or other skin diseases if you walk barefoot. If not otherwise stated, take medication after meals. Mission hospitals (United or other Mission Hospitals) are the best. Venereal diseases are more common in Asia than in the UK, North America or Australia.

On your return home get yourself checked for amoebas, worms and other tropical diseases which can take up to a year of incubation time. Do not read too much about salmonella, leprosy, leeches, gastric parasites and the threats of tropical diseases–you'll lose your desire to travel.

Food

You can avoid nearly all stomach and gastric disorders if you are careful in your eating habits. Eat less than at home. Only eat well-done meat. Do not eat ice cream. Only eat fruit which can be peeled (in Asia most fruit can be peeled). Do not eat lettuce or raw vegetables. This all sounds very nice and very theoretical. What are you going to do though, when tomatoes and cucumbers or apricots would provide a welcome change? Place them in boiling water for 30 seconds or wash them in 'pinky water'. 'Pinky water' is water with the addition of a few Condys crystals. When eating in a restaurant or hotel ask for a bowl and immerse the raw vegetables or fruit in this mixture for approx. an hour–they can then be eaten without any regrets. Condys crystals are harmless.

Drinking

The old raised finger warning must be heeded: Do not drink any water! By drinking water you can infect yourself with the following diseases: Diarrhoea, salmonella infections, dysentry, amoebas, typhoid, paratyphoid, hepatitis, cholera, etc. What are you going to do when the waiter persists in stating that the water is boiled? And if you have the valid suspicion that the boiled water has been filled into bottles that were previously only rinsed with tap water? There is only one way out–boil water yourself or make it drinkable by the addition of water disinfectant tablets. Products like Halozone, Hydroclonazone or Globaline are suitable. Make sure you obtain some that are usable after 15-20 minutes, not after 1 hour.

Iodine is also suitable to disinfect water. Add 4 to 8 drops to one litre of water, depending on degree of pollution, stir and wait 15 to 30 minutes. If the water tastes too strongly of chlorine or iodine; add lemon juice.

Water cleansing filters (Katadyn, Filopur) are only good for campers.

You should drink a lot (approx. 2 litres) in the tropics because you perspire heavily. It is unhealthy to drink less in the attempt to perspire less. Drink tea, fruit juices, Coke.

Visas

You need to obtain visas at home. You can also obtain them, in some cases, in the country prior to entry into the next, or sometimes at the border. You will find more detailed information for the relevant country under 'Entry Regulations'.

Photo Taboos

Do not photograph Moslems engaged in prayer. Be cautious with photographing women in Islamic countries, do not photograph military installations (except soldiers when they give you permission), no dams and harbour areas, no bridges and border crossings (in Iran, Pakistan and India) and no airports, railway stations or beggars. Pakistanis and Indians have a paranoid fear of spies and saboteurs. The least and most harmless that can happen to you is that they remove the film from the camera.

Souvenirs

A supermarket is nothing in comparison to the enticement of buying at a bazaar. However, do use this rule in a bazaar:

Haggle!! Give yourself plenty of time. When the Turkish bazaar dealer quotes you 200 Turkish Lira as starting price, offer 70 Lira. He might then drop to 150 Lira. Persist with your 70 Lira. He will give you good arguments for his product. Counter with good stories. You're only a poor student. The piece of jewellery that you wish to buy is for your sick sister. Even if the bazaar dealer does not believe these stories, he will honour them–as enjoyment of your story-telling talent. Meet him little by little. If you can't reduce the first quoted price to half, you'll be paying tourist prices.

Never quote a price first. Never pay the first quoted price as the dealer will not be pleased; he will think that he could have asked much more of this simpleton.

If you are keen on buying real antiques, old artifacts, gems or carpets gain information about these things at home and learn the authenticity tests. Antiques and old artifacts are 'new-antique' to 99%.

Language

English is the one language generally spoken and understood in all of Asia. It is an advantage to know at least 3 words in the local language: Good day, Thank you and Good bye.

Student Pass

Since 1982 only one standardised student pass is valid. This is issued by the International Association of Youth and Student Travel Bureaux (International Student Travel Conference).

There are two types:

Scholar card for students under the age of 20 and apprentices between the age of 16 and 26 who are doing a state-recognised apprenticeship

of at least two years duration
Student card for full-time university students and other students over
the age of 20.

The new cards were created to stop forgers from producing forged
student passes. Let's wait and see how long it takes before these new
cards can be bought as forgeries. Student passes are no longer as
thrilling on Asian trips as they were in the past because the largest
advantage–price reduction for trips–is tied to age limits and not the
student pass.

Climate/Weather

Turkey, Iran, Afghanistan and North-Pakistan have a winter which can
be as cold as in Northern Europe/USA but a much hotter summer.
South Pakistan has a Monsoon climate. Monsoon rains fall between
June and September. October till March is the best season to travel
around the Indian sub-continent as April and May are very hot (40 deg.
C and more).

Insurance

Do check whether your accident and health insurance covers trips to
Asia. Take out a luggage insurance if you take expensive camera
equipment with you. Should you fall ill in Asia, you will initially have
to pay the costs for doctors, medication and hospital (state hospitals
in India, Nepal, Pakistan and Sri Lanka are free). Keep the bills and
then have your insurance re-imburse you upon your return. Always have
a doctor's certificate made out in either English or French. For cases
of theft make a police report and obtain a confirmation.

The most reliable is a combined luggage-accident insurance. Do
inquire at a student travel agency.

Taxis

Taxis are relatively cheap in Asia. Always make sure that the meter
is switched on (unless you already know the price). If the meter does
not work, take another taxi. Do not pay any fees for luggage, night
excess or empty return trips if this has not been agreed upon prior to
the trip. Tips are not usually paid. Give the taxi driver the exact fare
since some have been known to take off with the change.

Tips

Asians are by now used to the fact that young backpackers from
Western countries do not pay tips. However: a small bakshish for the
room boy or the waiter in your favourite restaurant can speed up many
things.

Never give tips to civil servants since that can be misinterpreted as
a bribe. Offer them cigarettes or give them one of the disposable lighters
or a felt pen as a small souvenir.

Long Hair

Long hair does not pose a problem on this trip. Restrictions: you'll have to take into account that you'll be searched more thoroughly than others at the border when you look like a 'possible drug-carrying hippy'.

How to Travel

When to Start?

Cross-country travellers: It is best to start the Pakistan trip in the late summer so that you reach the Indian subcontinent after the monsoon period.

If you start in spring, you will meet the very hot pre-monsoon period in Pakistan, and if you travel for a longer period, end up travelling during the monsoon. The sky is continuously cloudy during the rainy season. Timing also depends on your travelling speed. But no matter what, the trip to or from Asia will fall into some unfortunate weather period unless you have unlimited travel time.

For big money earners: check when a start is favourable for taxation purposes.

For direct fliers: If you decide not to take the overland route and prefer to fly directly to the Indian subcontinent your flight date should lie somewhere during the autumn or winter period. It is boiling hot during the pre-monsoon period and during the monsoon it rains and rains and rains.

Travel alone?

It is quite safe for men to travel on their own. However, it is not advisable for women to travel on their own even if two women travel together. The problem usually solves itself en route. You will meet many other backpackers on your way, be it in the train, in hotels, at the border or while sightseeing. Join a group or form a group of three to five persons yourself. The group will most likely dissolve at the next target because some will want to continue directly while others will want to do some sightseeing.

Orientation

If you have to ask the way, do ask at least two locals. If the answer is the same, it might be correct. If the answers differ, ask a third person. Locals don't like to admit to the fact that they just don't know something. They give you any sort of answer so as not to lose face. They would also consider it as impolite not to be able to give you an answer. Don't show city or road maps to locals–it will only confuse them. They can't read maps anyway. Avoid asking leading questions. Don't, for instance say 'That's the way to the Taj Mahal, isn't it?' Phrase your questions in a neutral manner, as for example 'Which is the correct way to the Taj Mahal, please?'

These rules apply to the whole of Asia. You have to even double check in tourist offices. Never ask local women on the street. This could be severely misconstrued as an unseemly approach. Generally speaking, information gained from Western tourists travelling in the opposite direction is quite reliable. But don't believe everything since exaggeration is a wide-spread human feature.

How to Behave

Respect the religion. In Mohammedan countries: remove your shoes before entering a mosque or private home. Do not address women. Don't portray yourself to be a stuck-up Western person. Always give your partner in conversation the chance to maintain face. Don't eat or offer anything with your left hand as it is considered unclean (it is the hand used for toilet purposes).

Miscellaneous

Girls: if you pack bras and undies at the top of your suitcase, many customs officals will refrain from checking any further. If you are hassled by unwelcome guides or are sick and tired of the routine question 'Where do you come from' just answer 'No English'.

If you are offered food during invitation meals that you find absolutely repulsive, use the excuse that your religion forbids you to eat it. That will always be accepted.

Shorts are not really appreciated; either they look colonial (sub-continent) or unmasculine or plain ridiculous. Girls shouldn't wear shorts in muslim countries anyway–it's just as indecent to show your legs as it is to show your breasts in India. Don't believe all the horror and other stories that you are told by talkative travellers.

TRAVEL ADVICE

Cheap Flights

As a holder of a cheap ticket from the grey market you will of course not find yourself in a Lufthansa or Swissair jet. You also cannot–as with regular IATA tickets–change at random between IATA companies.

Cheap tickets are only valid for a particular airline. They are usually flights offering various levels of service and comfort. The spectrum stretches from 'luxury-grey' to 'red-grey'.

Generally these cheap flights cannot be booked directly with the airline but must be carried out through specialised travel agencies. If you haven't got any experience with cheap tickets, compare the offers that are usually printed in local city newspapers and alternative magazines.

General Hints

Watch out for the following points when buying cheap tickets:
It should be valid for a year.

You should be able to make, or change your flight reservations at any time and without charge during the trip.

As many stop-overs as possible at places of your choice (not the airline's choice).

Check if the hotel accommodation (airline's choice) is included in the price: usually the case with Eastern-bloc airlines.

Give preference to Far-Eastern airlines before you choose Eastern-bloc or Arab lines. Singapore Airlines or Thai International are known for their superb service.

It is far more comfortable to fly in Jumbo jets, DC10s or other large carriers than it is in narrow tubes like the DC8 or on the hard seats of a Russian Iljushin.

Be aware of the fact the flight time can be much longer than for direct flights since you will have to take detours into account (e.g. Aeroflot via Moscow to India).

Departure, transit (with possible change of plane) and arrival times during the night are also a disadvantage,

The more sections you book and buy at the same time (if possible with the same airline) the cheaper the kilometre price.

Travel with three or four persons and work out a rebate!

It is a fallacy that tickets can be bought cheaper on the Indian subcontinent even Bangkok is no longer a haven for cheap tickets.

However, only buy a one-way ticket if your travel plans are not definite. Reasonable tickets are available in all of Asia.

Cheap Flights from Germany/Europe

Don't be confused by the turmoil created by Lufthansa against the cheap-flight companies. Even if one or the other of these companies must relent under government pressure, enough of these airlines remain on the grey market and others will always crop up. You can now send in for a list (for the fee of a stamped envelope) of cheap-flight agencies in Germany (available from German Centre for Globetrotters (GCG), Mittenwalderstr. 7, 1000 Berlin 61).

The soviet Aeroflot line is also cheap from any West-European airport via Moscow to Delhi. Free sightseeing in Moscow is only possible with a visa and Intourist arrangement for over-night stay. Otherwise, you'll fly with a 'direct' connection. Price is approx. 1600 DM (US$1215).

Walter Kamm, globe trotter with experience in 100 countries and founder of the Globetrotter Travel Service has compiled current flight infos for this book. The Globetrotter Travel Service offers comprehensive free advice for travels on own initiative.: in Zurich Rennweg 35, Tel. 01/211 77 80, in Bern Muenzgraben 4, Tel. 031/21 11 21, in Basel Lindenberg 23, Tel. 061/33 22 88 (Switzerland).

The cheap flight rates are always less than half of the official rates. They are commercial flights with normal bookings. Tickets are valid for one year. Stop-overs are stated without additional costs. No age limits, no student pass necessary.

Prices used in this guide should be adjusted upwards. They are meant as guide-lines for budget planning. Enquire current prices in writing or per phone.

Readers' Tips

'I've had some rather unpleasant experiences with Aeroflot. Due to a non-scheduled stop-over in Taschkent (6 hours waiting time) we missed our plane in Moscow. We–approx. 20 persons–were detained for hours in a room at the airport. Our tickets were finally re-routed for the following day and we were accommodated at the airport hotel. We were not allowed to leave this building the whole day. We were all prisoners and a soldier sat guard at the door.

'We could only continue on to Frankfurt on the second day which meant that some passengers had missed important appointments. On arrival in Frankfurt it was discovered that for the majority, items such as cigarettes, souvenirs, cassettes, etc. had been stolen from our luggage. My new suitcase had been damaged during transport. Despite my two claims in writing, Aeroflot only replaced the ripped off security lock.'

'When we flew to Calcutta with Aeroflot, my girlfriend's backpack had disappeared in Moscow. It took weeks for the backpack to finally arrive. We continuously had to urge them to do something about it during this period. They wouldn't have lifted a finger of their own accord. We'll never fly with Aeroflot again.'

'Aeroflot is cheap but often loses the luggage–happened to me twice'

'When the political situation is such that overland travel to India is out, cheap flights from Athens are advisable. I paid approx. DM 475 with Egypt Airlines for the trip Athens-Karachi-Delhi.'

Other readers' tips are included throughout the text.

How to get there from Europe:

Overland to Pakistan

Despite military rule in Turkey, despite near-civil war in Iran, despite inner-political tension in Pakistan–it is still possible. Even if it's no longer as beautiful and varied as it used to be when one could travel through Afghanistan.

Route

Since there is only one border pass between the en route countries, the route is pretty well pre-determined.

There are no longer direct trains from Turkey to Teheran. The bus passes the border at Dogubayazit and continues to Bazargan.

Since the Russians are permanent visitors in Afghanistan you must travel directly to Pakistan from Iran. The southern route goes through

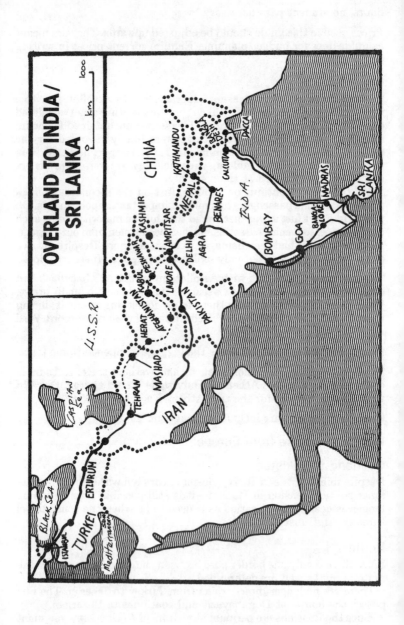

Belutschistan, the border crossing Taftan lies between Zahedan and Quetta and the train only operates on Friday.

Total distance: 10 000 to 11 000 kilometres, depending on starting point.

The largest portion of the costs falls towards the journey from Middle-Europe to Istanbul. Cheap possibilities: Low-rate train tickets (Eurotrain) in the summer months, foreign-worker's bus, hitch-hiking. Further possibilities: cheap flights (charter, foreign workers), hitch-hiking to South-Italy, from there a ferry to Greece, coastal vessel along the Yugoslavian coast.

It becomes cheap from Istanbul onwards.

Duration

Three to four weeks, but you won't get anything out of it and you won't have seen anything. If you add up two weeks each for Turkey, Iran, Pakistan and North-India it already adds up to two months.

You'd best start so that you reach Pakistan after the monsoon period, i.e. September/October. Then the best season starts on tha sub-continent (winter season). It is not advisable to travel through Turkey and Iran during the winter: snow in Anatolia, cold in Iran.

Visas

It is better to obtain visas in your home country, but you can get them en route in principle, always in the country prior for the following country. There are two exceptions:

Transit visa for Bulgaria–obtain at home since it costs three times as much at the border.

Transit visa for Iran–obtain at home (no longer available in Turkey). If you're coming from India, you can get it there (only in Delhi) or in Pakistan (only in Islamabad).

Visa for Afghanistan–currently not available except in rare cases for Kabul, if you get a permit (reporting, busines trip).

No visa required for Pakistan.

Visa for India available in Islamabad–means a detour from the normal route. Therefore better to obtain at home.

Don't forget to take a few passport photos along.

Miscellaneous

Car travellers require a Carnet de passage and third-party insurance. Petrol is cheaper en route then in Western Europe. However, it will still be cheaper doing the trip with the public transport system.

The overland trip is not very comfortable for women since it passes exclusively through Muslim territory from Istanbul to the Indian border.

Since one can't travel through Afghanistan anymore, the overland trip has lost a lot of its attraction. Additionally, the situation has become even more testy in the previously already unpleasant Iran since the fall of the Shah. The overland route can today only be recommended for absolute adventurers and backpackers on a low-key budget.

Fasting Times

The Mohammedan month of fasting (Ramadan or Ramazan) can make travel in Islamic countries unpleasant since even tourists are expected to observe the rules of fasting, not drinking and not smoking from sunrise to sunset during the 29 days of the Ramadan. The whole life in Mohammedan countries slows down, many offices and shops are closed in the afternoon, restaurants are closed during the day-exceptions are not usually made for tourists. It is considered most impolite to eat or drink in public during the day.

TO ISTANBUL

This is the most expensive part of the trip. Even though it is only 20 to 30% of the whole stretch (depending on your place of residence), it takes 60% and more of the total transport costs (calculated on the cheapest basis). It is really advisable to save here.

Bus
Numerous 'foreign worker' buses are available on the stretch from Central Europe to Istanbul. They are often cheaper than the train.

From West Germany:

The German Tourist Association has buses leaving from Dortmund, Bochum, Essen, Duisburg, Düsseldorf, Cologne (220 DM) Bonn, Frankfurt, Wurzburg, Nurenberg, Mannheim, Stuttgart (195 DM), Hamburg, Hannover and Berlin (215 DM). They leave every Tuesday and Saturday from the relevant railway station and a one night stop-over is obligatory in Nis/Yugoslavia (30 DM). You will get 10% discount with a student card. You can book in any DER office and in the offices of the German Touring Association in Munich, Stuttgart, Frankfurt (Am Roemerhof 17), Hanover and Cologne.

Bosfor Turizm, Seidlst. 2, Munich (Tel. 594002) also co-operates with the German Touring Association (see above) and sells tickets for the bus, which leaves each Tuesday or Saturday at 7 p.m. from Munich, Starnberger Station. The trip to Istanbul takes approx. 48 hrs. Costs DM 180,- exclusive 32 DM for the obligatory stay-over in Nis (Yugoslavia).

Each Friday and Sunday there is a direct bus connection from Bosfor Turizm (180 DM) which makes the trip in about 37 hrs. Students are given 10% rebate. Three pieces of luggage are permitted per person (you have to pay 5 DM for the first two pieces and a kingly sum of DM 30 for the third). No en route boarding.

From Switzerland:

The Express-Bus from Egat-Tur to Istanbul leaves Zurich each Saturday at 9.00 a.m. and costs 175 SFr. (return 320 SFr.). The trip takes approx. 44 hrs (no overnight stops). Book with Egat-Tur, Hafnerst. 13, 8005 Zurich (Tel. 44 77 11).

Varan Turzim also leaves from Zurich–Address is Klingenst. 9, Tel. 44 04 77. They leave every Saturday at 8.30 a.m.. Cost 175 SFr. and travel time is also approx. 44 hrs.

From Austria:

Every Tuesday and Friday at 7.15 p.m. with Varan Turizm from Suedbahnhof in Vienna, cost 1000 A Schilling (return 1800 Schilling); travels through to Istanbul without a night stop-over (36-40 hours). Students pay 10% less.

Varan Turzim is also available from Bregenz, Dornbirn, Innsbruck, Graz, Salzburand Linz to Istanbul. Information obtainable from the Head office in Vienna, Tel. 65 65 93

Bosfor Turizm also has buses on the route from Vienna to Istanbul. Information can be obtained from their office in Vienna, Argentinerst. 67, 1040 Vienne, Tel. 65 06 44.

What to take on the bus trip: drinks, some snacks and if possible, Yugoslavian Dinars. The Bulgarian transit visa is cheaper at home than at the border;

Rail
Munich, Main Railway Station starting at 5.34 pm with the Istanbul Express, arrival Istanbul at the second-next day at 11.30 a.m. (local time). Requires seat reservations.
Zurich Main Railway Station starting at 7.00 a.m. with a change in Venice. Leaves Venice 4.55 p.m., arriving in Istanbul two days later at 11.30 a.m.
Zurich Main Railway Station leaving at 8.21 a.m. with a change of trains in Schwarzach (Au). Continue at 8.40 p.m. and arrive in Istanbul at 11.30 a.m. on the second day.
Zurich Main Railway Station at 11.08 a.m., change in Innsbruck and Schwarzach. Leave Schwarzach at 8.40 p.m. and continue as above.
Vienna, Southern Railway Station; leave at 6.55 p.m., arrive in Zagreb at 1.23 a.m, change and continue journey, arriving in Istanbul on the third travel day at 11.30 a.m.

Note: trains are chronically late on the stretch to Istanbul. Tariff for second class to Istanbul (it costs about 50% more in first class and return tickets cost twice as much): from Munich 166.90 DM, sleeper surcharge per night 20 DM, seat reservation per route 3 DM.

From Zurich, via Schwarzach 209.40 SFr., via Venice 192.20 SFr. Sleeper costs 18 Sfr. per night for both routes and a reserved seat for the complete trip to Istanbul costs a total of 6 SFr.

From Vienna: 1274 Schilling, sleeper surcharge per night 140 Schilling, seat reservation 40 Schilling.

Reduced tickets are available for anyone below the age of 26 (approx. 20% but only on certain weekdays). Do enquire with your student travel agency.

Book seat reservations and sleepers earlier in the summer season.

Passport, luggage and ticket checks during the trip are usually uncomplicated, however they often occur in the middle of the night. You've probably just fallen asleep after the customs inspection when you're woken by the border guards for a passport check. A tip for the sleeper car attendant at the beginning of the trip will be very useful since you'll probably be spending two days on the train.

Plane
As always, this is the most expensive travel solution, but the quickest and least complicated. You'll fly cheaper with a student status, but the age limit is usually about 26 years. You might get a rebate of up to 60%.

From England:

Get to Germany, Austria and Switzerland by train, bus or hitchhiking or take Turkish Airlines or BA direct to Istanbul.

From USA:

Plane-The only sensible way-either to a European city like Vienna, Frankfurt or Munich. Check prices with your travel agent, or fly directly to Istanbul. Buy an around the world ticket and continue on after you have seen India, travelling via the Pacific.

   Alternatively you could choose to fly via the Pacific with a number of stopovers-direct to India and return home via Europe.

From Australia and New Zealand:

Air India, Qantas and many other major airlines call at Bombay or Delhi en route for Europe. You can often get a good deal through your travel agent or an STA Office.

   New Zealanders would have to fly direct to Singapore, or to Sydney, Melbourne or Brisbane to get a connecting flight to India.

Hitchhiking

It is quite possible to travel as a hitchhiker to Istanbul-and permitted everywhere (however not on the Freeways). Do reckon with three days to Istanbul.

   Good countries for hitchhiking are: West Germany, Belgium, the Netherlands and Austria. France, Switzerland and Spain are not as good. Italy, Greece and Yugoslavia are definitely debatable.

Don't think that you can hitchhike free-of-charge. There is practically no private transport from Pakistan onwards. Truck drivers earn 'pocket money' by taking passengers. Europeans either don't have to pay anything or three times as much. Haggle the price at the beginning of the journey but don't pay until you've arrived at your destination otherwise you'll run the risk of being dumped along the way. It is best to hitchhike as a twosome.

Dont use the thumb upwards sign in Asia, but wave vertically with the open hand.

Warning about the X-ray equipment at the Yugoslav-Bulgarian border: it is guaranteed to destroy films! Always remove film if they want to X-ray your luggage.

Car Travellers

Examples of distance to Istanbul: 2410 km from Zurich, 1980 km from Munich, 2390 km from Frankfurt, 1670 km from Vienna, 2860 from Amsterdam.

The route will take you across 'Europe's greatest death stretch', through the bottle neck Austria and the insufficiently safe Autoput in Yugoslavia. Roads improve somewhat in Bulgaria. Hopefully you have acquired your transit visa at home.

There are duty-free shops on both sides of the Bulgarian-Turkish border where they sell Western cigarettes and alcohol. Both are scarce and expensive goods in Turkey. You may import 2 bottles of hard liquor and 400 cigarettes into Turkey. Customs checks by the Turkish border guards are usually pretty strict.

Route Variations

Of course you need not choose the shortest, fastest and cheapest route via Belgrade and Sophia to Istanbul as described in this book. There are countless variations available. You could, for instance, first travel to Athens, get to know Greece and then continue to Turkey. You can however also fly from Athens to Delhi for approx. 13400 Drachma (= approx A$363, no student rebate) and not worry about continuing overland. Another possibility: with the train to Ancona or Brindisi (Italy), and then with the ferry to Patras in Greece. This is doubtlessly a lovely variation on the theme with a 30 hour boat trip. Prices vary from 90 to 110 DM (A$68-A$83) according to season (for the cheapest seats). Students can reduce this by about A$15.

TURKEY

The first Asian country on this trip. If you take it accurately, approx 3% of the 780.000 sq.km. is still left in Europe. 99% of the population in Turkey is Mohommedan. The country was ruled by a sultan until the year 1922. In 1923, Mustafa Kemal, called Ataturk (Father of all Turks) proclaimed the republic. He reduced the Islamic influence, introduced the Latin alphabet and enforced compulsory school attendance and forbade the women to wear the veil.

Turkey is an agricultural country (fruit, cotton, tobacco) with little industry. The military takes a strong position, having claimed power in 1980 and declared to return the country to a democratic-parliamentary rule.

GENERAL

ENTRY REGULATIONS

Visa not necessary (passport is sufficient), no vaccinations required for residents of West-Europe, Australia, New Zealand, Canada, U.K. or U.S.A. You can stay for three months. You can import 400 cigarettes, 2 litres of hard liquor and 250 grams of coffee which is in particularly short supply in Turkey. Western cigarettes (e.g. Marlboro) and spirits (whisky) are very sought after.

MONEY

Unit of currency is the Turkish Lira (in Turkish: Turk Lirasi), abbreviated to TL. One Turkish Lira is divided into 100 Kurus (phonetically: Kurusch), abbreviated Krs.

The rates for hard currencies fluctuate nearly daily due to this high inflation rate. Same rate for cash and cheques. The exchange rates are as follows:

1 US Dollar = 84 TL
1 Can$ = 68 TL
1 A$ = 61 TL
1 NZ$ = 50 TL
1 £   = 140 TL

Apart from the 5 TL notes you will find 5 TL coins, which can easily be mistaken for the 2 1/2 TL coins in size, feel and weight, but which are fairly rare. You can officially take 1000 TL notes with you, but no one asks any questions and you do not have to declare your foreign currency.

Money transfers from home are paid in TL by the bank, and you will only lose a few TL for charges. You can however, also request–provided that your required currency is not sold out–cash in Western currency, but at a great loss (more than 10%). You must also adhere to the one fact that is valid for the whole Indian trip: you can't turn your travellers cheques into cash, e.g, obtain a 10 dollar note for a 10 dollar cheque. Keep change dockets since you'll need them when changing TL back to hard currency. This is not possible at every bank.

HOTELS
Prices are often stated per bed (mainly in East Turkey). 15% service and 10% tax charges are usually only added in expensive hotels. Central heating costs 35 TL extra per day during the winter.

OPENING TIMES
Government offices: 8.30 a.m.-12.30 p.m. and 1.30-5.30 p.m., closed Saturday and Sunday.
Banks: 8.30 a.m.-12.00 noon and 1.30-5.00 p.m., closed Saturday and Sunday.
Shops: 9.00 a.m.-1.00 p.m. and 2.00-7.00 p.m. Not all shops close for lunch, others are open longer in the evenings. Stores are closed on Sunday with the exception of fruit shops and cafes.

Siesta is held in places along the Mediterranean coastline during the hot summer months. Everything, including government offices, close.

Sunday is the general public holiday.

DRUGS
As in many other drug manufacturing countries, (Opium is produced under state control in Turkey and Hashish planted illegally), the drug laws are very strict. Even with small amounts, you can expect imprisonment of several months if you can't buy freedom with a big bakshish. In Istanbul and apparently very pronounced in The Pudding Shop, police agents provocateurs are rather active and trap tourists to cash in on premiums. No big help can be expected from the Embassies. Conditions in Turkish prisons are really bad. The film 'Midnight Express' gives a very good impression of the situation.

MOSQUES
In tourist frequented areas you can enter mosques and take photographs of them. Remember to remove your shoes before entering them. Girls: cover bare shoulders and low necklines. Short skirts and shorts are despised. You can even take photos inside mosques, as long as you don't do it during prayer times.

LANGUAGE
Some words in Turkish, which has borrowed many words from French (kuafor) and other languages (Sandvic, Oksijen).

c = dsch, c = sch, i without the dot is silent, similar to a German O with diarsa, s with a cédille is a strong sch, j = a soft, voicy sch. The strange g with the accent on it is mute, i.e. Cagaloglu = Dschaalolu. In brackets: pronunciation and hints for understanding.

Good day . . . . merhabe
Mr. (form of address) . . . . Bay
Yes . . . . evet
No . . . . hayir
no, not, nothing . . . . yok
eat (verb) . . . . yemek
tea . . . . çai
water . . . . su
bread . . . . ekmek
eggs . . . . yumurta
please . . . . lüften
Thank you . . . . tesekkür ederim (teschekür)
very nice . . . . cok guzel (tschok güsäl)
that's fine, enough, finish, stop . . . . tamam
here . . . . burada (burda)
now . . . . simdi (schimdi)
yesterday . . . . dün
today . . . . bugün
tomorrow . . . . yarin (yaren)
time (2 o'clock) . . . . saat (saat iki)
2 hours . . . . iki saat
money . . . . para
how much (is it?) . . . . bu kaça (katscha)

CAR TRAVELLERS

No Carnet de Passage (customs pass) required only third party insurance (can be obtained at the border upon entry) if you do not possess a green card (European insurance slip for cars). Petrol prices per litre:

Super . . . . 72.20 TL
Standard . . . . 65.60 TL
Diesel . . . . 46.90 TL

Only use super-if you love your motor. Be cautious of the following: stones on the road, pot holes, sheep herds, bike riders, agricultural vehicles, oncoming buses and trucks (which usually drive in idle when coming down hill). Road works are generally never marked.

Avoid night trips. It is quite rare that Turkish drivers switch off the high-beam, provided that the lights work at all.

200 metres prior to reaching the Topkapi (old Istanbul city gate) on the E5, you will find an office of the Touring and Automobile Club of Turkey on the right hand side. Opened daily approx. from 8.30 a.m.-8.00 p.m., Tel. 21 01 52.

CAMPERS

The best of Istanbul's camping spots are 15 to 20 kilometres outside of the city. When approaching Istanbul leave the E5 and turn right onto the coastal road where the camping places are along the Marmara Sea: Florya, Yesilkoy, Atakoy. Very crowded and noisy during peak season.

The best know camping places in Turkey are the ones belonging to the Mocamp-Kervansaray-Chain (linked to BP stations). The Kartaltepe Kervansaray Mocamp is some kilometres ahead of the entry to Istanbul along the E5 (close to Yesilkoy airport).

Refer also to Istanbul/'Camper'.

'The camping places of the Mocamp Kervansaray chain are not always the best but surely the most expensive. The cheaper and nicer camping places are probably not next to the main road, but you will have more peace. I recommend: discover a little bit on your own'. (Markus Zimmermann, Zurich).

MAIL

Some postal charges to Europe:

Post cards . . . . 20 TL
Letter (up to 20 g) . . . . 30 TL
1 kg Seamail parcel . . . . 180 TL
1 kg airmail parcel . . . . 680 TL

Postcards and letters are sent by airmail and take about 5 days to Central Europe. Parcels must be taken unsealed to the post office, as the customs check takes place there.

WEATHER/SEASON

Mediterranean climate at the coasts (hot summers, mild winters), continental climate in the centre of Anatolia (hot summers, icy winters).

Istanbul has an extraordinarily severe winter (with snow) from October until April and even in summer it's rather cool in the evenings.

The best travel time is between May and September, Black Sea coast only in summer.

TIME

Local time–GMT + 2 hours (summer); GMT + 3 hours (winter).

MISCELLANEOUS

In a Tourist Office, request the brochure 'Turkey' in English, and the 'Turkey Road Map' with city maps of Istanbul, Ankara and Izmir on the rear side–both publications are available free of charge.

The Turks may, without exaggeration be counted amongst the most hospitable people in the world. If you're looking for contact with the people, you'll never be alone in Turkey, even as a sole traveller.

No tips are expected from tourists in simple restaurants.

Ramazan (Ramadan) is the Islamic month of fasting. In this period, even tourists are expected to refrain from smoking, eating or drinking alcohol in the period from sunrise to sunset. In East Turkey, Ramadan is adhered to particularly faithfully, not so however in Istanbul or the other tourist centres.

Some more words in Turkish -

Friend	arkadas (arkadasch)
House	evi
Waiter	garson
Switzerland	Isviçre
(Sweden	Isveç)
Germany	Almany
Austria	Avusturia
Australia	Avustralya
Good bye	Allaha ismarladik (esmarladek)
Reply greeting	Güle gule

Turkish Numbers

1	bir
2	iki
3	üç (ütsch)
4	dört
5	bes (besch)
6	alti (alte)
7	yedi
8	sekiz
9	dokuz
10	on
11	onbir
12	oniki
20	yirmi
21	yirmi bir
30	otuz (otus)
40	kirk (krk)
50	elli
60	altmis (altmesch)
70	yetmis (yetmesch)
80	seksen
90	doksan
100	yüz (yüs)
200	iki yüz
1000	bin

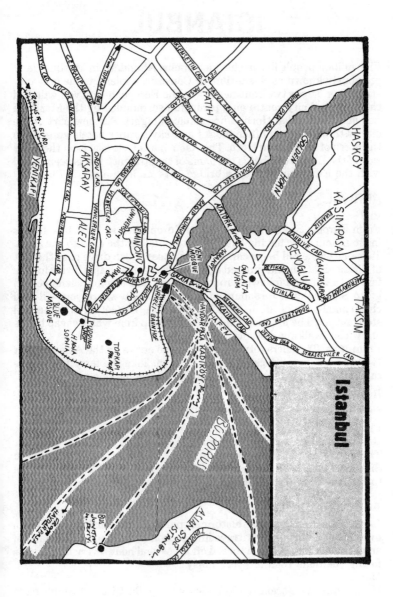

ISTANBUL

Five million people live in this metropolis. Abundant in Mosques (and previously known as Byzantium or Constantinople) it is the only city stretching across two continents. On the European side you will find the historical city centre on a peninsula surrounded by the Marmara Sea and the Golden Horn (a horn-shaped bight). The new part of the city with its modern office blocks and sky-scraper hotels spreads to the north of the Golden Horn. The Asian part of the city is on the other side of the Bosporus (that is the name of the straight). It has been linked with the European side by a bridge 1074 m. long since 1973.

ARRIVAL
Rail
From Europe: Sirkeci Station on the European side. Next bus stop is in Eminonu; after having left the station, follow the road to the right. Take one of the red-beige car or trolley buses which drive past the exit of Sirkeci Station and proceed up towards the mountains. Price for the fare is 15 TL. The following route numbers (not a comprehensive list) go to Sultanahmet (pronounced Sultanachmed), where you will find cheap hotels: 30, 32, 35, 35A, 44, 86, 91A, 92A, T4. Get off at the second stop and you'll be in front of the Pudding Shop from which cheap hotels are within walking distance.
From Asia: Travellers returning to Europe arrive on the Asian side at Haydarpasa (pronounced -pascha) Station. Take the ferry from there to Eminonu and the bus to Sultanahmed (connections see above).

Bus or Boat
Enquire about buses to Sultanahmet at each point of arrival.

Plane
Bus route 96 leaves Yesilkoy airport approx. every hour to Yenikapi. The fare is 15 TL. The airport bus (50 TL) drives to the terminal in Sishane. Leave both buses in Aksaray and take one of the many buses to Sultanahmed (fare is again 15 TL and another 4 to 5 stops).

ACCOMMODATION
Large selection in the historical part, Sultanahmed, but often overcrowded during peak travelling season of summer. Great lack of single rooms. The water is turned off for several hours every day. Rooms facing the main road are very noisy.
Hotels
Hotel Gungor, adjacent to the Pudding Shop. Tel. 26 23 19. Single room 300 TL, double room 500 TL, triple room 600 TL, 4-bed room 800 TL.
Hotel Yoruk (previously Hotel Yeni Topkapi), Incilicavus Sokak 35,

behind the Pudding Shop. Tel. 27 64 76. single room 400 TL, double room 600 TL. Partly furnished with a bathroom and view to the Golden Horn.

Hotel Akin, Incilicavus Sokak 12, Tel. 23 37 90. Double room 350 TL, triple room 480 TL, Dormitory 75 TL. Not very clean.

Sultan Tourist Hotel. Yerebatan Caddesi 35. Tel. 20 76 76. Double room 600 TL, triple room 900 TL, 4-bed room 1000 TL. Dormitory (attic location) 150 TL. Water available all day (tank). Clean, good manager, recommended.

Hotel Ayasofya, Yerebatan Cad. 33 Tel. 22 71 26. Single room 325 TL, double room 520 TL, triple room 600 TL.

Hotel Buhara, Alay Kosku Cad. 15. Tel. 25 76 04. Single room 350 TL (with bath 450 TL), double room 550 TL (with bath 700 TL), triple room 600 TL.

Yucelt Hostel (pronounced Yudschel), Caferiye Sokak 6 (below the Ayasofya), Tel. 22 47 90. Double room (with bath) 500 TL, bed in 6 or 8-bed dormitory 200 TL, quiet location, cafeteria garden (breakfast 80 TL). Youth hostel atmosphere. Hot water available between 8.00 a.m. and 12 noon.

Hotel Buyukayasofya, Caferiye Sokak 5, Tl. 22 29 81, Single room 300 TL, double with bath 600 TL, triple room 900 TL and 4-bed room 1000 TL.

Tourist Student Hostel, close to Hotel Liz. Only dormitory (4-5 bed rooms) for 100 TL. Not very clean.

Hotel Liz, Kucukayasofya Caddesi 42, (behind the Hippodrome), Tel. 26 64 99. Single room with bath 600 TL, double room with bath 650 TL, triple room 750 TL.

International Istanbul Youth Hostel (Turkish: Eskisehir Degrenci Yurdu), Cerrahpasa (-pascha) Caddesi 63, Aksaray, Tel. 21 24 55. 250 TL per bed in a 4-bed dormitory with youth hostel pass. It's 50 TL more without the pass. Approx. 300 beds, warm showers; bus routes, for example, 32, 35, 35A and 84 from Sultanahmed. Opened for tourists only during the main season (beginning of July till end of September).

Middle-class Hotels
Small selection in Sultanahmed: Hotel Holiday, Divanyolu Cad. 52 (same street as the Pudding Shop), Tel. 22 42 81. Not much more expensive than some of the cheap hotels, will however meet expectations put to a middle-class hotel. Single room 600 TL, double room 800 TL, triple room 1200 TL; with bath. Without bath: single room 500 TL, double room 700 TL.

Luxury Hotels
Divan, Cumhuriyet Cad. 2, Sisli, Tel. 146 40 21; Etap Marmara, Taksim Meydani, Taksim, Tel. 144 88 50; Hilton, Cumhuriyet Cad, Harbiye, Tel. 146 70 50; Sheraton, Taksim Parki, Taksim, Tel. 148 90 00.

Sleeping under the Stars
It is not advisable to spend nights in Istanbul's parks and the police

will often not permit it anyway.

'You're no longer permitted to sleep at the Hippodrome. A hitchhiker who spent a night there was thrown into jail for two days by the police. You can however sleep in the parks close by, but this is quite dangerous'

Campers

It is not at all advisable to spend the night in your own car away from a camping place since bands of professional car thieves are at work. Istanbul's camping places are at the outskirts of the city, some along the sea coast (see Turkey/'Camper').

'I had parked my VW camping bus at the Hippodrome, intending to spend the night there. The next day I was shocked to find that the complete roof rack including the luggage had been dismantled and stolen. All four wheels had been removed and had disappeared, the car was placed on four blocks. And that despite the fact that we had spent the night inside the car!'

FOOD

There are numerous restaurants in the direction of the hills, leading away from the Pudding Shop. The Pirlanta for example is good and cheap.

The double storey Pudding Shop (you can only eat downstairs) which is actually named Lale Restaurant, is not very good, but quite expensive. Yoghurt and Pudding are 30 TL each, Coke 30 TL, soup 60 TL and tea 25 TL (!). It's self-serve.

What to eat? Sis Kebab (schischkebab) of course. This is sometimes also called Saslik (schaschlik): grilled pieces of meat on a skewer, usually lamb. Two variations on the theme are Bursa Kebab (with tomato sauce and butter) and Doner Kebab, from the vertical spit.

Further meat dishes are Kofte (mince meat balls) and chicken (Tavuk). Fish (Balik) is usually very expensive. The cheapest fish can be bought at the swimming fish-friers next to Galata Bridge (approx. 60 TL) where the ferries berth.

Typical and tasty fare are Dolma, vegetables such as pepperoni or egg plant filled with rice and/or mince meat.

As a dessert: Yoghurt (pronounced Yo-urt), since the Turks invented it. Melons are also popular and there are two varieties: the sweet honey dew (Kavun) and the water melons (Karpuz). Or that wonderful 'Turkish Delight' called Baklava, a nut pastry. Usually the food is on show in the restaurant and if not, go to the kitchen and point to what you'd like.

DRINKS

What can you drink? Tap water is heavily chlorinated but you can drink it if necessary. It doesn't taste nice. Water in transparent bottles (usually labelled 'Maden Suyu') is free of charge in the long range buses and costs about 5-10 TL in Restaurants. It is not boiled, but does come from clean springs.

Try Raki as an aperitif. It is a brandy distilled with anise and turns white when mixed with water. Ayran is a salted mild drink which tastes unusual with the first sip but is very thirst quenching. Turkish Tuborg is definitely the best beer (half-litre bottles 40-50 TL). Wine is called Sarab (Scharab) and is cheap. Try Dikmen (175 TL for the 0.75 l bottle).

You should try the Turkish coffee, served in small cups and with water to sip in between, obtained in Yugoslavia. The reason: coffee is nearly unavailable in Turkey due to the import ban.

Tea is now called Tschai–this is valid for the rest of Asia (further to the East it is often only pronounced as Tsach).

MONEY

Opening times for banks: Monday-Friday 8.30 a.m.-12.00 noon and 1.30-5.00 p.m. Outside of these hours you can change money at change counters in the Sirkeci Station (left platform, 9.00 a.m.-7.00 p.m., seven days a week), passenger quay (maritime station, Karakoy, 8.00 a.m.-7.00 p.m., weekends 9.00 a.m.-7.00 p.m.) and with Turk Express, the representative of American Express in the Hilton Hotel (open daily from 8.30 a.m.-8.00 p.m.).

The official exchange rates are available everywhere (published daily in the Turkish Daily News).

There is no longer a black market for foreign currency. Whoever offers you a better rate of exchange on the street than the banks do must be a swindler who wants to get hold of your money with a nasty trick.

TRANSPORT

City Buses

The cheapest means of transport are the red and beige city car and trolley buses. 15 TL is a standard price. You must pay again after each change of bus. You will usually (at least most of the time) catch the right bus with a map of the city, some imagination and the aid of the always helpful Turks, particularly since the travel routes are always written up on the bus.

The T1 and T4 buses take an ideal ring route. T1 starts from Sultanahmet to the station/GPO, Eminonu, Galata Bridge, Karakoy, Dolmabahce, Taksim (centre of the new city), Galatasaray, Sishane, Ataturk Bridge, Unkapi, Aquaduct, Aksaray, Hurriyet Meydani then back to Sultanahmet. Line T4 drives this in the opposite direcion.

Common Taxi

Dolmus (pronounced Dolmusch) is a taxi for several people (common taxi) which usually drives fixed routes at fixed prices and tries to squeeze in as many passengers as possible (dolmus = full). Minimum fare is 20 TL. Sultanahmet to Taksim (far side of the Golden Horn) costs approx 40 TL.

The system works as follows when you're not close to a Dolmus station: place yourself at the side of the road and call your destination to the passing Dolmus (recognisable by the yellow and black chequered strip), usually the city suburb. If the Dolmus is going in that direction, he'll stop and if not, he'll just continue on his way. Sometimes the Dolmus chauffeurs call their destination out of the window. This system is widely spread in Turkey and even in Iranian cities.

Be careful: if you board a Dolmus as the first passenger you'll risk that the driver will not take on further passengers and burden you with the total taxi fare. So, insist on Dolmus when boarding one or only board when there are already other local passengers inside.

Taxi
Taxis usually look the same as Dolmus. Minimum fare is however 200 TL. Definitely agree on the price before starting the trip.

Ferries
Ferries from Eminonu or Karakoy to the Asian part of the city cost 10 TL (for further information see 'Sightseeing').

POST OFFICE/TELEPHONE

The GPO (Buyuk Postane) is close to the Sirkeci Station: up the street in the direction of Ankara Caddesi, second road to the right. Open daily (even on Sunday) from 8.00 a.m.-8.00 p.m. Only a few counters are open on Sunday and in the evening. The Poste Restante counter (for held mail) is open daily from 8.30 a.m.-5.30 p.m. You must pay 10 TL for each letter collected from the Poste Restante counter; passport must be shown.

There is a small post office in the Sultanahmet quarter in the court house (Adliye Saray). Letters sent c/o American Express will be forwarded to the representative, i.e. Turk Express, entry arcade of the Hilton Hotel, north of Taksim and open daily from 8.30 a.m.-8.00 p.m. Tel. 40 44 84. Bus No. 44, 63, 68, 74, C2, G2 from Sultanahmed.

'When you want to phone home, you walk about 100 metres to the right of the GPO until you reach a small building. Book your call, pay a deposit and then wait for about an hour.'

TURKISH in 5 minutes

The Turkish language uses quite a number of foreign words which usually stem from the French. The French word is written phonetically. This selection serves not only as an amusement but can be quite helpful in getting to know the system of circumscription.

akvarium	aquarium
Bagaj (bagage)	luggage
banliyö (banlieue)	boundary/precinct (city skirts)
bilet (billet)	ticket
büfe (buffet)	buffet
buji (bougie)	spark plug
bulvar (boulevard)	boulevard

feribot (ferryboat)	ferryboat
filtreli sigara	filter cigarette
garson (garçon)	waiter
gazete (gazette)	newspaper
istasyon (station)	station (train)
kamyon (camion)	truck
kartpostal (carte postal)	post card
kondüktör (conducteur)	conductor
kuaför (coiffeur)	hair dresser
kulüp (club)	club
kuset (couchette)	bed in sleeper
manastir (monastère)	monastry
müze (musée)	museum
oksijen (oygène)	oxygen
otobüs (autobus)	bus
pasaport (passeport)	passport
plaj (plage)	beach
sandviç	sandwich
sinema (cinéma)	cinema
taksi	taxi
tren (train)	train
tuvalet (toilette)	WC/toilet
vagon (waggon)	carriage (train)
vapur (vapeur)	(steam) boat
viski	whisky

CONSULATES (Embassies are in Ankara):

US Consulate, Mesrutiyet Cad. 104, Tel. 14 36 200-09
UK Consulate, Tepebasi, Mesrutiyet Cad. 34, Tel. 14 47 540
Bulgarian Consulate and Iranian Consulate–see Istanbul/'Continuation of the Journey'.

SIGHTSEEING

The three great sights worth seeing–Serail Topkapi, Hagia Sophia and the Blue Mosque–are placed next to each other. You can see them clearly when returning on the ferry from Harem, Haydarpasa, Kadikoy or the Prince Islands.

Topkapi Serail
(Turkish: Topkapi Serayi Muzesi). This is the palace complex of Turkish sultans with treasure chamber, harem and spectacular views. Open 9.30 a.m.-5.00 p.m. Closed Tuesday. Entrance fee is 160 TL on weekdays and 80 TL on Saturday/Sunday; the harem is 50 TL extra. Fee for cameras (on all days) is 150 TL (possible to smuggle them in).

Hagia Sophia
(Turkish: Aya Sofya Muzesi or Ayasofya, with emphasis on the second y). This is the one thousand five hundred-year-old byzantine basilica,

built as the largest church in the world, converted to a mosque in 1453 (added minarettes) and turned into a museum in 1953. Open 9.30 a.m.-5.00 p.m., closed Monday. Entrance fee is 70 TL on weekdays, 35 TL on Saturday/Sunday. Gallery (not inspiring) an extra 30 TL (weekend 15 TL). Camera charges are a stiff 150 TL (it's dark inside, so take a flash).

Blue Mosque

(Turkish: Sultan Ahmet Camii). Built in 1616 as architectural answer to the Hagia Sophia, it is the only mosque with six minarettes and considered the climax of Turkish mosque construction. It is open during the day, no entrance fee charged (unsuitable on Friday during mid-day prayer), no charges for minding shoes which have to be removed, a small tip is expected from tourists (approx. 2.50 TL). There is a Sound and Light show (free) for approx. 800 persons from May until September. The story of the mosque is told with light and sound effects. Show starts is at 9.15 p.m. from the 1st of May until the 15th August and a little earlier for the remainder of the show time.

Ferries

The numerous ferries criss-crossing the Bosporus are a sightseeing attraction all on their own–and one of the cheapest. Ferry connections are marked on many city maps (with dashed lines). Starting point is Eminonu/Sirkeci (e.g. for Kadikoy or the Prince Islands) or Karakoy (for Kadikoy and Haydarpasa) on the other side of the Galata Bridge. A ferry timetable can be purchased at some ticket offices for 50 TL.

'Ferries leave for the Prince Islands from a point close to Sirkeci Station. The islands are one huge park with numerous villas belonging to rich Turks. Marvellous, but the hotels are very expensive.'

'You can charter a boat at the Galata Bridge when you're in a group and drive around for 2-3 hours. Price is DM 2 each with 5 people and if you like, you can steer the boat yourself.'

City Buses

One of the cheapest sightseeing trips (15 TL) with city bus line T1 or T4, ring route (see 'Transport').

FURTHER PLACES OF INTEREST

Subterranean Cistern along the Yerebatan Caddesi, close to the Pudding Shop. Entrance fee 10 TL, cameras 20 TL. Opening times 9.00 a.m.-5.00 p.m. Closed Tuesday.

Gulhane Park (below Serail Topkapi) with mini-zoo, where you can look at cows(!) and dogs(!)–amongst other animals–behind bars. Entrance fee 5 TL.

Istanbul's red-light district: across the Galata bridge.

Galata Tower (61 metres high). Follow the Yuksek Kaldirim Caddesi (see above); you will find the tower on the left hand side a few minutes walking distance from the red-light district. You'll get a wonderful view of Istanbul but the lift costs 100 TL. Opening times 9.00 a.m.-2.00 a.m. (same opening times as the exclusive nightclub housed in the tower).

SHOPPING

The covered, labyrinthian Bazaar (Kapali Carsi) open 8.00 a.m.-approx. 7.00 p.m., except Sunday, is one great temptation with its 4000 shops. But don't buy any souvenirs yet, they'll get cheaper. Cruise and Hilton Tourists have jacked the prices up by paying the first quoted prices.

Leather goods are the best that Istanbul has to offer. A leather jacket costs about US$100.

Groceries: Migros self-serve stores along the Swiss design (and rather expensive for Turkish conditions) in the Ordu Caddesi, (direction of Aksaray), close to the entrance to the spice bazaar, which in itself is a shopper's paradise. There is a further Migros store close to the Bulgarian Consulate.

Buy medication (usually prescription free) here or wait till Pakistan. Medication is very expensive in Iran.

TURKISH BATHS

You shower, sweat, are scrubbed, washed, rubbed down, massaged and take a rest. Five minutes on foot from the Pudding Shop you'll find the Cagaloglu Hamami (hamam = bath), Yerebatan Caddesi 34, 300 years old, clad in grey marble one of the many (and not the cheapest) Turkish baths in Istanbul. A bath with soap, hair wash, bath towels and full massage costs 750 TL, self service 190 TL. No time limit, daily from 7.00 a.m.-10.00 p.m. For girls (entrance on the right hand side) only from 8.00 a.m.-7.00 p.m.

MISCELLANEOUS

Free-of-charge city maps, leaflets and maps of Turkey are usually only available in the Tourist Information Offices which are run by the Turkish Ministry for Tourism, as for example in Sultanahmet, Tel. 22 49 03, open daily from 9.00 a.m.-9.00 p.m. Furthermore in the entrance arcades of the Hilton Hotel, Tel. 40 63 00, opened 8.30 a.m.-6.30 p.m. Saturday/Sunday 9.00 a.m.-5.00 p.m.; on Yesilkoy airport, Tel. 73 73 99, in the harbour office at Karakoy, Tel. 49 57 76, daily from 9.00 a.m.-6.00 p.m. and not to be forgotten the Central Office at the Mesrutiyet Caddesi 57 in Galatasaray (Tel. 45 86 19).

The other Tourist Offices are run by the Istanbul city council and rarely have maps available, e.g. the office in Sirkeci Station (daily 8.00 a.m.-7.00 p.m.) and on Haydarpasa Station (Tel. 36 04 75).

Car travellers: The Touring and Automobile Club of Turkey has its main office in Sisli (Schischli) Meydani in the new city section, Tel. 46 70 90. It also has an information centre for car travellers.

Student passes: When you show a student pass and pay approx. US$3 you will get a genuine international student pass (ISIC) from 7Tur. Halaskargazi Caddesi 219/3 in the Osmanbey suburb, opened daily, except Sunday from 9.30 a.m.-6.00 p.m. (Tel. 47 35 66). Cenctur is directly in Sultanahmet, on Yerebatan Caddesi. It is also a travel agency which will furnish you with an ISIC pass at the above mentioned conditions. The International Student pass is also available from Intra Turzim (Tel. 40 38 91)

You have a right to the following concessions with the International Student Identity Card (ISIC):

10% (return ticket 25%) on the Turkish railroad system (TCDD)
10% on Turkish domestic flights with Turkish Airlines (THY) and 60% for European and certain other flights, provided you are not older than 28 years
10% (domestic) and 15% (international) with ships belonging to the Turkish Maritime Lines.

Foreign newspapers and magazines are available along the same street as the Pudding Shop. The only English language Turkish daily newspaper is the Daily News (25 TL, no edition on Sundays), available only in Istanbul, Izmir and Ankara. The Turkish monthly Magazine Middle East Review costs 100 TL.

There is a large bookshop on the Istiklal Caddesi 481, Beyoglu (new section).

Beaches are along the Marmara Sea, on the Bosporus and the Black Sea.

The easiest way to reach Florya: Suburban train from Sirkeci Station (Banliyo) leaves every 15 minutes in the direction of Halkali, price 10 TL, 40 minutes ride. Further travel means are by bus F (Taksim–Florya) from Aksaray (15 TL). There are two beaches at the Florya stop: Gunes and Belediye Plaj; sand beach, crowded on Sundays with rather dirty water.

There are beaches on the Prince Islands: three are open for choice on Buyukada (largest island). Take the boat from the dock near Sirkeci Station.

Swimming in the Bosporus is not very popular due to the currents and cold water. Kilyos on the Black Sea, has a fine sandy beach.

'Kilyos Beach is expensive and crowded. It's better to walk 2-3 km to the left and you'll find an empty and cheap beach.'

'You take the Bosporus ferry or the bus to Sariyer; from there take a Dolmus to Kilyos. Very nice beach, however exorbitant entrance prices. Whoever wants to bath free of charge will follow the road, that leads west and runs parallel to the beach (approx. 500 to 1000 m), then go the 150 m down to the beach.'

'Still missing vaccinations can be obtained at the vaccination centre in Karakoy on the other side of the Galata bridge (Sahil Saglik Merkezi) for a small fee.'

FURTHER TRAVEL

Rail

10% discount for single and 25% for return trips with TDCC (Turkish Railway) with the ISIC card. All trains in the direction of Asia leave from Haydarpasa Station (pronounced -pascha), abbr. to H. Pasa on the Asian side. Take the ferry to Haydarpasa from Karakoy on the northern end of the Galata Bridge. It leaves every 15 to 30 mins. between 6.00 a.m. and 11.30 p.m. The trip takes 20 minutes. Trains to Europe can be taken from Sirkeci Station, within walking distance from Sultanahmet.

Sleepers are very expensive, e.g. the Anadolu Ekspresi to Ankara costs about 1490 TL in a sleeper (for comparison: seat in first class 290 TL). Couchette only available in first class at a uniform rate of 40 TL.

Bus

Excellent connections with comfortable Mercedes buses to all parts of Turkey from the large bus station at the Topkapi. Turkish buses carry water (in bottles) and perfume(!) on board. The international buses also leave from Topkapi and go, e.g. to Baghdad, Tehran and Europe. Take one of the numerous city buses (e.g. 96) from Sultanahmet uphill to Topkapi. Buses leaving in the Eastern direction are also available from Harem bus station (Asian side); these are often somewhat cheaper, since the toll fee for the Bosporus bridge does not apply. Take the car ferry from Sirkeci Station to Harem.

You can buy bus tickets in the travel bureau in Sultanahmet or directly at the bus station Topkapi.

Plane

Despite great reductions (mainly on European flights) Istanbul is not a cheap flight centre. Enquire at the travel bureau in Sultanahmet or directly with the airlines about the cheapest offers.

In the following we list the discount regulations:

Student discount (ISIC card required): Turkish Arilines (THY) gives a 10% rebate on domestic flights. Student discount for Europe flights (and to Cairo, Tel Aviv, Baghdad, Amman) is approx. 60% for all airlines. However, you must not be older than 28 years (with some airlines only 26 years).

Youth fare: approx 25% youth discount is available on flights to the East (e.g. Tehran, Karachi). Youth Fare is also handled differently by the various airlines. The upper limit is usually 26 years (rarely 28).

Family discount: Turkish Airlines (THY) offers partners and their children, if they travel together, 10% family discount on Turkish domestic flights. The children must not be older than 23 years.

Car Stop

Is always possible. Short stretches in private cars, but you'll have to rely on trucks for longer trips. It is quite possible to travel from Istanbul to Tehran in a truck. Turks and drivers from Balkan states do ask for money now and then. Always settle price prior to starting the trip.

Ask for 'Truckstop' at Londra Camping (on the way to the airport). Take bus 89 or B from Sultanahmet.

From Istanbul to Europe

Rail

All trains to Europe leave from Sirkeci Station. It costs 3000 TL (2nd class) to Athens, departure 7.40 p.m. The train with car or connection to Zurich (2nd class 9700 TL), Vienna (2nd class 8000 TL) and Munich (8900 TL) leaves at 7.00 p.m. No student discount.

Bus

The cheapest version is to use one of the 'foreign-worker' buses to Munich or other cities. However, these buses are not very reliable. If there are not enough passengers, they will not run. You're also not insured. Tickets can be obtained at the travel bureau in Sultanahment or at Topkapi bus station.

Daily cheap buses at record prices of 3000 TL (can be haggled down to 2000 TL in some cases) to Munich. The fly in the ointment with these cheap buses: none of them have the necessary papers for entry into Germany. You'll have to take the train from Salzburg where–at least that's the standard regulation–the costs for the train are paid by the bus company. Tickets available in Sultanahmet. There are no such complications when taking the established companies, such as Bosfor Turizm and Varan Turizm. Their buses to Munich cost around 7000 TL; tickets are available in their city offices or at Topkapi bus station. There is a twice-weekly bus to Zurich for 6000 TL (e.g. with Varan Turizm). Buy tickets directly at Topkapi as they're not available in Sultanahmet.

Plane

This is the most expensive way even with student discount. Price example: Istanbul-Zurich costs approx US$485 and with student discount still US$200.

Ship

No tips for backpackers doing it on the cheap. The trip to Venice costs, e.g. between US$150 and US$450. Even with a student discount of 15%, it's still expensive.

Further information can be obtained from the Turkish Maritime Lines at the quay in Karakoy, Tel. 44 02 07, open Monday to Friday from 8.00 a.m.-5.00 p.m.

Car Travellers

You'll find further information and route details under 'From Europe to Istanbul'.

From Istanbul to Ankara

Rail

Five or six express trains daily which travel the 578 km to Ankara in

7 1/2 to 11 hours-plus delays.

Bogazici Ekspresi, departure 9.20 a.m. arrival in Ankara 6.30 p.m. only 1st class, 290 TL.

Mavi Tren, departure 1.30 p.m. or 10.50 p.m., arrival 9.00 p.m. (6.15 a.m.), 1st class 435 TL, 2nd class 210 TL, (only night version of Mavi Tren with 2nd class carriage).

Anadolu Ekspresi, departure 9.05 p.m. approx. 11 hrs. travel time, 1st class 290 TL, no second class.

Dogu Ekspresi, departure 11.40 p.m., arrival next morning at 9.06 a.m., first class 290 TL, 2nd class 210.

Toros Ekspresi, departure 10.35 a.m., travel time approx. 11 hrs. same prices as for Dogu Ekspresi, only on Tuesday, Thursday and Sunday and the latter two days as far as Baghdad.

Bus

Bus tickets for the 446 km to Ankara cost 450 TL (e.g. Gazanfer Bilge) to 660 TL. From Topkapi or Harem bus station (Asian side).

Plane

Daily several flights with Turk Hava Yollari (THY) to Ankara Esenboga, 3250 TL (approx. US$30), 45 minutes flight.

From Istanbul to Erzurum (East Turkey)

Rail

Direct from Istanbul To Erzurum (1728 km) daily with Dogu Expresi from H. Pasa station, departure 11.40 p.m., planned arrival in Erzurum on the morning of the second day at 9.32 a.m. Prices: 1st class 730 TL, (with couchette 770 TL), 2nd class 520 TL.

The Yolcu Tren (passenger train) is cheaper (440 TL to 620 TL). Very slow, at least 52 hours travelling time, not recommended.

Bus

Buses for the 1337 km to Erzurum cost 1300 TL, approx. 24 hrs. trip. You don't necessarily have to buy the ticket ahead, one or the other bus company always makes the trip.

Ship and Bus

A nice alternative. The 'Ege' leaves every Tuesday at 10.00 a.m. (the 'M/V Izmir' in January/February) from Denizyollari/Turkish Maritime Lines through the Bosporus and the Black Sea to Trabazon. Arrival there on Thursday at 1.00 p.m. From there with the bus to Erzurum.

Prices: between 500 TL (deck class) and 8500 TL (luxury class); 10% discount for student. Meals are not included in the lower classes (tourist class C, D, E and Deck).

Tickets available from Denizcilik Bankasi TAO/Turkish Maritime Bank Inc., Karakoy, on the right hand side when you cross Galata Bridge.

'Take the deck class, the sleeping rooms in the hull are dirty anyway. Also take provisions (and cigarettes). The food on the ship is expensive and poor quality. You can always buy provisions at the stops in between.'

Car
A nice alternative is to take the route via the coastal resort Izmir, Konya (city of the dancing dervishes) to Nevsehir (see Ankara/'Trip to moon landscape of Goreme'), then east to Erzurum.

Plane
Only with change-over in Ankara. Tickets for Istanbul-Ankara-Erzurum cost 5000 TL, daily connections. For details see 'From Istanbul to Ankara'/'Plane' and 'From Ankara to Erzurum'/'Plane'.

Directly to Iran and India
Visa for Iran
No tourist visas are currently being issued in Istanbul or Ankara. However, the situation can change, so we'll publish the address for the Iranian Consulate in Istanbul: Consulate of Iran, Turkogaci Caddesi, (crossing Yerebatan/Ankara Caddesi, 10 minutes on foot from the Pudding Shop) Tel. 28 50 53,. Open 9.00 a.m.-1.00 p.m. and 2.00 p.m.-4.00 p.m., except Saturday and Sunday.

Visa for India
In Turkey only available in Ankara.

Train
The direct train to Tehran, the Vangolu Ekspresi, was discontinued after the fall of the Shah. It is however possible, that the connection will be re-established.

Time table departure in Istanbul/Haydarpassa each Wednesday at 9.15 p.m. Arrival in Tehran Saturday at 10.25 p.m. (several hours delay are the norm). The stretch totals 2990 track kilometres and 52 miles on the Van Sea Ferry. If you're travelling 2nd class with a student discount, it would mean the cheapest (but not the most comfortable) way of getting from Istanbul to Tehran. No sleeping bunks in the 2nd class.

Bus
If there are sufficient passengers, a direct bus leaves daily for Tehran. Enquire at the travel offices in Sultanahmet or Topkapi bus station. Price: 3000 TL. Consider about 3 days for the trip, which is approx. 2550 km. Do check, whether the bus travels directly or whether you must pay for over-night hotel stops as well.

Plane
It's US$362 to Tehran and still approx US$273 with Youth Fare. There is no direct flight from Istanbul to India, only to Karachi (Pakistan) which is approx. US$580 Youth Fare.

Bus
There is a direct overland connection Istanbul-India with the occasional

bus. Enquire at the travel bureau in Sultanahmet. There is a bus to Delhi approx. twice a month for approx. US$110. Enquire precisely whether the bus is a direct connection or whether you have to change to another connection (which often doesn't arrive) along the way.

'Be careful with Magic Bus! This rip-off company is only after your money, it is rare that one of their buses arrives at the destination.'

ANKARA

2.2 Million inhabitants, 848m above sea level, Capital.

ARRIVAL

Train and Bus

Railway station and bus terminal (Otogar) are only 500 metres apart. When you want to reach the cheap hotels, take a city bus (15 TL uniform price, as in Istanbul) or a Dolmus (25 TL and possibly another 10 TL for luggage) to Itfayie Meydani (direction of Ulus). Minimum fare for taxis is 150 TL which is just enough to take you to the cheap hotels. Very often you'll be charged another 50 TL for your luggage. Double fare is charged from midnight till 6 a.m.

Plane

The THY bus costs 50 TL from Esenboga airport to the terminal at Ataturk Bulvari in the city suburb of Kizilay. You might be able to get off at Itfayie Meydani.

ACCOMMODATION

Hotels

The cheap hotel area is at the Itfayie Meydanie, a small square opposite the entrance to the Genclik Park. Reckon with about 250 TL per bed. The Anadolu Hotel or the Otel Uecler can be recommended.

Middle-class Hotels

Gul Palas Oteli, Bayandir Sokak 15, Tel. 18 21 87. Single room 900 TL, with bath 1200 TL; double room 1500 TL, with bath 1750 TL. Located within walking distance of the THY Terminal.

EMBASSIES

All embassies mentioned below are closed on Saturday and Sunday.
Australia: 83 Nenehatun Caddesi, Gazi Osman Pasa, Tel. 39 27 50-51.
New Zealand: No representative in Turkey. Embassies in Athens or Rome attend.
United Kingdom: Sehit Ersan Cad. 46/A, Cankaya, Tel. 27 43 10.
Canada: Nenehatun Cad. 75, Gaziosmanpasa, Tel. 27 58 03.
United States: Ataturk Bulvan 110, Tel. 26 54 70.

SIGHTSEEING

Citadel (Kale or Hisar) from Ulus through Hisarpaki Caddesi, then up the steps; view onto Ankara (in particular on the poor suburbs close by); ancient, picturesque houses within the fort walls.

Hittite museum, close to the citadel, opened 9.00 a.m.-6.00 p.m. (midday closed from 12.30–1.30), closed Monday. Entrance fee 20 TL, Saturday/Sunday 10 TL.

Ataturk Mausoleum, small mausoleum with personal artifacts of Ataturk.

MISCELLANEOUS

Tourist Office, Gazi Mustafa Kemal Bulvari 33, Tel. 29 29 30, open 8.30 a.m. to 8.00 p.m., Saturday/Sunday 9.00 a.m. to 5.00 p.m.

Turkish Airlines (THY) Office, Ataturk Bulvari, Zafer Meydani, Tel 18 92 11, open daily from 7.00 a.m. to 9.00 p.m. Departure point for airport bus (50 TL)

Good bookshop in Ataturk Bulvari 137/A. German, French and English newspapers from the previous day as well as magazines.

GPO is in Ulus. Each letter collected from the Poste Restante counter (held mail) costs 10 TL. The parcel post office (PTT Paket Merkezi) is a little below the GPO. Parcels (50–75 TL) are available there. You can also get your parcels sewn up there (40-60TL).

Tip for 'friends of high-proof goods': Whoever wants to have a drink before reaching the 'dry' Iran and the nearly dry Pakistan is well served in Hulya Sarap, a cellar pub at the crossing of Kosova Sokak/Azat Sokak (cheap hotels area). However no beer, only hard liquor.

A SIDE TRIP TO THE MOON LANDSCAPE OF GOREME

Goreme, 300 km south-east of Ankara is the centre of an extensive moon landscape, full of calcium cones, earth pyramids and stone needles (ghost chimneys) which have arisen from a volcanic tuff layer by erosion. Some early Christian minorities carved multi-story cave churches, monasteries (with byzantine frescoes) and dwellings from the soft rock pyramids.

ARRIVAL

By bus from Ankara (or Erzurum) in Kayseri, Nevsehir or Urgup. With the train in Kayseri.

ACCOMMODATION

The cheap hotels are along the Istanbul Caddesi in Kayseri (e.g the Zumrut Palas, approx. 230 TL per bed). There is no trouble finding hotels in the villages of Nevsehir and Urgup.

Camping
One of the many camping places: Hotel Pinar (Urgup), 100 TL per peson. 7 km out of Urgup, at the turn off to Goreme is the Paris Motel (Camping 175 TL per person). Another 500 metres further on in the direction of Goreme is the Kaya Mocamp and just before Nevsehir the Mocamp Goreme.

SIGHTSEEING

Rent a Dolmus if you want to see the whole area (Ortahisar, Goreme, Zelve, Avanos, Moon valley, Uchisar); daily rate (up to 10 persons) is 5000 TL (500 TL per person). It is even more expensive by taxi.

The cheapest version, if you're doing the sightseeing trip on your own: work out a route first-the Tourist Office will give you advice. Then use Dolmus, bus, hitchhike adn/or go on foot.

Some Dolmus rates: Urgup to Nevsehir 60 TL; Nevsehir to Avanos 50 TL, to Avcilar 40 TL. Dolmus do run, if they're full, but you have to take longer waiting times into account.

'One parking lot, one exchange and one post office counter-and of course the cave churches, that's Goreme. Can be reached from Nevsehir with Dolmus, leave at the Motel Paris in Urgup and walk the remaining kilometre. The short walk is worthwhile as you'll encounter wonderful stone pyramids. You have to pay an entrance fee for the cave churches: 50 TL, cameras 150 TL, open 8.00 a.m. to 7.00 p.m.'.

MISCELLANEOUS

The tourist offices in Urgup and Nevsehir are open daily. You can obtain city maps and locality maps.

The 3916 metre high extinct volcano with the small glacier near Kayseri is the Erciyes Dagi.

'The last christians were driven out in 1920. Unfortunately, almost all of the wall paintings in the cave churches fell subject to the non-reproduction laws of the Islamic conquerors. The testimonials of Christian culture were scratched out vehemently. However, one very important Christian quality survived in this area until now: the art of producing a good wine. We stocked up our supplies in a 'Serap Fabrikasi', which translated would mean vineyard.'

Further travel from Kayseri

Rail

Two connections daily with the Dogu Ekspresi to Erzurum at 5.50 p.m. and 2.36 a.m. The Dogu Ekspresi to Istanbul leaves at 2.03 a.m. or 10.42 a.m.

Bus:

Daily more than 20 buses to Ankara, costs 300 TL; buses to Erzurum 850 TL; daily direct connections to Istanbul. Some of these buses go via Nevsehir (150 TL).

Dolmus:

Dolmus to Urgup leave from the main square where the cheap hotels are. Fare-200 TL.

From Urgup

Bus:
The Lale Association drives to Ankara for 250 TL and to Istanbul for 450 TL (5 p.m.).

FURTHER TRAVEL/GENERAL

Visa
Any visas still required are available at the embassies in Ankara; all closed Saturday/Sunday.
Iranian Embassy: Tahran Caddesi 10. Tel. 27 43 20, opened 9 a.m. to 12 noon and 2 p.m. to 5 p.m.
Afghanistan Embassy: Cinnah Caddesi 88, Tel. 27 76 98, open 9 a.m. to 2 p.m. There is hardly any chance of obtaining a visa.

From Ankara to Erzurum

Rail
Daily 9.30 a.m. and 6.55 p.m. express train connection. 1st class 510 TL (with sleeping bunk 550 TL), 2nd class 360 TL. 1150 track kilometres, scheduled arrival 9.32 a.m. on the next day (Dogu Ekspresi) or 5.10 p.m., i.e. a minimum of 10 to 12 hours travel.

Bus
Fare is 900 to 1050 TL depending on the company, tickets and departure from the bus terminal Ankara, 15 to 18 hours travel, 891 km.

Plane
One flight daily, 3000 TL, bus from THY Terminal to Esenboga airport, bus fare 50 TL, 1 hour flight.

Car
The 891 km long stretch is not completely asphalt-layered. There is a stretch missing between Sivas and Erzincan (pass road). Snow chains are advisable in the winter. It is a lovely trip along the young Euphrates before you reach Erzurum.

From Ankara to Istanbul

Transit visa for Bulgaria/return travellers
The Bulgarian Embassy (Turkish = Bulgaristan) is on the Ataturk Bulvari 120, close to the German Embassy. Open daily from 10.00 a.m. to 12.00 noon with the exception of Saturday/Sunday. Return travellers stopping over in Ankara should obtain the transit visa here (850 TL) since it only takes a few minutes. The Bulgarion consulate is far out from the normal hustle and bustle in Istanbul.

Connections
Direct to Istanbul with bus, train or plane. Fares and detailed information can be found under 'From Istanbul to Ankara'.

ERZURUM

195,000 inhabitants, 1950 metres above sea level. Politically an unstable area (Armenia) with more military personnel than other Turkish cities.

ARRIVAL

Bus

If you do not arrive in front of the Ararat Travel office, take city bus No. 2 (10 TL) from Otogar (bus station); this stops in the proximity of Hotel Tahran. Taxi costs about 120 TL.

Rail

Go on foot to the Ararat Travel Office.

Plane

Airport bus for 30 TL to the THY Terminal in the city centre. From there on foot (it's downhill) or by taxi.

ACCOMMODATION

The buses to Tehran start in the morning between 5.00 a.m. and 7.00 a.m. in front of the Ararat Travel Office, Kazim Karabekir Caddesi 29B, Tel. 1 20 13. You should be there at least half an hour before departure. It is best to spend the night in one of the hotels in close proximity. Nuraniye, next to the Ararat Travel Office, single room 120 TL, double room 200 TL, triple room 240 TL, shower (if it has any water for a change), 20 TL extra and in winter 35 TL extra per person for heating. Hotel Tahran, a little further uphill, also has rooms with bath, double room 180 TL.

MISCELLANEOUS

The very helpful Tourist Office is located on the Cemal Gursel Caddesi, Tel. 1 91 27, open daily 8.00 a.m.-5.30 p.m.

FURTHER TRAVEL/GENERAL

Bus tickets

Tickets for long range buses are usually available at the Otogar (bus station) or from the Ararat Turizm Transport (Ararat Travel Office). The fare to Tabriz is 1500 TL, to Tehran 2000 TL and to Istanbul (usually from bus station) 1300 TL with the Ararat Travel Office. Be careful when buying tickets to Zahedan (Pakistani border) or to Munich: you usually have to change buses in Tehran or Istanbul, but you are never told about this. You lose time (waiting for connecting buses from the same company) and usually money as well. The ticket Erzurum to Munich (with changeover in Istanbul) costs 9000 TL from the Ararat Travel Office. You can however do the trip for only 4300 TL if you buy a ticket to Istanbul (1300 TL) and then take one of the numerous cheap buses to Munich for 3000 TL (see also 'From Istanbul to Europe'/'Bus').

From Erzurum to Ankara and Istanbul

Rail

There are two alternatives daily with the Dogu Ekspresi: 11.05 a.m. from Erzurum, only to Ankara, arrival the next day at 9.56 a.m; second express train 6.50 p.m. from Erzurum, arrival in Ankara on the next day at 7.21 p.m., continues to Istanbul, arrival on the third day at 5.02 a.m. Do calculate several hours of delay.

Bus

The bus to Istanbul costs 1300 TL.

Ship

The costs are 450 TL with the bus from Otogar to Trabon. The ship leaves every Friday at 2.00 p.m. to Istanbul; depending on class you'll pay between 500 TL and 8500 TL.

Side trips

The sight-seeing trip to the moon landscape of Goreme is very rewarding; The bus to Kayseri costs 850 TL. The trip takes approx. 13 hours; there are two connections per train on the Dogu Ekspresi with daily departures at 11.05 a.m. and 6.50 p.m., arrival the next day at Kayseri at 2.03 a.m. and 10.43 a.m respectively (detail information for Goreme can be found under 'Ankara').

From Erzurum to Iran

Rail

This is only possible via Russia. From Erzurum by train (1st class 110 TL, 2nd classss 80 TL) or bus (300 TL) to Kars; about 230 km trip. The border train from Kars via Akyaka to the Russian Leninakan apparently only runs on Tuesday. Then continue by train via Erewan, Dschulfa (Russian-Iranian border) to Tabriz and Tehran.

Bus

Early morning departure from the Ararat Turizm Travel Office. Buses are possibly unheated in winter, 5 to 8 hour trip. The trip can also be made (possibly somewhat cheaper) with local buses or the Dolmus.

Car

The shortest route (320 km) is across the 2500 m high Tahir pass. It is not recommended, since it is a very poor road. The new road, which circumvents the Tahir pass is under construction. Until this is completed, use the Military road (No. 40) which turns off left to Korasan. This stretch is 66 km longer but in good condition. Further advantage: less truck traffic since only Turkish trucks are allowed to use this route. It passes close to the Russian border and along the footland of the Ararat.

**TURKEY-IRAN
BORDER**

East Turkey has a bad name amongst campers. You will always hear of drivers that have been molested by children throwing stones at the cars, but seldom of muggings/robberies.

Don't refill your tank, Iranian petrol is cheaper. The first station is just behind the border. The border crossing is often blocked by trucks.

'A Carnet de Passage is required in Iran. If you don't have one you must take an official government guide who will accompany you to the Pakistani border. Expensive and depending on your haggling talent, anything up to US$800 will be charged. It is however possible to join other campers who are also without a Carnet de Passage, drive in a convoy and share the costs of the guide.'

'You can see an imitation of Noah's Ark on Mount Ararat. When coming from the direction of Igdir, a badly sign-posted path turns off to the left approx. 3 to 4 km before you reach Dogubayazit. You follow this path for about 8 km until you reach Noah's Ark. You will also find a cheap place for campers there.'

'Apart from Mount Ararat, the castle ruin of Ishak Pascha Kale with the mosque, about 5 km from Dogubayazit is worth seeing. It costs about 400 TL by taxi.'

BORDER-from Turkey to Iran

The Turkish-Iranian border station with Mt. Ararat, a 5165 m high, extinct volcano in the background is open from 7.30 a.m. to 7.30 p.m. (Turkish time). There is hardly any luggage control on the Turkish side. You can buy cigarettes and whisky in the duty free shop and there is no quantity limitation when departing for Iran ('unlimited for departing passengers'). The Iranian laws however prohibit the import of alcohol (total prohibition) and only cigarettes are permitted. Buy Winston. You can sell them for about thrice the cost in Tehran.–Careful: be warned of smuggling, it is too dangerous.

You have to fill in the disembarkation note on the Iranian side and declare all your money (cheques and cash). The total amount is stamped into your passport so that they can check whether you've been changing on the black market by comparing the available money and the official change receipts upon your departure (foreign currency control is handled casually when departing). You can of course declare less than you carry when entering Iran, but don't get caught.

If you haven't been able to get rid of your last TL on the Turkish side, you can exchange them on the Iranian side in the Bank of Melli at a bad rate. Luggage control (not very strict but there are further checks on the route to Tehran) is conducted approx. 2 km further along the route in the direction of Tabriz. There is a further bank in that customs building.

You'll have to allot about 2 hours for the border formalities.

Local time in Iran GMT + 2 1/2 hours (summer) GMT + 3 1/2 hours (winter)–Time difference to Turkey: 30 minutes.

RETURN TRAVELLERS

There is a very strict luggage control on the Iranian side of the common border. They are less strict with foreign currency checks, with which blackmarket dealers are supposed to be exposed. There is only a fleeting comparison between the sum stamped in the passport and the money available and official exchange receipts. No difficulties to be expected in standard cases.

The Turkish border is usually without problems. Fill in the form, no questions are asked about money. You can sell whisky and cigarettes from the Turkish duty free shop for double the amount in Erzurum. You can import 2 cartons of cigarettes (buy Marlboro) and 2 litres of spirits into Turkey. You can spend the time until everyone has bought their duty free goods by paying a visit to the Tourist Office. Reckon with about 5 hours in all for the border crossing.

Hitchhikers
Pass the border on foot if possible and then turn to hitchhiking. Truck

drivers are very reluctant to pick up strange passengers just in front of the border.

From the Border to Tabriz and Tehran

Bus
It is a 4 to 5 hour trip with the bus for the 273 km to Tabriz; a further 620 km to Tehran. If the driver permits a night stop-over (usually they just drive through) cheap hotels are available along Ferdowsi Ave.

Car
Good roads, good sign-posting throughout the whole of Iran. Numerous army check posts.

All petrol stations indicate the location of the next closest 'Filling Station', e.g. 'Next FS 21 km'.

A supermodern, toll-payable freeway starts in Qazvin, approx. 150 km before you reach Tehran.

ARABIC NUMBER

We tend to call our European numbers Arabic Numerals (to distinguish them from Roman numerals) but the real Arabic numerals do look quite different. Practically only Arabic numbers are used in Iran. They are read–as opposed to the writing–from left to right. We'll list the Farsi pronunciation of the numerals (with handwritten variations):

1	yek
2	do
3	se
4	chahr
5	panj (pansch)
6	shish
7	haaft
8	haasht
9	no
10	da
20	beest (biist)
30	chi
40	chehel (tschel)
50	panja
60	shaast
70	haftad
80	hashtad
90	novad
100	saad
200	dosaad

It is advisable to learn the numerals. They remain the same, with minor deviations from now until Nepal.

IRAN (PERSIA)

After the downfall of Shah Reza Pahlevi in 1979, Iran was declared an islamic republic. It is a desert country with 36 million inhabitants, most of them Shiite Moslems.

Economy: primary export is crude oil, others include cotton and carpets. Iran is the most expensive country of the trip and can be crossed in three or four days.

ENTRY REGULATIONS

You should really apply for visas in your home country before embarking on a trip through Iran.

The current situation is -

Australian and New Zealand citizens can obtain a visa within 3 weeks of applying for the duration of their stay.

For UK, Canadian and US citizens an application at the moment takes 2 months to process, and the granting of a visa is unlikely. There is no Canadian (represented by Denmark) or US embassy (burnt down).

MONEY

The unit of currency is the Rial.

The official rates of exchange are:

1 US$	=	71 Rials (Rls)
1 A$	=	48 Rls
1 Can$	=	53 Rls
1 NZ$	=	43 Rls
£1	=	120 Rls

The same rates apply for cash and travellers cheques.

Locally, 10 Rls are known as 1 Tuman, 20 Rls are 2 Tuman etc. If travelling by taxi, make sure whether the fare is in Rials or Tumans. There are 1, 2, 5, 10, 20 and 50 Rial coins. Some coins are inscribed only in Farsi. It is often very difficult to exchange foreign currency, especially cheques, at banks. American Express is especially disliked. There is no longer an American Express office in Iran.

Money can be transferred to Iran in approximately 24 hours but is not recommended as the entire amount must be withdrawn in Rials. And the exchange rate is not good.

Suggestion: go to the first floor of the Bank Markasi (Central Bank of Iran) in Ferdowsi Avenue. After a certain amount of agro you will be able to get a letter enabling you to withdraw a portion of the transfer, minus a 2% fee, in the desired foreign currency. The details will be entered in your passport for checking purposes (blackmarket deals).

Blackmarket: lucrative but illegal, of course. Currency infringements are dealt with harshly. Change your money with the hotel manager, not in the bazaar, even if his rate isn't quite so good.

OPENING TIMES
(in cities)

Shops: 8.30 a.m. to 12.00 noon, 1.00 p.m. to approx. 8.00 p.m.
Banks: 8.00 a.m. to 1.00 p.m., Thursday to 12.00 noon.
Offices: 7.00 a.m. (usually 7.30 in winter) to 2.30 p.m., Thursday to 1.30 p.m. Friday is generally a day off and everything is closed.

GENERAL TIPS

Avoid demonstrations and mosques. Take a minimum of photographs. Don't wear shorts (girls or boys). Be careful but not paranoid.

Car Drivers
The best roads of the trip. Information on driving conditions from the Touring and Automobile Club of Iran, 37 Varzesh Ave, Tehran, Tel.:31 90 40/41. An emergency service (same number) operates up to 50 km from Tehran. Petrol pumps usually have only Arabic numerals. Per litre petrol price:
Super: 40 Rls
Standard: 30 Rls
Diesel: 2.50 Rls

Mosques
Keep out! Fanatical Moslems could give you trouble.

Drugs
Dangerous–even relatively small quantities of hard drugs earn the death penalty. Leave them behind.

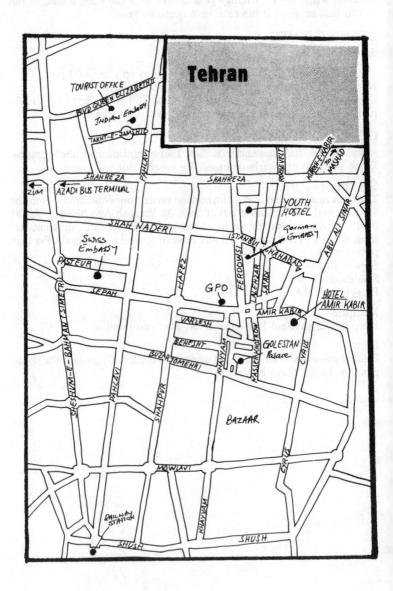

TEHRAN

Capital of Iran, 6 million inhabitants, 1180 metres above sea-level, situated on a slight slope at the southern end of the Alboroz (Elburs) Mountains. In the north of the city: the better suburbs and the modern, western business district. In the south: the older, poorer areas, bazaar and railway station. An expensive, hectic and sprawling city.

ARRIVAL

Bus

Usually to one of the two main bus terminals: the Azadi Terminal in the west of the city (from Turkey, Tabriz) and the Khazaneh Terminal in the south (from Mashad, Zahedan). Go to the cheap hotels in the city centre by communal taxi or municipal bus. A communal taxi costs 40 Rls from the Khazaneh Terminal. The municipal bus is cheaper.

Train

Tehran's main railway station is in the south of the city. Take municipal bus no. 63 or 213 (5 Rls). They stop close to Sepah Square, not far from the cheap hotels. Taxis are expensive.

Plane

There is no airport bus to the city. A taxi costs approx. 200 Rls. It's better to take a taxi to the Azadi Terminal and go from there by bus.

ACCOMMODATION

Hotel Amir Kabir, Amir Kabir Avenue, Tel. 30 22 21. Single 300 Rls, double 400 Rls, 2-bed dormitory 200 Rls each person, hand-basins in all rooms; clean enough and still the main rendezvous point in Tehran. Much more pleasant management than in the latter part of the 70s. But there's still a wall of signs at Reception telling you what not to do. Buy bus tickets here, for the shady Magic Bus Company, among others. Notice-board containing worthwhile informaton; simple, reasonable restaurant (guests only); checkout time 12.00 noon–general in Iran.

Many hotels won't accept backpackers.

The following is a list of other hotels in Amir Kabir Avenue or close by, where you can stay if the Amir Kabir is full. All have similar prices:

Hotel Tous (Tuss), opposite the Amit Kabir, Tel. 31 07 22, a bit hostile;
Aria Hotel in the lane behind the Amir Kabir, Tel. 31 30 11;
Hotel Khazar Sea in the lane opposite the Amir Kabir;
Hotel Ramsar (Hotel and Tourist Home only on its hoarding);
Bisetun Tourist Home (ditto), Tel. 31 28 93.

The youth hostel can be recommended, on Ferdowski Avenue, Kushk

Street, Behdasht Lane, Tel. 30 34 55/94. Single 300 Rls, double 400 Rls, dormitory (4 to 16 beds) 150/200 Rls; all rooms (incl. dormitory) with AC and heating in winter (free). Checkout time 1.00 p.m. No youth hostel card required. The youth hostel has a clean Korean restaurant.

Other cheap hotels near the railway station and in Nassar Khosrow Road.

Medium-priced hotel
(in the Amir Kabir area)
Hotel Asia. Tel. 31 83 20. Single 900 Rls, double 1200 Rls, all rooms with air-conditioning and some with bath. Checkout time 2.00 p.m.

EATING

The Amir Kabir Hotel has a restaurant offering a modest selection of dishes, at reasonable prices, but only for guests. A real hit with travellers on the way back from India–at last a real breakfast, only missing the coffee. Also recommended are the small shops and restaurants in the lane behind the Amir Kabir (soup approx. 60 Rls, a simple meal from 150 Rls).

TRANSPORT

Municipal buses
Bus destinations are written only in Farsi. Double-deckers cost 5 Rls and all others 10 Rls. Quite pleasant, not jam-packed as in India and Pakistan. Tickets can often be bought at bus stops or from fellow passengers. You need a new ticket each time you get off. There is no bus route plan.

Taxis
The orange taxis are the greatest rip-offs in Tehran. It's true that the meter may be running but the fare is charged per head, regardless. Single passengers can hardly get anywhere for less than 50 TL. Packs often cost 10 Rls extra. Tourists are always asked outrageous prices. Its cheaper to go by communal taxi. The driver usually calls out the destination and the taxis can scarcely be distinguished from private cars.

EMBASSIES AND CONSULATES

Australian Embassy: 123 Shahid Khalid-Al-Islambuli Avenue, Abbasabad, Tel. 62 62 02
N.Z. Embassy: Ave Mirza-Ye-Shirazi, Shahid Ali-Ye-Mirza, Hassani St. 29, Tehran, Tel. 62 50 61.
U.S. Embassy: No representative.
Canadian Embassy: No representative–see Danish Embassy
U.K. Embassy: British Interest Section of the Royal Swedish Embassy, 143 Ferdowsi Ave., Tehran, Tel. 67 50 11.
Indian Embassy: 166 Saba Street, Tel. 89 88 14, open 8 a.m. to 3.30 p.m., closed Fridays. One form to be filled out for visas, 3 passport

photos to be submitted and a wait of 24 hours.
Afghanistan Embassy, Abbasabad Ave/Pakistan Ave, Tel. 62 75 31.
Visas hard to get.

MISCELLANEOUS

The Tourist Office is situated on Elizabeth II Blvd, Tel. 65 70 64/5. Open
7.00 a.m. to 2.30 p.m. every day except Friday. Propaganda instead of
information but worth the trouble.

The General Post Office is on Sepah Ave (western extension of Amir
Kabir Ave), about 300 m from Sebah Place. Open 8.00 a.m. to approx.
6.30 p.m., closed Fridays. Each letter you collect from the Poste Restante
counter costs 5 Rls.

Tariffs to Europe:
Postcards–15 Rls
Letter up to 10 g–20 Rls
1 kg airmail–290 Rls
1 kg seamail–125 Rls

Express 37, registered 40 Rls extra.

There is no American Express Office.

Addresses were always hard to find in Tehran as there are hardly any
house numbers. In the wake of the revolution things have got worse,
with street names being zealously altered.

Car drivers: spare parts (including tyres) in Amir Kabir Ave or Qazvin
Ave. The latter leads to Tehran's camping ground at Gol-e-Sahra, but
it's probably closed.

Sightseeing: There is still a lot to see in Tehran. Previous sightseeing
attractions (crown jewels, Golestan Palace) have fallen victim to
Khomeni's clean-up campaign. As always, the Ethnological Museum
next to the Golestan Palace is open. Entry 30 Rls.

Souvenirs: Go to the stamp-sellers and letter-writers beside the GPO
and have a brass seal inscribed in Farsi (phonetic) with your name and
that of friends. It takes about 5 minutes and costs about 200 Rls.

There are two English-language daily newspapers: Kayhan
International and Tehran Times, both 25 Rls, four pages and the
mouthpieces of the government. Time and Newsweek, both 150 Rls,
are usually available although sometimes with censored pictures. Dailies
from England on Ferdowsi Ave for about 150 Rls. Ferdowski Ave also
has country and city maps of Tehran and other cities.

RETURN TRAVELLERS
Train
Enquire at the main railway station or Tourist Office whether the direct
train to Istanbul (Vangolu Ekspresi) has started running again. To

Moscow every Wednesday; change trains in Tabriz. Tickets from a small building to the left of the station.

Bus
Tickets to as far away as Munich can be bought (13-15,000 Rls) but this is not advised as you'll have to change to another bus in Istanbul at the latest. The average is one bus per day as far as Istanbul. Like all buses going westward, it leaves from Azadi Terminal (other bus lines include Iran Peyma, Mihan Tour, Levantour, TBT–all charge much the same fares).

Plane
To Istanbul every Wednesday, 26,570 Rls; international airport tax 750 Rls.

From Tehran direct to Delhi

Magic Bus goes there and back about twice a week, as do other freak buses. Beware of Magic Bus. Last year this company was still ripping off backpackers. It often doesn't get to its destination and only a portion of the fare is returned–usually in some currency you don't want, even if you paid in dollars.

'I'd like to warn everyone not to travel with Magic Bus. If you must, then only buy a ticket to a destination you're sure they'll reach, e.g. Istanbul-Tehran. Stretches like Athens-New Delhi are only a dream with this company.'

DETOUR TO MASHAD
From Tehran to Mashad

Train
Four trains daily to Mashad, 926 km, ordinary (passenger train) departs 2.30 p.m., arriving Mashad the next morning at 8.50 a.m. 12.30 p.m. departures arrive the next day at 7.00 a.m. Express trains: depart 5.15 p.m., arrive 9.20 a.m.; depart 4.00 p.m., arrive 8.00 a.m. Fares: 1st class 2315 Rls, 2nd class 1020 Rls, ordinary 780 Rls. No student discount. Trains are often booked out in summer (pilgrim season).

Bus
From Khazaneh Terminal, about a 20 hour trip, 940 km. Various bus lines such as Levantour between 7.00 a.m. and 6.00 p.m., more or less hourly, 600 Rls. Daily about 6 air-conditioned buses from Iran Peyma, 830 Rls. Buses sometimes booked out two or three days in advance (pilgrim season).

Plane
One flight daily with Iran Air, 3470 Rls, no student discount; no airport bus to Mehrabad airport.

ARRIVAL

Many bus lines stop in Nakh Rissi Street, close to the cheap hotels, from where buses set out for the Afghani border. From other bus stops and from the station in the north of the city by communal taxi to the cheap hotel area. The airport is only two or three km from the Nakh Rissi area.

ACCOMMODATION

There are cheap hotels in the Nakh Rissi Street area and in Naderi Ave, near the mosque.

There is a camping ground in the south-east corner of the city, near the airport and the route to the Afghani border. Best reached by a roundabout route.

SIGHTSEEING

Mashad (pron. Mash-had, with an almost non-exsistent 'a') is a holy city to Shiite Moslems. The Holy Shrine is the focal point for pilgrims. The blessed Imam Reza is buried under the shrine. In view of the current political situation and hostility to strangers, especially on the part of orthodox Moslems, a visit to the mosque is not advisable. Tourists are unwelcome in the entire area around the Golden Mosque and entry to the inner courtyards and the burial chamber has always been forbidden to non-Moslems.

From Mashad to Afghanistan

The Afghani Consulate is located on Khomeni Ave/Iman Ave, Tel. 44440. Open every day except Sunday from 8.00 a.m. to 1.00 p.m. Chances of getting a visa are practically nil.

AFGHANISTAN

Long the dream destination on the route to India, Afghanistan has been out-of-bounds for tourists since the Russian invasion of 1979. Of the approximately 20 million inhabitants of this barren, mountainous Moslem country, where resistance to the Big Brother from the North still continues, over 1 million live in refugee camps in the border areas of Pakistan and Iran. There's no way of accurately predicting how the situation in Afghanistan will turn out, but it's most unlikely that there'll be any opening up within the next few years.

From Tehran direct to Pakistan

Southern route via Beluchistan

At present, this route which avoids Afghanistan is the only possible overland route to Pakistan/India. In summer it's mercilessly hot and dusty but in winter, if it's snowing in Kabul, this stretch has a milder climate.

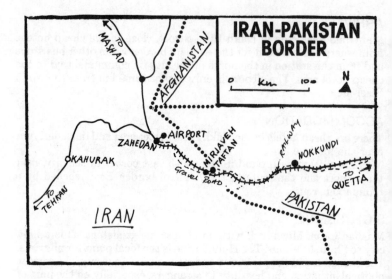

Bus

Numerous direct buses travel daily from Khazaneh Terminal to Kahedan, 1605 km. The journey lasts about 26 hours. TBT departs at 1.00 p.m. and Levantour at 3.00 p.m. Other bus lines on the route are Iran Peyma, KTM and Mihantour. Tickets are obtainable at the terminal or in one of the city booking offices: Levantour in Sepah Square, Tel. 30 27 23; TBT, Sephabod Zahedi, Tel. 89 12 21; Mihantour in a side street on lower Ferdowski, Tel. 67 84 40 and Iran Peyma, further up Ferdowski Ave, after the Swedish Embassy.

From Zahedan by minibus (50 Rls) to the Pakistani border at Taftan. Then onward in one of the numerous, brightly-decorated but totally overloaded and uncomfortable buses to Quetta. A horror trip of some 26 hours with one short sleep break, 70 Pakistani Rupees. Every two days or so there is a minibus for 100 Rs. It's not much better. No more Turkish or Iranian luxury coaches.

Rail

Recommended for train freaks only. Slower, more trouble and scarcely less expensive than the bus. There is no through-train from Tehran to Quetta.

From Tehran to Kerman costs 1730 Rls 1st class, 1085 Rls 2nd class. Then you go by bus from Kerman to the Pakistani border. For political reasons, the train across the Irano-Pakistani border from Kahedan to Quetta, 734 km, only travels the Pakistani Taftan-Quetta segment. Departure every Friday at 12.50 p.m., arriving in Quetta (according to the timetable) the next day at 7.15 p.m. First class 81 Rs, 2nd class 45 Rs. From this tariff comes a 25% reduction which the Pakistani

Government offers all tourists or 50% for holders of an international student card.

'The carriages are the worst I've ever seen. Dirty as cattle trucks. A 40 hour horror trip!' wrote one tourist.

Plane
At least one flight daily to Zahedan, 3900 Rls. In the case of domestic flights, the airport tax is already included in the ticket. From Zahedan by bus and train as above.

Car
Important tip: take along enough water-most of the journey is through desert. The route is: Tehran-154 km highway-Ghom or Quom (Golden Mosque)-270 km-Isfahan (city of mosques) (can be bypassed)-324 km-Yazd (Zarathustra's city)-387 km-Kerman (over 1 million inhabitants)-540 km-Zahedan. From Zahedan over very poor unmade roads (corrugated iron surface) to the border (about 100 km). Fill up in Zahedan or Mirjaveh. Once in Pakistan, drive on the left. From the Pakistani border there is 142 km of very bad road, some of it like corrugated iron, to Nok Kundi. The remaining 495 km to Quetta are tarred but the road is still broken up in places. Some petrol stations along the way but sometimes you need coupons-ask a bus driver. Only modest accommodation on the Pakistani stretch.

ZAHEDAN

The minibus from the bus terminus to the city costs 20 Rls, plus 10 Rls for luggage, Cheap hotels are only signposted in Farsi. Ask for the Hotel Rockn Abad (pronounced as written); clean, dormitory beds, 250 Rls, doubles and singles also available.

'There is a camping ground near the Pakistani Consulate, on the circle on the left after the station'

You can get Pakistani Rupees here from the money-changers (blackmarket). Officially they should only give you 100 Pakistani Rs but the border officials don't bother to check. You can also wait until Taftan (Pakistani border town). From Zahedan by taxi (350 Rls) or minibus (50 Rls) to the Pakistani border.

Return travellers: About 10 buses daily direct to Tehran, 1070 Rls, numerous army checkpoints on the way. It's worth buying cigarettes in Zahedan. A packet costs about 140 Rls.

BORDER-from Iran to Pakistan

The Iranian side is open from 6.30 a.m. until 6.00 p.m. There is no where to change money and no accommodation. Allow an hour for formalities by the Iranian border officials–first passport then luggage checking; they're not very strict. There is scarcely any luggage check in Taftan at the Pakistani border post which stands to one side and could easily be missed. Don't–you could be in trouble later for not having an entry stamp.

Taftan is a small shanty-town living on smuggling in the middle of the desert. The border fence separates it from Iran. It offers only few, primitive and expensive places to stay (room prices like those in Tehran).

MONEY

The bank in Taftan (the Muslim Bank) won't change money into Rials. Any excess rials should be exchanged for Pakistani Rs with money changers in the street. Ten Rs should cost about 250 Rls–a very poor rate if you've already changed them legally.

The time in Pakistan is 1 1/2 hours later.

The border for return travellers
Goods purchased on the officially tolerated blackmarket in Taftan are not allowed in. You'll get about 220 Rls for 10 Rs or 1 dollar. By comparison, the bank rate in Iran is only 81 Rls to the dollar. The border officials don't seem to know how many Rls you can take into Iran.

Beware! This situation could change overnight. Since the blackmarket rate for dollars (1 dollar = 170 to 220 Rls) is good, its is not worth the trouble buying rials on a large scale in Taftan and then-improbably-running into problems at the Iranian border for having too much Iranian currency on you. In Taftan you can exchange Rs for dollars at the Muslim Bank (1 dollar costs 10.5 Rs). If the bank has sold out of dollars it is still possible to buy them from the money changers, at an unfavourable rate to you. It's not worth exporting Pakistani Rs (export of 100 Rs allowed but no-one asks). You can still sell them in Zahedan but you'll never get rid of them in Tehran.

There is no luggage check on the Pakistani side. If you arrive in Taftan in the evening you can get an exit stamp at the customs building and then proceed directly to the Iranian border next morning. Reckon on about 1 hour for border formalities there. Quite strict luggage check-looking for drugs. You have to fill out a disembarkation card and declare any money. The amount is then entered in your passport. When you leave the country your receipts for changing money (if you've done it on the blackmarket then you won't have any) and any remaining money are checked to see if you're a blackmarket offender (any cash plus receipts for money changed officially should add up to the sum entered in your passport when you crossed the border). Sure, this amount hardly ever tallies with anyone leaving Iran and surprisingly even tourists who are unable to produce a single exchange receipt are never prosecuted. However, anyone who doesn't want to miss out on the lucrative blackmarket should still prepare a good story, just in case.

'Unfortunately we still have to urgently advise some backpackers who come to stay with us to return immediately to the border at Zahedan. Reason: the Iranian officials often forget the entry stamp. Without it you can't leave the country. If you're unlucky, they'll think you came in illegally. So, watch out!' (Management, Hotel Amir Kabir, Tehran).

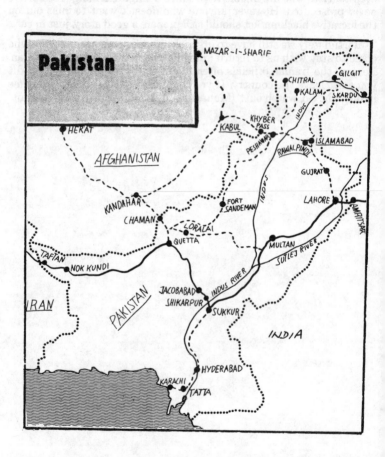

PAKISTAN

Pakistan was created from the Mohammedan areas of British-India in 1947. The nation's founder and first president was the Quaid-e-Azam (Great Leader) Mohammed Ali Jinnah who died in 1948. There were three wars against India (1948, 1965, 1971). During the last war, East Pakistan became the independent state of Bangladesh. Pakistan, with an area surface of nearly 800,000 square kilometres has a population of 84 million (97% moslems). It has the largest artificial irrigation system in the world and grows wheat, cotton and rice.

Numbers

1	ek
2	du
3	teen (tiin)
4	char
5	panch
6	chay (che)
7	saat
8	aat
9	now
10	das

7 words of Urdu

Practically everyone speaks some English. Still, we'll print 7 words in Urdu, the official language:

Good day	salam
Okay, that's fine	tighe
Ah, got it, yes	atcha (atscha)
Thank you	shukria
please	meharbani
how much (is it)?	kitnay paisa?
go away!	chelo

ENTRY REGULATIONS

All nationalities need a visa. The duration of the visa depends on the itinerary submitted with the application, but can be given in a matter of days if one is applying in transit in, say, India or Turkey. Normally the delay is 2 weeks. Visa fees are $3.50 for Australians, New Zealanders and Canadians, free for US citizens, and £24 for UK citizens. Vaccinations are only necessary for persons arriving from epidemic areas.

MONEY

The monetary unit is the Rupee (Rs), and one rupee equals 100 Paisa. In the colloquial language 1 Rupee = 16 Anna. Bazaar merchants often say 4 Anna instead of 25 Paisa, 8 Anna instead of 50 Paisa and 12 Anna instead of 75 Paisa.

Rough exchange rates guide

£1	=	31.00 Rs
US$	=	17.50 Rs
C$	=	14.00 Rs
A$	=	12.40 Rs
NZ$	=	11.00 Rs

Expensive hotels also exchange money, however at a slightly lower rate. There is no notable black market in Pakistan. Free money changers (legal) often give better rates than banks but do not accept cheques. In Pakistan there is only limited availability of cash dollars or other hard currencies for cheques or money transfers. American Express gives up to $100 in cash per person but with a fee of 24 Rs; other banks do not (except at re-changing at the border) pay foreign currencies. Travellers have in general had good experiences with money transfers to Pakistan; record times of 1 to 3 days are no exceptions.

ACCOMMODATION

There is no uniform check-out time. If the hotel listing under 'Accommodation' does not specify any, it means 'normal' check out time (12 noon). Very frequently you'll find the 24 hour system applies, i.e. you have the right to occupy your room for a full 24 hours after arrival. The hotels have come into somewhat of a bad light in Pakistan due to the many thefts. It is advisable to travel with your own lock and keep windows and doors closed at all times.

FOOD AND DRINK

Here, where the area gets even hotter, you should eat spicy food (curries, chillies) or salt tablets or a lot of soup to replace the salt lost through perspiration.

Specialities: Try Shami Kabab and Tikka.

Tuesday and Wednesday are vegetarian (no meat) days. Only chicken and fish are available in restaurants.

Soft drinks: 7UP, Pepsi Cola, Coca Cola and the excellent Mango drinks from Tops and Benz. RC Cola (Royal Crown Cola) tastes like watered down Coke and is just as expensive. Soft drinks are approx. 2 Rs in Lahore, 2.50 Rs in Quetta and approx. 4 Rs. in Taftan. Alcohol is only supplied to non-moslems in Pakistan and this only with a permit which is available for 10 Rs. from the Excise Office. Depending on local regulations, you are allowed 1 to 6 'units' per month. One unit corresponds to 250 ml spirits, 3 bottles of wine or 16 bottles of beer. You can sell your permit, but this is illegal. You'll get a max. of 100 Rs. per unit.

OPENING TIMES

Shops from 8.00 or 9.00 a.m.-8.00 p.m., in the winter usually only till 7.00 p.m. Lunch hour is from 1.00-2.30 p.m.

Offices and government department offices are usually open only from 8.00 a.m. to 2.00 p.m.

Banks are open 9.00 a.m.-1.00 p.m. Saturday till Wednesday, 9.00-11.00 a.m. on Thursday, and Friday is the general 'closed' day.

MAIL

Airmail charges to Europe

Post cards 1.90 Rs

Aerograms 2 Rs

Letters up to 10 g 3 Rs

Registered mail is 1.60 Rs. extra, express 2 Rs.

Sew packets in linen and then take them to the post office. 1 kg sea mail costs approx. 12 Rs, 10 kg, 40 Rs. Packets are automatically registered.

MISCELLANEOUS

Cities

Cities on the subcontinent are usually divided into the city and the cantonment. This division goes back to British colonial times. The city is the old part with the bazaars, often still surrounded by a ring wall and city gates. The cantonments are the geometrically planned and built residential areas, supplied with lots of greenery and inhabited by officers, or the well-to-do people and is the 'better' living area.

Mosques

You can enter mosques (always remember to remove your shoes!) and take photos inside in Pakistan. Be more careful in country areas when taking photos inside.

Women

As in the Iran, you also have a very hard life here. Unfortunately, there is no easy solution for the continuous molestation. In the mountain valleys of North Pakistan, women will generally be left in peace.

Media

The most important daily newspapers with their corresponding editorial headquarters: The Muslim (Islamabad), Dawn (Karachi), The Pakistan Times (Lahore and Rawalpindi), Morning News (Karachi). They all cost 1 Rs, with extra supplements and on Fridays 25-50 Ps extra, standard volume 10 pages, press censorship. Usually only Time and Newsweek (15 Rs each) are available from the international selection of magazines.

Car Travellers

Petrol prices (per litre): diesel 3.07 Rs, standard 5.01 Rs, Super 5.53 Rs. Supply shortages can occur in the mountain valleys of North Pakistan and other isolated areas.

Distances are given in kilometres; traffic is on the left side of the road.

Train

Three classes: 2nd class, 1st class and air conditioned (AC) class (about 5 times as expensive as second class). Bookings for all classes available up to 15 days ahead. A seat in first class costs 2 Rs, in second class 1 Rs; sleeping bunks: 1st class 20 Rs, 2nd class 15 Rs, bunks are included in AC class. There are expensive sleepers available in 1st and AC class. 2nd class is always more than full. Instead of four persons, you'll usually find 6 to a seat row. Reservations are not obligatory, but very advisable. Sleeping bunks are upholstered in 1st class but straight wooden bunks in 2nd class; no sheets or bedding available. You are permitted to use the bunks from 9.00 p.m.-6.00 a.m.

There is a 50% discount for all classes for people owning the International student pass (ISIC), no age limit. Tourists without the student pass are allowed a 25% discount. Apply for discounted tickets at the station with the Correspondence Clerk–all prices quoted in the book are without discounts.

Girls: ask for 'ladies' compartments' (separate compartments for women).

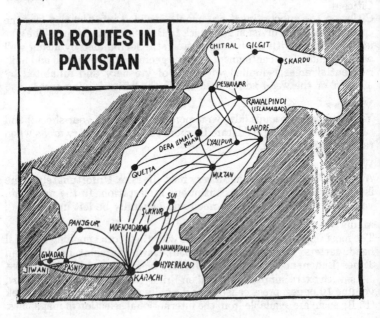

Careful: a lot of theft goes on in Pakistani trains. Particularly in North Pakistan backpackers will be searched for drugs.

Plane
If you pay for the flight in Rs, you'll usually have to present an official exchange receipt. Neither Pakistan International Airlines (PIA) nor other airlines give discounts to holders of the international student pass. The Youth Fare applied in many other countries is also not offered. Airport tax for international flights is 100 Rs.

Publications
The booklet 'Pakistan Tourist Guide' (10 Rs) is to be recommended as well as the half-yearly publication 'Focus on Pakistan' available for 30 Rs and in several languages. Both publications are available from Tourist Offices.

Weather
The most pleasant season in Pakistan is from November till March. It turns hot from April on, and May and June are the hottest months. July to September is monsoon time, warm and humid until October. December and January can be quite cold in the north. The season for the mountain region is the summer. In Peshawar, in the north-western corner of the country, the rain fall is distributed more evenly throughout the year. There is the typical monsoon climate in other areas of the country.

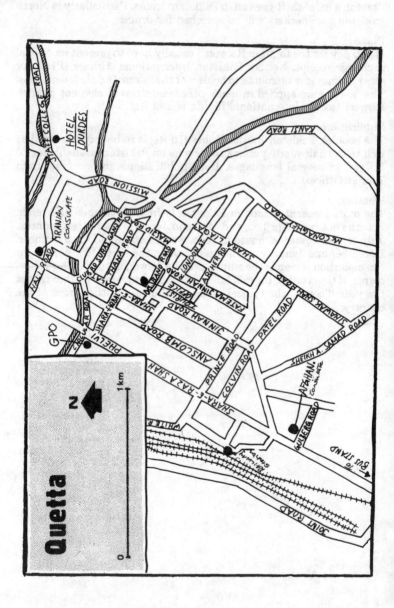

QUETTA

Population 200,000, 1676 m above sea level, capital city of Baluchistan, pleasant in summer due to high location

ARRIVAL

For 3 Rs with scooter from the station to the hotels in the bazaar area, 4-5 Rs to Hotel Lourdes. From New Quetta Bus Stop, the more remotely located bus station, it costs 5 Rs to the bazaar and 6-7 Rs to the Lourdes.

ACCOMMODATION

The hotels in Quetta are fairly expensive and usually fully booked in the summer (holiday resort).

Hotel City Baluchistan, Prince Rd, Tel 7 06 47, located at the bazaar perimeter, single rooms 30 Rs, double rooms 40 Rs, all rooms with bath, 24-hour mode.

Numerous other cheap hotels in the bazaar sector, double rooms from 25 Rs.

Lourdes Hotel, Staff College Rd., Tel. 7 01 68, double room 185/235 Rs, single room 116 Rs, 15% tax extra, all rooms with bath. Check-out time is 12 noon. Manager changes money (cash and cheques) at the current bank rates and for non-guests.

Be warned of Hotel Chilton (has a twin in Lahore). It is said that thieving is rife.

MONEY

Money changers in the proximity of the meat market pay 2000 Rls. for 1000 Pakistani Rs. You get an even better rate at the border in Taftan. Dollars are also available at the meat market. It is better in the Muslim Bank in Taftan (you pay 10.50 Rs. for 1 US$), provided that they haven't run out of US$; otherwise exchange with the local money changers on the street. No Western currencies available at banks in Quetta, they also do not engage in change transactions with Rials.

You can change money in the Lourdes Hotel outside of bank opening times.

MISCELLANEOUS

The Tourist Office in Jinnah Road (Tel. 7 30 53) is very good. Opening times 9.00 a.m.-4.30 p.m., officially closed on Friday, but someone is usually there.

RETURN TRAVELLERS

From Quetta to Iran

Visa: In Pakistan, the visa for Iran is only available at the Embassy in Islamabad; no visa at the consulate in Quetta or at the border, but you may have to wait over a month for it to be issued.

Train
A train leaves every Wednesday at 7.59 a.m. to the Pakistani border town of Taftan, arrival the next morning at 8.00 a.m.; 1st class 81 Rs, 2nd class 45 Rs.

Bus
Departure from New Quetta Bus Stop, 70 Rs, with about 10 buses leaving during the day. A mini-bus leaves from the proximity of the Tourist Office approx. every second day, 100 Rs.

From Quetta to Afghanistan

No visa available at the Afghanistan Consulate in Quetta.

From New Quetta Bus Stop with the bus, leaves approx. every 30 minutes during the day, 16 Rs, to Pakistani border station of Chaman; approx. 4 hour trip. Trip to Chaman is possible by train from Quetta. After arrival take scooter or taxi to the border.

From Quetta to Lahore

Train
Daily with the Quetta Express, departure 2.25 p.m., arrival in Lahore on the next day at 3.15 p.m., 2nd class 70 Rs with sleeping bunk 85 Rs., 1st class sleeper 145 Rs. Has direct carriages to Peshawar, arrival two days later at 6.10 a.m.

You have a right to a 25% discount as a tourist and a 50% discount as a student. See the Collectors Clerk at Quetta Station.

'Sometimes all seats are booked 3-4 days in advance, but it's better to wait because riding without a reservation is an absolute horror.'

Bus
Only possible with several changes as there is no direct bus. Not advisable.

Plane
Every Tuesday, Thursday, Friday and Sunday at 11.00 a.m. a flight to Lahore for 620 Rs.

Car
Three main routes:
The most adventurous and shortest route via Fort Sandeman is probably still barred for tourists for inner-political reasons (tribal area). Enquire at the Tourist Office in Quetta.

The 914 km route via Jacobabad/Dera Ghazi Khan. There is another more northern mountain route via Loralay to Dera Ghazi Khan, but the road is bad and in some areas, foreigners are only allowed to travel in the company of a policeman. During the monsoon period, the Indus ferry does not run from Dera Ghazi Khan but from 40 km north of the bridge.

The approx. 1150 km long route via Sibi, Sukkur, Panjnad, Muzaffargar, Multan is the third alternative-and it's all asphalt road.

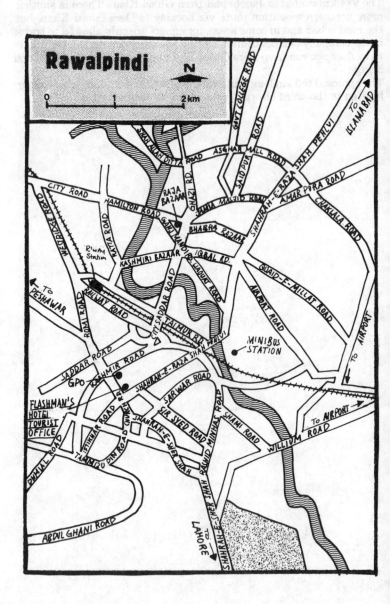

RAWALPINDI

Population of 700,000, 500 m above sea level; abbreviated to 'Pindi'.

ARRIVAL

With government buses to the large bus station located on the outskirts of the city. From there you take a scooter to the city, drivers usually refuse to turn the meter on. The minibuses (private) stop at various places; some behind the Moti Mahal Cinema, close to the Park Hotel. From there, the hotels listed under 'Accommodation' can be reached on foot or by scooter.

ACCOMMODATION

Hotel Taj Mahal, D.A.V. College Road, Tel 7 49 67, after the Park Hotel travel city-wards and take the first road to the left (Liaquat Rd.)–ask for Raja Bazaar. Single rooms 15 Rs, Double rooms 30 Rs, check-out time 2.00 p.m.

Hotel Pakeeza, next to Taj Mahal hotel, Tel. 7 40 70. Single room 25 Rs, double room 50 Rs, all rooms with bath, check-out time 4.00 p.m.

Hotel Al-Qamar, A-88/89 Jinnah Road, Tel. 7 24 82. Single room 25 Rs, double room 46 Rs, check-out time 5.00 p.m., all rooms with bath, recommended.

Camping in Flashman's Hotel on the Mall, Tel 6 48 11 costs 11.50 Rs per person. The same again if you want to use the swimming pool.

MISCELLANEOUS

The Tourist Information Office is in The Flashman's Hotel on the Mall, Tel. 6 48 11 (extension 12), open Saturday-Wednesday 9.00 a.m.-4.30 p.m., Thursday 9.00 a.m.-1.30 p.m., closed on Friday.

Ticket purchase and bookings for all classes at the station or with the Railway Booking Agency, Raja Bazaar, open daily from 6.00 a.m.-10.00 p.m.

Liquor Permit (6 units/month) at the Excise Office on College Road (do not confuse with D.A.V. College Road). Alcohol points of sale are in the expensive hotels (e.g. Flashman's).

FURTHER TRAVEL TO LAHORE/PESHAWAR

Bus
24 hour service from the main bus station; also minibuses. Fare: 25 Rs with minibus to Lahore, 24.25 Rs with standard bus (Deluxe 36 Rs); to Peshawar with minibus (15 Rs) or standard bus.

Rail
2nd class to Lahore costs 18.20 Rs and 11.30 Rs to Peshawar.

Plane
Daily connections. Depending on the type of plane, it costs 303 or 398
Rs to Lahore and 164 Rs to Peshawar.

To Quetta
Rail
Daily with Quetta Express, departure 5.06 a.m., scheduled arrival in
Quetta on the next day at 12.45 p.m., 2nd class 86 Rs.

To North Pakistan
See 'The Mountain Valleys of North-Pakistan'/'Journey'.

Side trip to Islamabad
Stop one of the many minibuses that travel on the Sharah-e-Raza Shah
Pehlvi and drive to Islamabad for 2 Rs.

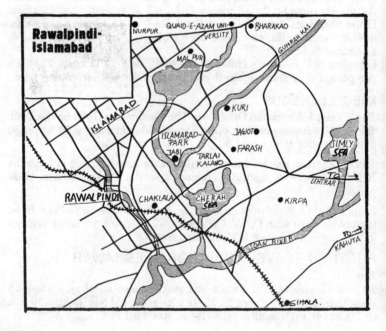

ISLAMABAD

Islamabad, population 100,000, 20 km distant from the sister city of Rawalpindi, is the capital of Pakistan. Islamabad was designed in 1961 and construction work is still not completed. There is nothing to see; a trip to Islamabad is only advisable if you still need a visa.

ACCOMMODATION

Very little choice. It's cheapest in the Foreign Tourist Camp, Aabpara. An overnight stay (whether under the stars, tent or car) costs 3 Rs per person. Occasionally the manager will fix the prices at 5 Rs. 24 hour mode, no comfort. Minibus stop Aabpara is close.

EMBASSIES

Embassies are not marked on the free Tourist Office City Map. You can only pick them out with the address specifications. Tracking down embassies is very time consuming, since Islamabad has a large area and no scooters.

US: Diplomatic Enclave, Ramna 5, Tel. 82 61 61-79.
Australian: Plot 17, Sector G4/4, Diplomatic Enclave No. 2, Tel. 82 21 11-5.
UK: Diplomatic Enclave, Ramna 5, Tel. 82 21 31.
NZ: Embassy in Pakistan is accredited to Iran.
Canadian: Diplomatic Enclave, G-5. Postal Address: GPO 1047
Afghanistan: 176 Shalimar, F-7/3, Tel. 2 25 66, open Saturday-Thursday, 9.00 a.m.-2.00 p.m. Visa applications must currently be approved by the Ministry of Home Affairs in Kabul. Waiting time: 2 to 6 months!
India: G-6/4, Tel 2 10 49. The Indian visa is available within 24 hours, in special cases on the same day.
Iran: House No. 3 & 5, Street No. 17, Shalimar 6/2, Tel. 2 26 94. Waiting period for visa can now be a month minimum.

Permit for Karakoram Highway
The permit to use the Karakoram Highway (Gilgit/Hunza) is only available from the Ministry of Tourism, College Road, F-7/2, Tel. 2 08 56. Fill in a form in quadruple, wait four days; the permit is free of charge.

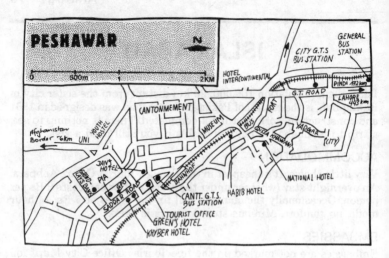

PESHAWAR

Population 300,000, 350 m above sea level, 'capital of the Pathanes', many Afghanistan refugees and fascinating old city centre.

ARRIVAL

Rail
The cheap hotels along Saddar Road are about 600 metres from the Peshawar Cantt station and you'd best take a scooter for 2 Rs to the hotels in the old city centre.

Bus
With the private buses at the General Bus Station. From there scooters to the cheap hotels on Saddar Rd. cost 6 Rs and 3 Rs to the National Hotel in the old city centre. It is cheaper (1 Rs) with the local minibuses which have their terminal at the General Bus Station and whose route passes close to the National Hotel and Saddar Road.

Also with the Government Transport Service (G.T.S.) at the city G.T.S. Station on Grand Trunk (G.T.) Road; with few exceptions it will then continue to the end station Cantonment G.T.S. Bus Station opposite the Tourist Office (cheap hotels in Saddar Rd. are within walking distance).

ACCOMMODATION

Within the Cantonment, diagonally opposite the GPO:
Khyber Hotel, Saddar Rd., Tel. 7 36 88, single room 12 Rs, double room 24 Rs, check-out time 4.00 p.m.
Green's Hotel, Saddar Rd., Tel. 7 43 04. Single room 18 Rs, double room 24 Rs. Clean, cooking facilities available, watched free parking place, 24 hour mode.
At the perimeter of the old city centre:
National Hotel 'inside Kabuli Gate', close to main bazaar street, behind Al-Farooq Hotel, Tel. 6 24 91, single room (no fan) 6 Rs, double room 12 Rs; atrium courtyard, age-old house in the colonial style, not very clean.
Police checks are not seldom in the cheap hotels of Peshawar.

Middle class hotels
Habib Hotel, Khyber Bazar, Tel. 7 30 16, single room 55 Rs (with A.C. 115 Rs), double room 90 Rs (160 Rs), triple room 140 Rs (220 Rs); 20% tax extra, heating costs in winter 36 Rs/24 hours, 24 hour mode.
Park Hotel, next to the Habib Hotel, Tel. 7 30 41, single room 75 Rs, double room 120/150 Rs, triple room 156 Rs, with A.C. an extra 60 Rs (no A.C. singles); check-out time 2.00 p.m.
Jan's Hotel, Islamia Road (opposite G.T.S. Bus Station Cant.), Tel. 7

20 56, single room 75.80 Rs, double room 125.80/151 Rs, triple room 156 Rs; all rooms with breakfast, 24 Rs extra for A.C. or heating in winter.

New Green's Hotel (next to Green's Hotel), Saddar Rd., Tel. 7 43 04, single room 75 Rs, (with A.C. 100/120 Rs), double room 100 Rs (150/200Rs), extra bed 20 Rs, for rooms with A.C. 40 Rs extra.

Campers

Camping in Dean's Hotel opposite Cantonment G.T.S. Bus Station is 20 Rs per person.

Other possibility: youth hostel on the university campus, 10 km outside of the city in the direction of the Khyber Pass.

MISCELLANEOUS

The Tourist Information Centre is in Dean's Hotel (see Campers), Tel. 7 64 28, open Saturday to Wednesday 9.00 a.m.-1.00 p.m. and 2.00-4.30 p.m., Thursday only 9.00 a.m.-1.30 p.m., officially closed on Fridays, but there is usually someone there.

Free money changers can be found at Memorial Place (Yadgar Chowk) in the old city centre and offer 10.50 to 11.10 Rs (better than at the bank) for cash dollars (US). They do not change travellers cheques.

The PIA office is at 33 The Mall, Tel. 7 54 61, open daily from 8.00 a.m.-6.00 p.m. No airport bus!.

Paperbacks, Newsweek and other magazines can be bought from the London Book Co., The Mall (close to PIA).

FURTHER TRAVEL TO QUETTA

Rail

The Down Khyber Mail with connecting carriage for the Quetta Express (from Rawalpindi) leaves daily at 10.15 p.m. scheduled arrival in Quetta on the second day at 12.45 p.m., 2nd class 96 Rs, with sleeping bunk 111 Rs.

Bus

Difficult and only possible with several changes.

Car: See 'Quetta'.

Plane

Change in Rawalpindi or Lahore, costs more than 1000 Rs. No airport bus to Peshawar airport.

To Lahore

Rail

468 km, three connections daily. Departure times in Peshawar Cantt: 6.20 a.m., 7.20 a.m., 10.15 p.m. The trip takes more than 10 hours, 2nd class 29 Rs (to Rawalpindi 11.30 Rs).

Bus

In the evenings there are 5 deluxe, overnight buses to Lahore, 56 Rs; numerous ordinary buses between 4 a.m. and 10 p.m., 38 Rs, departure point for all these G.T.S buses is the G.T.S. Cant. Bus Station at the Tourist Office; You can however get on at the G.T.S. Bus station along the G.T. Road, where you can also buy tickets. From the G.T.S. bus station you can continuously catch buses to Rawalpindi from approx. 5.00 a.m. to 7.00 p.m. Minibuses (private) leave from the General Bus Station. Day and night service, but only to Rawalpindi (15 Rs, 172 km). Change in Pindi, take minibus to Lahore for 25 Rs, 282 km or ordinary bus.

Further Travel to Chitral and Swat see 'The Mountain Valleys of North Pakistan'.

EXCURSION TO DARRA (40 km)

Darra is a small nest in the 'Tribal Area' and has reached fame through its gunsmiths. In approximately 150 workshops, anything from a small calibre gun to machine guns are produced as perfect imitations of all well-renowned brands of fire arms and sold without questions. Firearms, including ammunition can be bought without difficulty in Darra, but you'll have to reckon with problems at the checkpost along the way or at the latest at the next border.

How to make the journey

With one of the gaudy coloured private buses at the bus station after the bridge over the railway (when coming from the Cant. Railway Station), approx. 5.00 a.m.-7.00 p.m., every 15 minutes, 3.50 Rs.

EXCURSION TO KHYBER PASS/ AFGHANISTAN BORDER

The historic Khyber Pass which Alexander the Great crossed in his day, starts at Jamrud Fort, approx. 17 km outside of Peshawar and continues for 41 km (highest point is 1067 m). It is a bare, desert-like landscape up to the Afghanistan border at Torkham. The Khyber pass is tribal area and only the pass road is under Pakistani jurisdiction. The authorities are not allowed to deviate from the side of the road.

ARRIVAL
Bus
With the Jalalabad bus (7.15 a.m. from G.T.S. Bus Station, G.T. Road, a little later from G.T.S. Station Cantonment) you can travel to the Afghanistan border at Torkham; the remaining 74 km on the stretch Kabul to Jalalbad are only possible with a visa.

Other variation: take one of the numerous colourful private buses from the bus station past the railway bridge; it's 48 km to Landikotal, 4.50 Rs, travel time about 90 minutes. Then with a taxi (flat rate about 50 Rs) or with a Kollektiy car (2Rs) 8 km to Torkham.

Rail
Nice but very slow with the train (steam engine): departure 9.40 a.m. from Peshawar Cant., scheduled arrival 1.10 p.m. in Landikotal, then continue as described above. The train returns from Landikotal at 2.40 p.m., arriving in Peshawar at 5.50 p.m.

Take your passport!

LANDIKOTAL (Landi Kotal)
First degree smuggler's nest.

Simple accommodation available for between 3 and 5 Rs/person. However, sightseeing travellers who don't want to do 'business' are not very popular in Landikotal.

Torkham (Afghanistan border)
8 km from Landikotal, some huts, the PTDC Rest House, customs buildings and as the only attraction–the view to Afghanistan. The border is freely passable for tribal people.

ACCOMMODATION
In the government PTDC Rest House, directly next to the border barbed wire, a double room with bath is available for 75 Rs, for single occupancy for 50 Rs; you pay 10 Rs for a bed in a ten bed dormitory. Check-out

time is 12 noon, camping facilities and restaurant are available. Further accommodation is available from 5 Rs/person in the hotel next door.

MISCELLANEOUS

The Tourist Office is in the PTDC Rest House in Torkham, Tel. 81, open daily from 8.00 a.m. to sunset.

Be a little cautious-particularly at the border-with photography. Ask first. A sign in Torkham states that photographing tribal women is forbidden. Another sign in Torkham says that tourists should not spend the night in remote places along the Khyber Pass.

Car Travellers: Toll tax is 1 Rs/person, 4 Rs for the car. Spend the night at the PTDC Rest House in Torkham or cross the Khyber Pass before nightfall. It is quite possible that you will otherwise be sent back by the guards at the check posts.

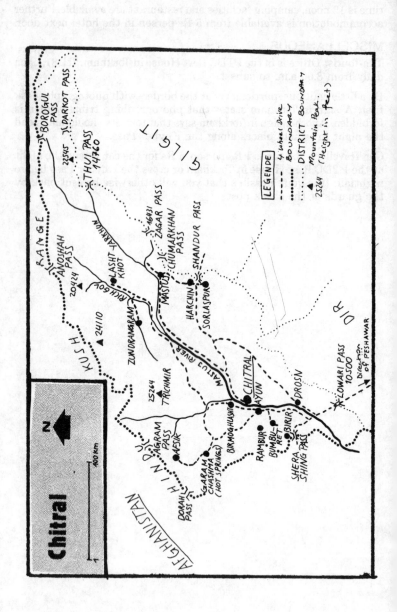

THE MOUNTAIN VALLEYS OF NORTH PAKISTAN

Probably the most beautiful scenery that Pakistan has to offer is its northern Hindukush and Karakorum valleys which are bordered in the west by Afghanistan, in the north by China and in the East by India. Here follows in brief some information on the most interesting excursions into this fascinating mountain area.

CHITRAL

ARRIVAL

Plane

The easiest way. PIA has daily flights (but only under good weather conditions) for 176 Rs from Peshawar to Chitral. Book early since these mountain flights (as all others) are usually fully booked several days in advance. The same applies to the return flight. Confirmed return flight reservations are not available in Peshawar.

The airport is on the outskirts, so it's best to take a jeep taxi to the village.

Bus/Jeep:

Only for adventurers-heavy approach route and only about 70 Rs cheaper than the plane. First with the bus to Dir, 8-10 hours trip, 23 Rs. The private bus departs at 3.00, 4.00 and 5.00 a.m. from the Dir bus stop in a rear courtyard in the old city centre in Peshawar (about 5 mins. from the railway bridge); the government buses leave at 5.00, 6.00 and 7.00 a.m. from the G.T.S. Bus Station at the Tourist Office and somewhat later the final departure from the stop on G.T. Rd, where you may also board.

Jeeps wait for the arrival of the buses in Dir and then continue to Chitral.

'Departure approx. at 4.00 p.m. You drive into the night. Several river crossings, a 70 km long glacier crossing and many narrow passes with deep drops along the side-we were thankful that darkness let us only take a guess at most of the dangers. We actually had 11 people plus luggage in a Willys Jeep.'

ACCOMMODATION

There is only a small selection of cheap hotels in Chitral. The best known budget hotels are the Dreamland (near the Tourist Office, direction of airport) and the Shapnam (on the other side of the 'Village Brook' and somewhat cheaper than the Dreamland). Accommodation is also possible with private persons and it's cheap (about 5 Rs/person), simple and pleasant.–There are also some expensive hotels, e.g. Trichmir View Hotel.

Accommodation can also be found in Ayun, Bumboret, Birir, Garam Chashma and other villages.

SIGHTSEEING

You must first obtain a permit from the Deputy Commisioner (D.C) in Chitral for any excursion. It is a mere formality. However, since a Swiss backpacker couple was murdered a few kilometres from the Afghanistan border in 1977, (a highly unexpected incident amongst this otherwise so peaceful mountain folk) one prefers to have every tourist obtaining a permit. You must specify your target and planned duration of stay.

Worthwhile excursions lead to the Kalash valleys, Garam Chashma (Hot Springs) etc. The jeep taxis maintaining communications in the valley are always hopelessly over-filled (they don't leave before they're more than full). Horrors!

There is a worthwhile excursion from Chitral to the Kafir Kalash, the black heathens, a non-muslim minority in the Berir, Bumboreet and Rumbur valleys. Rumbur is probably the most unspoiled because the road was only opened in 1977. From the jeep 'station' Chitral direct per jeep to Bumboret, or with a change in Ayun. Cheap hotels in Bumboret valley, Rest House in the main villalage Sheikh Anande. Take cigarettes and matches as presents for the Kalash. Women will only let you photograph them if you pay. Men will do it without payment.

Several day treks are possible from Chitral. You will need a trekking permit for this (see 'Trekking'). The standard trek takes you from Chitral to Gilgit.

Some go from Chitral to Gilgit, which is quite easily possible with the jeep Buni-Mastuj-Sorlaspur. Then continue with donkey and guide over Shandur Pass.

MISCELLANEOUS

All information on Jeep rates are available from the Tourist Office.

The 7705m high mountain at the end of the valley is the 'Trichmir'.

Vegetarians have a hard life in Chitral. Goats' meat is a part of every standard dish. You can practically only choose between chapattis, rice and green tea.

SWAT

ARRIVAL

Plane

Three times a week from Peshawar (136 Rs) and from Rawalpindi (165 Rs) to Saidu Sharif, the main town in the Swat valley.

Bus
167 km from Peshawar. Private buses leave pretty continuously from
the private bus station on G.T. Road, between 3.30 a.m. and 4.00 p.m.
costs, 15 Rs. Government buses leave every 30 minutes between 4.30
a.m. and 4.30 p.m. from the City Bus Station (also on G.T. Rd.), 15 Rs.
No boarding at G.T.S. Cant Bus Station; approx. 4 hours travelling time,
good road. Buses can also be taken from Rawalpindi.

ACCOMMODATION

Expensive but apparently the P.T.D.C. motels are good-e.g. in Miandam
and Kalam (single room approx. 100 Rs, double room approx. 160 Rs.)

GILGIT/HUNZA

ARRIVAL (to Gilgit)

Plane
From Rawalpindi 219 Rs. Very nice mountain trip.

Bus
No direct connection from Peshawar but apparently from Rawalpindi.

ACCOMMODATION

'The Tourist Cottage is located approx. 2 km outside of Gilgit. Costs
about 15 Rs for a single room. Very nice manager, excellent food. The
Hotel Jubilee in the centre is less clean.'

EXCURSION TO HUNZA

Northwards of Gilgit along the old Hunza Road to Nomal, then on foot
to Naltar, approx. 3000 m altitude in a side valley. The area is heavily
forested, many high mountains surrounded by glaciers. A lovely place,
but (in November) only 7 hours daylight a day. Return to Gilgit (46
km) by jeep.

N.B. You need a permit when you fly to Gilgit. When you do the trip
to Gilgit by bus you must obtain a permit to use the Karakoram
Highway in Islamabad. You also need a permit when you use the
Karakoram Highway from Gilgit to Hunza, even if you flew to Gilgit.
The permit is apparently only available in Islamabad (see Islamabad).
P. S. Even if you return by plane from Gilgit, it is advisable to obtain
a permit in Islamabad as flights are often fully booked.

SKARDU

You get there by plane: from Gilgit 110 Rs, from Rawalpindi 231 Rs.
Jeep: from Gilgit, approx. 12 hrs.

'We flew from Rawalpindi to Skardu, past the 8125m high Nang Parbat.
Skardu: a lovely place to go trekking, particularly in summer. We arrived
in November when snow was already falling to an altitude of 3500m

(Skardu is at an altitude of 2225m). We drove to Shigar by jeep and stayed in a very nice Government Rest House.'

TREKKING

Trekking permits are available from the Ministry of Tourism, College Road, F-7/2 in Islamabad. Price: 100 Rs per person and per trek; independent of duration.

LAHORE

Population 2.2 million, 214 m above sea level.

ARRIVAL

Rail and Bus
The main station (Lahore City Station) and G.T.S. (Government Transport Service) bus station are next to each other. Some cheap hotels are within walking distance, otherwise continue on scooters (see hotels).

Plane
No bus service only expensive taxis (35 Rs, but usually more for tourist) to the city.

ACCOMMODATION

General
Careful: the hotel scene in Lahore is the worst possible on the whole overland trip. Dozens of travellers in cheap hotels have lost all their possessions in the last years and/or have gone to gaol. Reason: shifty deals by the managers with the police, and thefts. The police usually do nothing. Stay clear of the Ringo Bell.

An old trick: The manager deposits a kilo of hashish under your bed and shortly afterwards, you'll be arrested by the police. You have no choice but to pay bakshish which is later shared by the management and the police. If you have no money, or not enough, you'll land in gaol. It is more common though, that the manager and his helpers will 'only' steal from you.

The following hotels are definitely dangerous:
Ringo Bell, 57 Mc Leod Rd (currently there is only a sign reading 'hotel for tourists' and it's possible that the hotel is being renamed); Hotel Venus, Hotel Picnic and the Chilton Hotel, 82 Brandreth Rd.

Hotels
YMCA, The Mall (Sharah-e-Quaid-e-Azam), close to GPO, Tel. 54 433. Single room 10 Rs, double room 20 Rs with bath 30 Rs, dormitory 10 Rs, check-out time 12 noon. Girls are only accepted when accompanied by a male, restaurant next door. From the station with a scooter, approx 4 Rs, but often fully booked, so call first. YWCA, 14 Fatima Jinnah Rd (previously Queens Rd.), Tel 54 707 (is to be replaced by a new number). Single room 20 Rs, double room 30 Rs, check-out time 12 noon, only for girls or married couples (otherwise state that you're engaged). Youth Hostel 7A Gulberg II, very remote and hard to find. 45 bus minutes from the station, take Bus No. 25 to Gulberg Main Market. Scooter to Gulberg II (the drivers don't know exactly where the Youth Hostel is) costs 14 Rs.

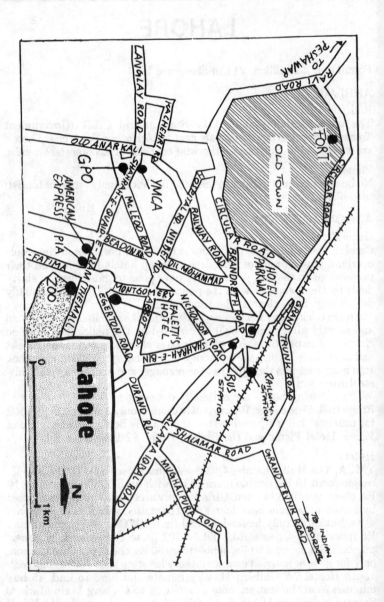

Lahore

Opposite the station you'll find a large block with some hotels classified as safe. All have the 24 hour mode, bath and same prices; single room 25 Rs, double room 50 Rs.

Hotel Clifton (not to be confused with Hotel Chilton), Tel 57 154, Hotel Chamber, Tel. 67 866, Hotel Shabistan, Tel. 56 744, Hotel Parkway, Tel. 57 259.

Middle class hotels

Hotel Asia, opposite the station, Tel. 57 429, single room 53 Rs, double room 81 Rs/98Rs (depending on size), 15% excise duty extra, check-out time 3.00 p.m., All rooms with bath and air conditioning.

Campers

In the YWCA (address see 'Hotels') an overnight stay in own tent or car costs 7 Rs per person; nice garden.

At the Youth Hostel.

Camping on the lawns of the Hotel Faletti, Egerton Rd., Tel. 30 36 60, 10 Rs per person, relatively clean, somewhat noisy, money changing possible.

FOOD AND DRINK

Numerous good Chinese restaurants. The restaurant Cathay, 60 The Mall (opposite American Express), Tel. 30 23 93 can be recommended. Expect about 15 to 25 Rs. More expensive Chinese restaurants are in the posh suburb of Gulberg; Mei-Kong, Kuo Chi and others.

Drinking: Tops and Benz fruit juices are excellent (approx. 2 Rs). Alcohol is only available upon presentation of a permit (see 'General'/'Food and Drink').

MAIL

The GPO is on the Mall (Sharah-e-Quaid-e-Azam), Tel. 58 072. Opening times: Held Mail counter Saturday to Wednesday 7.00 a.m.-6.00 p.m., Thursday 7.00-11.00 a.m. and 3.00-6.00 p.m.; other counters Saturday to Wednesday 9.00 a.m.-9.00 p.m., Thursday 9.00-11.00 a.m. and 3.00-9.00 p.m. For packets and registered letters 3.00-9.00 p.m. 20 Rs extra. The GPO is closed on Fridays.

American Express Travel Division, The Mall, open Saturday to Wednesday 9.00 a.m.-4.00 p.m., Thursday 9.00 a.m.-1.00 p.m., closed Friday.

SIGHTSEEING

Shalimar Gardens, 10 km outside of the city, Bus Nos. 3, 12, 17 from bus station; lovely gardens, established in 1642 by Shahjahan, the same who built the Taj Mahal; 2 Rs entrance fee, illumination and water games Wednesday and Saturday evening (only in the summer).

Badshahi Masjid, a mosque with stadium character, one of the world's largest (17th century); you can climb up the minarettes.

The Lahore Fort, opposite the Badshahi Mosque (similar forts in Delhi and Agra).

Golden Mosque (Sonahari Masjid) in the centre of the historical Walled City.

MISCELLANEOUS

Lahore city maps and brochures free of charge from the Tourist Office (PTDC Information Centre) in Hotel Faletti's in Egerton Rd., Tel. 30 61 78. Open Saturday to Thursday, 8.00 a.m.-7.00 p.m. (winter only till 6.00 p.m.) Friday 9.00 a.m.-4.30 p.m.

Good book shop: Lion Art Press Ltd., next to American Express. Large selection of Bartholomew Maps; 'Indian subcontinent', cost 49 Rs.

Airlines: The Pakistan International Airlines (PIA) office is a few steps away from American Express, Indian Airlines next to Hotel Faletti's.

Reading rooms: The American Centre and the Goethe Institute are both quite remote in the suburb of Gulberg.

RETURN TRAVELLERS

Two variations:

1. Lahore-Quetta-Tehran (directly from Pakistan to Iran)
The Quetta Express leaves Lahore daily at 11.00 a.m., arrival in Quetta on the next day at 2.15 p.m.
   From Quetta by train and/or bus to Tehran (information in the corresponding chapters).
2. Lahore-Peshawar-Kabul-Tehran
(Route via Afghanistan)
Currently closed for Westerners

Rail
3 good connections daily via Rawalpindi to Peshawar, 1st class 53 Rs, 2nd class 29 Rs.
5.45 a.m. departure with 13 Up Awam Express, arrival in Peshawar Cantonment at 4.35 p.m.
8.30 a.m. departure 5 Tezrao, arrival Peshawar Cant. 8.25 p.m.
7.10 p.m. departure Khyber Mail, arrival next day at 6.10 a.m.

Bus
Buses to Rawalpindi run day and night. It is more comfortable with one of the minibuses, departing from the stand near the station; fare is 25 Rs, with A.C. 50 Rs. The government buses (no minibus service) depart from the large bus station next to the railway station; 24.25 Rs, deluxe 36 Rs to Rawalpindi; to Peshawar, 450 km, 9 hour trip, more than 10 connections daily; fare: ordinary 38 Rs, deluxe 56 Rs.

Plane
PIA flies once daily direct from Lahore to Peshawar, all other flights stop over in Rawalpindi; 466 Rs.

BORDER-from Pakistan to India

FROM LAHORE
Rail
There is only one connection per day from Lahore to Amritsar, departure 2.15 p.m., scheduled arrival in Amritsar 6.25 p.m. Tickets for 2nd class: for the Pakistani section 4 Rs and for the Indian stretch 3 (Indian) Rs.

Border formalities (fairly strict) at Lahore Station and at the Indian border station Attari Road.

Money exchange: approx. the same rates on both sides, you'll receive approx. 75 Indian Rs for 100 Pak. Rs. Officially it is not permitted to take more than 100 Pak. Rs. out of the country; it is not allowed to import Ind. Rs. Expensive articles such as cameras are occasionally stamped into the passport to prevent you from selling them.

Bus
A border crossing is only possible at the Wagah/Attari crossing. This is 27 km east of Lahore. The border is open daily from 8.30 a.m.-3.30 p.m. Pakistani time (9.00 a.m.-4.00 p.m. Indian time). Reckon with about 1 hour formalities on the Pakistan side (Wagah) and on the Indian side (Attari Road).

Bus 12 (2 Rs) and Minibus 12 (3 Rs) drive to the border from the station, which is a good one hour drive. Taxi drivers often ask fantastic fares of anything up to 100 Rs. Can be done for half though. Share the costs with other travellers.

Border
The border set-up stretches for approx. one-and-a-half kilometres. Take a coolie if you have a lot of luggage. On both sides you will encounter the passport control, followed by the luggage control which is pretty strict since they look for drugs. You can exchange any remaining Pak. Rs on both sides of the border. Time difference between India and Pakistan is half an hour.

To Amritsar
Bus
Buses run continuously to Amritsar, the next city (29 km), 2.45 Rs; somewhat more expensive with minibus. A taxi costs approx. 70 Rs.

Plane
There is no plane connection from Lahore to Amritsar. Pakistan International Airlines (PIA) and Indian Airlines have four flights each per day to Delhi, 1068 Rs.

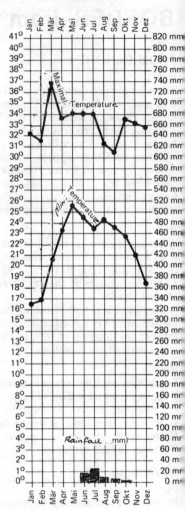

WEATHER GRAPH

The Golden Temple, Amritsar

Taj Mahal

A typical Indian train

INDIA

Predominantly Hindu subcontinent with Islamic cultural influences in the North. Population of 683 million, of which about 80% are Hindus and 10% Moslems. After China, India has the largest population of any country in the world (about every fifth person in the world is Indian), but is only about the seventh largest in terms of area with 3,288,000 km2.

It has been a democracy independent of England since 1947, resulting from the partition of British India. Agrarian state with about 70% illiteracy.

ENTRY REQUIREMENTS

A visa is required for India. You can get a 30-day visa at home or from an Indian embassy overseas. For a tourist is takes about 2-3 days to obtain the visa, and extensions are possible.

Anyone travelling overland who wants to get a visa along the way will find the address of the Indian embassy in the relevant capital city.

At the moment no vaccinations are prescribed.

Entry requirements over the last few years have become noticeably relaxed. Previously, anything that customs officials believed to be valuable (camera, tape recorder, etc.) had to be noted in your passport, to prevent you from selling it during your stay.

In a few areas of India, the normal tourist visa is not valid. For these 'restricted areas' you need a special permit which you normally have to apply for at the Ministry of Home Affairs in Delhi (see 'Delhi'/'Permits for prohibited areas'). If you want to visit one of these prohibited areas, it could be worthwhile–because of the long delays–applying for the permit at the Indian embassy before leaving home.

Extending your visa

You can extend your Indian visa at any of the Foreigners' Registration Offices found throughout India. Theoretically you are allowed a further month. But in practice you will probably be fobbed off with only a couple of weeks. The length of extension given to tourists varies from place to place. In addition, of course, anything is possible with bribery (in Bombay and Panjim/Goa visas even for a year are issued for 300 dollars). Ask other travellers about their experiences. In general, officials in small places off the beaten track seem to be more generous. The extension is usually free. Take passport photos with you; you will need up to four.

Instead of applying for a visa extension, you can of course also leave the country and get a new visa from an Indian embassy. Nevertheless it is just as hard to get the second 3 months. The Indian Embassy in Colombo is especially stingy.

CLIMATE/TIME TO TRAVEL

India has three seasons:

Hot season: April to beginning of June.

Monsoon (rainy season): beginning of June to end of September.

Less hot season: October to March.

In fact, October can still be warm and humid; the comfortable time for travelling really starts in November. Except on the East coast, where the Small Monsoon (Northeast Monsoon) prevails down to Sri Lanka.

December and January in the North of India can be decidedly cool, particularly at night. It is dry and there are no mosquitoes. Snow falls in Kashmir and other high areas.

April is the beginning of the great heat and dryness. Then it is up to 10 degrees C. cooler in South India (because of the influence of the sea) than in the North, where the climate is continental.

The hot season, from April to May, is also the holiday period. Then the Indians-those that can afford it-escape to the Hill Stations (hill country).

At the beginning of June the (Southwest) Monsoon reaches the tip of the Indian subcontinent and works its way north until the beginning of July. It then travels back again in the opposite direction. So the monsoon season lasts longer in the South than in the North.

When the rains come and the sun is covered by clouds, the temperature suddenly drops several degrees Celsius, and it becomes humid, which is more unpleasant than just the heat. Floods occur, especially on the Ganges Plain, disrupting travel. Kashmir has almost no monsoon season.

RELIGION

India's principal religion is Hinduism (about 80% of the population). Then there are the 10% who are Moslems. Sikhs and Christians are a fairly large minority with about 2% of the population. A small minority is the Jains, who are almost unknown in the West, and the Buddhists, who predominate in Sri Lanka (for information about Buddhism, see 'Sri Lanka'/'General').

Without some knowledge of the major Indian religions you will not really be able to come to grips with life on the subcontinent. A brief summary is contained below. In practically no other country in the world is everyday life and religion so inextricably entwined as in India, and only by direct contact with the country and its inhabitants will you be able to grasp its true dimensions.

Hinduism

The Hinduism practised today originated during the three millennia before Christ in the fusion of traditional root religions with the beliefs of the Aryan nomads invading North India-Vedism, which is characterised by its sacred texts.

Spiritual and temporal life are bound up in the caste system, in which

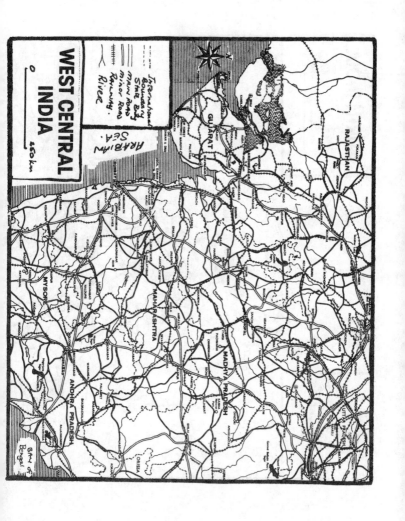

WEST CENTRAL
INDIA

0   250 km

- - - International Boundary
- - - State Boundary
—— Main Road
—— minor Road
+++ Railway
∿ River

ARABIAN SEA.

GUJARAT

RAJASTHAN

MAHARASHTRA

MADHYA PRADESH

MYSORE

ANDHRA PRADESH

ORISSA

UTTAR PRADESH

Bay of Bengal

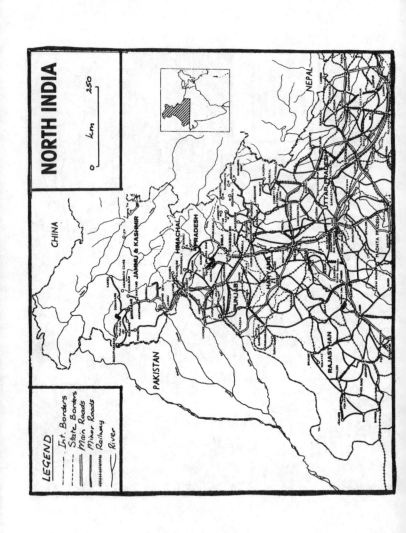

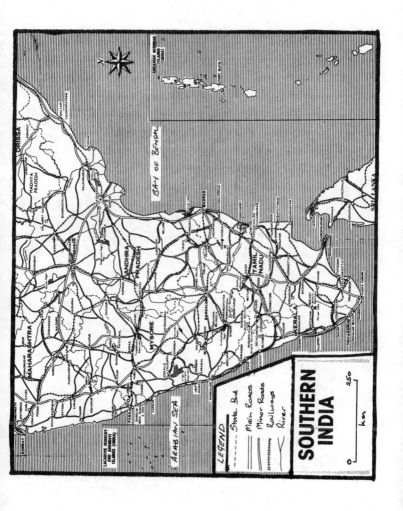

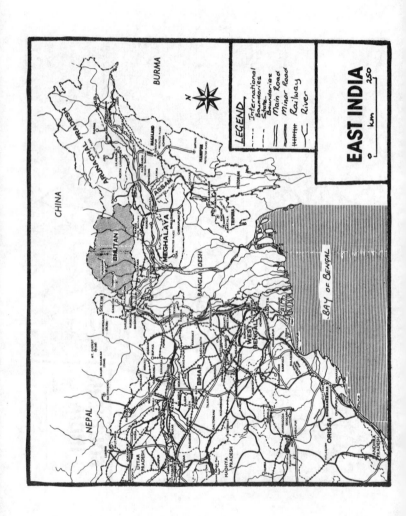

the Brahmins are the highest caste. According to this system, the privilege of religious observances belongs to this priestly caste. (Even today in India it follows that he to whom religious leaders submit can get secular power for himself.)

In the 8th century before Christ the oldest philosophical and religious writings of the Hindus were set down in the Upanishads. Written in the holy literary language, Sanskrit, these contain the thoughts, meditations and prayers necessary for a life of holy fulfilment.

Despite the great array of gods (at any given time, a believer will seek appropriate direction among them) Hinduism recognises no God as such. This perception can be crudely explained in this way:

Especially worshipped is the holy Hindu trinity consisting of:

Brahma, the four-headed creator of the universe, with his female parallel Sarasvati, the goddess of art and knowledge.

Vishnu is the preserver-he is portrayed sitting on a lotus, lying on a snake or flying on the bird Garuda-his companion is Lakshmi, goddess of happiness and beauty.

Shiva, on the bull Nandi, is the god of war, the destroyer, and also the re-creator. His female counterpart is Parvati, one of the most glittering figures of Hindu mythology.

This holy Hindu trinity is, however, not seen as living gods (in the Christian sense), but, rather, they are perceived as a manifestation of the absolute which cannot be understood. A Hindu calls this eternal, infinite principle 'Brahman'. The aim of the believer is not to reach one or other god, but to become part of the absolute.

Apart from the gods of the trinity Hinduism recognises a whole host of other gods, for example the beloved elephant god Ganesh, whose image you will come across all the time in India. At the same time the two most important teachers of the religion, Rama and Krishna, are worshipped as incarnations of Vishnu. And when Buddha began a counter-movement to Hinduism, the Hindus took him in as well: as an incarnation of Vishnu.

This flexibility of Hinduism towards other religions (you will even come across Christ as an incarnation) explains amongst other things why no missionary concept exists as in Christianity or Islam. There is no single path to salvation.

The foundation of the practising Hindu is the guru-disciple relationship, in which he is brought to spiritual wisdom. The means of becoming one with the absolute is meditation, through which a separation from everyday life can occur. Yoga in many forms is a further means of freeing the consciousness, of attaining 'enlightenment'.

The hierarchical caste system divides Hindus into five groups: priests, warriors/rulers, merchants, farmers and the casteless untouchables. This ranking results from the concept of reincarnation, according to which every soul, on the basis of its conduct in its previous life (Karma), returns as an animal or in the form of one of the five human groups. Hindu attitudes, particularly towards animals have their origins in this:

believers are against any killing of animals whatsoever.

The notion of reincarnation also substantiates the view of death as being a foregone conclusion without any threat. The soul simply migrates to a new, young body. The renewal continues until the soul has found its way back to its beginning, to Brahma, as part of the eternal.

The teachings of the Sikhs

These go back to the teachings of the guru Nanak who lived from 1469 to 1539. This holy man is worshipped by Hindus, Muslims and Sikhs alike. The belief of the Sikhs-they were originally a Hindu sect-consists above all of becoming one with the creator through constant repetition of his name, through leading a righteous life and through sharing one's earthly goods. Nine other gurus incarnate followed Nanak. The sixth of these, guru Hargobind, made the Sikhs during the troubles of his times into a warlike society, which is still a part of the Sikhs' image today. Another incarnation, guru Gobind Singh, established the brotherhood of converted Sikhs, called the 'Khalsa' (pure). This guru established today's outward image of the Sikhs: he introduced the turban, uncut hair and the bracelet worn on the right wrist that signifies the link with the creator.

Gobind Singh led all gurus back to the words of the holy book of the Sikhs, the Sini Guru Granth Sahib, which is worshipped by Sikhs as a living guru. This guru 'book' is kept in the golden temple at Amritsar, the centre of the Sikhs.

One frequently finds Sikhs to be good businessmen. One of the saddest chapters in Sikh history, however, was the bloodbath with the Muslims that took place when Pakistan separated from India in 1948, which made the most brutal inroads on their numbers.

Jainism

At the same time as Buddhism, Jainism developed, diverging from strict Brahman Hinduism. It was founded by Mahavira, who was renamed Jaina (conqueror) after his awakening. He taught a life according to the following strict rules: no killing, no stealing, no lying, chastity and renouncing any selfishness. Jainism recognises no castes, but recognises death and reincarnation and redemption from this cycle.

Jains do not hunt or fish and steer clear from farming so that they do not kill any living creatures. They are also strict vegetarians. The Jains do not recognise God as such. They worship Jiva, which is a body of enlightened individuals. Every living creature can attain this absolute level of perfection. The path to it is by meditation and especially asceticism.

Islam

Islam recognises only one god, Allah, to whom every person must submit. Mohammed was his prophet. His utterances and writings, which Allah proclaimed through him, were set down by Mohammed's successors in the Koran. A practising Moslem prays daily, observes fasts and observes moderation in eating and drinking. His place of pilgrimage is Mecca. Since the partition of India from Moslem Pakistan, to which many Indian Moslems fled, 80 million members of this religion remain in India today. The fundamental difference from Hinduism has during the course of history sometimes prevented the peaceful coexistence of these two religions. There have always been power interests that have and still do set the two religions against one another. Two of the darkest chapters since the Arab invasion of India in the 13th century were the bloodbath after the partition of British India into West and East Pakistan and Hindu India, and the 1965 and 1971 wars between India and Pakistan.

ACCOMMODATION

Hotels

In the better hotels foreigners have to pay with hard currency or travellers cheques or with rupees for which they can produce official exchange notes. (This rule also applies to air tickets.) You pay with rupees at cheap hotels.

In India a 12.00 noon check-out time is usual. Above all in South India, however, there exists the 24-hour system, i.e. a guest is entitled to his/her room for a full 24 hours from the time of arrival. If in the 'accommodation' chapter you find no check-out time listed for a hotel, assume that it has the normal check-out time (12.00 noon).

A good tip for backpackers wanting a medium range of accommodation are the state government-run tourist bungalows which you will find all over India. They are not all that expensive, but are mostly clean and have rooms with showers.

As the owner of a railway ticket you can stay overnight–admittedly for only one night–in the good-value railway retiring rooms which are often found even at the smaller stations. There are sometimes even rooms with air-conditioning. However, these overnight rooms are often already booked out by other railway travellers.

You can stay overnight for free in waiting rooms, though it is impossible to sleep in 2nd-class waiting rooms (they are always packed). There are showers for the 1st-class waiting rooms. In a few temples you can get free accommodation and sometimes even free food. All the same you should not take these free gifts thoughtlessly, as they are intended primarily for locals and pilgrims.

If you take a room with a wash basin or shower, always check immediately that there really is running water and that it runs away. If it does not, bargain for a lower price. Hot showers are sometimes available even in cheap hotels. But they usually do not work.

Best test of a hotel room: look at the wc. In mosquito-infested areas, check that the mosquito net has no holes. Do not chase the geckoes (white lizards) out of the room. They eat mosquitoes and other insects. They will not do anything to you.

'American plan' or 'full board' means all meals included.

Be careful when staying in dormitories, waiting rooms and even temples, as a lot of stealing goes on. For this reason it is worth travelling with your own padlock.

FOOD

Meals are divided into vegetarian and non-vegetarian. Vegetarian is usually half the price of non-vegetarian. As Indian cooking is traditionally vegetarian, the preparation of vegetables is incredibly varied. It is not worth eating non-vegetarian in cheap restaurants. The meat is tough and full of bones and everything is drowned in chillies to disguise the poor quality of the food.

If you cannot do without meat: you cannot really go wrong with chicken. You will seldom find steak or beef as the slaughter of cows (except in Kerala and West Bengal) is forbidden. There is always good cheap food in railway refreshment rooms in all the larger stations (station buffets). Snacks: pokora (chopped meat or vegetables cooked in pastry) are very tasty. Samosas are similar. In cheap restaurants one eats with the (right) hand. Western guests are sometimes given cutlery (a spoon for chicken, for example). Another method: shovel up pieces of meat, dhal (lentil soup) and vegetables with a piece of chapatti (thin unleavened bread). Or buy yourself a spoon.

Food trip: allow yourself the treat of eating Indian food once in one of the good restaurants (usually in luxury hotels). Even the curries there are not too spicy.

In South India the cooking is much spicier that in the North and is unbearable for most Western palates. Alternatives: eat Western-style food in stations or expensive hotels, or in the few Moslem restaurants. Or make do with fruit, tomatoes, onions, unleavened bread, sweets and tea.

In simple restaurants in South India very cheap (from 1.25 Rs) standard meals are available, consisting of rice and various curries. The whole thing is often served on a banana leaf and there is of course no cutlery, but you can have as many servings as you like. A few South Indian specialities: paratha (a sort of chapatti with lots of ghee), iddli (rice cake, e.g. for breakfast), wada, masala dosa, puri, etc. In a good restaurant also try alu gobi (potatoes with cauliflower) and alu (potatoes with spinach).

In addition you will find in India a rich variety of different fruits (mangoes, bananas, pineapple, coconuts, giant tangerines, etc.)

Sweets: The Indian equivalent of a Mars Bar is called 5 Star; the best-known brand of ice-cream is 'Kwality' (Indian ice-cream compares well with european as far as flavour goes, but hygiene is not always the best); absolutely harmless and available everywhere are glucose biscuits.

After a meal the bill is sometimes served with a plate of aniseed and a few toothpicks. Often a sign that a small tip is expected.

DRINK

Water is served with meals in restaurants; of course it has been neither filtered nor boiled. The national drink is tea (chai). Costs about 50 Ps. Coffee is in fact always Nescafe, best prepared like tea in the tea-shops of South India. Soda is likewise generally available. Be careful of the the cheap (about 25 Ps) soda that you get in heavy glass bottles in South India. It is usually no more than ordinary water with carbon dioxide which is bottled in people's homes. Water-lovers: In any restaurant or chai shop you can get-after astonished looks-a glass of hot water. If you don't like it like that you can fill a water bottle and let it cool. Milk in India-despite the large number of cows-is quite hard to come by. You can find good milk, packed in plastic bags, e.g. in Goa.

Cold drinks: Limca, lemon-flavoured and prepared according to an Italian recipe, is the favourite. Indian Fanta is called Gold Spot. Instead of Coca Cola (banned in 1977) there is Thumbs Up, Campa Cola etc. Cold drinks normally cost 1.50 Rs. But in a few places they are very expensive (in Ladakh you will pay up to 5 Rs a bottle). Cold drinks are also often faked. The writing on the label and the cap should at least match.

Otherwise: Lassi, fruit juices, milkshakes (all three very popular with backpackers, but hygiene usually leaves something to be desired). Fresh coconut milk is different: it's supposed to be so sterile that it was used in wars as a substitute for blood transfusions. A coconut costs on average about 1 R.

There is total prohibition only in the state of Gujarat.

MONEY

The unit of currency is the Indian Rupee (R, plural Rs). It is divided into 100 (naya) paisa, abbreviated to P. or Ps or NP (for Naya Paisa).

Travellers cheques get a better exchange rate than cash. These are the approximate exchange rates, which are currently being established again:

US$	=	17 Rs
£	=	25 Rs
Can$	=	11 Rs
NZ$	=	9 Rs
A$	=	10 Rs

Different banks have different exchange rates on the same day. Try the State Bank of India for the highest rate. Never forget to have a receipt made out for any exchange transactions. Today there is no real black market to speak of anymore in India. Swindlers still try, however, to entice tourists with offers of high exchange rates in order to trick their money out of them.

Outside banking hours (but at a mostly worse rate of exchange) you can change money in the large hotels. In fact this service is intended principally only for the hotel's guests.

Bank drafts: In India you get the equivalent sum paid out in rupees or in dollar travellers cheques, but never in the cash of a hard currency. Also you cannot change travellers cheques into cash dollars. Many backpackers have had bad experiences with changing money in India. Delhi especially is infamous for travellers being stranded for weeks because their bank drafts from home don't work out. More information in 'Preparing to travel'/'Money remittances'.

Wages: an ordinary labourer earns about 200 Rs a month, and the middle class about 2000 Rs/month. The average yearly income of an Indian is the equivalent of $190.

Beware of cheating when getting change: it is best always to pay with exactly the right amount. Anyhow there is always a chronic shortage of change in Indian tills, and everyday you will hear 'no change' accompanied by a shrug of the shoulders. When you are changing money at the bank make sure that you get the majority of the sum in small notes.

Banknotes

Never accept a ragged, torn, sticky-taped, dirty or in any other way damaged banknote–you will find it almost impossible to get rid of. You can exchange it at the State Bank of India, at the Reserve Bank and sometimes at other banks. You can give ragged notes away as baksheesh.

MAIL

The main post offices (GPO), where the poste restante is, can be nerve-racking for posting letters. If you want to register a letter, you must first have it weighed and the postage calculated at the Enquiries desk, then you have to queue at the Stamps counter to buy the stamps, and then queue at the Registered counter to have the letter registered.

Charges for airmail to Europe:
up to and including

20g	2.60 Rs
50g	4.65 Rs
100g	6.20 Rs

Maximum weight is 2kg (66.90 Rs). Registration fee is 2.25 Rs, aerogrammes cost 2.70 Rs, postcards (airmail) 2.25 Rs. Express mail is unknown in India.

Parcels

Sending parcels home from India is surprisingly less complicated than from some other countries (e.g. Nepal). First find a box (try in a wine shop), then carefully tie it up, label it, sew the parcel in cloth (you can have it done at a tailor's for a few rupees) and then address it again (with a ballpoint or water-resistant felt-pen). Somewhere on it you should also put your passport number. The best thing to do is to write near the sender's address: 'I'm a bona-fide tourist, my passport number is . . .'

At the post office you must than fill out four copies of the customs declaration form in which a detailed list of the contents of the parcel must be given, together with their approximate total value. The value of the contents cannot exceed 500 Rs (after other declarations 1000 Rs). But you can of course declare the value as less than it actually is. The parcel should not be longer than 100 cm, and length plus circumference should not measure more than 180 cm. Parcels are always registered automatically. The parcel is most unlikely to be checked by Indian Customs, but it will almost certainly be by the border authorities in your own country.

Here are approximate parcel rates to Europe by seamail:

1kg	30	Rs
3kg	38	Rs
5kg	45	Rs
10kg	60	Rs
15kg	80-95	Rs
20kg	105-125	Rs

Maximum weight for parcels sent by seamail is 20kg. They take about 3 months to reach Europe. Rather surprisingly, the percentage of parcels which never reach their destination is very small.

Airmail: up to 250g about 30 Rs, then (as for surface mail) for every additional 250g about another 6 Rs. Takes about a week. Maximum weight 10kg.

Postage is rounded off to the next highest rate, so if a parcel weighs 6kg you have to pay for 10kg.

You can send printed matter (books, etc.) most cheaply by bookpost. Do not sew up the parcel as one end must be 'open' (= 'easy to open').

TELEPHONE

In India telephoning within a state or from one place to another is usually more than a small miracle. If, for example, you want to phone Delhi from Jaipur (Rajasthan)–270km–you have to wait several hours to get a line.

Even when you book a call as an (expensive) 'urgent call', you have to wait 1 to 2 hours. And the line is appalling. The same is true of the rest of India.

So one would expect an overseas call to be terrible. But, surprisingly, it is really not so bad. The best thing to do is to register the call days in advance. But do not expect that everything will come off at the right moment. Reversed-charge calls (the person you are calling pays for the call) are called 'collect calls'.

TRANSPORT

The Indian Railway is the cheapest form of transport in India, especially over long distances. But for everything connected with the railways you need time, money, nerve and elbows. Indian railways are an adventure–and a chapter on their own. Here it is.

Indian railways have four classes:

2nd class: wooden benches, designed for four plus one passengers per row, but mostly hopelessly overcrowded, luggage racks, fans, 4 toilets per carriage, very dirty (3rd class was abolished and combined with 2nd class).

There are two types of 2nd class sleeping carriages: 2-tier and 3-tier. 2-tier are so-called sitting-cum-sleeper coaches; in other words, you sit on the seats at night and do not sleep–assuming, of course, that the carriage is not fully occupied. The upper berth above the seats is slightly padded. 3-tier sleeping carriages work on the European couchette principle. There are three levels to sleep on: on the seat itself, on a middle berth or on the top berth. The berths are not padded, but are made of bare wood. Despite differences in comfort and room, 2- and 3-tier cost the same (5 Rs).

ACCC class (air-conditioned chair car): air-conditioned carriages, which run only over a few long routes. Three plus two padded seats per row, like aeroplane seats, but the armrests cannot be raised, so you cannot stretch out–if there are empty seats. Some seats have their back to the engine. Little room for luggage. Air-conditioning means cooling in summer, heating in winter.

1st class: padded seats in compartments of four or, less often, two. Every seat also has a berth, i.e. at night there are only as many passengers as the compartment has berths for. The compartment can–and in fact must–be locked from 9.00 p.m. to 6.00 a.m.

No bed-linen unless you order and pay for it in advance (4 Rs per night), fans, very spacious, fairly clean, four toilets per carriage with showers in two of the toilets, drinking water, cleaners ('sweeper service'), meal service, an attendant (sleeping-car conductor), lots of room for luggage.

AC class (air-conditioned class): air-conditioned first-class carriages with five compartments for either two or four people. Same advantages as 1st class, plus a washbasin in the compartment, carpets, bed-linen included; air-conditioning means cooling in summer and heating in winter.

There is also an AC 2-tier sleeper, 4-bed-compartment (48 beds) curtain system, without cabins.

Tickets

Usually separate ticket offices for 2nd and 1st class, as well as for the different trains (up, down). Always ask if you are standing in the right queue. You can often get your reservation at the same ticket office. You can rely on waiting times of up to several hours–at least for men.

Women: queue at the ticket offices reserved for women, where there are fewer people. You can even buy tickets for your travelling companions there. If there is no separate ticket office for women, you are allowed to go to the head of the queue.

Check your change! Cheating with change is by no means unknown at Indian ticket offices.

Reservations

You can sometimes make reservations for sleeping berths at the same ticket office where you buy your ticket. But usually you have to queue at another ticket office. First get a requisition form at Reservations or Enquiries. On this you have to fill out the names (up to six travellers), desired date of travel, route and, possibly, train number and destination. In the space marked 'preference' you can indicate whether you want an upper, middle or lower berth. The upper one is the most comfortable, unless the night-light and fan disturb you.

In 2nd class reserving seats is almost always optional (only a few special trains like the Pink City Express and the Taj Express have only reserved seats). You always have to reserve sleeping berths. It's possible to make reservations (seats and berths) in all classes for up to one year in advance.

Your ticket shows only your carriage number. But a passenger list is stuck on the outside of the carriage giving exact seat allocations. If you are unlucky all the names will be written in Hindi or else so incredibly illegibly that only with great difficulty will you be able to find which seat you have been allocated.

Reservations are compulsory in 1st and AC classes. You can also get tickets and reservations–for an extra charge–at small travel bureaux and near some stations (e.g. opposite New Delhi Railway Station). If you cannot get a berth for the day you want to travel: black-marketeers sell reserved seats in the station before the train departs, but this is illegal. If you buy a reservation with an Indian name, the conductor will notice, and you'll have to smooth your way with a tip. For reservations always ask, too, about the 'quota for foreigners'. This consists of a number of seats set aside on some trains especially for tourists.

Indrail pass

There are no longer any student reductions, since the Indrail Pass was introduced on 1 May 1977. It entitles tourists to unlimited train travel during a specified period.

Here is the list of charges (in US$)

Valid for	2nd Class	1st (ACCC)	AC
7 days	20	50	100
15 days	35	75	150
21 days	40	100	200
30 days	50	120	240
60 days	75	170	325
90 days	95	210	375

Has to be paid for in US dollars or other hard currency. Rail reservations can be made up to one year in advance and are free for holders of an Indrail Pass. If you've booked everything and suddenly decide to change your plans, let the reservation lapse as otherwise you have to pay a

10Rs cancellation fee. An Indrail Pass is non-transferable and cannot be refunded if it is lost. It is available in Delhi, Bombay, Calcutta, Madras, Secunderabad and Hyderabad.

Fares and reservation fees

You can calculate fares yourself from the table above. Note the large difference in fares between classes.

AC class is usually more expensive than the airfare for the same journey. For 2nd class there are on the one hand Mail and Express (faster) trains and on the other hand Ordinary or Passenger (slower) trains. The fares on the slower trains are about 25% cheaper than on the faster ones. The prices given here are all Mail/Express fares, but it could be that only Passenger trains run on the route you want.

Reservation fees:
10 Rs for seat or berth in AC class
4 Rs for seat or berth in 1st class/2-tier AC
2 Rs ACCC class
2 Rs 2nd class sleeper
1 R 2nd class seat

Additional charges for sleepers
5 Rs for first and second nights in 2nd class
15 Rs in addition to price of ticket in 2-tier AC sleeper (for up to 1000 km) and 25 Rs if the distance is greater than 1000 km.

Extra charges for some 'Superexpresses'
20 Rs AC class
10 Rs 1st class/2-tier AC
6 Rs ACCC class
2 Rs 2nd class

How to travel by train

Every Indian town has at least two stations, e.g. Baripur Jn (Junction) and Baripur Cantt (Cantonment). Check carefully which station your train leaves from. Calcutta's stations are called Howrah and Sealdah. At Benares the station on the through-road is called Mughal Serai and is 17 km by rail south of Varanasi Jn. Delhi Jun means Old Delhi or Delhi Main Railway. Only New Delhi is New Delhi Railway station.

Trains leave fairly punctually from stations where they start their journey. Along the journey delays of several hours can build up. So don't plan tight connections. If you miss a train: for up to three hours after the train's departure you can get a refund on your ticket but you have to pay 6-12 Rs as a cancellation fee in 2nd class (1st class 18-36 Rs).

Boarding an Indian train is pure horror: you'll be ruthlessly pushed and trodden on. If you haven't got a reservation, you have no choice but to fight like mad or get a powerful coolie to win you a seat in return for a good tip (about 5 Rs). Women may sometimes find a place in the 'ladies only' compartments which are reserved for women. Even 1st class carriages fill up with passengers who have either 2nd class tickets or even no ticket at all–until the conductor throws them out.

To find the seat/berth reserved for you, look on your reservation ticket for the carriage number and then find the corresponding carriage. On the outside of the carriage are stuck lists of names with the places reserved for them.

Train journeys are mostly hot and dusty–take something to drink with you. In addition, in both steam and diesel trains the amount of soot produced is considerable. A layer of black will have coated your face by the end of every fairly long journey. During the journey tea (usually in disposable clay cups), soft drinks and food can be bought at all stations (even at night). There are seldom dining cars, but on all major trains you can order meals which will be brought directly to your seat. It can be very cold on trains in winter.

Warning: No where is as much pinched as on Indian railways, especially in 2nd class. Use your backpack as a pillow at night, or fasten it to yourself. Hide your passport and money in your sleeping bag or between your legs in your trousers. Before going to sleep take off your watch and hide it; some travellers have had theirs pinched from their wrists. Don't let other travellers see anything valuable you may have with you (transistor radio, camera, jewellery), as the temptation is great. Best protection against theft: keep watch with other travellers!

Travelling without a ticket is possible, but is hardly worthwhile. You'll be penalised if your're caught–even as a foreign tourist.

Timetables

You can find almost all express train connections in the all-India timetable 'Trains at a Glance' (2 Rs, available at train stations). Absolutely all train connections, though for only a specific part of the railway system (e.g. Western Railway, Southern Railway, etc.), in the 'Zonal Timetables' (all nine cost 1 R each). Summer and winter timetables are hardly any different from each other. 'Railway summer' is from 1 April to 30 September. A free, summarised timetable, 'Tourist Railway Time Table' is available from some Govt of India Tourist Offices.

The various railways (Northern Railway, Western Railway, etc.) are reproduced in different colours on the multi-coloured Railway Map of India (1:4.2 million): 10 Rs. The 'All India Railway Tourist Guide with Latest India Railway Maps' is cheaper (4 Rs).

You are entitled to your sleeping berth from 9.00 p.m. to 6.00 a.m. It can happen that before you lie down to sleep you have to eject uninvited passengers from your bed.

India has the fourth-largest railway network in the world. Every day approximately 61,000 km of track carry about 10 million people. Result: 2nd class is always hopelessly crowded and reservations are not always possible even for tourists (despite the 'quota for foreigners'). In addition, you will notice again and again that extra passengers travel even on carriage roofs.

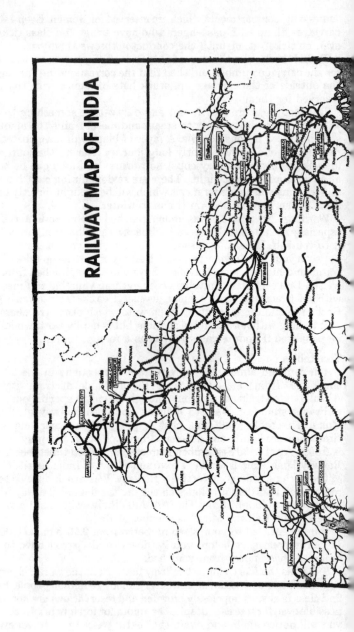

RAILWAY MAP OF INDIA

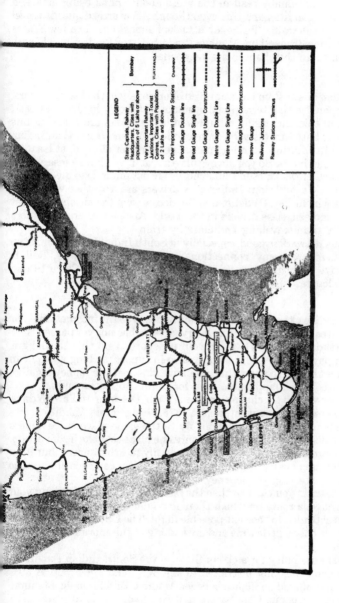

LEGEND

State Capitals, Railway Headquarters, Cities with population of 5 Lakhs or above	Bombay
Very Important Railway Junctions, Important Tourist Centres, Cities with Population of 2 Lakhs and above	VIJAYAWADA
Other Important Railway Stations	Chandrapur
Broad Gauge Double line	
Broad Gauge Single line	
Broad Gauge Under Construction	
Metre Gauge Double Line	
Metre Gauge Single Line	
Metre Gauge Under Construction	
Narrow Gauge	
Railway Junctions	
Railway Stations Terminus	

You will continually read in the press about trains being attacked by 'dacoits' (bandits), and this even though a few armed guards travel on many of the trains. Trains are attacked almost only in a few States in North India (Rajasthan, Madhya Pradesh, Uttar Pradesh and Bihar), and even there the chances are very small.

Bus

The Indian bus system has improved enormously in the last few years, but compared with international systems is still only mediocre at best. In spite of this, increasing numbers of backpackers are choosing bus over rail as buses are (usually) more comfortable and faster than Indian railways. In addition, standing passengers are not allowed, at least on long-distance buses. So you always have a seat, if you have a reservation and a ticket. However, even Indian buses are not immune to breakdowns and delays. In addition: Indian bus drivers are, together with their colleagues in Turkey, Pakistan and Mexico, among the absolutely most reckless and senseless drivers in the world. Also, buses are a bit more expensive than travelling 2nd class by train.

The bus network is good, especially in South India. In addition, from Delhi there are many connections to surrounding towns. Rail is 'imperative' only for some long routes, namely Madras-Calcutta and Delhi-Calcutta.

Air

Indian Airlines, the internal airline (as opposed to the international Air India) gives a 25% reduction to everyone who has not yet passed their 30th birthday. You have to show your passport to get this Youth Fare. You can pay in dollars and usually also in rupees (as long as you can produce a receipt to show that you have changed the money legally). The Youth Fare is applicable even for flights to Kathmandu.

Another way to fly cheaply in India: with 'Discover India' - 15 days' flying, as much as you want, for US$375. No age limit. Validity starts with your first flight. You cannot fly to the same place twice, unless it is for a detour for which there is only one place to make a connection. So you cannot fly from one place repeatedly to other places, but have to make a circular journey (or at least start). You can even change the route after starting the journey.

A good trick: you can lengthen the period of validity by booking your last flight on a route on which there is no daily connection. Then the ticket is extended to the next possible flight. The US$375 is worthwhile if you have only a little time and are looking at the enormous distances in India.

A final possibility for a cheap flight is the South Indian Excursion Fare, which is also not restricted to any particular age-group. A 30% reduction is offered on flights between Madras, Tiruchirapalli, Madurai, Trivandrum, Cochin, Coimbatore and Bangalore. This discount offer is valid for 21 days from the first flight, as long as the same route is

INDIAN AIRLINES — NETWORK

not flown twice. In addition, the concession is offered only to tourists who fly in from Sri Lanka or the Maldives and who want to return there after their South Indian trip. You have to be able to produce your return ticket upon request.

Air tickets have to be paid for in hard currency or travellers cheques, or a bank receipt for currency exchange has to be produced, showing that you have officially changed the appropriate sum. The rupee exchange rate is fixed.

During the travel season, book your seat well ahead. Seats on the main routes are sometimes booked out days in advance. Space on flights to Srinagar (Kashmir) is scarce. The main travel periods for Indian tourists are the hot months and also the autumn festivals Dussehra/Ramlila/Durgapuja and Divali/Deepavali. Take-off is very often delayed. Security checks before boarding. No photography allowed at airports.

No airport tax is charged for internal flights. Otherwise: 50 Rs for citizens of neighbouring countries and 100 Rs for others. Prices: all given in this book are–unless otherwise indicated–without any kind of reduction.

Since 1981 there has been a new, second national airline. However, Vayudoot, as it is called, is of no interest to budget travellers as it has extremely restricted offers.

DRIVERS

For India you need a car permit. Third party insurance is also compulsory.

Warning: Drive on the left-hand side of the road! Take special care with wandering (holy) cows, children, teams of oxen, pedestrians and railway crossings.

Distances are given in kilometres. There is no really good road map of India. The 'Road Map of India' is bad. 'Indian Subcontinent', in the Bartholomew World Travel Map series is better. A free India map available from some Tourist Offices is also quite good.

You have to take your car out of India after six months at the latest.

You also have to pay duty on the car if you give it away or if it is burnt up in an accident.

Petrol prices per litre:
Diesel: 2.67-2.82 Rs
Regular: 5.50-5.91 Rs
Super is available only in towns. In Delhi, for example, it costs 5.67 Rs.

Shortages in petrol supply can occur from time to time (apparently for diesel especially). Emergency supplies are organised by the District Authority Collector/Food and Supply Office. Petrol costs about twice as much on the black market.

HITCHHIKING

From the financial point of view hitching in India is hardly worthwhile. Firstly because public transport is cheap and secondly because drivers who pick you up often expect a tip. However, by hitching you have the opportunity to come into closer contact with Indians.

BUREAUCRACY

The Indian bureaucracy is excessively large (to provide employment for as many people as possible) and demands a lot of asiatic composure. You will be sent from window to window, have to wait hours, and have to fill out dozens of forms.

This applies to border controls (customs) railway workers, Indian Airline employees, post office staff, banks and government departments.

Allow plenty of time and remain polite. Outbursts of temper will only lengthen the waiting time (sometimes officials are impressed by colonialistic behaviour). Ask to speak with the boss if you feel an official is wrong, or ask nicely for the complaints book–that usually helps. There is usually a complaints book in all Indian offices and businesses, and the staff are not permitted to refuse to let you make an entry. Sometimes you only have to ask for the complaints book, but first make sure that you are at the right window. Approach Sikhs when you can. Use a few of the Hindi words which you have learned. Take some reading material with you to fill in the time. Always carry your passport with you.

OPENING TIMES

The day begins much later in moslem countries. Shops are open from 9.00 or 10.00 a.m. until 7.00 or 8.00 p.m. Offices are usually open from 10.00 a.m. to 4.00 or 5.00 p.m., and closed for lunch from 1.00-2.00 p.m. Monday-Friday, and are open 10.00 a.m.-1.00 p.m. on Saturday. Banks are open 10.00 a.m.-2.00 p.m. Monday-Friday (not closed for lunch) and from 10.00 a.m.-noon on Saturday. Everything is closed on Sunday.

PHOTO TABOOS

There are restrictions on taking photographs of anything that is remotely connected with the military: electricity power stations, dams, radio stations, border crossings, railway stations, bridges–even the Howrah Bridge which is Calcutta's landmark. Indians have a fetish about spies and saboteurs.

LANGUAGES

India has so many languages that the Indians themselves communicate in English. You can get by with English; you need only three Hindi words:

good day . . . . namaste
ah, yes, I understand . . . . atcha
thank you . . . . dhanyabad

For numbers there are again Lakh (100,000) and Crore (10 million).

WEIGHTS AND MEASURES

India has officially adopted the metric system. Kilometres are abbreviated to kms and pronounced 'kayems'. Kilograms are abbreviated to kgs and pronounced 'kaygees'.

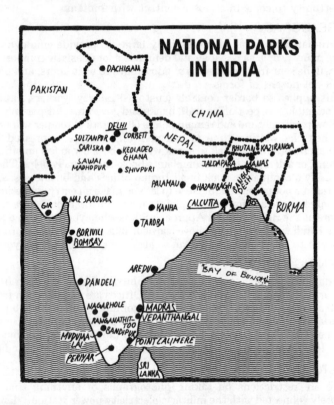

NATIONAL PARKS IN INDIA

Hardly any other country in Asia can have as many national parks and sanctuaries as India. Only a few are closed to tourists. The fauna in the parks varies according to geographical position: so you will find Indian lions only in Gir and the white rhinoceros in North India (Kaziranga and Manas, both in Assam). The main attraction is, of course, his majesty the tiger, which like the leopard lives almost throughout India, but can only be seen with luck (the best chances occur in Kanha/Madhya Pradesh). A few other representatives of the Indian animal world: Indian elephant, sloth bear, Himalayan brown bear and Himalayan black bear (both only in North India), wild buffalo (North India), gaur (a type of buffalo erroneously called 'bison' in India), deer, antelope, crocodile (the rare, up to 5 metre long gavial is found only in the drainage area of the Ganges), Ganges dolphin (also only in the Ganges and nearby rivers) and of course monkeys and countless types of birds. In North India you will see rhesus monkeys everywhere (even in towns); south of the Godavari River the bonnet monkey takes over. On the other hand the common langur is met throughout India.

The best time to visit parks is during the dry season, when the grass is not too high and you can make out the animals more easily. Some parks are closed during the monsoon season.

Note: You cannot compare an Indian animal park with Africa's game parks where herds of several hundred animals are no rarity and you feel you are in a giant open-air zoo. Asia is, rather, a continent of shy, single animals.

Tips on books: 'The Book of Indian Animals', published by the Bombay Natural History Society (60Rs): a classic with lots of colour plates, revised over and over again. Ideal park reading matter are the records of the adventures of Kenneth Anderson and Jim Corbett. Both men's works are also available in paperback (Anderson: Rupa Paperback, Corbett: O.U.P.).

Two park areas are discussed in detail in this book: Bandipur/Mudumalai and Periyar.

PRESS

There is no censorship. The media is anti-Pakistani and openly sympathetic to the Soviet Union. International news is generally given only a small amount of space.

Daily newspapers: The large Indian newspapers all appear daily and on Sunday also have magazine-type supplements. Cost is 50 Ps (only The Patriot, true to its leftwing image, costs 40 Ps) sometimes with a few paisa as 'air surcharge'. The local news reported in the individual dailies varies quite markedly.

The major daily papers:

Indian Express (Sunday issue The Sunday Standard): published from New Delhi, Bombay, Madurai, Vijayavada, Hyderabad, Bangalore, Ahmedabad, Cochin and Chandigarh. Available throughout India, it has the largest circulation with about 550,000 copies daily, but in none of the largest towns is it number 1.

The Times of India: published from New Delhi, Bombay and Ahmedabad. Dominates the advertising market in Bombay where it is the best-selling newspaper. Found less often further South.

Hindustan Times (Sunday issue The Hindustan Times Weekly): found almost exclusively in North India. Best performer in Delhi.

Statesman (Sunday issue The Sunday Statesman): with editions in Delhi, Bombay, Madras and Calcutta, where the the Statesman is the market leader.

The Hindu: is printed in Madras, Coimbatore, Bangalore, Hyderabad and Madurai. Available practically only in South India.

Magazines:
The Illustrated Weekly of India: by far and away India's largest and most popular weekly magazine, retail price is 2 Rs. Content: multi-coloured hotchpotch of articles of interest to tourists, a small dose of politics as well as news and other entertainment.
India Today: political magazine, the 'Spiegel of India', fortnightly, retail price 4 Rs. 160 pages packed with information, interviews and correspondents' reports from all Indian States, seriously researched. Little international news.
Destination India: monthly, 5 Rs, unfortunately rather hard to get hold of. A geographic magazine dealing exclusively with India.
From the forest of international publications only the two US magazines Time and Newsweek are generally available (15 Rs). Also fairly widespread is the Hong Kong-produced Asiaweek (12 Rs).

MISCELLANEOUS

Fares for shared rickshaws and scooters apply to the whole rickshaw, not per person. Don't let yourself be cheated if a rickshaw driver at first quotes one rupee for a specified distance and then tries to sting you and your companions for another rupee each.

Indian cigarettes are pretty bad; foreign brands are not imported. The cheapest: Charminar (filter, 20 per packet, 2 Rs), Bluebird (filterless, 20 per packet, 1.30 Rs). Bluebird are hard to get in North India.

Time difference: GMT (winter time) plus 5 hours 30 minutes.

Pests: see also 'Before the journey'. Best mosquito coils are Tortoise (pack of 10–3.50 Rs). By the way mosquito coils are not toxic.

Mass tourism: for European tour operators India ranks relatively low. Their trump card on the Indian subcontinent is Sri Lanka.

Treatment in State hospitals is free.

Only souvenirs over 100 years old may not be exported.

The power supply runs at 220 volts.

AMRITSAR

Population 650,000, 214 m above sea level, 'Sikh capital'.

ARRIVAL

Train

Numerous cheap hotels right opposite the railway station. Costs 1.50-2 Rs to the Golden Temple by cycle-rickshaw.

Bus

It's about 1 km to the Youth Hostel from the bus station. Cycle-rickshaw to the railway station about 1.50 Rs.

Air

Indian Airlines bus into town, 5 Rs, stops at the Indian Airlines office in the Mall.

ACCOMMODATION

The Guru Ram Das Niwas (Sarai) is a free hotel for pilgrims (and also tourists), about 5 minutes' walk from the Golden Temple (starting from the main gate): 228 rooms of which three (even more if there's large demand) are for tourists. Also 18 sleeping cells. Free board. In contrast to rules elsewhere there is no maximum period of stay, i.e. you can stay for free as long as you want and eat what you want. Nevertheless one shouldn't abuse this hospitality.

In the Guru Ram Das Niwas at the Golden Temple you can stay for free for 2-3 weeks. In winter there are blankets and mattresses. Two meals per day in the large eating area (cover your hair).

More free accommodation in the Guru Nanak Niwas, also near the Golden Temple. 66 rooms.

The New Akal Guest House is also under the management of the Golden Temple. 26 rooms for 20 Rs each, all with bathroom and 'air-cooled'; 24-hour system.

Hotel Pegasus/Hotel Palace, opposite the main railway station, near the Tourist Office. Tel. 41 800. Basically a single hotel, but has been made into two for tax purposes. Single 20 Rs, double 35/40 Rs (60 Rs with air cooler), all rooms have a bathroom; 24-hour system.

Vikas Guest House, 52-A, Rani Jhansi Marg No. 4, tel. 45 354; double 16/20 Rs, 35 Rs with 'cooler'. A bit out-of-the-way (about 2 Rs by rickshaw), but quiet and clean.

Tourist Guest House, 13555 G. T. Road; single 12/15 Rs, double 20/25 Rs. Double with bathroom 25/30 Rs, with bathroom and cooler 45/50 Rs, 4-bed dormitory 6/7 Rs per person. 2 Rs extra for a hot shower for guests without bathrooms in their rooms, meals ordered in advance.

The Tourist Guest House is recommended; clean, shower. On the route

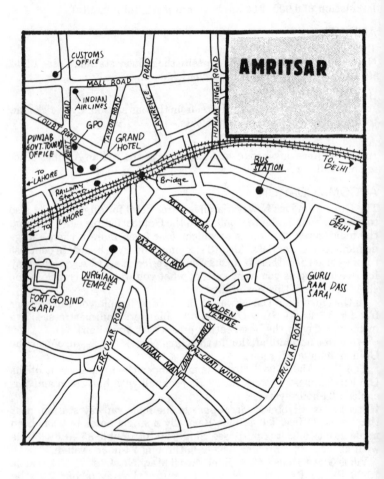

from the Youth Hostel to the railway station, just before the railway bridge on the YH side.

Youth Hostel, 1 km from the bus station, leaving the town on G. T. Road, tel. 48 165; double 20 Rs, dormitory 8 Rs, 70 beds, but no single rooms, expensive restaurant.

Good cheap hotel: Hotel Paris, a few metres from the Tourist Guest House.

Middle-class hotels

Grand Hotel, Railway Road, opposite main railway station, tel: 33 821. Single 50 Rs, double 75 Rs; single with air conditioning costs 100 Rs and double 125 Rs. All rooms have baths. 10% service charge.

Hotel Astoria, Queens Road, tel: 51 418. Single 35 Rs, double 65-95 Rs (45-85 Rs for single occupancy), extra bed 20 Rs. Prices for rooms with AC: single (only one single room with AC) 65 Rs, double 125/135 Rs (single occupancy 85/95 Rs), 10% service charge, all rooms have baths.

Numerous other cheap hotels near the railway station (e.g. Volga) and near the Golden Temple.

Campers/Drivers

At Mrs T.Bhandari's Guest House, 10 Cantonment, tel: 43 737/41237; camping costs 10 Rs per person. Beautiful private house surrounded by trees, very clean. Also rooms let in bungalows: double 240 Rs, 300 Rs with AC, single occupancy 125 Rs and 155 Rs respectively. All rooms have baths and breakfast, 20% service charge.

In the Tourist Guest House on G.T. Road camping costs 8-10 Rs per car, 15 Rs with electricity supply. The cheapest place for campers is the Youth Hostel (also on G.T. Road): 4 Rs per person.

Car garage: at the Customs Office on the Mall, tel: 33 843. Charges (all types of vehicles): first 7 days free; the next 7 weeks 100 Rs/week; thereafter 300 Rs/week.

FOOD AND DRINK

Free board in the Sikh Community Kitchen near Guru Ram Das Niwas. Mealtimes 11.30 a.m.-3.00 p.m. and 7.30-10.00 p.m.

Excellent cooking in the vegetarian and non-vegetarian Refreshment Rooms at the railway station. Full vegetarian meal with dessert 6 Rs.

Fish and chips in the restaurant on the left near the entrance to the Palace/Pegasus Hotels, approx. 10 Rs.

Shopping: in season, good mangoes 4 Rs/kg; pineapples 2 Rs each. Beer from 6 Rs for a 650 ml bottle in the small shops opposite the railway station.

SIGHTSEEING

The Golden Temple, the Sikhs' holy place, stands in the middle of a large water tank. It's made of gilt copper sheets. The Temple was built in its present form by Sikh Maharajah Ranjit Singh (1780-1839). The original temple was built at the end of the 16th century. Deposit your shoes, socks, and cigarettes at the information office on the right of the entrance. You can also get a compulsory head-covering there in case you don't have a hat. You can photograph in the Temple complex but not in the Golden Temple itself, where there are non-stop readings from the holy book (Granth) and music. A Sikh Museum has unattractive pictures of holy men and heroes in the entrance building to the Temple. Opening times: the Golden Temple itself is open in winter from 3.00 a.m. to 10.00 p.m.and in summer from 2.00 a.m.to 11.00 p.m. But the area around the water tank is open 24 hours a day.

The Baba Atal Tower (beautiful view, free) has roughly the same opening hours as the Golden Temple. The Museum–also free–is open all year from 7.00 a.m.to 7.00 p.m.

A tip: anyone who is not a great sightseer and wants to see everything in a quick trip should take the door on the left near the Information Office and go up the stairs. You come to a balcony with wonderful views over the Golden Temple.

SIKHS

What you must know in Amritsar: Amritsar is the holy city of the Sikhs. They are members of a monotheistic, casteless religious sect that was founded by the Guru Nanak (1469-1538). The holy place of the Sikhs, the Golden Temple, stands in Amritsar.

You can recognise Sikh men immediately by their outward appearance: they have long beards, and long hair intricately twisted into a knot on the top of the head and covered with a turban. Sikhs are not allowed to cut their hair as it is considered to be the source of all energy. This is one of the irreligious precepts, as is the prohibition of tobacco, drugs and alcohol. While the prohibition of tobacco and drugs is taken very seriously, only a devout religious minority sticks to the prohibition of alcohol.

In the Sikh religion hospitality is also very important. The best example of this is Amritsar itself, where even tourists can eat and sleep for free. This free board and lodging also exists in other Indian towns. Still, one should not forget to help out without payment in the kitchen or elsewhere in return for this free service.

There are roughly 10.5 million Sikhs in India (1.9% of the population). Sikhs are talented and well-to-do business people; begging Sikhs are a very rare sight.

MISCELLANEOUS

The Punjab Government Tourist Office is in the building of the Hotel Pegasus, opposite the station, tel: 42 164, open 9.00 a.m.- 5.00 p.m., closed Sunday.

To the right of the entrance to the Temple is the Golden Temple

Information Office, tel. 47 583, open every day from 7.00 a.m. to 8.00 p.m.

The enquiry office at the station is open every day 6.00 a.m.-10.00 p.m.

The Indian Airlines office is open every day 10.00 a.m.-5.00 p.m.

The Bus Stand enquiry office, tel: 45 558; open every day 5.00a.m.-10.30 p.m.

Post office: if the GPO is shut, try the post office on the square in front of the railway station; open till 10.30 p.m. Another post office is near Guru Ram Das Niwas.

Health: cheap blood, stool and urine tests at Lions Poly Clinic by the railway bridge (near the Tourist Guest House), tel: 45 737. Open weekdays from 8.30 a.m.-1.00 p.m and 4.00 p.m.- 6.00 p.m. (In summer 7.30 a.m.-12.00 noon, 5.00-7.00 p.m.)

Central Telegraph Office, open 24 hours, in the same building as the GPO.

FURTHER TRAVEL

From Amritsar to Lahore
Train
The border train leaves the main railway station (Amritsar Jn) daily at 9.15 a.m. Tickets are available before departure on platform 3, on showing your passport. 2nd class: 3Rs. The train is well occupied, but not overflowing. Scheduled arrival at the Indian border station of Attari Road is 9.52 a.m., train leaves again at 11.40 a.m., scheduled arrival in Lahore is 12.15 p.m., but is usually later.
Bus
The Wagah border-crossing is open from 9.00 a.m. to 4.00 p.m. But you ought to be there at 3.00 p.m. at the latest. No difficulties to be expected either on the Indian side or the Pakistani (Attari) side. At the Bus Stand in Amritsar take one of the numerous buses to the border, 29 km, 2.45 Rs, a bit more expensive by minibus. Taxis charge a flat rate of about 70 Rs.

MONEY
Officially you are not permitted to take Indian rupees out of the country. You are allowed to take up to 100 Rs (Pakistani) into Pakistan. However, with some exceptions, currency controls are not taken very seriously. The exchange office at Amritsar station gives 110 Rs(Pak) for 100 Rs(Ind), about the same rate as at the Indian border.

BORDER FORMALITIES (Rail)
Attari (Atari) Rd: fill out a red embarkation card; passport checks and often questions about money. Then luggage checks, only quite cursory.

Paradoxically, you are not allowed to buy Indian rupees at the State Bank of India counter after clearing Customs. You can change your remaining Indian rupees for Pakistani rupees at an exchange counter near the State Bank. Western currencies often appear to be unavailable; no Pakistani rupees are given for travellers cheques. Reckon on about two hours for all the passengers to get through Indian Customs before the train resumes its journey.

Lahore: Customs formalities take place on the platform; reckon on about 45 minutes. Passport and luggage checks (not strict), fill out one form (Gate Pass); possible to change money at the National Bank of Pakistan. Before you can leave the station you still have to pay in arrears for your ticket for the Pakistani part of the journey from Attari Rd to Lahore, 4 Rs (2nd class).

From Amritsar to Delhi

Rail

Six good direct connections from the main railway station (Amritsar Jn), 447 km: Depart 6.40 a.m. (summer: 6.35 a.m.), except on Wednesday, by the expensive AC Express. Arrive New Delhi at 2.50 p.m. (summer: 2.40 p.m.).

Depart 9.45 a.m. (summer: 9.40 a.m.) by Amritsar-Dadar Express. Arrive Delhi 10.05 p.m.

Depart 12.55 p.m. by Flying Mail. Arrive New Delhi 9.50 p.m.

Depart 4.20 p.m. by Janata Express. Arrive Old Delhi 5.40 a.m. (summer: 5.25 a.m.).

Depart 6.50 p.m. by Tata Nogar Express (except Tuesday, Thursday, Sunday). Arrive New Delhi 4.35 a.m.

Depart 10.50 p.m. by Frontier Mail. Arrive Old Delhi 6.25 a.m. (summer: 6.30 a.m.).

Fares: 2nd class 25.35 Rs, 1st class 110.50 Rs, ACCC class (AC Express only) 54.50 Rs AC class 206 Rs. All night trains have 2nd class sleeping carriages.

Bus

Regular buses depart from the Bus Stand between 6.30 a.m. and 9.30 p.m.; 36.40 Rs; approx. 10-hour journey, 442 km.

Air

Daily flight by Indian Airlines, 318 Rs, about a 50-minute flight. Airport bus from Indian Airlines Office on the Mall, 5 Rs.

Additional connections

Rail

Bombay (1985) km): depart Amritsar main railway station 6.40 a.m. (summer 6.35 a.m.) by AC/Pashim Express (Thursday, Friday, Saturday only). Arrive next day at Bombay Central at 4.40 p.m., 755 Rs in AC class, another 155Rs in ACCC class.

Street scene, New Delhi

Crowd at Republic Day Parade, New Delhi

Agra Fort

Depart 9.45 a.m. (summer: 9.40 a.m.) by Amritsar- Dadar Express.
Arrive Dadar (a Bombay suburb) next day at 5.20 a.m.
Depart 10.50 p.m. by Frontier Mail, arrive Bombay Central 8.05 a.m.
Fares for mail-express trains: 2nd class 81.45 Rs, 1st class 346 Rs. All
trains travel via Delhi.

Howrah (Calcutta, 1829 km): depart 6.40 a.m. (summer: 6.35 a.m.)
by AC Express (Monday, Tuesday, Sunday only). Arrive next day at
4.55 p.m.; AC class 732 Rs, ACCC class 150 Rs.
Depart 4.50 p.m. by Amritsar-Howrah Express, arrive Howrah next
day at 3.45 p.m.
Depart 7.10 p.m. by Amritsar-Howrah Mail, arrive next day at 7.55 a.m.
Fares on Mail/Express trains: 2nd class 78.60 Rs, 1st class 335.50 Rs.
Trains to Calcutta travel via Varanasi (Benares).

Bus
Chandigarh: numerous buses between 4.40 a.m. and 11.00 p.m.; deluxe
28.90 Rs, ordinary 18.90 Rs. There's also a direct bus to Manali.

You will find additional connections in the chapters on further travel:
'From Amritsar to Lahore', 'From Amritsar to Delhi' and 'Kashmir'/
'Expeditions'.

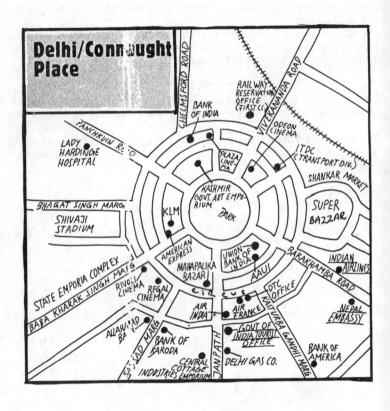

NEW DELHI

Population 6.2 million; 239 m. above sea-level. The Indian capital is composed of the modern government and residential quarter known as New Delhi (a planned city, built from 1911 onwards), and Old Delhi with the Fort, Great Mosque and bazaars. The city centre is the circular Connaught Place in New Delhi.

ARRIVAL:
Rail
At Delhi Jn (Old Delhi) or New Delhi Railway Station. Taxi and scooter-drivers are often unwilling to turn on the meter and want to travel only for flat rates. A scooter from Old Delhi Railway Station to Main Bazaar or Connaught Place costs about 6 Rs; flat rate by taxi about 15 Rs. You can walk from New Delhi Railway Station to the cheap hotels in Paharganj (Main Bazaar), scooters cost 2.50 Rs to Connaught Place, taxis about 8 Rs.

Bus
At the Kashmiri Gate Inter State Bus Terminal, right up in the north of the city. Scooters from here to the cheap hotels in Paharganj cost about 6 Rs, rickshaws 4 Rs. Scooters to Connaught Place also about 6 Rs. Cheapest option: by bus 101 to Connaught Place.

Air
Palam Airport, about 15km southeast of the city. 8 Rs to Connaught Place by EATS (Ex-Servicemen's Airlink Transport Service).A taxi into the city costs, depending on the destination, about 30 Rs, a scooter 16 Rs. 20% surcharge at night. Cheaper: bus 780 to Super Bazaar near Connaught Place.

ACCOMMODATION
Hotels
In the Main Bazaar, which is known to many scooter-drivers only as Paharganj, there is the cheap hotel district. Hotels are often booked up: you have to get to them early or make a reservation by phone.

Hotel Vishal, tel. 52 76 29/52 16 56. Dormitory 10 Rs, single 20/25/30/35 Rs, double 25-55 Rs; the more expensive rooms have bathrooms. Still one of the best hotels in the Main Bazaar, although it was once better. Lovely roof garden. If you want to go away for a few days, you can leave your luggage at the hotel.

Venus Hotel, 1566 Main Bazaar, right next to the Vishal, tel. 52 62 56.

Single 12 Rs, double 15 Rs, double with bath 20/25 Rs, triple (with bath) 30 Rs. One of the cheapest hotels. There tends to be lot of junkies here. Roof garden.

Vivek Hotel, 1541/50 Main Bazaar, tel. 52 19 48. Single 20-40 Rs, double 25-95 Rs; some of the more expensive rooms have baths and air-coolers.

Hotel Sapna, 5135 Main Bazaar, tel. 52 82 73. Single 20 Rs, 25 Rs with bath; double 25 Rs, 40 Rs with bath.

Kesri Hotel, tel. 52 82 46. Single 15 Rs, 25 Rs with bath; double 25 Rs, 40-50 Rs with bath.

Connaught Place district: accommodation generally smaller, more private, friendlier and cleaner than competitors in the Main Bazaar. The small guest houses in Janpath Lane are especially recommended.

Mr S. C. Jain's Guest House, Pratap Singh Building, Janpath Lane, tel. 35 34 84. In the 4-bed dormitory 12 Rs per bed, double with washbasin 35 Rs. Checkout time 10.00. Hot water 2 Rs per bucket. Small, peaceful, pretty little garden, clean and highly recommended. Warning: as the manager doesn't pay the scooter-drivers a commission (which is somehow always charged to you everywhere else), the drivers usually insist that his guest house is full. Phone or call in on the off-chance.

Soni Guest House, Janpath Lane (on the right after the Delhi State Co-operative Bank), tel. 31 29 48. Dormitory 10 Rs, single 25 Rs, double 35 Rs. Relatively clean. Safety deposit boxes provided.

Mrs Colaco's, 3 Janpath Lane, tel. 31 25 58. 10 Rs per bed in the 4-bed dormitory, single 25 Rs, double 35 Rs.

Sunny Guest House (not to be confused with the Soni G.H.), 152 Scindia House (lane behind Air India, 'off Janpath'), tel. 42 909. Single 30 Rs, 40 Rs with bath; double 50/60 Rs. 10% service charge. Hot water available on request. Clean, fridges available.

Ringo Guest House, 17 Scindia House (behind Air India), tel. 40 605. Single 33 Rs, double 49.50 Rs (55/65 Rs with bath), triple 77 Rs. Luggage deposit 1 R/day. Restaurant for guests only.

In Chankyapuri, the embassy district, which is a bit out of the way: One 120-bed youth hostel at 5 Nyaya Marg, tel. 37 62 85. With a youth hostel membership card a dormitory bed costs 15Rs, without card 18 Rs. Men and women separated. You are not allowed to stay in your room between 10.00 a.m. and 5.00 p.m., and if you come back after 11.00 p.m. you have to pay a 2 Rs fine. Restaurant and cooking facilities available. 'Boy scout' atmosphere. You can change money next door at the Canara Bank.

Opposite the Indonesian Embassy: Vishwa Yuvakendra International Youth Centre, Circular Road, tel. 37 36 31. 8 Rs in the dormitory (2 x 16 beds); single 25 Rs, 45 Rs with bath; double 35 Rs, 55 Rs with bath.

Middle-class hotels
The two Ys, neither of which is restricted to either sex:

YWCA International Guest House, 10 Parliament Street (Sansad Marg), tel. 31 15 61. Single 85 Rs, double 140 Rs (single occupancy 115 Rs), extra bed 40 Rs; 10% service charge; breakfast inclusive. All rooms have baths and AC.

YMCA Tourist Hotel, Jai Singh Road, tel. 31 19 15. Single 45 Rs, 74 Rs with bath; double with AC 80 Rs. 145 Rs with bath and AC; extra bed 25/40 Rs. 10% service charge. Maximum stay is officially 15 days.

Other suitable hotels with AC:
Hotel Continental Annexe, entrance on Parliament Street, Hanuman Road, first cross-lane on the right, tel. 31 12 08. Without AC: double 80 Rs (single occupancy 60 Rs), extra bed 20 Rs. With AC: double 100 Rs (single occupancy 70 Rs), extra bed 25 Rs.

Hotel Continental, 65 Regal Building, tel. 31 00 11. Single (without bath) 125 Rs, double (with bath) 175 Rs. 25% tax. All rooms have AC.

Hotel Bright, M-Block, 1st floor, Connaught Circus (opposite Super Bazaar), tel. 35 04 44. Single 37.50 Rs (44.50 Rs with bath), double 52.50 Rs (59.50 Rs with bath) extra bed 17 Rs. Additional charge for cooler 6 Rs. At least part of the hotel is planned to be converted to AC.

Hotel Blue, one floor above Hotel Bright, tel. 35 22 22. Single 40 Rs (50 Rs with bath), double 55 Rs (70 Rs with bath), extra bed 25 Rs. Doubles have coolers.

Hotel Palace Heights, D-Block, 2nd Floor, Connaught Place (behind Odeon cinema), tel. 35 13 69. Single 25-70 Rs, double 55-90 Rs. The better rooms have baths and coolers.

Camping
Delhi's two official camp sites are:
Tourist Camp, Nehru Marg (opposite Irwin Hospital), tel. 22 28 01. Situated halfway between New and Old Delhi. Rather noisy. Also has rooms: single 16 Rs, double 22 Rs. The camp site's 2-man tents cost 20 Rs/night each; dormitory tent 9 Rs/person; sleeping outside 8 Rs. Parking fee for vehicles 8 Rs, plus 3 Rs for each person sleeping in the vehicle. Additional charge for electricity 2 Rs. Sleeping in your own tent: about 7 Rs/person. The Tourist Camp is the major meeting place for backpackers in Delhi. Freak-buses also leave from here.

Tourist Camping Park, Qudsia Gardens, opposite Interstate Bus Terminal, in the north of the city, tel. 22 31 31. Dormitory 10 Rs (4 beds), double 20 Rs. Communal bathroom with hot water.

Tents: 6 Rs for the site plus 2 Rs/person. Parking: 6 Rs for the place and 2 Rs/person for everyone sleeping in the vehicle. Cafeteria and garden restaurant.

FOOD AND DRINK

Restaurants
Kake-da-Hotel, 74 Municipal Market, Connaught Circus, opposite L-Block. Perhaps the best of the many small restaurants (dhabas). Packed at mealtimes.

Restaurant Manoranjan, Janpath, opposite Swissair/Lufthansa. A sort of garden restaurant. Even some Chinese cooking.

Lots of small, cheap restaurants in the building called Mohan Singh Place, first building on the left after the Rivoli cinema if you're coming from Connaught Place. Even milkshakes there (2.50-3Rs)–if you're game. Milkshakes are cheaper in Paharganj (1.50Rs).

Lots of small, cheap and clean restaurants in the A.C. Palika Bazaar. Sometimes open till 10.00 p.m.

Restaurant Metropolis, Main Bazaar (Paharganj). By far and away the best in the Main Bazaar. Large choice. Indian, Chinese and European cooking. Unfortunately has gone downhill a bit in the last few years, but is still a fast-food experience.

Less well-known is the food at the Cafe Gaylord and the Cafe India, two favourite and not very clean hang-outs in Paharganj.

Food 'experiences'

Moti Mahal, Netaji Subash Marg. The most famous chicken restaurant. Not for vegetarians. Examples of prices: full Tandoori chicken 20 Rs, half 10 Rs, soft drinks 3 Rs. Beware of Moti Mahal imitators who trade under the same name but have nothing to do with the original Moti Mahal.

The numerous ice-cream parlours on Connaught Place are a really special experience. Two of the best are right after American Express, Wenger House, around the corner: Keventer's–about 2.50 Rs per 'slice'; also has excellent bottled milk. Bonanza Ice Cream Parlour–approx. 20 varieties; about 2.50 Rs a bucket.

Standard Restaurant, 44 Regal Building (near the Regal cinema) on Connaught Place. Recommended by various travellers.

For gourmet backpackers: European food in the Hotel Sheraton's Restaurant Mediteranee, e.g. Italian scampi 30 Rs approx.

Shopping

Vegetables, fruit and sometimes even a few western foods at The Oriental Fruits Mart, 23-E Connaught Place/junction of Barakhamba Road.

Western-style shopping centre: Super Bazaar on Connaught Circus. The chemist is open 24 hours every day, other departments 10.00 a.m.-7.00 p.m. Closed on Sunday. The groceries and toiletries departments are also open on the first and second Sunday of each month.

Confectionery, bread and sausages in the basement of the luxury hotel Oberoi Intercontinental. Examples of prices: black bread 7 Rs, 100g of chocolates 15 Rs, salami 4 Rs.

Swiss confectionery in Wenger & Co. Pastry Shop, A-Block.

on the first and second Sunday of each month.

Confectionery, bread and sausages in the basement of the luxury hotel Oberoi Intercontinental. Examples of prices: black bread 7Rs, 100g of chocolates 15Rs, salami 4Rs.

Swiss confectionery in Wenger & Co. Pastry Shop, A-Block.

TRANSPORT

City buses

A bus route fare table (1.50Rs) and the 'Abstract Time Table' (50Ps) are available from the Delhi Transport Corporation (DTC) on Connaught Circus, Scindia House (back courtyard)–both useful aids for getting around.

Route descriptions are also published in the various Delhi travel guides.

City buses are (as everywhere in India) hopelessly crowded, especially during peak hours.

Motor rickshaws

Scooters are the cheapest mode of transport in Delhi. Basic rate (turning on the meter) 1 R; the fare is calculated according to the tariff displayed on the meter (the 1 R basic rate is included in this) plus another extra rupee (in fact, exactly 95 Ps). Actually, drivers are often unwilling to turn the meter on. Haggling is usually no use; try the next scooter.

The bell-ringing motorbike monsters you see on the streets are called four-seater car rickshaws. There's room for four or more passengers next to the reasonable Sikh driver. They go from Connaught Place (opposite the Regal cinema).

Fares to:

Minto Bridge	75 Ps
Turkman Gate (Ramlila Grounds)	1 R
Delite Cinema (Asaf Ali Road)	1 R
Delhi Gate	1.25 Rs
Darya Ganj	1.25 Rs
Fountain (Chandni Chowk)	1.50 Rs

The last route passes the Tourist Camp (Nehru Marg), Moti Mahal Restaurant, Jama Masjid Mosque and Red Fort.

Cycle rickshaws are found almost only in Old Delhi.

Taxis

Taxis are substantially more expensive than scooters. The basic charge is 2 Rs. Calculating the fare: the amount shown on the meter plus 2 Rs plus luggage charge. At night you have to be prepared for an additional charge of up to 50%.

POST/TELEPHONE

Delhi has two General Post Offices. If your mail is not addressed specifically to the New Delhi GPO, but to the Delhi GPO, you will find it at the Old Delhi GPO, near (Old) Delhi Main Railway Station.

The New Delhi GPO is open 10.00 a.m.-5.00 p.m., and only till 3.00 p.m. on Saturday; closed on Sunday. Poste restante 8.00 a.m.-7.00 p.m.

The poste restante counter at Old Delhi GPO is open every day except

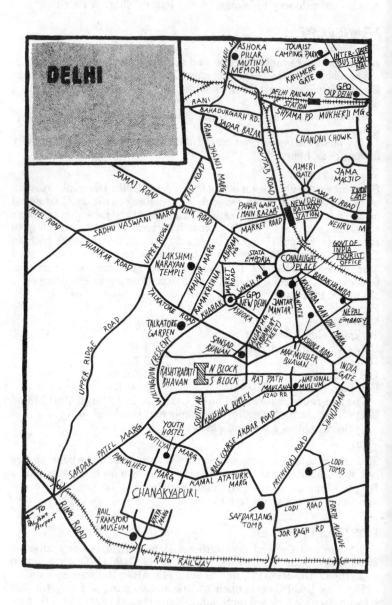

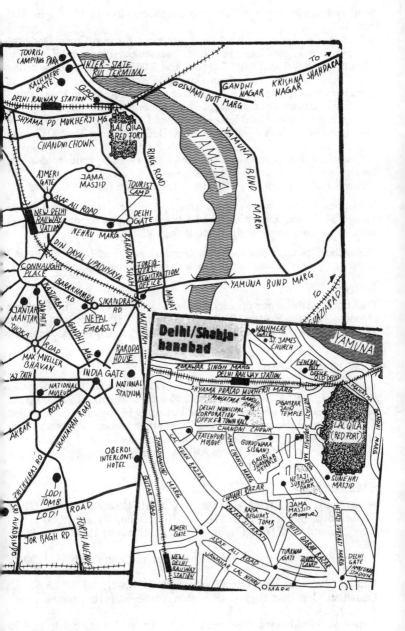

Sunday from 7.00 a.m. to 6.00 p.m. (registered letters 10.00 a.m.-4.00 p.m. only).

Mail sent c/- American Express at American Express Travel Division, Wenger House, A-Block, 1st floor, Connaught Place. Mail service: Monday-Friday 10.00 a.m.-1.00 p.m. and 2.00 p.m.-4.00 p.m, Saturday 10.00 a.m.-12 noon, closed on Sunday. Produce American Express travellers cheques or pay 9 Rs. Letter-forwarding 25 Rs. Parcels and registered letters are not accepted by American Express.

Warning: all registered letters addressed to the New Delhi GPO or c/- American Express end up at New Delhi Delivery Post Office on Market Road.

Don't have any parcels or registered letters sent to your embassy as no-one will take delivery of them there.

Small but efficient Post Office on Connaught Circus.

Telephone: phone overseas at, amongst other places, the Central Telegraph Office, Janpath. Open 24 hours. Possible to make overseas calls even from some budget hotels (e.g. Vishal).

Some tourists have reported that the desk clerks at New Delhi GPO often show only a fraction of the letters available. So insist.

MONEY

One bank with longer opening hours: State Bank of India, Evening Branch, Monday-Friday 10.00 a.m.-6.00 p.m., Saturday 10.00 a.m.-12 noon and 2.00-4.00 p.m. Situated near the Madras Hotel at Connaught Circus.

EXTENDING YOUR VISA

At the Foreigners' Registration Office, Hans Bhavan, Bahadur Shah Zafar Marg, tel. 27 31 90, Open 10.00 a.m.-1.30 p.m., 2.00-4.00 p.m., closed on Sunday and every second Saturday in the month. You need four photos for the extension. The Delhi office is considered to be very stingy. If the length of the extension period doesn't suit you, turn to the (superior) Ministry of Home Affairs, Khan Market; open for tourists between 4.00 and 5.00 p.m. only.

EMBASSIES

Australian, Aust. High Commission, Aust. Compound, No. 1/50-g Shantipath, Chanakyapuri, 110-021, New Delhi, Tel. 60 13 36/9.

New Zealand, N.Z. High Commission, 25 Golf Links 110003 Tel. 69 73 18.

United Kingdom, British High Commission, Chanakyapuri, 1100-21 Tel. 60 13 71.

United States, Shantipath, Chanakyapuri, 110021, Tel. 60 06 51.

Canadian, Canadian High Commission, 7/8 Shantipath, Chanakyapuri, 110021.

Nepalese, Barakhamba Road, tel. 38 65 92. Open Monday-Saturday 8.30

a.m.-1.00 p.m., closed on Sunday and the second Saturday in the month.
A 30-day visa costs 90 Rs. Take three passport photos.

Sri Lankan, 27 Kautilya Marg, tel. 37 02 01. Open Monday-Friday 9.00
a.m.-1.00 p.m. As the three-month visa is no longer available, you can
give the embassy a miss. A one-month visa is issued on arrival in Sri
Lanka.

Bangladeshi, 56 M.G. Road (Ring Road), Lajpat Nagar III, tel. 61 56
68. Open Monday-Friday 10.00 a.m.-12 noon. Take two photos. 24-hour
wait.

Bhutan, Chandra Gupta Marg, tel. 69 92 27. Entry to Bhutan possible
only as a member of a guided tour.

Burmese, 3/50 F, Nyaya Marg, tel. 69 02 51. Open Monday-Friday 10.00
a.m.-12 noon. The seven-day visa costs 40 Rs; take three photos with
you; one day's wait; entry possible only by plane.

Thai, 56N, Nyaya Marg, tel. 61 59 85. Open Monday-Friday 9.00 a.m.-12
noon. A 60-day tourist visa costs 40 Rs. 24-hour wait.

Pakistani, Shanti Path, tel. 69 03 01. Open 9.30 a.m.-12.30 p.m. Friday
only till 11.30 a.m., closed Wednesday and Sunday.

Iranian, 5 Barakhamba Road, tel. 38 54 91. Open Monday-Friday
9.00-11.00 a.m. A two-week transit visa is sometimes available on the
same day, but usually on the next.

Afghanistan, B 54 Greater Kailash, tel. 69 41 86. Open 9.00 a.m.-12
noon, closed on Sunday and the second Saturday in the month. The
chances of getting a visa within a useful period of time are very poor.

PERMITS FOR "PROHIBITED AREAS"

Entry to some areas of India is not allowed or is restricted. Among
these restricted areas are the north-eastern states (Assam, part of West
Bengal, Meghalaya, Nagaland, Tripura, Mizoram, Manipur, Sikkim),
parts of Kashmir, and the Laccadive, Nicobar and Andaman Islands.

You can apply for permits at Indian embassies overseas, in some cases
at Foreigners' Registration Offices or at the Ministry of Home Affairs
in Delhi.

In general the Ministry of Home Affairs (Lok Nayak Bhawan, Khan
Market, tel. 61 19 84) has jurisdiction over prohibited areas on the
Indian mainland; open for tourists on weekdays from 4.00 p.m. to 5.00
p.m. For the Laccadives and Andamans apply to the Ministry of Home
Affairs, North Block, tel. 37 41 03; open 10.15 a.m.-1.00 p.m. and
2.00-5.15 p.m., closed on Sunday and the second Saturday in the month.
Permits for Darjeeling (which belongs to West Bengal) at the Foreigners'
Registration Office (see 'Extending your visa' for address).

Sikkim

Fill out two forms, make a written request, take two passport photos
and wait about three weeks. The permit is free. Only four days are
granted for Gangtok and surrounding areas. A seven-day extension is
supposed to be possible in Gangtok. Sikkim is planned to be opened

up more for tourism. A relaxation of conditions of entry and length of stay may occur.

Darjeeling
If you fly direct to Bagdogra, you will be issued with a supposedly non-extendable 15-day permit. The overland route is possible only with a permit. You can get seven days for free and without any problems at the Foreigners' Registration Office in Delhi (or Calcutta), and a further eight days in Darjeeling itself.

Laccadives
Permits are granted only for the tourist island of Bangara. For the fine sum of $20 the Travel Corporation of India, Hotel Metro, Connaught Place, will arrange everything for you. Apply at least one month before you want to travel (see also 'The Island World of the Laccadives').

Andamans
The 15-day permit (valid for Port Blair and surrounding area) is free, wait four weeks (see also 'Expeditions'/Calcutta and Madras respectively).

Other restricted areas
Permits for other restricted areas are very hard or impossible to get hold of.

SIGHTSEEING

Jantar Mantar, an open-air stone observatory built between about 1710 and 1724, still in operation today on Parliament Street. Admission free.

Red Fort, Old Delhi: huge red seventeenth-century fortress. Admission 50 Ps, free on Friday. The Fort is open every day from sunrise to sunset, and its museum is open from 9.00 a.m. to 5.00 p.m. Every evening (between 7.00 and 10.30 p.m., depending on the time of year) a sound and light show in English; tickets for 3 Rs or 5 Rs available at the Fort booking office and at a few other booking offices elsewhere.

Jama Masjid, Old Delhi, the largest mosque in India with space for about 20,000 people. Admission for non-Muslims 7.00 a.m.-12.30 p.m., and 2.00-5.00 p.m. Photography fee 1 R, filming fee 10 Rs. Good views from the top over the Red Fort and Old Delhi. Hundreds of beggars gather on the steps of the mosque for Friday prayers (at midday).

Qutab Minar, 71 m high minaret built in the thirteenth century. 15 km south of Delhi; 504 bus from Super Bazaar or 502 from the Red Fort, 45-minute journey. You can climb the minaret.
   The 530 bus goes straight to the Qutab Minar. Departs about every 20 minutes, the last bus on weekdays leaves about 10.30 p.m. Can be caught from the bus stop about 20 metres from the Air France office at Connaught Place.

National Museum, Janpath. Open 10.00 a.m.-5.00 p.m., closed on

Monday. Admission 50 Ps. Gives a good insight into Indian art and history.

Also visit the Zoo, which was planned by Carl von Hagenbeck. Admission 50 Ps. Closed on Friday, open other days till about 5.00 p.m. (6.00 p.m. in summer). Main attractions: the white tiger and clouded leopard.

Cheapest DTC sightseeing tour: New Delhi (9.00 a.m.-1.00 p.m.) costs 6 Rs, Old Delhi (2.00-4.45 p.m.) 5 Rs, the two tours combined 10 Rs. Reservations, tickets and departures from DTC, Scindia House, Connaught Circus.

SOUVENIRS

The 20 or so Government emporia are a real shopping paradise. These are the government-run shops of the individual Indian states. They are situated in the three State Emporia Buildings on Baba Kharak Singh Marg (previously Irwin Road), near Connaught Place. You can find everything in them, from Mysore sandalwood soap to gemstones, spices and textiles. A shopping stroll through India without travelling. All the shops are air conditioned, open between about 10.00 a.m. and 6.30 p.m, various lunch-hours, closed on Sunday. Fixed prices. Most of the state shops have tourist information.

In case you don't go to Nepal: Nepalese and Tibetan souvenirs are available in the Tibetan Market on Janpath, north of the Imperial Hotel in the direction of Connaught Place.

Spectacle frames and lenses are considerably cheaper in India than in Europe.

Dentists in Delhi are supposed to be better than elsewhere in India.

Delhi's shopping centres are the area around Connaught Place and the bazaars (e.g. Chandni Chowk in Old Delhi).

INFORMATION OFFICES

Government of India Tourist Office, Janpath 88, tel. 32 00 05. Open 9.00 a.m.-6.00 p.m (8.00 a.m.-6.00 p.m. in summer), Saturday and holidays 9.00 a.m. (8.00 in summer) to 1.00 p.m., closed on Sunday. Helpful and obliging.

Tourist offices of the Indian states of Haryana, Jammu & Kashmir, Rajasthan, Himachal Pradesh and Uttar Pradesh in the Chandralok Building, 36 Janpath. All open Monday to Friday from 10.00 a.m. to 5.00 p.m., closed on Sunday and the second Saturday in the month. About 20 tourist offices of various Indian states in the State Emporia Buildings (see 'Souvenirs').

More tourist offices at the Interstate Bus Terminal (6.00 a.m.-10.00 p.m. daily, tel.22 90 83), Old Delhi Railway Station (7.00 a.m.-9.00 p.m. daily, tel. 25 10 83), New Delhi Railway Station (6.00 a.m.-9.00 p.m. daily, tel. 32 10 78) and the India Tourist counter at Palam Airport.

UP AND AWAY

Airlines: Indian Airlines: Kanchenjunga Building, Barakhamba Road, tel. 4 00 71. Open 24 hours a day, but tickets sold 9.00 a.m.-7.00 p.m. Air India: next to the Government of India Tourist Office on Janpath, tel.34 42 25. Open every day 9.30 a.m.-5.30 p.m.
Most of the other airlines are also situated in the Connaught Place district.
Royal Nepal Airlines (RNAC), Hotel Janpath, 44 Janpath, tel. 31 259.

Cheap-flight travel agents: The largest concentration of these is in the restaurants and hotels of Paharganj (Main Bazaar) and around Connaught Place (e.g. Students Travel Information Centre); cheap airline tickets also available in the Tourist Camp.
Some examples of prices from the Students Travel Information Centre, Hotel Imperial, Janpath, tel. 34 47 89:
Europe from 3200 Rs, Bangkok 2485 Rs (25% cheaper with an international under-26 student card), Singapore 3790 Rs (25% discount up to 27 years old even without a student card).

Palam Airport
The 780 bus leaves Super Bazaar every 30 minutes until about 11.00 p.m.; fare is 60 Ps. The EATS (Ex-Servicemen's Airlink transport Service) leaves from its office in the Malhotra Building, F-Block, Connaught Place, Janpath, tel. 4 65 30; fare is 8 Rs. It serves all international flights. It's also possible to catch it at some hotels, which are on the route to the airport (e.g. Hotel Imperial, the YMCA).
All-inclusive taxi fare is about 30 Rs, the scooter fare is about half that.
At the airport, the tourist office, post office and State Bank of India are open round the clock. It's possible to change any unspent rupees back into dollars at the State Bank counter as long as you can produce at least one exchange receipt to cover the amount you are changing back. Airport tax must be paid at the State Bank counter before you check in; 50 Rs for nationals of neighbouring countries, 100 Rs for others. Even Afghanistan and the Maldives count as neighbouring countries.

AWAY

Freak buses: Freak buses depart from the Tourist Camp and (seldom) Connaught Place. Watch for notices in backpackers meeting places. Approximate prices: $300 to Central Europe, $130-$180 to Istanbul or Athens, $35-$45 to Kathmandu, about $40 to Goa.

Rail/Reservations
The tourist quota is administered by the Railway Tourist Guide, Baroda House, tel. 38 78 89. Open 10.00 a.m.-5.00 p.m., closed on Sunday and every second Saturday in the month. However, tickets and definite reservations are not available from Baroda House; you will be referred

with a form to the railway station appropriate to your destination or to the Northern Railway Office on State Entry Road. You get Indrail Passes at Baroda House, at the Northern Railway Reservation Office on State Entry Road, and also at Everett Travel Service at Connaught Place.

MISCELLANEOUS

Health: cholera vaccinations at NDMC Townhall, Parliament Street. Open weekdays 7.30 a.m.-1.00 p.m., 2.00-7.00 p.m. 5 Rs with certificate stamped.

Gammaglobulin vaccination (innoculation against jaundice) is available only from doctors. Doses and therefore prices vary according to body weight; about 30-50 Rs. Doctors and laboratories for stool, blood and urine analysis are mostly in the Connaught Place district. In the same area, chemist Kemp & Co. (1-E Connaught Place) and the chemist in the Super Bazaar–both open 24 hours a day.

Ambulance: tel. 102.

According to some reports at the Irwin Hospital, medicines, treatment and hospital accommodation are free. It's diagonally across from the Tourist Camp.

Swimming: the swimming pool in Talkatore Park (25-m. pool) is open for 50-minute sessions from early morning until about 9.35 a.m., and again in the evening from 5.30 to 9.20 p.m.

It costs 22 Rs to swim in the swimming pool of the Hotel Imperial, Janpath. Open 8.00 a.m.-10.00 p.m.

International student cards (and stamps) are available on production of a student identity card at the Students Travel Information Centre in the Hotel Imperial (see also 'Cheap-flight travel agents').

As in all Indian towns, in Delhi English street names from colonial days have been 'Indianised'; so many streets have two names, the English and the Indian one.

More information in 'Delhi Diary' (1 R, weekly, includes calendar of events), 'Delhi & New Delhi Guide for Businessmen & Visitors' (4 Rs), Wrangler 'Delhi Tourist Guide' (4 Rs), Darshan 'Delhi & New Delhi' (3.50 Rs), and 'Know Thy Delhi' (3 Rs); all available at Connaught Place. A free publication, 'Delhi Welcomes You' (monthly) is available in some hotels. All these publications have errors and inaccuracies.

Quite good and cheap maps of India (unfortunately only a small selection) from the Map Sales Office, Survey of India, on the left near Central Cottages Emporium, 1st floor, Janpath; open weekdays 10.15 a.m.-1.30 p.m. and 2.00-5.00 p.m.

Good bookshops around Connaught Place (e.g. B.E.D. Galgotia & Sons, 17-B Connaught Place).

Foreign newspapers and magazines can be read for free in the Max Mueller Bhavan, 3 Kasturba Gandhi Marg (formerly Curzon Rd), not far from Connaught Place; the reading room is in the rear building; open Monday-Saturday 11.00 a.m.-6.00 p.m.

US newspapers and books in the air conditioned reading room of the American Library, USIS Building, 24 Kasturba Gandhi Marg; open Monday-Saturday 9.30 a.m.-6.00 p.m.

Other reading rooms: British Council Library, Rafi Marg, and Alliance Francaise, D-6, NDSE, Pt. II.

If you are in Delhi on 26 January, don't miss Republic Day: a military parade with decorated elephants and camels, warrior tribes, folkloric groups, and cultural events during the three-day folk festival.

The automobile club, the Automobile Association of Upper India (AAUI) is at 14-F, Connaught Place, on the intermediate ring road between (inner) Connaught Place and (outer) Connaught Circus, tel. 4 51 38. Open 10.00 a.m.-1.00 p.m., 2.00-4.00 p.m., Saturday 10.00 a.m.-1.00 p.m., closed on Sunday.

Camping gas containers can be refilled at the Delhi Gas Co., 76 Janpath (near the Tourist Office).

CONNECTIONS FROM DELHI

Check out the following chapters on further travel ('From Delhi to. . .'). Other connections can be found for some other destinations under 'Further travel'.

Further information
Rail: from Enquiries in New Delhi Railway Station (tel. 34 37 27; open 24 hours) and Enquiries, Old Delhi R. St. (tel. 25 55 60; open 24 hours).
Bus: all Government buses and even some deluxe buses depart from the Interstate Bus Terminus, Kashmiri Gate, general enquiries tel. 22 90 83.
Air: the Indian Airlines office is situated in the Kanchenjunga Building, Barakhamba Road, tel. 4 00 71. Open 24 hours every day for information.

For some airfares and possible services from Delhi see 'India General'/'Flights'.

From Delhi to Amritsar
Rail/Bus/Air
For lists of services and fares see 'From Amritsar to Delhi'.

From Delhi to Agra
Rail
The quickest service is the Taj Express, one of India's super-trains. 7.10 a.m. every day from New Delhi, arrives Agra Cantt at 10.20 a.m.; 2nd class 15.55 Rs.
On the Taj Express's arrival tickets are sold on the train or in the main Agra Cantt railway station for a whole day's sightseeing tour that starts at 10.30 a.m. This connecting sightseeing tour is organised by the Govt. Tourist Office and ends at 6.30 p.m. at Agra Cantt railway station.
Return journey by the Taj Express leaves Agra Cantt at 6.55 p.m.; about a 3-hour journey. So you can make a one-day trip to Agra and spend nearly 9 hours there.
Three other good 'normal' trains depart from Delhi at 7.55 a.m., 10.15 a.m, and 3.20 p.m; 2nd class 12.55 Rs.

Bus
Ordinary, 16.50 Rs, approximately hourly between 5.30 a.m. and 6.30 p.m.; deluxe 19.75 Rs, about 5 buses between 7.30 a.m. and 4.30 p.m.; 204 km. All buses depart from the Interstate Bus Terminal at Kashmiri

Gate. Private bus companies in Delhi organise one-day trips to Agra for 45 Rs return. See advertisements in hotels. Bus tours organised by the Tourist Office in Delhi cost 110 Rs.

Air
At least one flight every day by Indian Airlines; 130 Rs.

From Delhi to Bombay (and Goa)

Rail: Four good services from Delhi to Bombay Central:
Depart Old Delhi 7.55 a.m. (New Delhi 8.20 a.m.); 4 Frontier Mail.
Depart Old Delhi 1.55 p.m. (New Delhi 2.20 p.m.); 24 Janata Express.
Depart New Delhi 4.05 p.m.; 26 AC/Pashim Express.
Depart Old Delhi 9.25 p.m. (New Delhi 10.25 p.m.); 20 Bombay Express.
Fares in second class about 62 Rs; 1390 km; travelling time between 24 hours (Frontier Mail) and 32 hours.
Two trains travel via Agra (Taj Mahal) and Manmad (for Ajanta and Ellora):
6 Punjab Mail departs Old Delhi 6.10 a.m. (New Delhi 7.55 a.m.). Arrives Bombay Victoria Terminus next day at 12.40 p.m.
58 Amritsar-Dadar Express departs New Delhi 9.30 a.m. Arrives Bombay/Dadar on day after next at 5.20 a.m. Dadar is 6 km north of Bombay Central and 9 km north of Bombay V.T.
Second-class return fare for the 1550 km journey about 68 Rs.
All these trains have second-class sleepers.

Bus: Only overland buses coming from Europe or Kathmandu to Goa. Delhi to Goa costs about $40. Departure dates on notice boards in appropriate restaurants, hotels, travel agents and meeting places in Delhi.

Air: Several flights every day by Indian Airlines and Air India: 687 Rs.

OTHER SIGHTSEEING TRIPS

Instead of travelling direct from Delhi to Bombay, there are interesting diversions if you get off and stay at Agra, Jaipur, Ajanta/Ellora (see 'Bombay').

You can of course make more stops (e.g. Ajmer/Pushkar and Udaipur). But it's not worth staying in Ahmedabad.

From Bombay to Goa
All information under 'Bombay'.

From Delhi to Kashmir
(See Kashmir/Arrival)

From Delhi to Nepal

Direct from Delhi to Kathmandu

Rail/Bus

Twice-weekly direct rail service to Muzzaffarpur, 130 km south of the Nepalese border: the 154 Jayanti Janata Express leaves Old Delhi Thursday and Sunday 7.05 p.m. (6.25 p.m. in summer). Arrives Muzaffarpur Friday and Monday at 4.45 p.m.; 1224 km; 22-hour journey; 62 Rs (2nd class). Very poor rail services (change at Sagauli) after the Indian border crossing at Raxaul. Better to take a bus from there; 10 Rs; 3-4 hour journey; 137 km.

Daily service to Muzaffarpur with only one change (in Barauni) on the 86 Assam Mail; departs Delhi 9.40 a.m., arrives Barauni 5.55 a.m.; then 2 connections to Muzaffarpur.

Other direct travel possibilities in the Nepal/Pokhara direction from Delhi via Lucknow; 4 express trains every day; 7-10 hour journey; 507 km. Five trains daily from Lucknow to Gorakhpur; about an 8-hour journey; 275 km; 41.85 Rs in 2nd class. Bus from Gorakhpur to the Indian-Nepalese border crossing at Sonauli; about 7 Rs; 85 km.

Air

At least one flight every day from Delhi to Kathmandu by Indian Airlines or Royal Nepal Airlines Corporation (RNAC). US$125, $94 with youth discount. The flight via Patna (change planes) is a bit cheaper: normal fare US$110, $82.50 with youth discount.

From Delhi to Kathmandu via Benares

Three express trains every day from Delhi to Benares (Varanasi); about an 18-hour journey; 831 km; 2nd class 45.15 Rs.

Also some super-express trains, which do not run every day: the 176 Neelachal Express (day train; departs New Delhi Tuesday, Thursday and Sunday; 12 hours); the 82 AC Express (night train; departs New Delhi Monday, Tuesday and Friday; 13 hours); and the 154 Jayanti Janata Express (night train; departs Old Delhi Thursday and Sunday; 12 1/2 hours).

In addition 6 other expresses daily, which travel to Mughal Sarai (suburban station in Varanasi). These expresses continue on to Patna, which is also a good starting point for trips to Nepal.

From Benares to Nepal via Gorakhpur

Rail:

Since the extension of the meter gauge (narrow gauge) to Breitspur, rail services on the 233 km route between Benares and Gorakhpur have been improved. At the time of going to press no new timetable details were available (previously, the journey took more than 7 hours, changing trains in Bhatni).

Anyhow, take a bus from Gorakhpur to the Nepalese border (96 km), as only 3 slow trains a day travel to the border station of Nautanwa (82 km; 3-hour journey).

Bus

Direct bus to the Indian border at Sonauli (also Sunauli); departs

Varanasi early in the morning at 5.00 a.m; 20 Rs; about a 9-hour journey. Otherwise 5 or 6 buses daily from Benares to Gorakhpur; even a deluxe bus at 9.30 a.m and 3.00 p.m; 5-6 hour journey; 195 km.
Connecting bus from Gorakhpur to Sonauli 7 Rs; 3-4 hour journey; 96 km.

Sonauli/Ghairawa Border

Sonauli and the Nepalese border town of Bhairawa are about 4 km apart. Reckon on one hour for formalities. Time is 10 minutes later in Nepal. 100 IRs = 145 NRs (Nepalese rupees). After crossing the border take a rickshaw or share-taxi to Bhairawa.

On to Pokhara and Kathmandu

Express buses leave Bhairawa for Pokhara 4 times during the morning and once in the early afternoon; 29 Rs; 6-10 hour journey. Minibus 35-38 Rs; 6-8 hour journey; 180 km.
Daily flight from Bhairawa to Kathmandu by RNAC; 540 Rs; 45 minutes.
Drivers: 180 km on the Siddharta Rajmarg to Pokhara. It's worth stopping in Tansen. Drive on the left in Nepal. Petrol is expensive.

ACCOMMODATION

Pashupati Lodge, Main Chowk (main street). Double with WC/shower 27.50 Rs.

From Benares to Nepal via Raxaul

Rail

There is one very good, fast service a day, with only two changes and includes a steamer trip on the Ganges.
Depart Varanasi on the 14 Upper India Express at 1.30 p.m.; 230 km; arrive Patna 7.00 p.m. Rickshaw from Patna Junction railway station, about 3 km to the Mahendrughat on the Ganges. Depart 8.50 on the paddlesteamer; 1 1/2 hours upstream, about 40 km, to the Palezaghat railhead. The boat is usually very full (try 1st class). Arrive Palezaghat at 10.20 p.m. Board the 78 Mahendrughat Narkatiaganj Express. Depart 11.00 p.m.; 293 km to Raxaul at the Indian-Nepalese border; arrive 11.42 a.m. (12.50 p.m. in summer). 2nd class costs 32.55 Rs; total of 564 km; nearly 22-hour journey.
There is another daily service which involves changing trains three times, but is a bit cheaper, shorter (450 km) and quicker (18 hours). Here is the new timetable:

Depart Varanasi...................	9.00 p.m.–262 km, 72 Down
Arrive Sonpur....................	6.55 a.m.–change trains
Depart Sonpur...................	7.50 a.m.–58 km, 520 Down
Arrive Muzaffarpur...............	9.45 a.m.–change trains

Depart Muzaffarpur.............. 10.15 a.m.–101 km, 449 Up
Arrive Sagauli................... 1.41 p.m.–change trains
Depart Sagauli.................. 2.00 p.m.–29 km, 356 Down
Arrive Raxaul................... 3.00 p.m.

The last three times are a bit later in the summer timetable. If you are too tired to wait for the late train in Sagauli, take a local bus for the last 24 km to Raxaul; 2 Rs.

The 154 Jayanti Janata Express leaves Varanasi twice weekly (Monday and Friday) for Mazaffarpur via Patna and (with a slight detour) Barauni.

Depart Varanasi................ 7.35 a.m.
Depart Patna.................. 11.44 a.m.
Arrive Mazaffarpur.............. 4.45 p.m.

At a little more than 9 hours, this is the quickest service; 462 km; 2nd class to Mazaffarpur costs 26.90 Rs. Bus from Muzaffarpur to Raxaul; 10 Rs; about a 4-hour journey; 137 km.

'The best service from Muzaffarpur to Raxaul is the bus, hourly, travelling time 3 hours, 10 Rs.'

Rail and Bus
The Nepal Travel Service, Kothi Parade (next to the Govt Tourist Bungalow) in Benares sells tickets for the trip to Kathmandu by bus and rail for 105 Rs, which includes reservations, hotel (Sagar Lodge, Birganj) and breakfast. For those who feel they need to know the itinerary:

9.25 p.m. Depart Varanasi on the 72 Fast Passenger (sleeper); 208 km
4.35 a.m. Arrive Chapra (5.15 a.m. in summer)
7.15 a.m. Depart Chapra by bus; approx 220-230 km
2.00 p.m. or a bit later arrive Raxaul, cross border, spend night in Birganj
5.30 a.m. the following morning. Bus to Kathmandu

You can of course make this trip off your own bat, following this timetable. 2nd class to Chapra costs 9.75 Rs, bus to Raxaul 20-25 Rs; 7-8 hour journey. One train also goes from Benares to Chapra in the morning, but then you are most unlikely to catch a bus to Raxaul in Chapra. Chapra is also written 'Chhapraa', 'Chupra' and 'Chopra'.

Air
Daily direct flights by Indian Airlines from Benares to Kathmandu; US$65, US$50 with youth discount; 45-minute flight; sit on the left for views of the Himalayas.

For about half the cost you can fly from Patna, which is only 4 1/2 hours by rail (15 Rs, 230 km) east of Benares. At least one flight daily by RNAC or Indian Airlines; US$34, US$27 with youth discount; 45-60 minute flight (depending on the type of aeroplane). It's 8 km from Patna City to the airport. RNAC office in Patna: Hasan Manzil, Fraser Road, tel. 2 32 05. Indian Airlines Office in Patna: South Gandhi Maidan, tel. 2 25 54.

Car

It's altogether about 600 km to the border: Benares–250 km, Patna–48 km, Bakhtiarpur–43 km, Mokamah–bridge over the Ganges–20 km, Barauni–103 km, Muzaffarpur–84 km, Motihari–29 km, Sagauli–24 km, Raxaul (border crossing).

A car ferry over the Ganges at Mandanpura, near Patna, to Palezaghat, then about 88 km to Muzaffarpur. This shortens the journey by 126 km.

'The ferry crossing takes about 2 1/2 hours as the ferry goes quite far upstream and the Ganges at this point has a very strong current so in places the ferry can travel hardly faster than walking pace.'

RAXAUL/BIRGANJ BORDER

The Indian border town is called Raxaul, the Nepalese town Birganj (also 'Birgunj). The two places are 5 km apart.

If you want to be driven over the border by tonga it costs about 10 Rs. The driver will wait until the formalities have been completed.

On the Indian side there is first the passport control and then customs. Indian rupees are not allowed to be taken out of the country but in fact officials at this border usually turn a blind eye. Many travellers are coming back to India. In case you want to change your Indian rupees back and the exchange counter is closed (after 6.00 p.m.): you can still change your money on the Nepalese side; also possible at the streetside money-changers in Raxaul. There are 145 Nepali rupees (NRs) to 100 Indian rupees (IRs).

On the Nepalese side there is first the Immigration Office (passport control) where, if you haven't already got one, you get a 7-day visa for 122 NRs and a passport photo. You are given a Foreign Exchange Transaction Form, on which you are supposed to make sure are entered all the exchange transactions you make while in Nepal. Only by showing this form when you leave Nepal can you change back any unused Nepalese rupees.

There is a branch of the Nepal Rastra Bank in a free-standing, white building next to Customs; you can buy Nepalese rupees here. You can even get them for Indian rupees, even though it is actually illegal–no-one bothers about it. You get 136–145NRs for 100Rs (145 is the official exchange rate). The counter closes at 6.00 p.m. You can also change travellers cheques at the Sagar Lodge, Birganj.

Border formalities take about one hour. Luggage is hardly ever searched.

Put your watch forward by 10 minutes (Indian time plus 10 minutes).

ACCOMMODATION

In Raxaul: Tourist Lodge or Railway Retiring Rooms.

'National Lodge & Restaurant, Blockroad, near the station and bus. The manager will organise everything for you, buses and trains etc., in return for a little baksheesh.'

Better accommodation in Birganj, e.g. Hotel Star; dormitory 8 Rs, single 20 Rs; Hotel Koseli or Sagar Lodge. Hotel Diyalo, right opposite the large bus station in Birganj, has rooms with and without air conditioning.

Tips for spending the night in Patna: Hotel Gayland, New Dak Bungalow Road; rickshaw from the station 1 R.

Hotel Grand next to the Tourist Office. Clean single rooms with shower and WC for 15 Rs.

The Hotel Nilgiri. New and very clean. Single with bath about 20 Rs, double with bath 25 Rs.

Drivers

Fill up before leaving India; Nepal has the most expensive petrol on this trip. Few petrol stations along the way. Drive on the left in Nepal. Border is closed between about 10.00 p.m. and 6.00 a.m. Even so, it's possible to get through with luck, cheek and/or baksheesh (not necessarily in that order).

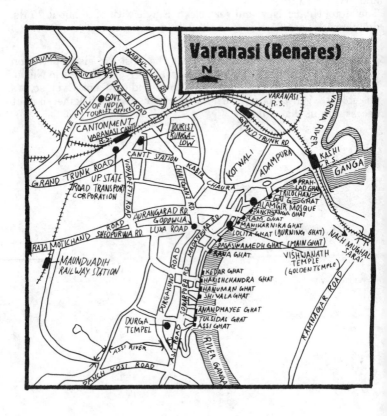

BENARES (VARANASI)

Population 800,000; 81 m above sea-level. Holiest city of the Hindus. Countless pilgrims come to Varanasi (the English called it Benares) from every distant corner of India to bathe in the holy waters of the Ganges, or die there.

ARRIVAL

Rail

If you arrive at Varanasi Jn (Cantt) railway station: Tourist Bungalow and other cheap hotels are within walking distance; take a rickshaw to the other hotels. A rickshaw to the Main Ghat on the Ganges, where there are also budget hotels, costs 2 RS (but you'll always be stung for a bit more).

If you arrive at the suburban station of Mughal Sarai: make the approx. 17 km trip to Godaulia (Godowlia), the centre of Benares, by train or local bus.

Bus

The bus station is near Varanasi Cantt railway station.

Air

An Indian Airlines bus (10Rs) goes from the airport, which is 22 km outside the city, to the district where the expensive hotels are (Clark's, de Paris, etc.). Get off at de Paris; the cheap hotels are within walking distance or go by rickshaw to the other budget hotels at Cantt railway station or on the Ganges (Main Ghat).

ACCOMMODATION

Warning: most of the hotels listed here don't exist, are being renovated or are already full–according to the rickshaw drivers. Reason: these hotels don't pay the drivers any commission.

Hotels near the Ganges (Main Ghat)
Sri Venkateswar Lodge, 5/64 Desashwamed Ghat Road, near Main Ghat on the Ganges, rather hard to find, in a back street, tel. 66 800. Single 8 Rs, double 16 Rs, triple 21/24 Rs; 24-hour system; highly recommended.
Central Hotel, Dasashwamed Road, tel. 62 776. Single 5-15 Rs (17-20 Rs with bath), double 7-25 Rs (30-50 Rs with bath); 24-hour system; restaurant in the hotel.
Bellevue Lodge, Dasashwamed. Single 10 Rs, double 15 Rs (20 Rs with bath), triple 25 Rs.
Yogi Lodge, 8/29 Kalika Gali, in a lane in the old city. Single 10-15 Rs, double 15-20 Rs, dormitory 5-7 Rs. 10% extra tax. Roof garden. Simple restaurant.

Om House Lodge, D. 12/26, Nichi Brahmapuri (Bans Phatak), in the middle of a maze of lanes in the old city. Single 6 Rs, double 12/15 Rs. Roof garden. Safe for valuables. Bicycle hire (6 Rs/day). The manager gives yoga lessons and arranges music lessons.

Hotel Moti Mahal, near Central Hotel. Dormitory 5 Rs, single 10 Rs, double 15 Rs.

'We had a double room for 15Rs. Very clean, large beds, four windows, communal kitchen with utensils provided.'

Other cheap hotels
Govt Tourist Bungalow, Parade Kothi, a few minutes' walk from the main railway station, tel. 55 415. Single 12 Rs (15 Rs with bath), double (with bath) 25 Rs, triple (with bath) 30 Rs, dormitory bed 5 Rs. 24-hour system. Own restaurant and U. P. Tourist Office counter.

Hotel Relax, right by the entrance to the Tourist Bungalow, similar prices.

Hotel Garden View, D 64/129, Amar Niwas, Sigra-Quarter, tel. 63 026. Single 15-20 Rs, double 25-45 Rs, triple 30-45 Rs, deluxe room 45-65 Rs. All rooms have baths, warm water and music. A bit off the beaten track and noisy, but the people managing it are nice and will organise train reservations.

The Hotel Empire, centrally located in Godaulia, is good. Single with bath costs about 25 Rs.

Hint for travellers on the cheap
The cheapest accommodation is in houseboats on the banks of the Ganges (cost only a few rupees), but there are no creature comforts. Naturally impossible during the monsoon floods. Warning: lots of thefts!

Middle-class hotels
(No middle-class hotels on the Ganges)
Hotel Ajaya, Lahurabir, tel. 53 440. Single 20-50 Rs (75 Rs with AC), double 30-60 Rs (90 Rs with AC), extra bed 10-20 Rs. 10% extra tax. All rooms have bath. 24-hour system. Restaurant available.

Hotel Ashok, Vidyapeeth Road, tel. 54 391. Similar prices as Hotel Ajaya. Also AC and 24-hour system.

The Hotel Faran is good and worth the money. Double room with bathtub and WC 60 Rs. Also, the restaurant is good and cheap.

Campers
Hotel Over Lander's (formerly Hotel River View), turn right (signposted) off the street that leads to Clark's Hotel. Camping 2 Rs per person. Large parking area. Also has rooms: single 20 Rs, double 35 Rs, dormitory 6 Rs. 10% extra tax. All rooms have bath. English colonial-style house. Near the Varuna River.

Tourist Dak Bungalow, 59 Cantonment, near the Tourist Office, tel. 64 461. Parking fees: small car 6 Rs, VW bus 10 Rs. Rooms: in the old wing–single 30 Rs, double 50 Rs, extra bed 15 Rs; new wing–double 60 Rs, extra bed 20 Rs. All rooms have bath, and in the new wing some have air-coolers. Pretty surroundings. Quiet. But an expensive restaurant.

RESTAURANTS

Monga Underground Restaurant, near Central Hotel, on the road to the Main Ghat. Good, cheap Chinese cooking.

Aces New Deal Restaurant, Godaulia, opposite KCM cinema. If you're coming from the Main Ghat, go right at the first large cross-roads, and the restaurant is a few metres along on the right-hand side. Backpacker meeting-place with ice cream and western food.

'The cheapest food is in the Varanasi Guesthouse near the river. Four-course meal with rice and tea is 7Rs.'

'Kwality Restaurant: highly recommended, good plentiful food, but not particularly cheap.'

SIGHTSEEING

Benares (Varanasi to the Indians) is one of the oldest cities in the world (3000 years) and the centre of Hinduism. The main sights lie on the banks of the Ganges with its 64 ghats and countless gurus, believers and saddhus. No other Indian city radiates such atmosphere and fascination as the old part of Benares.

Boat trip on the Ganges at dawn, when the faithful come to the ghats (steps on the riverbank) to bathe, pray and be blessed by brahmins under sunshades. Rowing boats leave from the Main Ghat (Dasashwamedh Ghat); 3-5 Rs per hour.

Burning Ghat (Manikarnika Ghat), where dead Hindus are ceremonially cremated; 24-hour service. Thousands of believers come to Benares to die. Their ashes are scattered on the holy Ganges. Photography is not allowed but in return for a bit of baksheesh (5 Rs per photo, though you'll at first be asked for more) it's possible to photograph the cremation area from the boat. But everyone should decide for themselves whether this is tasteful or not.

Vishwanath Temple (Golden Temple) in the old city. The centre of Shiva worship. No entry for non-Hindus; but you can watch the temple activities through a peep-hole in a back street and photograph the temple's golden roof from a neighbouring house, but of course not for free. It's important to establish the price first, otherwise you'll be asked afterwards for an exorbitant sum.

Right on the Main Ghat and visited by hardly anyone is Jai Singh's Observatory (there's another one in Jaipur). Entrance free. Good views over the Ganges.

Durga or Monkey Temple: Hindu temple on Durgakand Road in the south of the city, with 'holy' monkeys running about. The gallery is open to non-Hindus.

Bharat Mata Mandir (Mother India Temple) with huge marble relief of the subcontinent.

Tulsi Manas Mandir (Marble Temple) situated in a garden, surrounded by Disneyland-like statues of gods.

Wander through the crooked, narrow streets of the old city on the riverbanks. A fascinating adventure. See the highwater marks drawn on the fronts of the houses along the banks. This will give you some idea of the huge body of water that pours through Benares in the monsoon season, flooding temples and houses.

Two sightseeing tours depart daily from the Tourist Bungalow: 1. River trip/temples/university; about 5.30 a.m.-12.00 noon; 9.75 Rs; 2. Sarnath/Ramnagar Fort; about 2.00-6.00 p.m.; 10.25 Rs. Ramnagar Fort (15 km) is a maharajah's palace, and Sarnath (8 km) is a place of pilgrimage for Buddhists: Buddha preached his first sermon here.

SHOPPING

Benares is both famous and infamous for its silk. Much of what is sold as silk here is nothing of the kind or is at least not pure silk. The price per square metre varies between about 15 Rs and 30 Rs. Guys will accost you all the time in the street, wanting to take you to 'their' shop or 'their' factory. Don't get mixed up with them–you'll pay high prices as a secret commission will be tacked on. Benares is a good place to buy Indian musical instruments. A sitar costs between 400 Rs and 2000 Rs, depending on the quality; tablas 150-200 Rs.

Other souvenirs: chillums (from 50 Ps), marble statues and incense.

'Cheap, attractive flutes from the pedlars on the Main Ghat. Especially attractive are snake-charmers' flutes–from 8 Rs. Very fragile, and difficult to travel with.'

'You can be ripped off buying musical instruments. Many shops promise to send your purchase to your home address. But to do that they need a licence, which most shops don't have. Also, you'll be enticed with false promises and statements. For example, Ravi's Classical Music Centre has nothing to do with Ravi Shankar and also doesn't actually manufacture the instruments.'

'Worth buying: silk brocade, sandalwood-boxes and -bangles.'

'Brass statues of Indian gods that believers buy as mementoes of their pilgrimage are available for a few rupees. Also attractive and cheap: enamelled decorative plates.'

MISCELLANEOUS

Govt of India Tourist Office, 15 B The Mall, Cantt, tel. 64 189. Open 9.00 a.m.-5.00 p.m., 9.00 a.m.-1.00 p.m. on every second Saturday in the month and holidays, closed on Sunday. Large choice of multilingual leaflets.

Another Govt of India Tourist Information Counter at Babatpur airport.

U.P. Government Tourist Bureau, Parade Kothi (in the Tourist Bungalow), tel. 63 186. Open 10.00 a.m.-5.00 p.m., closed on Sunday and every second Saturday in the month.

U.P. Tourist Information at the railway station. Open every day 9.00 a.m.-7.00 p.m., tel. 53 887. Few leaflets.

What's good for a devout Hindu is not necessarily good for a tourist: one sip of water from the holy Ganges, which contains the untreated sewage of several million people, could be fatal.

Swimming: for 10 Rs you can use the swimming pools of the Hotel Clark's and Varanasi Ashok (not to be confused with Hotel Ashok).

Post/telephone: GPO, Bisheswarganj, Kotwali district. Poste restante open 10.00 a.m.-6.00 p.m., closed on Sunday. The Central Telegraph Office is in the Cantt, near the Tourist Dak Bungalow. Another post office there too.

Money: change travellers cheques at, amongst other places, the Benares State Bank, 52/1 Luxa Road, near the Main Ghat.

Visa extensions: at the Foreigners' Registration Office, Srinagar Colony.

FURTHER TRAVEL

(For other connections see 'From Benares to Nepal')

Rail
Some important services depart from Cantt Railway Station (Reservation Office, tel. 6 49 20; open all day).

To Calcutta:
52 Jammutawi-Sealdah Express, departs 1.29 a.m.
82 New Delhi-Howrah Express, 5.35 a.m., Monday, Tuesday, Friday.
14 Upper India Express, 1.30 p.m.
50 Amritsar-Howrah Express, 7.56 p.m.
6 Amritsar-Howrah Mail, 5.35 p.m.

To Delhi:
113 Ganga-Yamuna Express, departs 1.05 p.m. Tuesday, Wednesday, Saturday, Sunday; other days 1.25 p.m.
175 Neelachal Express, 9.35 a.m., Monday, Wednesday, Saturday.
13 Upper India Express, 6.46 p.m.
157 Kashi-Vishwanath Express, 2.15 p.m.

To Bombay:
194 Maha Nagiri Express, 11.10 a.m., Tuesday, Friday.
28 Express (only to Dadar), 11.00 a.m.

To Amritsar:
49 Howrah-Amritsar Express, 9.26 a.m.
5 Howrah-Amritsar Mail, 10.15 a.m.

To Madras:
140 Ganga-Kaveri Express, 7.05 a.m., Tuesday, Sunday.

To Agra:
Upper India Express, departs 6.46 p.m., through-carriage to Agra.
Krishna Agencies, a one-man-band, will take care of train reservations
for a fee of 10 Rs. The guy calls into the budget hotels on the Ganges
every evening. Thanks to his connections, he's successful even with
trains that are officially booked up.

Bus
The bus station of the Uttar Pradesh (U.P.) State Transport Corporation
is in the Cantonment, near the railway station. Services to Gorakhpur
(see 'From Benares to Nepal') and Allahabad.

Air
Calcutta: three direct flights weekly, 423 Rs. Also three flights weekly
to Delhi, 430 Rs. Flight to Agra (change planes at Khajurahao), 350
Rs. See also 'India-General/Air'.
Further information from Indian Airlines, Mint House Motel, Cantt,
tel. 64 146.

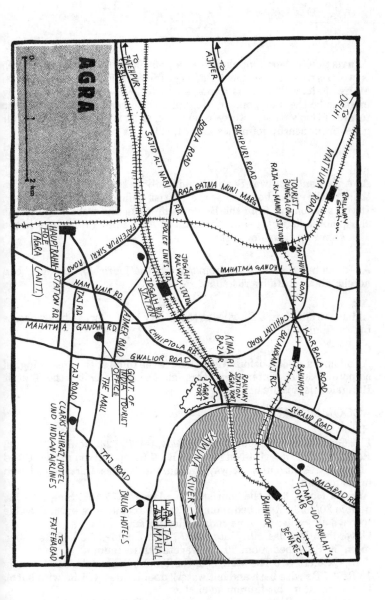

AGRA

A diversion to Agra (population about 500,000, 169 m above sea-level) is worthwhile. India's most famous sightseeing attraction, the Taj Mahal, is here. The Taj is a monument to love, and is considered by many to be the high point of Moghul architecture. Unfortunately the future of this vast structure doesn't look at all hopeful: waste sulphur gases from nearby refineries are attacking its masonry.

ARRIVAL

Rail

At Agra Cantt Railway Station (main railway station). It is 3 km from there to the cheap hotels near the Tourist Office; 2 Rs for a rickshaw. If you are coming from the Benares direction and want to go to the cheap-hotel district, get off the train at Agra Fort. From there to the Taj Mahal by rickshaw costs 2 Rs.

Bus

At Idgah bus station. 2 km from there to the Tourist Office and cheap hotels; about 2 Rs by rickshaw.

Air

Indian Airlines bus, 6 Rs, goes to the luxury hotel Clarks Shiraz; passes by the Tourist Office.

Car

At Sikandra, 10 km before Agra, there is the tomb of the great Moghul emperor Akbar. Enter Agra through the Delhi Gate; the Tourist Bungalow is nearby.

ACCOMMODATION

Hotels

U.P. Govt Tourist Bungalow, Delhi Gate, tel. 72 123. Double 25 Rs (35 Rs with warm water), 4-bed room 65 Rs, 7 Rs per person in the 10-bed dormitory. A bit out-of-the-way. Restaurant. Garden. Caravans allowed (2 Rs/person).

Ashoka Hotel, near the Tourist Bungalow, tel. 75 108. Single 15 Rs, double 20/25/30 Rs, 4-bed room 50 Rs. All rooms have bath. Possible to have air cooler in some rooms. Restaurant.

Goverdhan Hotel, Delhi Gate, tel. 73 313. Double 25/30/40 Rs, 4-bed room 50 Rs, 6-bed room 80 Rs. Vegetarian restaurant.

Agra Caterers, 510 The Mall, near the Tourist Office, tel. 72 271. Single 15 Rs (25 Rs with bath and hot water), double 20 Rs (35 Rs with bath). Not very clean. Restaurant available.

Bengal Lodge, Rakabganj Road, Chippitola District, tel. 72 400. Single 15 Rs (25 Rs with bath), double 25 Rs (40 Rs with bath). Air cooler possible in all rooms for 10 Rs.

Guest house of the former Major Bakshi Sardar Singh, 33/83 Ajmer Road, tel. 76 828. Rooms are let only in the new building. Single (only two) 30 Rs, double 50 Rs. 10% extra tax. All rooms have bath and warm water.

Khush Mahal, Mrs Naval Framjee's guest house, just around the corner from the Tourist Office. Single 15 Rs, double 25 Rs. Car parking 5 Rs. Colonial-style house.

Hotels in the Taj Mahal district

India Guest House, at the South Gate. Single 8 Rs, double 12 Rs, triple 16 Rs. Small and simple.

Relax Hotel. Dormitory 6 Rs, double 12/15 Rs. The hotel's restaurant is one of Agra's backpacker meeting-places.

Shajahan Hotel. Dormitory 4 Rs, single 10 Rs (15 Rs with bath), double 12/15 Rs (20/30/40 Rs with bath). Restaurant and roof garden.

Mumtaz Mahal, at the tonga stand. Not to be confused with the luxury hotel Mumtaz Ashok. The Mumtaz Mahal 'can't' be found by many rickshaw drivers as it doesn't pay any commission. Dormitory 3 Rs, single 6 Rs, double 12 Rs. Check-out time 10.00 a.m. Simple restaurant (also for people not staying in the hotel). For years the favourite meeting-place for backpackers in Agra.

'The Mumtaz Mahal is still very good. Bus no. 7 from Agra Cantt to the Taj, then 5 minutes on foot.'

Middle-class hotels

Grand Hotel, 137 Station Road, tel. 74 014. Single 70 Rs, double 95 Rs, extra bed 25 Rs, deluxe double rooms 125 Rs; all rooms with bath and AC. Rooms in the old wing with bath but without AC: single 50 Rs, double 65 Rs, extra bed 15 Rs. Bar and restaurant. Camping is possible as well, 10 Rs/head.

Hotel Jaiwal, 3 Taj Road, tel. 64 141. All rooms have bath and AC. European plan (without board): single 60 Rs, double 80 Rs. American plan (with board): single 130 Rs, double 190 Rs.

Camping

Highway-Inn, Vibhab Nagar. Charges in the Main (and Economy) Wings: sleeping in the vehicle 4 Rs (3 Rs) per person, parking fee 4 Rs (2 Rs), 2-man tent 4 Rs (2 Rs). Rooms also let: dormitory 9 Rs (6 Rs), double 22/35 Rs (16 Rs). Large, quiet site. Restaurant. Bicycle hire. 25% discount for students and holders of youth-hostel cards.

Empress Hotel, Mahatma Gandhi Road (M.G. Road), near the Tourist Office, tel. 75 548. Parking fee 10 Rs per day. Rooms: single (with bath) 16 Rs, double 30/35/40 Rs. 10% service charge. 24-hour system. Petrol station and repair workshop nearby. Colonial-style house, over 100 years old. Large garden.

Further camping accommodation at the Tourist Bungalow, Grand Hotel and in Mrs Naval Framjee's guest house (see 'Hotels').

SIGHTSEEING

Bus sightseeing tour organised by the Government Tourist Office, starting after the arrival of the Taj Express. The buses leave from in front of Agra Cantt railway station at 10.30 a.m., going to Fatehpur Sikri in the morning and around Agra itself in the afternoon. Ordinary bus 20 Rs, AC bus 30 Rs; admission fees included; 1.50 Rs cheaper on Fridays, when there are no admission fees.

Taj Mahal, 3 km from the city centre. Open till 10.00 p.m. Loveliest by the light of the full moon (the Taj is open till midnight on the day of the full moon as well as four days before and four days after). Watch out for pickpockets!
   The Taj is a burial mosque of white marble decorated with gemstones. The Moghul emperor Shah Jahan had it built between 1636 and 1658 for his favourite wife Mumtaz Mahal. They are buried side by side in the Taj.

Agra Fort, 3 km from the city centre. Vast fort (16th century) of red sandstone and white marble pavilions, like Delhi's.

Tomb of Itimad-ud-Daulah, 6 km from the city centre: burial mosque (17th century) of white inlaid marble; its shape is reminiscent of a jewel casket.

Fatehpur Sikri, 37 km west of Agra. Palace complex of red sandstone. 16th-century capital of the Moghul empire, where the emperor Akbar lived with his four wives (one Muslim, one Hindu, one Buddhist, one Christian) and his harem of 800 women, and ruled with his four advisers (one Muslim, one Hindu, one Buddhist, one Christian). Akbar abandoned this seat of government after 16 years because of the shortage of water. Local buses depart from Idgah bus station to Fatehpur Sikri about every 30 minutes throughout the day; about 4.50 Rs. Admission to Fatehpur Sikri 50 Ps, to other sights 2 Rs.

All sights are some distance from the new city centre. Reckon on about 75 Ps per kilometre or 5-7 Rs per hour for cycle-rickshaws. Cheaper: hire a bicycle (from 2 Rs/day) or use the city buses.

'Like, for example, Benares, the rickshaw scene in Agra is a real pain. They charge inflated prices and want to take you to shops the whole time so that they can cash in on the commission. I had a good time with Mr Mool Chand, who runs a small teashop opposite the Hotel Empress with his family. His speciality: sightseeing trips lasting several hours in his rickshaw.'

EXCURSION TO BHARATPUR BIRD SANCTUARY

Bus or train from Agra to Bharatpur (54 km), then rickshaw to the park. The trip can also be made from Jaipur.

Accommodation
Either in Bharatpur or in the Forest Rest House in the park itself (may be possible only with an advance reservation).

Sightseeing
With a guide by boat on the lake, which is 1.5 metres at its deepest point.
Fauna: Waterbirds especially, but also a few mammals such as deer and hyenas.

SHOPPING

Government shops of Rajasthan, Kashmir and several other Indian states in the arcades near the Taj. Also in the Taj District are innumerable shops where musical instruments, gemstones and marble craft objects are sold.

'Large choice and fixed prices at the Marble Arts Palace, 159 Garden Road, Baluganj. The shop is also a training centre; you can watch the masters and apprentices at work and you don't have to buy anything. It's quite a contrast to other training schools in Agra.'

'Many statues, especially the white ones, aren't made of marble but of chalk. You can test them by drawing the edge of the statue along a dark surface. Chalk leaves clear lines, whereas marble leaves no mark at all.'

MISCELLANEOUS

Govt. of India Tourist Office, 191 The Mall, tel. 72 377. Open 9.00 a.m.-5.00 p.m., 9.00 a.m.-1.00 p.m. on every second Saturday in the month and holidays, closed on Sunday. Also a Govt. of India Tourist Office counter at the airport.
Govt of U. P. Tourist Office, 27 Taj Road, tel. 75 852.
Govt of U. P. Tourist counter at Cantt Railway Station, tel. 61 273. Open every day 10.00 a.m.-5.00 p.m.
Rajasthan Tourist Information, Shopping Arcade (near the Taj Mahal), tel. 64 582. Open 10.00 a.m.-5.00 p.m., closed on Sunday, holidays and the second Saturday in the month.
Railway Enquiry, Cantt Railway Station, tel. 72 121. Open 24 hours every day.
Idgah Bus Station, tel. 64 198. Reservations between 10.00 a.m. and 5.00 p.m.

Foreigners' Registration Office, 16 Idgah Colony (for visa extensions).

The GPO and Central Telegraph Office are both on the Mall, near the Govt of India Tourist Office. Another (small) post office near the Taj Mahal.

Banks: the Allahabad Bank in the Hotel Clarks Shiraz is open longer. Opening hours: 12.00 noon-5.30 p.m., Saturday 12.00 noon-4.00 p.m., closed on Sunday.

Swimming: in the swimming pools of some hotels (Clarks Shiraz, Lauries Hotel, among others). Reckon on about 10 Rs.

FURTHER TRAVEL FROM AGRA

To Bombay
Rail: only one good service (the other trains travel at night): 6 Punjab Mail, departs Agra Cantt 11.16 a.m. (11.31 a.m. in summer), 1343 km, arrives Bombay V.T. 12.40 p.m.
Air: change planes in Jaipur

To Benares
The 355 Agra-Bareilly Pr., departs 6.30 p.m., takes a through-carriage from Benares. 2nd class with sleeper 33.30 Rs.
Air: change planes in Khajuraho.

To Delhi
Quickest and most comfortable is the Taj Express (but possible only with reservations), departs 6.55 p.m.; 2nd class 15.55 Rs. Taj Express reservation office is open 9.00 a.m.-12 noon and 2.00-6.45 p.m. If it's already booked out, take one of the other express trains, e.g. Toofan Express: departs 1.50 a.m., arrives New Delhi 7.25 p.m., Old Delhi 7.55 p.m.
Bus: services between 5.30 a.m. and 7.30 p.m.; ordinary 4.50 Rs, deluxe 19.75 Rs.

Other rail services
132 Jayanti Janata Express, every day except Thursday and Sunday, departs Agra Cantt 12.16 p.m. (12.36 p.m. in summer) for Ernakulam/Cochin, Mangalore.
16 Grand Trunk Express departs 10.42 p.m. Arrives Madras Central the day after next at 8.35 a.m. 1993 km.
Other services to Madras: 8.00 a.m. and 7.37 p.m. (summer 7.47 p.m.).
8 Toofan Express. Departs Agra Cantt 2.32 p.m.. Arrives Howrah (Calcutta) next day at 6.15 p.m. 1242 km.

Other bus services
Jaipur between 6.30 a.m. and 10.45 p.m. about every hour. Ordinary 18.30 Rs, deluxe 30 Rs.
Bharatpur (54 km) service between about 6.30 a.m. and 11.00 p.m. 5 Rs.

KASHMIR

A trip to Kashmir is highly recommended, especially in summer, when India is hot and steamy. Kashmir is cooler and dry and has hardly any monsoon season. And from here you can make a detour to Ladakh, in 'Little Tibet'.

'Happy Valley', 'Paradise on Earth', 'Switzerland of Asia' - Kashmir has been given many flattering descriptions. Indian Moghul kings and British colonial officers alike would escape the monsoons to this attractive valley situated 1600 m above sea-level. The Moghuls laid out gardens to transform Kashmir into a paradise, following descriptions in the Koran. The English developed the houseboat.

Today anyone can stay cheaply on a houseboat on Dal Lake and be rowed through lagoons and canals in a shikara (gondola).

The season is from April to October; in winter it is too cold; in May and June there are too many Indian tourists; in July and August the lotus flowers blossom, and in autumn the saffron-fields flower.

From Amritsar to Kashmir

Rail/bus: Only one good rail service from Amritsar: departs Amritsar 9.55 p.m., arrives Jammu 4.20 a.m. Or bus to Jammu: regular services between 5.15 a.m. and 4.00 p.m.; 14.75 Rs; about a 5-hour journey; 215 km.

Then bus from Jammu to Srinagar: B-class bus leaves the General Bus Stand about 6.30 a.m.; 23.55 Rs. In fact a whole fleet of them leaves but, if you possibly can, it's worth making reservations days in advance. Also, some A-class buses depart from the Tourist Reception Centre in Jammu in the mornings; 30.50 Rs.

The buses wait right outside the railway station for passengers arriving on the morning train.

The bus from Jammu to Srinigar takes about 10-11 hours for the 293 km trip; lovely journey over two mountain passes, through cedar forests and pretty valleys.

Drivers

Stop at the Tourist Check Post in Lakhanpur (just after Pathankot), 2.50 Rs toll tax. 9 Rs road-toll at the Bannihal Toll Post 170 km after Jammu. Lovely countryside to travel through on the National Highway (NH) 1A, which is mostly two-lane, and through the Jawahar Tunnel (2211 m. above sea-level, 2 1/2 km long) to the 'Happy Valley'.

All along the way, 'witty' sayings with terrible rhymes warn you to drive safely (e.g. 'keep your nerves in the sharp curves').

Lots of military traffic. If you're unlucky, you'll find yourself at the end of a convoy of 100 army vehicles. But the convoys often stop to close ranks.

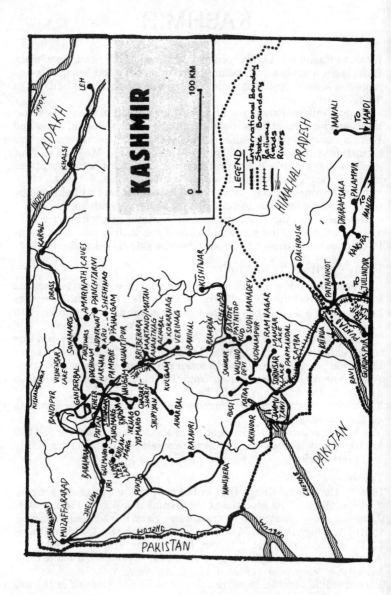

Delhi-Srinagar

KM
891 — BARAMULA, GULMARG, SRINAGAR, BANDIPUR, NUNAR, JHELUM, PAHALGAM
835 — BIJBEHARA, KHANABAL, ANANTNAG, ISLAMABAD, KAZIGUND, BANIHAL, BATOTE, RAMBAN
586 — UDHAMPUR, DOMEL, JAMMU, BHADARWAH, CHENAB, SAMBA
478 — KATHUA, LAKHANPUR, PATHANKOT, RIVER RAVI, MUKERIAN, TANDA, RIVER BEAS, JULLUNDUR, PHAGWARA, PHILLAUR, SUTLEJ
311 — LUDHIANA, KHANNA, SIRHIND, RAJPURA, AMBALA, MARKANDA
211 — PIPLI, KARNAL, PANIPAT
85 — SONEPAT, RIVER YAMUNA
0 — DELHI

KASHMIR - WEATHER

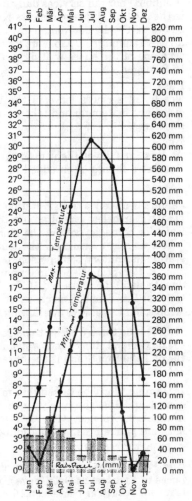

Jan Feb Mär Apr Mai Jun Jul Aug Sep Okt Nov Dez

Max. Temperatur

Minimum Temperatur

Rainfall (mm)

Air

One flight daily by Indian Airlines Amritsar-Srinagar; 269 Rs. Two flights daily from Jammu to Srinagar; 130 Rs; often booked out!

From Delhi to Kashmir

Rail/bus: Four rail services daily from Delhi to Jammu Tawi. The best is the Jhelum Express: departs New Delhi 8.50 p.m., arrives Jammu 9.25 a.m. Or the 33 Jammu Tawi Mail: departs Old Delhi 9.20 p.m., arrives Jammu 10.40 a.m. Fare for the 585 km: 2nd class 32.55 Rs. Then take one of the buses waiting at Jammu Tawi railway station direct to Srinagar.

Bus

Nearly all services leave in the morning; 590 km; 46.50 Rs. Stay overnight in Jammu and take a connecting bus to Srinagar the next morning.

Air

At least one direct flight daily with IA from Delhi to Srinagar; 483 Rs. Extra flights often added in the high season.

JAMMU

Jammu is merely a transit station for Srinagar; it's not worth staying here. Nevertheless one often has to make a forced stay here as buses leave for Srinagar only in the mornings.

You can stay overnight in the Tourist Reception Centre at the railway station (dormitory 3 Rs/person, but there are also doubles) or in the Tourist Reception Centre in Jammu itself on the Vir Marg, tel. 5324: double 40-50 Rs, extra bed 10 Rs. You will find cheap hotels near the General Bus Stand. The cheapest overnight stay is in the Ragunath Temple, but it is always overflowing with pilgrims. Only for emergencies!

'Bright blue three-wheeler taxis go from Jammu Tawi railway station to the General Bus Stand, which is in the town; only 1 R per person. Beyond the Bus Stand is the bazaar, where there are plenty of cheap hotels.'

In Jammu, don't be talked into making a reservation for a Srinagar houseboat. It's absolutely unnecessary as houseboats are always available in Srinagar. Also, reservations made here usually don't work out, and you're buying a pig in a poke.

FURTHER TRAVEL

Bus: For services to Srinagar see also 'From Amritsar to Kashmir'. All buses to Amritsar or Delhi leave from the General Bus Stand. 15 buses leave for Amritsar between 5.15 a.m. and 4.00 p.m., and for Delhi at 4.40, 5.25, 5.55, 6.40 and 7.20 a.m.

Rail: Direct service to Amritsar departs Jammu Tawi 10.35 p.m., scheduled to arrive in Amritsar 5.25 a.m.
Four services daily to Delhi: 3.30, 5.40, 9.25, and 10.05 (10.40 in summer).

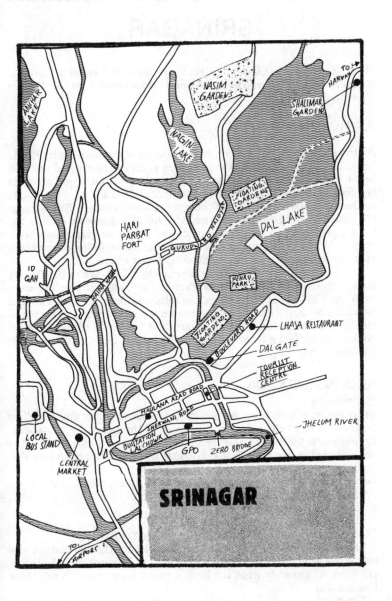

SRINAGAR

SRINAGAR

Population nearly 1,000,000. 1610 m above sea-level. Capital of Kashmir. Srinagar is situated on Dal Lake and is criss-crossed by the Jhelum River, tributaries and canals.

ARRIVAL

At the Lal Chowk bus station or the Tourist Reception Centre (State buses), where hordes of Kashmiris descend on you to try and talk you into a houseboat ('very good price'). The only solution, if you arrive at the Tourist Reception Centre, is to dash right into it and gasp for breath, as the houseboat-hirers are officially not allowed in there. But because the police on duty are not immune to a bit of baksheesh, even in the Centre you won't be completely protected from persistent houseboat-owners. You can choose your accommodation (hotel or houseboat) here at a special counter or get involved with one of the touts.

Another possibility: whether you arrive at Lal Chowk or the Tourist Reception Centre (TRC)–go by scooter to Dal Gate (you can also walk from the TRC, about 10 minutes; the minimum fare by scooter should be from 1.60 Rs). From there you can have a look on foot or be rowed around in a shikara until you see a houseboat you like. Shikara (oarsmen) always ask for fantastic prices at first. But one hour should be possible for from 5 Rs.

ACCOMMODATION

Houseboats

There are fur classes of houseboat; the prices are similarly ranked. When business is bad (which seems to be most of the time), the houseboat-owners settle for less than the recommended prices. Three meals a day are included in the price, but individual arrangements can always be made.

Deluxe class costs 220 Rs per person, 325 Rs for two.

A class single 150 Rs, double 220 Rs

B class single 100 Rs, double 170 Rs

C class single 65 Rs, double 115 Rs

D class (Doonga class) single 45 Rs, double 60 Rs

The more expensive the houseboat, the cleaner the bed clothes, the better the sanitary fittings (washbasin, WC and shower) and the better the food. Ask exactly what the food is, or you'll end up with rice three times a day.

The prices also vary according to position: Chinarbagh, canals and the Jhelum River are the cheapest moorings, being surrounded by streets and traffic, and Dal Gate is also quite noisy. The best is Dal

Lake proper. Nigin Lake (also 'Nagin') is very isolated and you'll be dependent on buses for getting into town.

Tips on Houseboats

Travellers on a budget should be careful to choose a houseboat that you can get to on foot, as otherwise you have to pay extra all the time for shikaras (especially at night, when fantastic prices are charged). Many houseboats have their own shikara, but of course it's not always there when you need it.

Also make sure that you get a good houseboat-man, as normally you will be living on the same boat as the houseboat-family. Houseboats usually don't have any doors.

There are about 1000 houseboats in Srinagar. The following selection is meant to be simply a guide. Many other houseboats could be recommended.

Chinar/Helen/Helen of Troy: three houseboats next to each other on Dal Lake, not far from Nehru Park. Reached only by shikara, they belong to the very serious family of Gaffara Surma & sons. Large, luxuriously furnished rooms with bath, very clean, good fodd. Like most of the deluxe boats, a place for 'luxury' travellers. Reservations: Gaffara Surma & Sons, tel. 76309, P.O. Box 99, Nehru Park, Dal Lake, Srinagar. Haifa, tel. 77796, owner Iqbal Chapri. This deluxe houseboat is moored on a tributary of the outlet from Dal Lake, the 'crossing' is at the gate near the Park Hotel. One of the boats that you share with the houseboat-family. And in this case it's worth it! Iqbal Chapri must be the best kown and most successful houseboat-owner in Srinagar. For years he has been fighting for the survival of the houseboats, and makes himself unpopular with his allegations of corruption and his criticism of State support for the recent development of hotels that threaten the existence of the houseboats. He's also an excellent debater and writer. Trekking enthusiasts can turn to his son Ibrahim, who is an expert on the native flora and fauna and has a wide ethnographic knowledge of the native people.

Other houseboats:
Convey/Young Dream House: very centrally located (near Dal Gate); reach it on foot or by shikara. Favourite meeting-place for backpackers. Owner: Abdul Salam Dar and family, who, like most houseboat-owners, are Muslims. Young Dream House: D-category, 15 Rs per person, lodging only; 25 Rs with breakfast and lunch. Convey: B-category, board and lodging 110 Rs for a double; TV and tape-recorder available. Abdul Salam Dar also rents out chalets (from 10 Rs) and rooms. There is always space here as the rents are high.

'At Abdul Salam Dar's I paid 25 Rs (breakfast and dinner inclusive) a day for a room in an old house with a lovely view of houseboats and canals. As a bookworm and diary-writer, I could find fault with only one thing: the electricity quite often didn't work. And no wonder, if you see the fantastic tangle of wires that carries the expensive juice.'

Hotels

Hotel Heaven Canal, centrally located near Dal Gate, with views of houseboats and canals. Double 40-90 Rs; 20% discount in the off-season; 7% service charge; all rooms have bath.

Hotel Crescent, also near Dal Gate. Reckon on 60 Rs for a double.

Tourist Hostel, in the Tourist Reception Centre. 4-bed dormitory 7 Rs/person, double 70/80/90 Rs; 25% extra tax.

'In the Neptun Guest House, on the right after Zero Bridge, you can get a double for 20 Rs. Quiet position, lovely garden and a cheerful old eccentric for a manager. Clean showers.'

Campers

Mirza Camping & Parking Sites, Nagin Lake Beach (about 8 km away from the Tourist Reception Centre, Srinagar), tel. 78864. Staying overnight in own tent or vehicle 7 Rs per person. If you want, you can also hire a two-man tent for 5 Rs. Rowing boats are also hired out: about 2-3 Rs/hour or 6-10 Rs/day.

FOOD AND DRINK

Good-value (and good) restaurants: Grand Hotel, Residency Road; Indian Coffee House on Sherwani Road, good coffee; Restaurant Lhasa, in a side-stree off the Boulevard with good but not particularly cheap Chinese and Tibetan food.

'You'll find good Chinese, European and Indian food in the Restaurant Capri (1st floor). Very clean. From the Tourist Reception Centre, go along Sherwani Road towards the town and then first right.'

Good, cheap South Indian specialities at the street stalls in front of the Tourist Reception Centre: masala dosa 2 Rs, wada 50 Ps, 'Madras coffee' 1 R. You can get fish and chips at the fish shop at Dal Gate. Beer costs 13 Rs in restaurants.

Self-catering: check out the many dry-fruit shops; tutti frutti 5 Rs/150g, walnuts 2 Rs/100g. Food shops in Srinagar are generally well stocked. Bread is usually available, 100g Amul butter (often rather rare) costs 3.30 Rs, 250g honey 10 Rs, 350g strawberry jam 10.50 Rs, 250g apricots 4 Rs, 1kg cherries 8 Rs.

TRANSPORT

Shikaras (gondolas)

The gondolas, which can take a maximum of 5 adults, are called shikaras. For certain trips there are official set prices which are displayed on large boards on the river bank. Here are the prices, in simplified form: from every landing-place (ghat) on the Boulevard and from Dal Gate to Gagribal (opposite Nehru Park) a shikara ride costs

one-way/return
- to Charchinar
    (island with 4 maple trees) and Cheshmeshahi Moghul garden 18/25 Rs

- to Nishat Moghul garden.............................18/27 Rs
- to Nishat and Shalimar Moghul gardens.............25/40 Rs
- to Nasim/Hazratbal.................................20/30 Rs
- to Nagin (Nigin) Lake..............................20/30 Rs
- to Vier (via Dal Gate lock,
  then down the Jhelum River to the flood-gate).......20/30 Rs

The fares are a few rupees higher from the ghats on the Jhelum River (greater distance), except to Vier (8 Rs cheaper/return 5 Rs cheaper). If you get out and want the oarsman to wait: waiting costs 2 Rs/hour.

According to the above fares, the return trip to the Moghul gardens should last 6 hours at the most, and 5 hours to Nasim and Nagin, otherwise it'll cost overtime.

An extra oarsman costs-any trip-25 Rs for a maximum of 6 hours. Crossing to a houseboat costs about 2 Rs, but children ride for 50 Ps.

The trip from Dal Gate to Nehru Park is 6 Rs, 10 Rs return.

The shikara men don't always stick to these prices and usually ask for double. If you don't know the journey, it's better to bargain for an hourly rate: about 5 Rs, plus 2 Rs/hour for waiting.

Shikara prices are always higher on Sundays and during the Indian season (May, June, October).

You can, of course, hire a shikara for yourself and paddle around in the maze of canals. Ask your houseboat-man. Reckon on a minimum rental of 6 Rs per day.

Taxi/scooter/bicycles

The official taxi fares to major destinations are displayed on a large board opposite the Tourist Reception Centre. Scooter-fares are calculated by the meter plus 50 Ps.

You can hire bicycles at Dal Gate for 4 Rs/day.

SIGHTSEEING

Lovely views of Dal Lake, the lagoons and the town from Shankaracharya Hill which rises about 300m above the lake. Viewing platform reached by taxi from Gagribal; the taxis may charge a special fare for the trip.

A shikara trip on your own to get to know everything goes something like this: Dal Lake, Kabutar Khana (the Maharjah's picnic house), Charchinari (island with four maple trees), Nishat Gardens and Shalimar Gardens (Moghul gardens; get out and have a look around), Floating Gardens, Nagin Lake, Rainawari (village), Dal Lake. This takes about six hours and costs about 30 Rs.

Another interesting shikara tour is to go through Srinagar on the Jhelum River.

Always haggle hard about the price!

There's a Souns & Light Show in English every day at about 9.00 p.m. in the Shalimar Gardens (admittance: upper class 7.50 Rs, lower class

3 Rs). Daily sightseeing tours organised by the Tourist Reception Centre; 15 Rs.

TRIPS

Excursions to the mountain resorts of Gulmarg (2730 m above sea-level, India's ski centre) and Pahalgam (2130 m above sea-level; pony-riding is the main attraction) may be sensational for Indians, but for Europeans they're not. You can get to both places by taxi or bus (see 'Further Travels') or even on Tourist Office day trips. An official sightseeing tour to Gulmarg costs 32 Rs and to Pahalgam 30 Rs.

There are no organised trips to Dachigam National Park, about 20 km from Srinagar. First obtain a permit from the Wildlife Warden (in the same complex as the Tourist Reception Centre), tel. 5411; open Monday-Saturday, 10.00 a.m.-4.00 p.m. To get there: local bus from Lal Chowk Bus Stand to Harwan, about every 30 minutes. Admission to the park costs 20 Rs; you're allowed to wander about, with some restrictions; no accommodation in the park itself.

SOUVENIRS

The inhabitants of Kashmir produce a gigantic selection of souvenirs and craft. There are Kashmir shawls, embroidery, wood carving, painted paper mache, enamel, leather goods, jewellery and carpets–from the cheapest (numdahs) to the most expensive hand-knotted ones.

Only a small minority of shops have set prices on display, e.g. the Kashmir Govt. emporium, in the Govt. Central Market or at Suffering Moses, but all these shops are relatively expensive.

Things to watch out for: Leather and fur goods: as with anything, good quality. The leather must feel supple, and not brittle. Look at the thread used and at the seams. Leather pants and jackets cost around 320 Rs, leather bags 125-225 Rs, and shoes around 100 Rs.

Wood carvings: the wood must be dry and have been stored out of the weather, otherwise it will split later. It is really walnut? Sometimes wood is painted to make it look like walnut.

Embroidery: articles with fine short stitches will keep their colour longer, and the larger the area embroidered, the better and more expensive. Remember that most of these articles cannot be washed, only dry cleaned.

Woollen materials: Judge quality by the feel. It usually takes between 3 and 5 days to have it made up. Even leather goods should not take any longer.

MISCELLANEOUS

The Tourist Reception Centre is the place to get all your information and they also handle hotel and houseboat bookings. It is also the bus depot and Air India have their office there, as well as the Wildlife Warden.

There is also a trekkers' information booth, kiosk, restaurant and the State Bank of India.

Business hours: accommodation bookings and tourist information are open daily (even nights); the State Bank of India is open Monday 10.00 a.m.-3.00 p.m., Tuesday closed, other days 1.00-5.00 p.m. Indian Airlines are open daily 10.00 a.m.-5.00 p.m., Tel. 73 27 0/ 73 53 8.

The GPO on the Jhelum River is closed on Sunday. Poste restante is open from 10.00 a.m.-6.00 p.m. weekdays, Tel. 76 54 1. If mail is not collected within 30 days it is returned to sender.

Visa extensions–not for more than one month at a time–at the Foreigners' Registration Office, Tel. 73 39 4, not far from the Tourist Reception Centre, near the Linz Restaurant, follow the little streets. Open from 9.30 a.m.-3.30 p.m. (winter 10.00 a.m.-4.30 p.m.) closed on Sunday. You must take four photographs with you.

Dal Lake is polluted because of the open air toilets in the numerous houseboats, and other untreated drainage water, and it is a paradise for algae, but not for swimmers. In spite of that if you really want to swim you naturally can go. On some houseboats there are special bathing boats.

Special maps: Tourist guide maps to Ladakh, Srinagar city and Kaskmir (2 or 4 Rs).

FURTHER TRAVEL

(For details of transportation to Ladakh see 'Trip to Little Tibet').

Rail

Reservations for the train to Jammu can be made at the Northern Railway city booking agency Badshah Chowk (around the back) open daily, except Sunday, from 10.00 a.m.-3.00 p.m. Reservations have to be made at least three days before your departure. The booking agency is not very helpful though. Often they do not get the reservations quite right. You can also but tickets and make reservations at the Kashmir Travel Agency but you pay an extra fee of 10 Rs there.

Bus

To Jammu: The government run buses of the Jammu and Kashmir Road Transport Corporation depart from the bus terminal at the Tourist Reception Centre. The fleet of buses start at approximately 7.30 a.m. and the number of buses is dependent on the demand. Because there are only a limited number of buses it is better to book early especially in the season (no reservation fee).

Prices: AC Bus 98 Rs, Super Deluxe 60 Rs (via Verinagh 66.50 Rs) A-Class 30.50 Rs (via Verinagh 33.70 Rs) B-Class 23.55 Rs.

There are also a few privately owned B-class buses which run to Jammu. Diamond Motor Services, for example, depart from their office in the Ab Lal Chowk daily around 7.00 and 9.00 a.m. for 23.50 Rs.

Local buses (only B-class) depart from the Lal Chowk Bus Stop to Gulmarg, Pahalgam and other villages. There are also some buses from private companies which have their offices nearby. The Kashmir Motor Drivers Association charge only 18 Rs to Sonamarg and 22 Rs to Pahalgam.

Air
From Srinagar their are flights to Jammu, Amritsar, Chandigarh and Delhi. You can take a taxi to the Airport for around 36 Rs, or travel on the Air India bus for 6 Rs.

TRIP TO LITTLE TIBET (LADAKH)

Ladakh, the eastern province of Jammu & Kashmir, is part of Tibetanlama culture and is also known as Little Tibet. Until the summer of 1974 tourists were not allowed to visit it. Since the Chinese invasion of Tibet (in 1951), Ladakh has been one of the last refugees of lamaistic culture that is still accessible to Westerners (except for Bhutan). It is a poor, barren mountain area where sumptuously painted monasteries (gompas) sit like fortresses on crags and ridges. The main reason for going to Ladakh is to visit these monasteries and see the religious art. It's possible to go only between about mid-May and mid-October, when the mountain passes are open.

ARRIVAL

Bus

The starting point is Srinagar. 434 km of asphalt road to Leh, capital of Ladakh. Buses depart from the bus station near the Tourist Reception Centre: A class 70 Rs, depart 8.30 a.m., from twice-weekly to daily, depending on demand; B class 51.90 Rs (25.50 Rs as far as Kargil), one bus daily at 8.30 a.m. The bus trip takes two days, with an overnight stop in Kargil. The bus continues from there the next morning, leaving between 6.00 and 7.00. More information about Kargil later. All areas one mile north of the road to Leh are forbidden to tourists.

Air

Indian Airlines flies every Saturday and Sunday from Srinagar to Leh for 358 Rs. A beautiful flight over the mountains with views of Nun (7135 m) and Kun (7077 m) and in the distance the 8611 m high K2 (Godwin Austin), the second-highest mountain in the world, and Nanga Parbat (8126 m). The flights go only when weather permits (sit on the left-hand side for the mountain views). There's a flight every Monday to Leh from Delhi via Chandigarh. Especially during the season, flights to Kashmir and Ladakh are often hopelessly booked out.

Truck

Even before the buses start travelling from Srinagar to Leh at about the beginning of June, the first trucks start going, transporting provisions and other goods to Leh. The drivers are willing to carry people for a whole heap of money. If flights are booked out or cancelled and the buses are not yet running, this is, apart from taxis, the only way to get from Srinagar to Leh. A seat costs you between 50 Rs and 60 Rs; the journey usually takes two days (overnight stay in Kargil or,

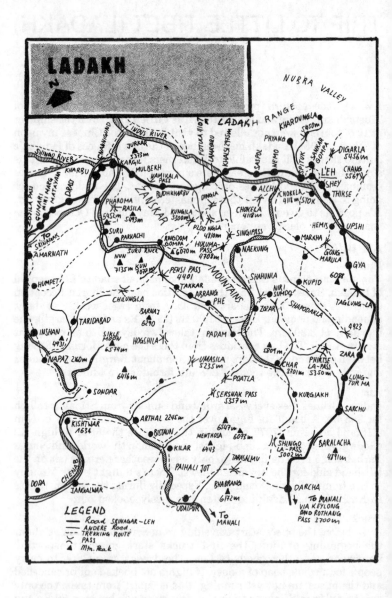

LADAKH

N

NUBRA VALLEY

LADAKH RANGE

INDUS RIVER

SHINGO RIVER

WAKHAGUND

JURKAR

KHARBU

KARGIL

MULBEKH

FOTULA JOT

LAMAYURU

KHALSI 2711m

SASPOL

NEMO

PHYANG

KHARDUNGLA 5450m

SANKAR GOMPA

SPITUK

LEH

DIGARLA 5456m

CHANG 5561m

SHEY

THIKSE

STOK

ZOSILA PASS

ZOJILA PASS

MINI MARG

MATAYAN

DRAS

PHAROMA RASILA 5452m 5493m

SURU

PARKACHI

BUDHKHARBU

NAMIKALA PASS

DINGLA

ZANSKAR

KUNGILA 5300m

PLDO NGLA

SINGIPASS

CHOKELA 4118m

ALCHI

CHOKELA 4118m

STOK

HEMIS

UPSHI

TO SRINAGAR

AMARNATH

SURU RIVER

NUN 7135m

KUN 7077m

RINGDOM GOMPA 6070m

HUKUMA PASS 4708m

NAEKUNG

MARKHA

GONGMARULA

GYA 6088

HUMPET

CHILUNGLA

PENSI PASS 4401

TAKKAR

ABRANG PHE

ZOPAR

SHAHUNLA

NIRI SUMDO

SHAPODAKLA

KUPID

TAGLUNG-LA

4923

INSHAN 4931

TARIDABAD

BARNAJ 6290

SIKLE MOON 6574m

HOGSHILA

PADAM

UMASILA 5235m

POATLA

5809m

CHAR 3701m

PHIRTSE LA-PASS 5350m

ZARA

LUNG-TUR MA

NAPAZ 2160m

6416m

SONDAR

ARTHAL 2245m

BISTAUN

KISHTWAR 1634

KILAR

SERSNAK PASS 5357m

KURGIAKH

SARCHU

DODA

CHENAB

JANGALWAR

PAIHALI JOT

MENTHOSA 6443

6547m 6073m

TARASALMU

UDAIPUR

BNABRANG 6172m

To MANALI

SHINGO LA-PASS 5002m

BARALACHA 4891m

DARCHA

TO MANALI VIA KEYLONG AND ROTHANG PASS 3700m

LEGEND
— Road SRINAGAR–LEH
— ANDERE Road.
···· TREKKING ROUTE
)(PASS
▲ Mtn. Peak

less often, Drass). Have warm clothes at hand as it gets very cold on or in the truck. The trucks leave from no single place in Srinagar. Ask your houseboat-man! More information about truck journeys under 'Leh'/'Further travels'.

Taxi
A taxi from Srinagar to Leh costs, flat rate, about 1000 Rs and a normal Ladakh tour 3500 Rs. Some travel agents organise jeep tours of Ladakh: journey only to Leh 1000 Rs, every additional sightseeing day 500 Rs.

WHAT TO TAKE
Sleeping bag, Nivea cream (Ladakh is very dry), flashlight (in order to see the wall paintings in the temples, which are often dark), waterbottle, penknife, warm clothes. Perhaps also a mattress and tent, if you want to be independent and stay overnight in any of the usually isolated monasteries. Campers: take meat and vegetables with you; they're more expensive in Leh than in Srinagar.

You can leave anything you don't absolutely need on your houseboat in Srinagar.

Drivers
Take enough petrol for the journey; petrol stations in Kargil and Leh. Three mountain passes, of which the first, Zoji-La, is in catastrophic condition on both sides of the pass. The Zoji-La is in fact not the highest, but is by far and away the pass worst affected by snow on the road to Leh and is therefore a key point.

Here are the distances:
Srinagar-84 km-Sonamarg-24 km-Zoji-La Pass (3528 m above sea-level)-18 km-Matyam-21 km-Drass-23 km-Tasgam-34 km-Kargil (2665 m)-40 km-Mulbekh-15 km-Namika-La (3730 m)-15 km-Nudhkharbu-21 km-Fatu-La (4108 m)-15 km-Lamayuru-27 km-Khalsi (Khalatse)-35 km-Saspul (4 km detour to Alchi gompa)-26 km-Nimu-36 km-Leh (about 3550 m).

Military convoys often travel on this strategically important road. When they do, dozens of trucks take over the road. You may have to wait for them. It's best to ask at check points about the convoy times, which follow certain regulations.

There are few camping places along the way. Try the Rest Houses and Bungalows in Sonamarg, Drass, Kargil, Mulbekh, Budhkharbu, Lamayuru, Khalsi (1 km after the village). Warning: there are badly signposted speed breakers along the whole route!

KARGIL
Population 3000; 2665 m above sea-level; a village of shacks, with nothing to see. Anyone making the trip overland must stay here usually for one night. There is enough accommodation. Numerous hotels near the bus stand. Try, for example, the Hotel Evergreen, double 25/35 Rs, single occupancy 15 Rs; new and clean. Less well recommended is the

Dak Bungalow, tel. 29: usually occupied by officials and not very pleasant military types; no singles, double 25 Rs, extra bed 5 Rs.

'Recommended: Hotel De Luxe. Dormitory (camp-bed with a cover) 5 Rs, triple 20 Rs.'

The Tourist Office is located in the Dak Bungalow complex. Open every day including Sunday. If no-one is there, enquire at the reception desk.

Changing money: try at the State Bank of India office on the main street.

There is electricity between about 7.30 p.m. and 11.00 p.m., if the noisy diesel generator is working.

Buses to Srinagar or Leh leave Kargil between 6.00 a.m. and 7.00 a.m. Going towards Leh, the landscape becomes more and more barren, with hardly anything growing in it.

LEH

Capital of Ladakh; population about 9000; 3500 m above sea-level; situated about 10 km from the Indus in the middle of a bleak mountain wilderness. A small Tibetan town with lots and lots of charm. You'd feel as though you were in Nepal or China if it wasn't for the ever present Indian Army which is nevertheless very friendly to tourists. But Leh is significant not only for being an outpost of the Indian Army: in recent years it has been the centre of a now unstoppable tourist boom. Leh can no longer be described as a 'secret'.

ARRIVAL/ACCOMMODATION

Warning: accommodation prices often vary according to the time of year. Most hotels are closed during the hard, ice-cold winters and open only in the middle of May/beginning of June, when the tourists arrive. The prices then escalate accordingly. So the tariffs given here are simply standard prices. The high season is June to October.

Private citizens in Leh are officially not allowed to let rooms to tourists, so as not to compete with the hotel industry, which is often not in Ladakhi hands (especially the better hotels). Naturally, many locals don't take much notice of this regulation.

Every foreigner arriving in Leh has to be registered. You have to register in a book either on the aeroplane or at the checkpoint before Leh.

Whether you arrive at the bus station or the airport, touts will definitely be waiting for you. Because of the great competition you can (and must) first haggle about the price. The touts take over the cost of a jeep taxi from the airport.

A few brief notes about hotels:

Hotel Moon Land, the hotel with the registration number 1, the first hotel started in Leh. Single 15 Rs, double 25 Rs, breakfast 6 Rs, lunch and dinner 10 Rs each. The manager is an all-round genius who repairs everything from typewriters to radios and, for instance, even pulls teeth for 10 Rs!

Palace View Hotel Kidar. Rooms cost between 10 Rs and 15 Rs.

Palace View Guest House. Single 15 Rs, double 25 Rs.

Himalaya Hotel, tel. 104. Single (without bath) 30 Rs, double (with bath) 60 Rs, camping 10 Rs/tent (more if there are more than two people). Parking 5 Rs per vehicle. Lovely surroundings with mountain views.

Hotel Khar-Dunglla, situated a little above the 'tree' (see town map). No singles, double 50 Rs (single occupancy 25 Rs). In the season rooms

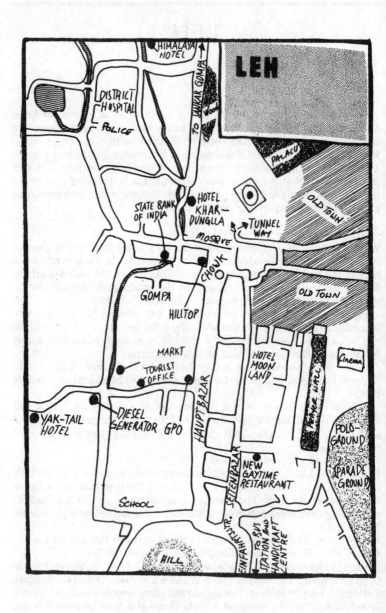

let only with full board; then a double costs 150-250 Rs. Co-operates with travel agents.

New Antelope Guest House, near the Himalaya Hotel, tel. 86. Double 30 Rs.

Tsemo-La (formerly the Glacier View Hotel). Opened in 1981. Claims, with 32 rooms, to be the largest hotel in Leh. Is managed by the Holiday Inn Bombay and Eastern International Hotel Ltd company. Rooms let usually only with 'American plan' (full board). Single 225 Rs, Double 325 Rs. 30% extra taxes. All rooms have bath and hot water (own generator). Travellers cheques are accepted. The first bar in Leh is supposed to be opened in the Tsemo-La.

Yak-Tail, tel. 118. No singles, double (full board) 250 Rs; without board, a double costs 50-150 Rs; 25% reduction for single occupancy. No camping, but parking possible (5-10 Rs, depending on the size of the vehicle); sleeping in the vehicle costs 10 Rs/person (the parking fee is included in this charge). Jeep-hire.

Hotel Khangri, tel. 51, near the diesel generator (like the Yak-Tail). 22 rooms. European plan (room only): single 125 Rs, double 150 Rs (200 Rs with bath); American plan: 50 Rs extra per person. Apparently the only hotel that is open in winter (about 25 Rs per day extra charge for heating). You can pay with cash or travellers cheques. Campers: parking 5 Rs, tent with 2 people 10 Rs.

Hotel Kang-lha-chchen, tel. 144. Only full board: double 350 Rs, single occupancy 280 Rs.

FOOD AND DRINK

Restaurants in Leh are of only average quality and the choice is rather limited. All about the same quality and rather expensive for what they offer are the Himalaya Restaurant, the Golden Dragon and the Hilltop. The New Gaytime Restaurant (near the Polo Ground) is a bit better: one plate of plain rice costs 2 Rs, vegetables 3 Rs, dhal 2 Rs, tea 50 Ps. The Dreamland Hotel is also quite good. Cold drinks are very expensive and cost a minimum of 3.50 Rs in restaurants.

The Pamposh Hotel (on the way from the Main Bazaar to the 'tree') is a simple chai-shop with excellent curds (1.50-2 Rs) and flat bread–also to take away.

You will also find cheap provisions in other chai-shops; samosas 50 Ps each.

Also try Tibetan specialities in a restaurant–such as moe moe (steamed dough, often with meat), tupka (noodles with meat) and chang (barley beer; only occasionally available).

Self-catering: the range of provisions available in Leh has improved with the arrival of tourism. But prices are usually higher than in Srinagar. Depending on the season there are mangoes (8 Rs/kg, 6 Rs in Srinagar), cherries (from May onwards, 4 Rs/250 g) and apples. Also available are yoghurt (curds), flat bread, meat, eggs, chocolate, radishes, tomatoes (6 Rs/kg) etc. Bananas are rather scarce. Mineral water ('Himalayan Spring Water') costs 8 Rs a bottle.

HEALTH

In Leh there are only two poorly stocked chemists. However, it's not necessary to take medicines with you as the most important ones are available. After arriving at such an unaccustomed elevation (3500 m), many backpackers suffer from altitude sickness; a few go straight to bed. Take things in stages to acclimatise yourself. The air in Leh (and most of Ladakh) is extremely dry. Treat dry lips and red, swollen hands with Nivea cream (14 Rs/50 g) or the Indian imitation product Pond. If you have diarrhoea, stool tests are possible in the District Hospital. But you must insist on having one. Otherwise you will be given a prescription for any old antibiotic. If you are given a prescription for medicines that aren't available in the two chemists, try the military hospital. If they are available there you'll be given them for free. Diagnosis in the District Hospital is also free; open 10.00 a.m.-1.00 p.m. and 2.00-4.00 p.m.; closed on Sunday; tel. 95.

Ladakh is definitely a jaundice area.

SIGHTSEEING

Directly behind the old town rises a rocky hill with the palace, Tsemo Gompa and Leh monastery. The building of the palace (uninhabited today) began in 1553, and it is still owned by nobility. It can be visited during the day; there are wall paintings and thankas to see. Also worth a visit is Tsemo Gompa, built in 1430. Excellent views from the 'castle hill' over Leh and the Indus Valley.

The old town of Leh is a sightseeing attraction in itself, forming a sort of semi-circle around the castle hill. What is right for Benares is also right for here: stay alone with your fantasies and your dreams or wander through the crooked idyllic streets armed with diary, pencil and/or camera. It's worth it.

Photographers: don't be too 'bloodthirsty'; be tactful. Ladakhis don't particularly appreciate (understandably) enthusiastic souvenir hunters snapping them around every corner. To photograph without causing offence, perhaps ask if you can take a shot or wander round with the camera and wait for them to ask you. Indeed there still are Ladakhis who take a childlike innocent joy in being photographed by one of these strange adventurous foreigners. All they expect in return is that you send them one of these precious pictures or give them a photo of yourself. But as most Ladakhis are illiterate, taking their address always causes much mutual frowning and helpless laughter.

'Hardly any other place in India has as much charm as Leh, and Ladakh in general. Here are a few impressionistic pictures: women wearing turquoise-decorated top-hats over matted plaits that haven't been washed for years (water is short, and Ladakhis have a different concept of hygiene from us 'clean' Europeans); old Tibetan men, their long hair elaborately plaited, with prayer wheels and shoes with turned up toes;

yaks; sand storms; wonderful play of colours between the desert, blue sky and snow-covered mountains; and shepherds who suddenly appear out of the desert wastes on your journey through the moonscape of Ladakh.'

SOUVENIRS

In the Handicraft Training Centre, near the radio station, there are masks, rugs, dragon paintings and thankas. No antiques (anything over 100 years old cannot officially be taken out of India). Thankas cost from 70 Rs to 500 Rs, depending on size and workmanship. You can also have a thanka produced on request. But it usually takes several weeks to paint one. The Handicraft Training Centre (tel. 21) is open every day except Sunday from about 10.00 a.m. to 4.00 p.m. Fixed prices.

Prices are also fairly fixed in the souvenir shops in the town, unless the proprietor of the shop is an immigrant Kashmiri. The Curio House, near the Pamposh Hotel Curd Shop, is recommended: stylish necklaces, daggers, silverware, red-coral jewellery, bangles, decorated boxes and, of course, Ladakhi turquoise.

MISCELLANEOUS

Tourist Reception Centre, tel. 97. Open 7.00 a.m.-8.00 p.m. (summer), 9.00 a.m.-approx. 6.00 p.m. (winter). Have a look through the information file on Leh and Ladakh; lots of useful information.

Indian Airlines, tel. 76, situated in the Ibex Guest House near the Tourist Reception Centre. Open every day except Wednesday from 10.00 a.m. to 5.00 p.m. There is often no-one there.

GPO, tel. 82. Open 10.00 a.m.-6.00 p.m. (summer), until 5.00 p.m. on Saturday, closed on Sunday.

Shops are closed for lunch between about 12 noon and 2.00 p.m.

Visa extensions: enquire at the S.P. (Superintendant of Police).

Books, magazines, newspapers: try in the Main Bazaar. Little choice. Newspapers often unavailable.

Wonderful black-and-white photographs of Ladakh from the photography shop near the 'Tree'. Taken by the proprietor (Ali Shah) and in post-card format; they cost 2 Rs each.

TREKKING IN LADAKH

With its still relatively undisturbed environment and people, Ladakh is a great temptation for trekking enthusiasts and adventurers. But it's entirely possible that in a few years the trekking paths here will be as worn as those in Nepal. Trekking in Ladakh is an adventure and it ought to remain so. So no comprehensive details of the various trekking routes are given here–only some information, tips and suggestions.

A large proportion of Ladakh is still restricted: broadly speaking, everything that lies more than one mile north of the road between the Zoji-La Pass and Leh. The road from Leh to Manali is open to tourists as far as Upshi (the prohibited area starts one mile east of the road). See also 'Leh-Manali Road'. Permits for the prohibited areas are not available in Leh. If at all, the only place to get them is at the Ministry of Home Affairs in Delhi. You can book complete trekking arrangements in some travel agencies in Srinagar and Leh. Boat trips on the Zanskar River (embarking at Padam) are also offered.

Equipment: Ladakh is still hardly organised at all for trekking tourism. So don't expect any hotels, restaurants, provisions etc. along the way. Whereas in Nepal nearly everything is available along the way, here you still have to carry everything with you (or have it carried by porters or animals). A good sleeping bag is imperative (it gets very cold at night), and also a good lightweight tent so that you can be really independent. Besides these, take enough provisions (better to buy them in Srinagar) and a water bottle (water is rather scarce on many treks in Ladakh). You can also hire trekking equipment in Leh–but there's little choice!

A pony or mule costs about 50 Rs per day, a guide about 70 Rs a day during the trek and about half that on rest days. Few treks in Ladakh can be done without a guide.

The Major Treks
For detailed information see also the literature listed in 'General'/'Maps and publications'. The trek lengths given below are only for the outward journey. If you want to trek back along the same route, you must allow extra days.

Pahalgam-Panikhar (Suru): bus from Srinagar to Pahalgam (2130 m) from where you trek to Panikhar in eight days at the most. A road goes from Panikhar to Kargil (67 km); possible to get a lift in a truck. The trek goes over the 4400-metre high Gulol Gali Pass and the Lonvilad Gali (about 4700 m, crossing a glacier on the way down). Pahalgam-Panikar is 88 km.

Sanko (Sanku)-Drass: a mini-trek (a bit more than 40 km) that can be done in three to four days.

Kargil-Padam (Padum): allow about 10 days for the walk to Padam. From there there are two more 10-day routes to Darcha: over the approx. 5100-metre high Shingo-La Pass or over the Phirtse-La Pass (5350 m). Bus from Darcha to Manali (daily service). A road has been built from Kargil to Padam, but not all the bridges have yet been completed and the road is very bad. You can enquire in Kargil about the condition of the construction work and about travel possibilities.

Lamayuru-Padam: allow about nine days for the approx. 170 km trip. A difficult trek and not recommended without a local guide. You have to cross various passes, among them the 5200 m high Singila and the Humula (also called Humulala; the altitudes given for this pass vary between 4700 and 5000 m).

Padam-Kishtwar: a six-day trek over 114 km. The highest point is the Umasila (5235 m). You can complete the last part of this trek (from Galar to Kishtwar, 29 km) by bus. There are direct buses to Srinagar from Kishtwar. Local guides and porters are also very much advised for this trek.

There are many more treks possible from Padam; and from Kishtwar you can trek to Lihenwan in the Kashmir Valley in seven days.

MONASTERIES (Gompas)

The first monastery on the Srinagar-Leh road is in Mulbekh, where Little Tibet really begins. There is also a huge stone relief of a Maitreya (Buddha) on the right of the road. Spectacular monastery: Lamayuru, situated on a hill in a valley basin. 2 km before Saspul (Saspol), turn right after a bridge across the Indus on to a jeep road to Alchi (about 4 km, 1 hour on foot), where there is an interesting monastery (Indian-influenced paintings, large Mandalas). Around Leh there are half a dozen monasteries (within striking distance): Tsemo (1 km, on the castle hill), Sankar (3 km), Spituk (8 km), Phyang or Fiang (15 km); to the east: Shey (16 km), Tikse (19 km), Hemis (42 km), Stok (13 km), Stakna (about 30 km). The largest monastery in Ladakh is Hemis, where hundreds of lamas and novices live. Also there is the largest prayer drum (takes two men to move it–with great effort) and the largest thanka (displayed only once every 11 years) in Ladakh. There's a whole collection of monasteries here and there throughout the areas prohibited to tourists.

The best time to visit monasteries is early in the morning or towards evening, when the temples are open to locals. During the day, the lamas are either not there or are not willing to open the temples for tourists. In any case: leave a few rupees in the collection plate.

Take off your shoes before entering the temples. You can keep your socks on; thick socks are good protection against the cold floors and oil drips from the butter lamps. You can take photographs even during prayers; there are no objections to photography, but here and there you may be asked for money. Drivers: to reach Hemis, first go to Karu (35 km), then turn sharp right after the bridge; Hemis is 7 km further on.

TRANSPORT

Taxi

Excursions, sightseeing trips and the journey back to Srinagar can be made by jeep-taxis (which don't have meters) as well as by public transport. You can have a look at the official fares for individual journeys in the Tourist Office in Leh. The drivers often want to charge more. On the other hand, it sometimes happens that the fares, which are always flat rate (i.e. for the whole taxi and not per person), are underbid when business is bad.

Examples of fares (from Leh): 300 Rs for a day trip to the four monasteries of Hemis, Tikse, Shey and Stok; the official fare for the journey to Kargil is about 1000 Rs (1700 Rs for a return trip) and to

Srinagar about 1800 Rs (which can be beaten down to 1000 Rs). For trips longer than a day, you have to reckon on an overnight charge of at least 80 Rs per night.

As well as the jeep-taxis, some 'Ambassador Taxis' also operate; they all have meters.

Bus

Ladakh is accessible from Leh by a fairly good, if also (as is usual in India) often overburdened, bus network. Also buses don't run every day on all the routes. A timetable of bus services is set out at the Tourist Office. But as changes occur all the time, you'd do better to enquire at the bus station. Here are some services from Leh (summer timetable):

To Stok: daily at 8.00 a.m. and 4.30 p.m.; return journey to Leh 9.00 a.m. and 5.30 p.m.

To Shey: daily at 8.15 a.m. and 4.20 p.m.; return journey at 9.10 a.m. and 5.10 p.m.

To Spituk: daily at 8.30 a.m. and 4.50 p.m.; return journey 9.30 a.m. and 5.10 p.m.

To Sakti: twice daily. Get out at Karu for Hemis and then 7 km on foot.

Leh-Manali Road

On the Leh-Manali Road, tourists are allowed as far as Upshi, 49 km south of Leh. If you want to go further (only private vehicles or trekking–no buses), you need a permit, which is available only from the Ministry of Home Affairs in Delhi and is very difficult to get. The road to Manali is 475 km long and travels through an almost uninhabited area. The highest pass is the Taglung-La (5328 m above sea-level). The road is open for only about two or three months in the year, between July and September, when the next snow falls. Take all provisions and sufficient petrol with you. Also water; the Taglung to Pang stretch (69 km), for example, has no water. The first relatively large village on the route is Keylong, 360 km from Leh. One mile to the east of the road the area prohibited to tourists begins.

Beacon Highway

As for the Leh-Manali Road, a permit has to be applied for in Delhi for travel on the Beacon Highway; tourists hardly ever get one. The Beacon Highway leads over the Khardungla (Khardung-La) into the Nubra Valley. At 5600 m (other sources give it as 'only' 5450 m high), the Khardungla is supposed to be the highest road pass in the world.

MISCELLANEOUS

Festivals: of the many festivals that take place in Ladakh, only the most important is mentioned here–the Hemis Festival, which takes place once a year, in the second half of June (occasionally the beginning of July), and includes mask dances and archery. The Hemis Festival is, however, no longer a secret: travel companies discovered it a few years ago and now fly tour groups in every year especially for the occasion. Once again, one fears for the survival of a genuine tradition.

Fauna: for years various animal parks have been planned for Ladakh, but it appears that to date none of these projects has materialised. Despite this, the majority of the mammal fauna is protected. Here are some of the shy representatives of Ladakhi fauna, which can be seen only with a great deal of luck and persistence: Ovis ammon (a mountain sheep; both sexes have horns); ibex (a type of goat whose horns grow to more than a metre); and, a great rarity, the snow leopard, which is called Shan or Shun in Ladakh. The snow leopard is found almost exclusively above the tree-line (if at all), and is relatively small (about 1.10 m long, excluding tail) compared with its relatives in the Indian jungle. The wild yak is similarly rare. But in its domesticated form it is found all over, for example, Leh.

In Ladakh you won't find any scooters or rickshaws.

FURTHER TRAVEL FROM LEH

Leh is a terminus and all routes lead back from here to Srinagar. Even by air you have to change planes in Srinagar, unless you fly to Chandigarh.

Bus
The buses to Srinagar leave Leh early in the morning. Try to make a reservation well in advance, as the buses are often booked out, especially in the season. For all other information see 'Trips to Little Tibet (Ladakh)'/'Bus'.

Truck
Even before the road to Srinagar is open to bus traffic, the first trucks travel from about the beginning of May. The truck station lies between the Polo Ground and the Bus Stand. Enquire about travelling by truck a few days in advance. You usually have to leave a deposit. You don't have to travel as far as Leh; and can get out along the way. The journey to Srinagar costs 50-60 Rs and to Kargil about half that. Once you have come to terms with the driver, note the number of the truck as otherwise you'll have great difficulty finding the truck the next day. Departure time: about 5.00 a.m. Overnight stop usually in Kargil, less often in Drass. But there are some drivers who make the journey without a break. As the trucks travelling to Srinagar normally have no freight, you usually have a comfortable place. It's a bit more expensive to travel in the driver's cabin (where 2-8 passengers sit) than in the 'high seat' built above it or in the back of the truck. From the (uncovered) high seat you have a wonderful panoramic view, but it gets icy cold up there and if it rains you have to shelter under the covering on the back of the truck. When there is a spell of bad weather just before or just after the season, snow can fall on the Zoji-La Pass before Srinagar and your truck is then cut off before the pass. Hard luck if you have lots of luggage: the only thing you can do is start walking the rest of the journey to Sonamarg if you don't want to go back to Drass. The Zoji-La, which is affected by snow and prone to rockfalls, marks the border

between Kashmir and Ladakh and is a real problem on the Leh-Srinagar road. The Pass can be crossed on foot weeks before the trucks can travel across it, but it's fairly tough-going and is possible only with good equipment and, possibly, guides.

Take food with you for the truck journey. There are some check points along the way where luggage searches are occasionally carried out.

Taxi

You must allow about 1000Rs (flat rate) for a taxi journey to Srinagar.

Air

There's an Indian Airlines flight from Leh to Srinagar every Saturday and Sunday, 358 Rs. You'll have a good view of the mountains if you sit on the right-hand side of the plane.

Every Monday there's also a flight from Leh to Chandigarh, and from there to Delhi.

In the season these flights are usually booked out way in advance. Then, if there's bad weather and some flights are cancelled, the situation becomes chaotic. And even the few extra planes that Indian Airlines puts on in the main holiday season don't help very much.

BOMBAY (MUMBAI)

With a population of about 7,000,000, Bombay is India's second-largest city, after Calcutta. It lies on a sharp, marshy peninsula which originally consisted of seven small islands. The former fishing district is today a modern, westernised city of skyscrapers, and India's most important financial and industrial centre. Bombay is, besides, one of the most significant centres of the Indian film and recording industries. In Dharavi (about 400,000 inhabitants), it has the largest slum district in Asia.

ARRIVAL

Rail
Either at the Bombay Victoria Terminus (VT) railway station or at Bombay Central railway station, which is the terminus of the Western Railway.

From Bombay VT take bus 1, 6 Ltd, 103 or 124 to Electric House (45 Ps), where the cheap hotels are, or walk to one of the cheap hotels nearby. From Bombay Central take bus 70 or 124 to Electric House or Mereweather Road (45 Ps). If you arrive in Dadar on the 58 Amritsar-Dadar Express, take a local Western Railway train to Bombay Central (45 Ps) or Churchgate (45 Ps), and a bus from there.

Bus
Arrivals either at Bombay Central railway station (State buses) or near Victoria Terminus (private companies).

Air
International flights land at Sarah International Airport. Other flights land at Santa Cruz Airport, not far from the international airport. EATS buses from Santa Cruz Airport into the city (Hotel Taj Mahal Intercontinental or Air India) cost 13 Rs; from Sarah International Airport 16 Rs; about a one-hour journey. The cheap hotels on Mereweather Road are situated just near the luxury Taj Mahal Hotel. Taxis from Santa Cruz into the city cost (flat rate) about 55 Rs and from Sarah about 60 Rs; extra charge for large pieces of luggage. This fare is not identical to the tariff shown on the meter. It is about 100% higher. The total payable is worked out according to the 'Small Taxi Tariff Card', a conversion table that every taxi driver is supposed to have. But in any case the drivers don't bother about the official tariff with tourists.

ACCOMMODATION

Bombay has a chronic shortage of cheap hotel rooms. The best time to try and get a room is in the morning. Many of the cheap hotels don't

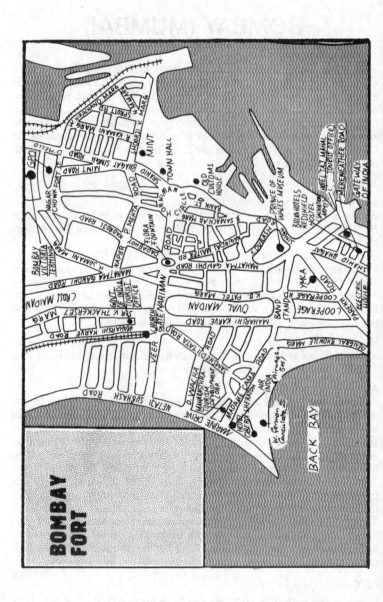

BOMBAY FORT

BACK BAY

GPO
MAGAR CHOWK FORT
SPROTT RD.
HIRACHAND MARG
SHROFF R KAMANI MARG
D'MELLO
D'MELLO ROAD
NATIVYA
MINT ROAD
SHAHID BHAGAT SINGH ROAD
BHAGAT SINGH ROAD
MINT
TOWN HALL
DAHIP
NADIVYA MARG
H. SOMANI MARG
BOMBAY VICTORIA TERMINUS
NAOROJI ROAD
P. MEHTA
NAPIER
DADABHOY
FLORA FOUNTAIN
ROAD
DHC CIRCLE
ROAD
BANK ST.
OLD CUSTOMS HOUSE
PRINCE OF WALES MUSEUM
BILLA HOTELS REDSHIELD HOSTEL
SALVATION ARMY
HOTEL TAJ MAHAL
TOURIST OFFICE
MERERWEATHER ROAD
GATEWAY OF INDIA
MAHATMA GANDHI ROAD
S. SAMACHAR MARG
NAGINDAS MAITRA RD
THEATRE
SHAHID BHAGAT
MAHATMA GANDHI ROAD
GOVT. OF INDIA TOURIST OFFICE
CROSS MAIDAN
STR V THACKERSEY MARG
MAHARSHI KARVE ROAD
VEER NARIMAN
CHURCH GATE NARIMAN
K.B. PATEL MARG
OVAL MAIDAN
BAND STAND
YMCA
COOPERAGE RD
PARCHU COOPERAGE RD
ELECTRIC HOUSE
MAHARSHI KARVE ROAD
NETAJI SUBHASH ROAD
VEER
JAMSHEDJI TATA ROAD
D. WACHA
MAHARASHTRA TOURISM DEVELOPMENT CORP.
MADAME CAMA ROAD
AIR INDIA
ROAD
GENERAL BHONSLE MARG
MARINE DRIVE
HOTEL NATRON OBEROI
AIR INDIA (Airways) Bus
W. German Consulate

have actual rooms; the bedrooms are simply separated from each other by wooden partitions and often don't have any natural light (Oliver, Sea Shore, etc.). The guest houses in the Mereweather Road district are often full of long-stay guests and Arab tourists, and are even fuller when a ship has just docked with Indians from Kenya or the Arab countries.

Hotels

Mereweather Road district:

Salvation Army Red Shield House, 30 Mereweather Road, tel. 24 18 24. Dormitory bed 30 Rs, double 75 Rs, family room 37.50 Rs/person. Full board. Checkout time 9.00 a.m. Men and women separated.

Carlton Hotel, Florence House, 12 Mereweather Road, tel. 23 06 42. Single 45 Rs, double 45-80 Rs. Small rooms, very clean.

Oliver Guest House, 6 Walton Road (near the Red Shield), tel.24 02 91. Single 26 Rs, double 50 Rs. Checkout time 10.00 a.m.

Stiffles Hotel, 8 Ormistone Road (opposite Red Shield House), tel. 23 15 18/23 09 60. Single 25 Rs (50 Rs with bath), double 50 Rs (60/80 Rs with bath), double with bath and AC 120 Rs.

Rex Hotel, same address as Stiffles, 3rd and 4th floors. All rooms with bath: single 50 Rs, double 70 Rs, double with AC 110 Rs. Warm water for three hours a day.

Sea Shore Hotel, 1-49 Kamal Mansion, 4th floor, Arthur Bunder Road (near the Radio Club), entrance round the corner. Single 25 Rs, double 40 Rs, 4-bed room 100 Rs. Try to get a room with a view of the harbour.

India Guest House, same address as the Sea Shore Hotel, one floor below. Only has doubles, 60 Rs.

Kerawella Chambers Guest House, 4th floor, 25 Strand Road (same building as the Strand Hotel), tel. 24 19 04. Double 60 Rs.

Cowie's Guest House, diagonally across from the Oliver Guest House, tel. 23 06 42. Single 70 Rs, double 160 Rs. Clean.

Whalley's Guest House, Apollo Bunder, tel. 22 18 02. Single 55 Rs, double 85/115 Rs, dormitory 15 Rs. Breakfast included.

Other cheap accommodation

Railway Retiring Rooms in the Victoria Terminus, tel. 26 80 41 (extension 273). Single 30 Rs, double 50 Rs, extra bed 20 Rs.

In the Railway Retiring Room at Bombay Central, tel. 37 72 92, ext. 4175. Doubles 40 Rs. Clean. Warning: Railway Retiring Rooms are only for railway passengers and tickets must be shown on demand.

Middle-class hotels

YMCA International House, 18 YMCA Road, near Bombay Central railway station, tel. 37 06 01. Single 29 Rs (49 Rs with bath), double 38 Rs (68 Rs with bath), extra bed 19 Rs. 5% service charge extra. Also has some rooms with AC. Clean.

YWCA International Guest House, 18 Madame Cama Road (near Museum bus stop), tel. 23 51 61. Single (with AC) 60 Rs, double 90 Rs

(100 Rs with AC), 4-bed room 180 Rs, extra bed 45 Rs. 5% service charge extra. Breakfast included.
Both the Y's are for men and women.

Campers/Drivers
Camping on Juhu Beach, in the North of Bombay.
Address of the automobile club: Western India Automobile Association (WIAA), Lalji Narainju Memorial Building, Churchgate.

FOOD AND DRINK

The Olympia Coffee House and the Leopold are good: clean, large choice; beer and Nescafe are even available. Both near Electric House. Also good, and right opposite the Olympia Coffee House, is the Cafe Apsara.

Some Chinese restaurants in the Gateway of India district, but they are expensive.

Dipti's House of Pure Drinks, diagonally opposite Stiffles Hotel. Small bar with lots of fruit juice drinks and ice creams.

As everywhere in India, you should beware of the tap water. By drinking it you risk jaundice and other diseases.

TRANSPORT

There are no cheap motor-scooters and no rickshaws in Bombay, only expensive taxis. Taxis have meters. You can buy the 'Small Taxi Tariff Card' for 50Ps from street vendors. Extra charge of 50 Ps for larger pieces of luggage.

The single cheap means of transport is the BEST (Bombay Electric Supply and Transport) buses. Buy a BEST bus guide or town guide, which shows all the bus routes (e.g. 'Pocket Bombay Guide', 2 Rs) from any newspaper-seller.

'Ltd' after a bus number means 'limited stops', i.e. express bus; usually 5-10 Ps more expensive than normal buses. Telephone information about bus routes: 44 65 21/44 78 39. Bus information: BEST Transport House, 1st floor, near Electric House.

POST/TELEPHONE

The General Post Office (GPO) near Victoria Terminus railway station is open Monday-Saturday and on holidays between 8.00 a.m. and 8.30 p.m., Sunday 10.00 a.m.-5.00 p.m.; poste restante counter Monday-Saturday 8.00 a.m.-6.30 p.m., holidays 10.30 a.m.-5.30 p.m., closed on Sunday.

Overseas phone calls can be made at the Overseas Communication Service, near Flora Fountain.

STREET NAMES

Finding addresses in Bombay can be confusing since English (colonial) street names have been 'Indianised'. So, for example, French Road is now called Dr. Atmaram Ramchandra Rangnekar Marg. Of course, many locals still use the old names.

You will find a list of the old and new names on the first page of the Bombay phone book and in city guidebooks e.g. 'Pocket Bombay Guide'. The de-colonialisation didn't stop even at Bombay itself: on 30 June 1981 Bombay was officially renamed Mumbai.

SIGHTSEEING

A city sightseeing tour in an AC bus costs 25 Rs and lasts from about 9.00 a.m. to 2.00 p.m. Departs from the Government of India Tourist Office, but you can join it at the Taj Mahal Hotel. Runs every day except Monday. Reservations at the Maharashtra Tourist Development Corporation (MTDC) Hutments on Madame Cama Road.

Two city tours in the afternoons, about 2.30-5.30 p.m.: one by the MTDC (20 Rs) and one for 25 Rs by the TCI.

Also two sightseeing tours daily (starting at about 8.45 a.m. and 10.30 a.m.) of Bombay's suburbs. They cost 35 Rs and 30 Rs and start at the Government of India Tourist Office and the Taj Mahal respectively. MTDC has no suburban tour on Mondays. The cheapest suburban tour is by BEST, 15 Rs, but it runs only on Sunday (approx. 8.45 a.m.-5.30 p.m.). Departs from the Taj Mahal Hotel and Indian Tourist Office. Tickets from the Assistance Centre, Transport House (by Electric House), 1st floor, or–if all the seats have not been sold–on the bus itself before it leaves.

Cheapest sightseeing: on one of the red double-decker buses, 132 or 133, which travel clockwise and anti-clockwise respectively through Bombay (ring road). The best way of getting a first impression. Get on the bus by Electric House. The round trip costs about one rupee (but if you interrupt your journey you have to buy a new ticket).

Sightseeing on your own: bus 106 from Churchgate up Malabar Hill to the Hanging Gardens, with their bushes and trees pruned into shapes of animals and people. Opposite are the Kamala Nehru Gardens, with a wonderful view over the Bay of Bombay (outlined at night by lights, the 'Queen's Necklace'). Also on Malabar Hill are the Towers of Silence, where Bombay's Parsis (followers of Zarathustra) leave their dead to be consumed by vultures. The Towers of Silence are hidden behind trees and are not open to tourists; there's a model of the Towers of Silence in the Prince of Wales Museum (closed on Monday). Walk down from Malabar Hill via Mani Bhavan, Laburnum Road, to the Mahatma Gandhi Museum; from there to Chowpatty Beach and along Marine Drive (Netaji Subhash Road), past the Taraporevala Aquarium (closed on Monday), and back again.

Other attractions:
Haji Ali Dargah (tomb), a holy place in the sea which is reached by a 300-metre long footbridge bordered by countless beggars. Take one of the numerous buses (81, 83 to 86, 132, 133 etc.) from Hutatma Chowk (Flora Fountain). Buses 132 and 133 also pass by Electric House.

From just by the Gateway of India boats leave every 30 minutes between 8.30 a.m. and 1.30 p.m. for Elephanta Island, which has sculptures in caves. About a one-hour journey; 9 Rs return. Also from the Gateway: short harbour trips for 3 Rs.

Trips to the rock temples of Ajanta and Ellora: a bus leaves the MTDC office on Madame Cama Road every day at 8.30 a.m. for Ajanta/Ellora; transport only 65 Rs. A bit cheaper by public transport, but more complicated.

TRAVEL SEASON/WEATHER

Tropical climate (near Bombay is the northern limit of the coconut palm) with pleasant winters and very strong monsoons. Many people lose their lives every year when houses collapse during the monsoons.

SHOPPING

Street vendors sell contraband: US cigarettes, batteries, perfumes etc.

For vegetables, fruit, spices, meat and fish: Crawford Market (now: Mahatma Jyotiba Phule Market) on the corner of Dr. Dadabhai Baoroji Road and Lokmanya Tilak Road. The market building with its tower was built in the second half of the nineteenth century and is reminiscent of Les Halles in Paris.

Chor Bazaar is the flea market and thieves' market at the crossroads of Sardar Patel Road and Maulana Azad Road.

Large selection of LPs (Indian music and pop; about 50 Rs each) in, amongst other places, the bookshop of the luxury Taj Mahal Hotel, where you can also find newspapers from England and current affairs magazines (Time, Newsweek etc.).

MISCELLANEOUS

Government of India Tourist Office, 123 Maharshi Karve Road (Queens Road), opposite Churchgate Station (alongside), tel. 29 31 44. Open 8.30 a.m.-5.30 p.m., closed on Sunday.

Tourist Information Counter in the Taj Mahal Hotel. Open 8.30 a.m.-3.30 p.m., closed on Sunday.

Other tourist counters at Sarah International Airport and Santa Cruz Airport as well as in Bombay Central and Victoria Terminus railway stations.

Divisional Tourist Office, Government of Maharashtra, Madame Cama Road, tel. 24 17 13.

Money: the American Express office is open 11.00 a.m.-3.00 p.m. Monday-Friday and 11.00 a.m.-1.00 p.m. on Saturday. Stay away from the black market; don't be lured by high exchange rates as you will usually be cheated. Black market money-changing goes on especially at the Gateway of India and in front of the American Express office.

Prostitution: Bombay must be the city with the most prostitutes in the world. The centre of commercial love is the poor district around Falkland and Foras Roads, where crudely made-up and betel-chewing girls wait behind wooden bars in 'cages', trying to entice passers-by, suitors and the curious into their bed cubicles which are separated only by curtains from the outside world and from neighbouring cubicles.

Hardly any of the very young girls sit in the 'cages' of their own accord: they have been cast out by their families, sold in times of terrible need by their parents in the country to professional dealers, or plainly and simply abducted. Helpless, without much money, unwanted by their families and taboo as marriage partners for any Indian man, they don't stand a chance in Indian society.

Cinema: good selection of foreign (English-language) films; details in the daily press.

Health: Kemp's Chemist by the luxury Taj Mahal Hotel is open around the clock.

Visa extensions: Apply for extensions at the Deputy commissioner of Police, Gymnasium Road, opposite Crawford Market.

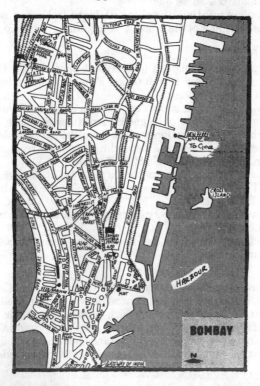

Swimming is not allowed at Chowpatty Beach in the middle of the city (and in any case the water is filthy).

Other places: at Juhu Beach, a long beach in the North of the city, also not very clean. Bus 4 Ltd or 84 Express from Flora Fountain (Hutatma Chowk) to Santa Cruz Station Road. Or suburban train from Churchgate Station to Santa Cruz, then bus 231 to Juhu Beach. Allow about 1 hour for the journey. Hardly any shade at the beach.

One of the few jobs possible in India: extra for one of Bombay's numerous film companies. Film people call in now and then to the backpacker hotels in the Mereweather Road district. The Sunrise Restaurant, which was once the centre for film jobs, doesn't exist any more. About 70 Rs per day; girls more sought after than guys.

FURTHER TRAVEL

Flights to Europe and Southeast Asia

Enquire about cheap flights at the Students Travel Information Centre, Hotel Bombay International, 29 Marine Drive, tel. 23 34 04; or at Space Travels, Nanaghay Mansion, 4th floor, Sir Pherozeshah Mehta Road (Sir P.M. Road), tel. 25 56 52.

At the time of printing, the cheapest flight to Europe was offered by the Polish airline Lot via Warsaw 'to anywhere in Europe', 3400Rs.

Internal Travel

Rail: The quota for foreigners (places kept specially for tourists) is organised by the Railway Tourist Guide. Enquire at the railway station from which you are leaving.

To Delhi: 6 good services every day; 2 go via Agra (5/37 Punjab Mail, departs Bombay VT 4.30 p.m., and 57 Amritsar Express, 10.40 p.m. from suburban railway station Dadar). All other services depart from Bombay Central. The distance, depending on the route, is about 1390 or 1550 km. See also 'From Delhi to Bombay'.

To Ernakulam and Trivandrum: the Jayanti Janata Express departs Bombay VT at 3.35 p.m., arrives Trivandrum on the day after next at 11.45 a.m.; 2062 km.

To Poona: several services every day from Victoria Terminus; 192 km; about a 4-hour journey.

Other direct services every day to, amongst other places, Howrah (Calcutta) and Madras.

Bus

Services leave from Maharashtra State Road Transport Corporation Bus Terminal, opposite Bombay Central railway station, Bellasis Road, or from private bus companies, which mostly have their departure points on Mahapalika Marg and other streets near Victoria Terminus. There is a limited selection of long-distance buses, especially if you're heading northwards; private companies operate southwards as far as Bangalore.

To Poona: numerous services every day. The State buses leave from the State Bus Terminal. Ordinary buses 13.50 Rs, luxury 22 Rs.

Air
The office of Indian Airlines is situated in the Air India Building, Nariman Point, tel. 23 30 31. For some airfares and destinations, see 'India General'/'Flights'.

Ship
To Karachi/Pakistan: apart from the ship service to Goa, the passenger service to Karachi is of interest to anyone who wants to tie at least one sea journey in to the overland route. One ship per month.
The fare to Karachi is about 500 Rs and 700 Rs, depending on class. Arrive in Karachi the day after next. The ship continues from there to Dubai-Bahrain-Kuwait.

From Bombay to Goa
Ship
The most recommended means of getting there. Every day (except Tuesday) between September and the end of May, Mogul Lines ships travel from Bombay to Goa. No ships during the monsoon season. The 417 km-long journey down the coast, during which the steamer puts to shore several times, lasts 21-22 hours.

Fares: lower deck 33 Rs, upper deck 52.50 Rs, cabins 120, 135, 160 and 400 Rs (depending on the degree of comfort). Meals are not included, but are available cheaply on board. Departs 10.00 a.m. from the New Ferry Wharf in Bombay harbour. Take bus 43 from the cheap hotel district to the Central Railways Goods Depot, and change there to bus 41 or 42. Buses 41, 42 and (at certain times) also 48, 49, 50 go direct to the Ferry Wharf. Tickets are available there at the Mogul Lines booking office; tel. 86 40 71. The office is open Tuesday-Sunday, 10.30 a.m.-1.30 p.m. and 2.00-3.00 p.m. Tickets are also available at the MTDC on Madame Cama Road, opposite the Hotel Oberoi, tel. 24 11 713.

You can sleep on benches or on the floor. There's no great difference between the upper and lower decks. The coolies in blue shirts are allowed on to the ship earlier than the passengers to reserve the best seats with their luggage. So when the gates open at 9.30 a.m. and everyone crowds on board, there's hardly a bench left to lie down on at night, and you'll have to sleep on the floor–unless you hire a coolie for a few rupees.

Rail
Best service: depart Bombay VT at 8.45 a.m. on the 307 Miraj Express, arrive Miraj at 8.00 p.m. Change to the 206 Gomantak Express, get out in Madgaon (arrives about 8.00 a.m.) and continue by bus. Arrive Vasco Da Gama terminus at 9.05 a.m.; 769 km.

Bus
Four buses every day from the Maharashtra Bus Station opposite Bombay Central railway station.

Depart 5.15 p.m. Ordinary bus. 54 Rs. Arrive about 10.00 a.m. at Panaji (Panjim); get out at Mapusa (Mhapsa) for Calangute Beach.

Depart 10.00 a.m. 70Rs. Arrive early next morning in Madgaon.

Depart 6.00 p.m. Luxury bus. 72Rs. Arrive about 11.15 a.m. the next day at Panaji; get out at Mapusa for Calangute.

Depart 3.30 p.m. Luxury bus. 79 Rs. Arrive in Panaji about 8.45 a.m. the next day.

Private buses to Panaji depart from Mahapalika Marg (near Victoria Terminus). Ordinary (also called 'semi-luxury') 55 Rs, luxury 75 Rs, AC buses 88 Rs.

Allow between 16 to 20 hours for the approx. 600 km trip.

Air

One flight daily to Dabolim, 277 Rs. Airport transport (EATS bus) departs from the Air India Building or the Taj Mahal Hotel.

POONA (Pune)

1.3 million inhabitants, 559 m. above sea level. Since the Bhagwan Shree Rajneesh left for the United States in August 1981, his Ashram is deserted and Poona has lost its importance for the tourists.

ACCOMMODATION

Numerous, for Indian conditions rather expensive 'cheap' hotels are in the station area.

The National Hotel is directly opposite the station (single room 15 Rs, double room 30 Rs); further hotels are in Wilson Garden Road, approx. 300 m from the station; Hotel Alankar, single room 25 Rs, double room 35 Rs; Central Lodge, single room 10 Rs, double room 17 Rs, both hotels operating with the 24 hour mode.

FURTHER TRAVEL

To Bombay

Train, bus, plane or collective taxi (54 Rs. per person, drives only to suburb of Dadar, departs close to station).

To Goa

The 307 Miraj Express coming from Bombay leaves Poona at 1.50 p.m. (further information under 'From Bombay to Goa').

Bus: government company daily at 5.30 a.m. from the State Transport Bus Terminal to Mapusa/Panjim (Panaji), 38 Rs. A private company also runs to Mapusa/Panjim: tickets (40.50 Rs) available at Ambika Petrol Depot service station on Connaught Road (close to station). Do book seats the day before, it's approx. 12 hours for the trip to Mapuse (for Calangute Beach).

GOA

Goa (900 000 inhabitants), 3611 sq. km. was a Portuguese colony from 1510 to 1961. Half the population is catholic, Portuguese is still spoken. Together with Daman and Diu (both ex-Portuguese), Goa politically represents a union territory under direct rule of Delhi.

ARRIVAL
Ship
Landing at 7.00 a.m. or 8.00 a.m. at Panaji Quay. This is usually pronounced 'Panjim'. Proceed from the docking point with city bus or on foot (10-15 minutes) to the New Bus Stand where the buses for Calangute Beach (15 km, 1.10 Rs) and Colva Beach (50 km) leave via Margao.

A 'common' taxi Panaji-Calangute costs about 20 Rs, i.e. 5 Rs/person plus perhaps luggage extra and scooters usually cost approx. 20 Rs.

Train
Leave at Madgaon (Margao). Take local bus from bus station to Colva (6 km), 75 Ps, last connection approx. 8.30 p.m.
Or to Calangute: Direct bus from Margao to Mapusa (pronounced Mapsa), 4.65 Rs, then local bus Mapusa-Calangute (75 Ps). Or by ferry from Cortalim-Agacaim.
There are regular ferries on week days (55 Ps) from final rail station Vasco da Gama/Marmagao to Dona Paula. From there with the bus to Panaji (55 Ps).

Bus
Get off in Mapusa, 13 km short of Panjim if you want to go to Calangute Beach. Local bus from Mapusa to Calangute Beach (approx. 8 km), 75 Ps, common taxi approx. 5 Rs/person.

Plane
Indian Airlines bus from Dabolim airport to Panjim, 29 km.

ACCOMMODATION
Numerous cheap hotels and accommodation with fisherfolk in Calangute and Colva. Price principle: the further from the beach the cheaper. Beds start from 8 Rs per day; huts, houses and rooms with families 150-400 Rs/month-depending on season and comfort (electricity or water supply). At least in the main season private persons do not like renting for short periods.

Caution: always lock accommodation carefully as Goa is another place where theft is very common. When going out in the evenings, do take a flashlight as you might have trouble finding your house in the dark.

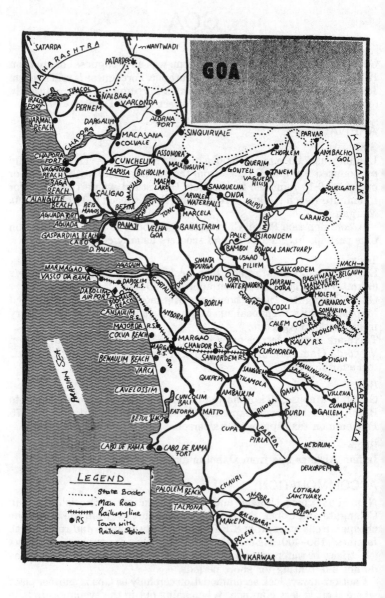

Some accommodation is in the city centre, but mainly on the beach (with the exception of the Tourist Dormitory).

Tourist Dormitory, Calangute, somewhat distant from the beach, 8 Rs per bed in 5 and 8 bed rooms; single room 20 Rs, double room 25 Rs.

Tourist Resort Calangute (state run), middle class format; Dormitory 5-8 Rs, single room 25 Rs, double room 35 Rs, additional bed 10 Rs. All rooms with bath and verandah; often fully booked during the Indian holiday season, approx. 50% price reduction during the monsoon period. There is an official limit of 8 days to duration of stay.

Royal Hotel, double room 25 Rs, extra bed 5 Rs.

Calangute Beach Guest House, single room (common bathroom) 20 Rs, double room 35 Rs (with bath 75 Rs).

Concha Hotel, double room (with bath) 132 Rs, double room with bath and A.C. 165 Rs.

Further Accommodation

Along Calangute Beach: camping under palm trees at the Baia de Sol (formerly Motel Lomir) at the northern end of Calangute Beach ('Baga Beach').

The Baia de Sol is also a middle class hotel, double rooms (no single rooms available) 93.50 Rs or 110 Rs in the new section. Can be reached by bus from Calangute (last bus approx. 8 p.m.), motorbike or on foot.

Colva Beach: Tourist Cottages, approx. the same prices as Tourist Resort Calangute.

Panjim: hotels in all price classes in the city.

FOOD AND DRINK

The cheapest: fresh fruit such as pineapples, coconuts, bananas, etc. Seafood is also very good: shark, octopus, prawns and shrimps. Buy fish to fry yourself at the market or straight from the fishers.

Goa is India's wettest state: not only no prohibition but also the cheapest beer (approx. 6 Rs for the bottle in a restaurant); local wine, particularly sweet wine is available. The local coconut-palm spirit is called Fenni.

Supplies in Calangute

Self-suppliers are best off buying at the market in Calangute. There is a larger choice in Mapusa (excursion), with bus. Large and interesting market, but only on Fridays.

Calangute probably has the richest kitchen in India. The Sea View Restaurant (opposite the Tourist Resort) offers Goan specialities and general seafood dishes in a large variety but without finesse. The Epicure offers approx. the same quality (but smaller selection).

Restaurant Summervine is a specialist for 'continental food'. Menus change daily and cost between 20 and 30 Rs. Accompanied by a mini-orchestra with piano and violin.

BEACHES

Goa has endless, palm lined sand beaches which are separated from each other by peninsulas, rocks or estuaries. The best known and developed beach is the 7 km long Calangute beach, 15 km from Panjim. Anjuna beach known as the 'hippy beach' joins to the north where you can-as on several other beaches-live in self-made houses free of charge. The famous Christmas party is celebrated here. Still further to the north are Vagator Beach and Chapora Beach.

South of the Mandovi and Zuari river mouth lies the broad Colva beach (connected by road from Margao). A string of nearly empty beaches join in the Southern direction: Fatrade, Betul, Palolem, Varca, etc.

TRANSPORT

Taxis don't have meters. Offical fare (for car taxis): 1.60 Rs for the first kilometre, 90 Ps for each following kilometre. Bike taxis (can fit 2 passengers) are an important means of transport in particluar in Calangute. But they are somewhat expensive. The 2-3 km from Calangute to Baga Beach cost 3 Rs.

You can hire motorbikes for approx. 40 Rs per day in Calangute, Margao and some other places.

SIGHTSEEING

Panaji (formerly Panjim) the capital is a picturesque place with Mediterranean charm and lovely old houses. Panjim's lovliest church: Church of Our lady of Immaculate Conception (17th century).

Old Goa (Velha Goa), 10 km east of Panjim, was the centre of Goa in the former Portuguese colonial times. Many churches, amongst them the Basilica Bom Jesus (16th century) with the silver sarcophagus, which contains the incorrupt body of the Jessuit missionary St. Francis Xavier (1506 to 1552).

The Tourist Office in Panjim offers 8 sightseeing tours in Goa, ranging from the three hour 'Beach Special' (7 Rs) to the whole day Goa Tour for 22 Rs. Sightseeing tours from Calangute are also possible with private organisers.

FESTIVALS

You'll find a comprehensive list of christian and hindu festivals in the brochure called 'Welcome' (available from the Tourist Office).

3rd December: Feast of St. Francis Xavier, Old Goa; 8th December: Feast of Our Lady of Immaculate Conception (Goa's patron); 24th December: Christmas in tropical surroundings!, 6th January: the Epiphany.

In the spring, approx. one month before Easter: procession with more than 40 life-size statues of saints.

The largest religious feast is celebrated every ten years, when the beautifully decorated remains of St. Francis Xavier are displayed in a glass coffin. This will be the case in 1994.

BUYING A HOUSE

It is nearly impossible for foreigners (including British) to buy property or houses in India. You can still try though: hand in an application to the Reserve Bank of India and then prepare to wait for anything up to 9 months. Unfortunately, your application will probably not be successful i.e. you will be granted a 49% ownership title and the remaining 51% will have to remain in Indian hands (look for a trustworthy local partner).

Alternative: lease for 99 years (leasehold estate) which practically means a purchase. If you have a house on rent you won't usually encounter great difficulties with visas, even after long stays.

MISCELLANEOUS

Tourist Offices: The Department of Tourism, 1st floor, Rua Afonso de Albuquerque, Panjim, is open daily from 10.00 a.m. to 12.30 p.m. and 2.30 p.m. to 5.00 p.m., public holidays 10.00 a.m. to 11.30 a.m., closed on Sundays.

There are further Tourist Offices in the Municipal Building, Margao and in the Joshi Building in Vasco da Gama; also on the Dabolim airport and at the New Bus Stand in Panjim.

Calangute: no state Tourist Office. You will obtain information from the Tourist Resort Calangute and from the Tourist Bureau Lions Club (Mr. and Mrs. Barbosa).

The Indian Airlines Panjim office is in Dempo House, Tel. 2890.

Only take necessities to the beach when you go for a dip. It is absolutely silly to sleep on the beach accompanied by your possessions.

The held-mail counter at Calangute GPO is open from 10.00 a.m. Mail is often filed under the wrong letters.

Market: During the week there is a fish and vegetable market in Calangute on the market place, on Saturday a flea market atmosphere around the GPO area. There is a big market with a wide variety of goods (not only groceries) each Friday in Mapusa. It is quite a rewarding visit. Once in a while you'll find an illegal Backpacker's market along Anjuna Beqach.

The Press: since the East Coast Times is no longer available, The Navhind Times (35 Ps) is the most important local paper with no competition in Goa. There are some Portuguese papers which are threatened by extinction and the monthly magazine 'Goa Today' (1.50 Rs).

FURTHER TRAVEL

To Bombay

Ship

Daily departure from Panjim except Wednesday and depending on tide either at 9.00 a.m. or 10.00 a.m.; no ships during the monsoon period. Fares and further information see 'From Bombay to Goa'. Tickets are available from M/V.S. Dempo & Co., opposite Customs Wharf; bookings for cabins up to 30 days in advance and for deck up to six days in advance from 10.00 a.m. to 12.30 p.m. and 3.00 p.m. to 5.30 p.m. On the day of departure tickets are sold from 7.30 a.m. to 30 minutes prior to departure.
(Also see 'From Bombay to Goa')

Train

Departure from Margao or terminus Vasco da Gama, no train from Panjim. Two trains: Vasco da Gama, departing at 9.25 p.m., arriving Miraj 8.20 a.m., change and continuation of the trip at 9.10 a.m., arrival in Bombay V.T. in the evening at 9.30 p.m. (not good when looking for a hotel); the Vasco da Gama leaves at 11.25 a.m. arrives at Miraj at 9.40 p.m., change and continuation at 11.55 p.m. arriving in Bombay V.T at 12.25 p.m.

Bus

Several government and private buses daily to Bombay. Expensive but faster than by train.

Plane

Indian Airlines bus from Panjim to Dabolim airport costs 10 Rs. Daily flights to Bombay for 277 Rs.

To Bangalore

Train

This is only half as expensive by second class railway ticket as it is with the direct bus but you have to change trains. In addition, Calangute holidayers must first take the bus to Vasco da Gama or Margao since Panjim has no connection to the Indian railway network. Reservations can be made at the Tourist Office in Panjim. The train leaves Vasco da Gama at 11.00 a.m. You can however board at Margao. Arrival in Bangalore on the next morning at 7.15 a.m.

Bus

A fairly comfortable bus departs daily from the New Bus Stand in Panjim to Bangalore at 4.15 p.m. for 68.30 Rs. The trip takes approx. 15 hours. Tickets are available from the counter of the Karnataka State Road Transport Corporation (KSRTC), opposite the GPO. Book at least three days in advance!.

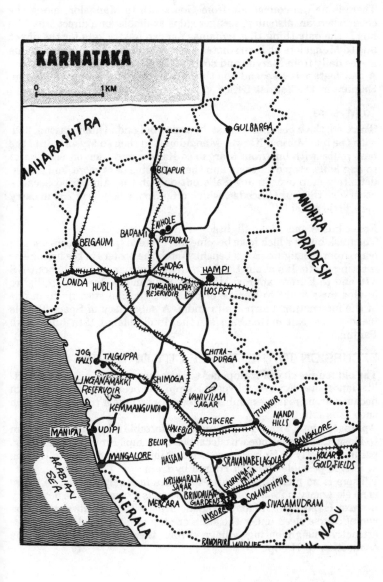

To Mangalore

There is no rail connection from Goa south to Mangalore along the coast; there are also no passenger ships available for a direct trip. The bus is the only thing that remains. You can buy tickets for the direct bus to Mangalore at Keni's hotel, 18th June Road in Panjim. The bus leaves daily from Margao and costs 46 Rs. You must book well ahead. A new feature is a second bus that drives to Mangalore from Panjim. Enquire at the Tourist Office.

To Mysore

'There are three possibilities: 1st, by train via Londa-Hubli-Hassan, 2nd: with the bus Margao-Karwar-Mangalore and then to Mysore. 3rd.: the best route, with bus from Margao to Karwar and then on via Kumta to Jog Falls, stop over there and then continue to Mysore. You should definitely stop over in Jog Falls but only in the rain period because otherwise the four Cascades, which drop from a height of 253 m carry very little water.'

Freak buses and cheap flights
The freak buses which have become more rare in the past years usually leave from Calangute (Baga beach). Watch the posters in the hitchhiker meeting spots. It's about US $3 to Delhi, Katmandu/Nepal about US $70 and to Europe approx. US $350. You can also buy cheap flights in Goa for a flight to Europe or other destination starting from one of the international airports in India. A subsidiary of Space Travels (headquarters are in Bombay) is in the Hotel Fidalgo, 18th June Road, Panjim.

EXCURSION TO THE TEMPLE CITY OF HAMPI

The old temple city of Hampi lies to the east of Goa in a nearly desert-like landscape. For several years Hampi has been undergoing a boom because an increasing number of tourists include a trip to Hampi in their Goa trip.

Approach route: From Goa the most comfortable is by bus from Panjim to Hospet, then continue with local bus to Hampi. From Bangalore also per bus directly to Hopset and then continue with local bus to Hampi. It is also possible to reach Hampi by train.

There is no mentionable infra-structure in Hampi as yet. i.e, there is no electricity, no water on tap and no hotels (no one has the necessary licence). Expect to 5 Rs for a room (no beds) with a private person; you can of course sleep under the stars or stop off at the hotel in the less attractive neighbouring village. From there you will get a bus connection to Hampi.

BANGALORE

Bangalore, approx. 1000 m above sea level, capital of Karnataka (previously Mysore) has the greatest percentage increase in population of all Indian cities and takes fifth place after Madras with a population of 2.6 million. Bangalore is one of the cleanest cities in India but doesn't have many sights worth seeing.

ARRIVAL/ACCOMMODATION

The main station (City Railway Station) and the KSRTC bus stand are next to each other. Cheap hotels can mainly be found on the eastern side of the bus stand where the numerous private buses arrive. The Janatha Lodge is not very cheap but very good, single rooms cost 13 Rs, double rooms 25 Rs, extra bed 5 Rs; all rooms with bath, warm water between 9.00 a.m. and 12 noon, room service, very clean.

MISCELLANEOUS

Tourist Offices: The Information office of the Commissioner of Tourism is at 9 St. Mark's Road, Tel, 579 186. A further information desk for tourists is at the City Railway Station.

Publications: Bangalore's largest daily paper is the Deccan Herald. Information for tourists is given in the 'Bangalore City Guide' (5 Rs), and the 'Bangalore Time Guide' (with train, bus and plane timetable, 1.50 Rs.).

Shopping: Try the Mahatma Gandhi Rd, the fashionable shopping centre of Bangalore for Western consumer articles.

The GPO is on the Race Course Rd.

Indian Airlines Office: Karnataka Housing Boad Building, Dist. Office Rd.

FURTHER TRAVEL

Rail

To Bombay (1211 km): departure 6.25 a.m., arrival in Bombay V.T on the next day at 8.10 a.m.

To Madras (356 km): departure 1.45 p.m., 7.30 a.m., 9.50 p.m., approx. 6 hr. trip.

To Trivandrum (950 km): departure 9.05 p.m. (in summer 8.45 p.m.), arrival on the next day at 4.30 p.m., a further train only twice weekly, departure at 11.50 a.m.

To New Delhi (2491 km): departure 1.30 p.m. (only Monday and Thursday), arrival next day at 1.30 p.m. Other timetable in summer,

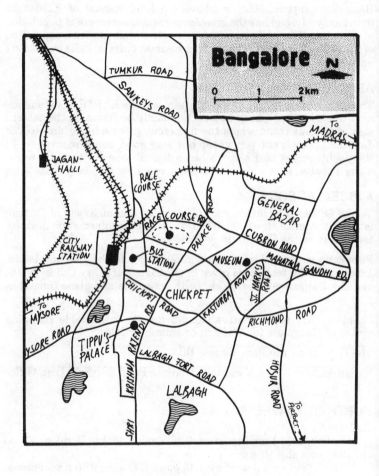

departure Bangalore 10.30 p.m.(Monday, Thursday), arrive New Delhi 1.35 p.m.

To Goa: no direct connection to Margao.

To Mysore: (139 km): Mail/Express trains at 6.30 a.m., 7.30 a.m., 10.30 a.m., 2.15 p.m. 5.00 p.m. and 6.15 p.m.

Bus

To Mysore: Continuous connection with the government KSRTC buses, 12.10 Rs, approx. 3 hour trip. Private companies also drive to Mysore. A guided sightseeing tour from Bangalore to Mysore and return costs approx. 50 Rs.

Further connections: government buses do drive to some destinations outside of Karnataka, e.g. Bombay, Madras (35 Rs), Mangalore, Ooty, Ernakulam and Panjim (one bus daily, 68.30 Rs). A whole network of private buses ensures excellent connections within the whole of southern India.

Plane

Direct flights to Delhi, Bombay, Madras, Mangalore and Cochin. Further details under 'India General'/'Flights'.

MYSORE

Mysore, 770 m above sea level 400 000 inhabitants, is one of the most attractive cities of South India with the Maharajah Palace. There are numerous other sights in and around Mysore.

ARRIVAL

City Railway Station or Central Bus stand or, if you arrive with a private bus company, at their office.

ACCOMMODATION

There are numerous hotels in proximity of the station and the Central Bus Station which is close to the Maharajah Palace. Two cheap hotels at the Central Bus Stand: Central Hotel, Ghandi Square, single room 15 Rs, double room 25 Rs, all rooms with bath and some with a beautiful view. Just around the corner in a side street is Geetha Lodge, single room 10 Rs, double room 20 Rs, all rooms with bath. It's a bit noisy during the night as there is an open-air cinema next door.

The summer residence of the Maharajah of Mysore was converted to a luxury hotel. The Hotel Rajendravilas Imperial is on Chamundi Hill with a beautiful view of Mysore and offers the usual services of a first class hotel.

Food Tip

The Gunhouse Imperial Restaurant is opposite the Maharajah Palace. It is definitely not the cheapest, (minimum charge is 12 Rs) but one of the smartest restaurants of Mysore. The pride of the Gunhouse Imperial is the 'barbecue' prepared over an open fire.

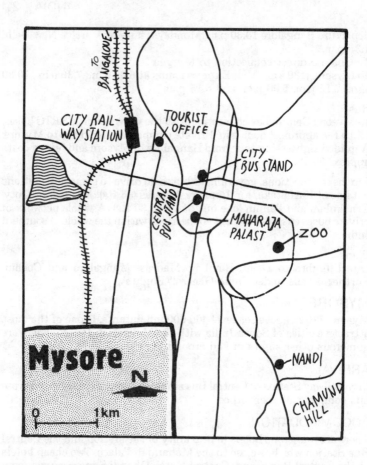

SIGHTSEEING

If you want to see 'everything' you're better off joining one of the government or privately run sightseeing tours. Whole fleets of decrepit Tata buses are on the road daily. The tour with Tourist Corporation Karnataka costs 22 Rs (entrance fees not included) and takes 12 stressed hours in which you'll see about as many sights. Included are the government silk factory, sandalwood factory, zoo, Chamundi Hill, Maharajah Main Palace, and in the evening the main city attraction (at least for Indians) the Brindavan Gardens.

Maharajah Palace: The palace is opened from 10.30 a.m. to 5.30 p.m. and illuminated from 6.30 to 7.30 p.m. on Sunday. Entrance fee 2 Rs, tours free of charge, photographs prohibited within the palace.

Chamundi Hill (1160 m): take a taxi or local bus (80 Ps); 13 km from Mysore. The Chamundeswari Temple is on the peak (beautiful view of Mysore), a little further down the Nandi, a stone-hewn bull of approx 7.5 x 5 m size.

Brindavan Gardens: 19 km from Mysore, at the foot of the Khrishnarajagar Dam which dams the Cauvery River, contains gardens with small lakes and water plays which are illuminated in the evenings, starting from 7.00 p.m., Entance fee is 1 R, and an additional 5 Rs for cameras.

FESTIVALS

The most important festival, celebrated at the end of September/ beginning of October is definitely the Dusshera Festival which lasts 10 days. It is celebrated throughout the whole of India but definitely has more importance in Mysore where it is called Navaratri (Nine Nights) by the locals. The highpoint of the festivities is the tenth day when the 'Maharajah' or his representative passes through the streets in a triumphal procession accompanied by camels and elephants.

MISCELLANEOUS

Tourist Office: Govt. of Karnataka Tourist Information, Exhibition Buildings, Tel. 22 0996. Ask for the 'Karnataka Tourist Information' brochure which contains a lot of useful information, besides containing a city map. The office is open from 10.30 a.m. to 1.30 p.m. and 2.15 p.m. to 5.30 p.m. Monday to Saturday; it is closed on Sunday and every second Saturday of the month.

Accommodation in Bandipur National Park: Reservations with the Field Director, Project Tiger, Government House Complex, Tel. 20901, open daily from Monday to Saturday, 10.30 a.m.-1.30 p.m., and 2.15 p.m.-5.30 p.m., closed every second Saturday of the month. Careful: Reservations are obligatory! You will receive the interesting brochure 'A Guide To The Tourism Zone of The Bandipur Tiger Reserve' from the Project Tiger Office for 3 Rs.

Information on the Maharajah Palace and Dusshera Festival can be found in 'Dasara Cultural Festivities' (5 Rs).

Mysore is well known for silk and sandalwood (incense, little boxes, etc.).

Excursion to Sravana Belgoal
This place, holy to the Jains, is located approx. 100 km from Mysore. The centre of veneration is the 17 m high, 1000 year old Gomateswara statue situated on a hill.

FURTHER TRAVEL

To Bangalore: numerous good train and bus connections.

Bandipur/Mudumalai and Ootacamund (Ooty) only bus connection, buses to Ooty, 161 km, fares 13.65 Rs depart from Central Bus Stand, approx. 5 hours drive. A reservation (50 Ps) a day in advance can be highly recommended. The first bus leaves at 6.15 a.m., the last at 3.00 p.m. All Ooty buses go via Bandipur/Mudumalai but not all stop there. Enquire before doing the trip. Fare to Theppakadu (Mudumalai National Park): 10.55 Rs.

To Ernakulam: Approx. two bus connections daily (do not go via Ooty).

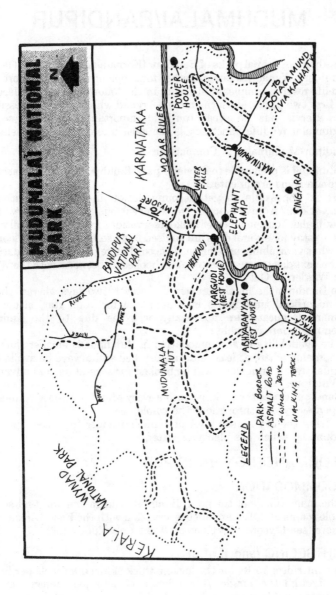

MUDUMALAI/BANDIPUR

The adjoining animal parks of Bandipur (Karnataka), Mudumalai (Tamil Nadu) and Wynad (Kerala) together form one of the most important wild-life reserve complexes in India. In the following we only discuss the first two parks, since the remote Wynad which is only accessible from Kerala has no great touristic importance. The 320 sq.m. Mudumalai Wildlife Sanctuary is the most interesting for travellers.

Bandipur-Mudumalai; A Comparison

Mudumalai is preferable to its sister park Bandipur for many reasons. Here are some arguments:
1. It is impossible to get accommodation in Bandipur without reservations from Mysore. No reservations are necessary for Mudumalai. You can however make reservations from Ooty and all who wish to stay for several days are advised to do so. Otherwise you'll only get what is available and might have to change your accommodation on the next day because someone has booked 'in between' with the Wild Life Warden in Ooty.
2. In Bandipur the 'maximum period of stay' is two days whereas there are no official time limits in Mudumalai for your stay, although permanent guests are not really welcome due to the limited accommodation available.
3. The availability of accommodation in Bandipur is smaller than in Mudumalai, where at least a dormitory bed will always be available. Frequently, all bungalows will be booked for several days in advance in Bandipur.
4. Bandipur closes the park to visitors every Monday while Mudumalai is open every day throughout the whole year.
5. During the dry season a lot of animals wander from Bandipur to Mudumalai which has plenty of water.

INFORMATION ON BANDIPUR

ACCOMMODATION

In the main village of the park, Bandipur village you will find some double rooms at 20Rs. Advance reservation with the Field Director in Mysore (see Mysore/'Miscellaneous') is an absolute must!

SIGHTSEEING (and tariffs)

Elephant rides: 30 Rs for the lovable thick-skinned animals per hour ride through the jungle. A maximum of four passengers can be accommodated besides the Mahout.

Jeep rides: the price is fixed at 5 Rs/km., 6 people can be accommodated.

Guided tours/on your own: Bandipur unfortunately does not supply guides for trips on foot through the park. Walking around on your own on the park paths is of course officially forbidden. The asphalt road to Mudumalai is of course an exception.

INFORMATION ON MUDUMALAI

ACCOMMODATION

Immediately on arrival at the Park's main village Theppakadu, report to the Reception Centre where one will often only be able to give you dormitory beds without prior reservation. Within the whole park area, there are seven Guest Houses with approx. 50 beds and three dormitories with room for a further 54 persons. A double room costs 15 Rs for the first person and 10 Rs for the second person and you'll pay 3 Rs for a bed in one of the clean dormitories. Accommodation with private persons is not possible within the park area.

If you don't like it in the accommodation offered within the park area, you can always try the Masinagudi Village, approx. 8 km from Theppakadu. You can try hitchhiking or bus to get there.

WILDLIFE

The fauna in the parks of Mudumalai and Bandipur corresponds to the fauna of all other South-Indian parks: tigers, leopards, wild dogs, elephants, Gaur (Indian Buffalo, erroneously called 'Bison' in all of India), sloth bears (the most dangerous animal in Indian parks), hyenas, jackals, various small feline types, many wild pigs, 4 types of deer (spotted deer, also called Chital, Sambar, Barking Deer and Mouse Deer), two types of monkeys (Commond Langur and Bonnet Monkey) many types of birds (e.g., the peacock is seen everywhere) and rarely snakes (e.g. python and cobra).

Whoever thinks he's landed in a sort of open-air zoo where all the species of India's animal world will stand for a portrait snap will leave sorely disappointed.

FOOD

Supplies are–at least for the gourmet–a small problem in Mudumalai. The two Chai shops in Theppakadu offer practically only Chapatti, Idli, rice and a few vegetables. A more substantial meal will only be found at the Guest Houses on advance order. Each of these Guest Houses has a cook who will often be amicable and sell groceries that are not readily available in Mudumalai to tourists for a small additional fee. You'll shop at cheaper prices in Masinagudi where you'll obtain just about anything.

SIGHTSEEING (and tariffs)

Elephant rides are available at 6.00 a.m. and 4.00 p.m. They take about two hours and cost around 20 Rs. Four paying persons can be accommodated apart from the Mahout.

Jeep and Van: Excursions by bus and van also take place in the mornings and evenings, provided enough people are available for the tour. Rates: the jeep costs 2 Rs/km (up to 6 persons can be accommodated) the van is 3 Rs/km for up to 8 persons, then the km fare is increased by 50 Ps per person (up to a max. of 20 persons). You will have to consider another few Paisas for the guide. You'll travel about 35 km on the park roads on a 2 hour jeep tour which will cost you about 15 Rs each with a full load.

Campers: You can travel freely along the two main thoroughfares of Mysore-Ootacamund and Theppakadu-Masinagudi. But it is obligatory to take a guide along the proper park roads (2 Rs/hour).

Wandering around the park: Officially you should be issued with a guide for 2Rs/hour. Usually you will however receive the answer 'no guides available'. This is just one of the reasons why visitors roam around the park on their own and even spend the night in the open. Whether this will be tolerated for very much longer by the park administrators is questionable. However, some routes are sanctioned for tourism by the park administration: e.g. the Circular Road, the route to the Moyar waterfalls or the approach routes to some of the viewing towers. The two main asphalt thoroughfares to Ootacamund (Ooty) and Masinagudi are of course freely traversable.

Additonal fees: For each guided sight-seeing trip you will have to pay 1 R 'sanctuary fee', 2 Rs for still cameras and 10 Rs for movie cameras (the last two fees are per day and not per park excursion). Campers pay an additional parking fee for their car, which ranges from 5 to 7.50 Rs/day depending on size.

MISCELLANEOUS

The information centre is the Reception Centre, which is also responsible for accommodation and sightseeing trips. You will often also be able to obtain the booklet 'Mudumalai Wildlife Sanctuary' by E.R.C. Davidar (2.10 Rs) from there.

There is no medical support available in Mudumalai.

There is a small post office in Theppakadu. However, letters mailed from there to Overseas often take up to three weeks to reach their destination.

The biggest threats to the animal park are not posed by poachers but by the forest fires which break out annually during the drought period. It is a problem many other parks have. In no case should you light an open fire or throw cigarette butts away.

The work and excursion elephants live in the Elephant Camp which is in Theppakadu on the other side of the bridge over the Moyar. It is best to go there in the late afternoon when all elephants are there and being fed.

FURTHER TRAVEL

Stop a bus on the through-road to Mysore (97 km) or Ootacamund (Ooty). It's 64 km to Ooty (5.65 Rs, nice three hour trip climbing from 1000 metes to 2200 metres).

OOTACAMUND (Ooty)

Ootacamund (Ooty for short) has approx. 70 000 inhabitants and was a popular high-altitude health resort for the English during colonial times. Not only the architecture is reminiscent of those times but also horse racing and golf courses.

The season for Ooty is during the hot pre-monsoon time from April to June and during the autumn months of September to October. Winters are cold in the 2286 metre altitude of Ooty. The temperature drops down to freezing point in January. The prices sink with the readings on the thermometer. Accommodation is approx. 40% cheaper during the 'off season'.

ARRIVAL/ACCOMMODATION

There are some cheap but quite shabby and often bug-ridden lodges around the C.T.C. bus station. The Krishna Prabha Lodge asks 8-10 Rs for a single room and 15 Rs for a double room. You'll find better, and not very expensive hotels when you walk approx 1 km in the direction of Charring Cross (city centre), along the smelly stream.

R.K. Lodge, Commercial road, Tel. 2022, single room 15 Rs, double room 25 Rs, nice clean rooms but common shower in need of renovation.

YMCA, 58 Commercial Road, rooms 10/25 Rs (price depends on number of persons), also for girls. The YMCA is often blocked by permanent guests are nor very clean.

Nahar Tourist Home, Commercial Road, opposite Tourist Office, single room 30 Rs, double room 50 Rs, all rooms with bath.

Note: all prices quoted here are for 'off season'; they climb by about 40% during peak season.

Hotel Fernhill Imperial (Tel. 2055) is a former holiday palace of the Maharajah of Mysore, situated a little outside of Ooty. It lies in the centre of a large park, the air filled with the scent of eucalyptus and soft wood trees. The hotel boasts a restaurant, a coffee shop and venues for tennis, mini-golf (putt-putt) and billiards. The 'Off Season' (and 'Season') prices: single room 120 Rs (170 Rs), double room 200 Rs (270 Rs), suite 270Rs (350 Rs).

FOOD/SHOPPING

Some good restaurants along Commercial Road. Try the Chung Wah Chinese Restaurant if you like Chinese food. Reckon with a minimum of 10 Rs for one meal.

Furthermore, you'll find some articles of food in Ooty that are quite rare throughout the rest of India: honey, cheese, mushrooms, strawberries (the last two depend on season). Furthermore, Ooty is a centre of the South-Indian tea plantations (Nilgiri Tea) and there are numerous medicinal farms in the hills surrounding Ooty where Camphor, Quinine (against Malaria), Eucalyptus oil and other products are grown or won (see also 'sightseeing'). Visit one of the shops where the combined products from the Nilgiris (that's what the mountains of Southern India are called) are offered for sale.–The many bakeries are also worth a visit.

Shopping centres: 'Everything under one roof' boasts a sign at the supermarket (proximity of Charring Cross). The selection is however, not quite as large. The Municipal market (located betweeen bus station and Charring Cross) is no less well equipped. You can buy nearly anything from writing paper to a banana.

SIGHTSEEING

Mariamman Temple: When walking from the bus station in the direction of Charring Cross, you'll find this temple on the left hand side after a few minutes walk. Fruit and other things are offered there daily. It is particularly festive on Friday: Procession with a musical band. The temple may be entered by non-Hindus.

Botanic Garden: this is Ooty's main attraction and probably the loveliest Botanic Garden in India. It is located on a mountain side and offers a beautiful view, 25 Ps entrance fee, open daily from 7.00 a.m. to 7.00 p.m., expansive and suitable for walks.

Ooty Lake: an artificial lake, surrounded by eucalyptus and soft-wood trees, you think you are in Switzerland. The sea is not suitable for swimming since it is cold and rather badly polluted. But you can hire boats.

MISCELLANEOUS

Tourist Ofice: just before you get to Charring Cross in the same building as the supermarket, Tel. 2416, open Monday to Saturday 10.00 a.m.-5.00 p.m.

The Wild Life Warden (for Mudumalai reservations), N. Mahalingam Building, Coonoor Road, Tel. 3114 closed on Sunday.

The best bookshop is Higginbothams in the supermarket building. You can obtain the booklet 'Welcome to the Nilgiris' for 2 Rs from there.

Row boats on Ooty Lake cost, depending on size and season, between 4.50 Rs and 12 Rs per hour: paddle boats 6-12 Rs per hour, and motor boats 30-45 Rs per hour.

Riding: The owners down at the lake ask between 10 and 20 Rs per hour for one of the attractive, small built horses. You must haggle!

FURTHER TRAVEL

To Mysore(161 km): only possible with the bus, 13.65 Rs. The road goes through the National Parks of Mudumalai and Bandipur where some of the buses stop on request.

To Ernakulam/Cochin: Daily 5 buses from Ooty to Palghat, 10 Rs, approx. 5 hours drive. Change in Palghat: it is a further 5 hours to Ernakulam and the bus (approx. 10 connections daily) costs 11.50 Rs. The trip can however also be made by train or train and bus: the Nilgiri Railway leaves daily at 11.20 a.m. and 2.00 p.m. and covers the mountainous stretch from Ooty to Mettupalaiyam in approx. 4 hours. Change to bus there or continue by train via Coimbatore Jn to Ernakulam (or Trivandrum).

SURROUNDING OOTY

Dodabetta: this is the highest mountain in the Nilgirs and Tamil Nadu with its 2633 metres. It has tea plantations on its sides. A traversable road leads up to the peak. You can do the trip on foot from Ooty, reckon with about 3 hours for the climb or take a bus driving in the direction of Kotagiri and get off at Four Road Junction. It is not far to the peak from there. The easiest way is to hire a taxi with friends and divide the fare amongst yourselves.

A trip to the Dodabetta can be combined with a visit to the medicinal farm of the 'Chincona Department', which is on the 'rear side' of the Dodabetta. However, this requires a permit which can be obtained from the Chincona Department in Ooty (a few minutes walk from the YMCA).

However, this is no official tourist trip but a sightseeing tour devised for botanists or other persons interested in medicinal plants. If you are not overly interested in plants do not bother the employees on this farm and restrict visits to the Botanic Garden.

COCHIN/ERNAKULAM

Cochin, with its 500,000 inhabitants is the second largest metropolis in Kerala and an important port city. It consists of four parts:

1. (Fort) Cochin/Mattancherry: the romantic old section of Cochin located on a peninsula and harbouring the Main GPO, displaying Chinese fisher nets and other sights.

2. Ernakulam: the modern city centre located on the mainland, boasting the bus station, Ernakulam Railway Station and the K.T.D.C. Tourist Reception Centre.

3. Willingdon Island: this is an artificial island reclaimed from material removed from the harbour and located between (Fort) Cochin and Ernakulam. The Cochin Harbour Terminus, airport, Govt. of India Tourist Office and Hotel Malabar are located there.

4. Some other islands such as Bolghatty Island, Gundulu Island, Wallarpatt Island, etc.

ARRIVAL

Train

At Cochin Harbour Terminal, a main station on Willingdon Island, or at Ernakulam Railway Station (more appropriate when searching for hotels).

Bus

At Ernakulam Bus Station (not far from the Railway Station); numerous cheap hotels immediately adjacent to the bus station.

Plane

On Willingdon Island. If you do not wish to stay at the expensive Malabar hotel, take the ship or public bus (bridge) to Fort Cochin/Mattancherry or to Ernakulam where you'll find the largest choice in accommodation. An airport bus is supposed to be in service to Ernakulam (Indian Airlines Office) .

ACCOMMODATION

Ernakulam: low priced accommodation adjacent to Bus Station; Opposite are Ninans Tourist Lodge, single room 15 Rs, double room 20 Rs; Hotel Blue Nile, single room 12 Rs, double room 22 Rs; Hotel Luciya, same price as the Blue Nile, all three hotels with bath in all rooms and clean. There are many small, cheap Lodges in a side street: e.g. Casino Lodge, St. Anthony's Lodge, Priya Lodge-reckon with about 7 Rs for a single room in these Lodges; the double room costs 15 Rs. Willingdon Island: few accommodation facilities and low in attraction. Exception: the expensive Malabar Hotel. This is located on the northern tip of the island with a beautiful view and swimming pool. Single room

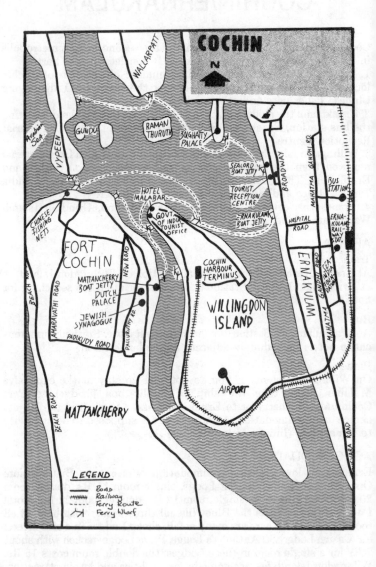

One means of transport, an Elephant near Agra

Srinagar — looking across a city of Houseboats

A Shikara on Dal Lake, Kashmir

165.20 Rs, double room 234.20 Rs, all rooms with A.C.
Fort Cochin/Mattancherry; only a few simple Lodges in the oldest and
most picturesque section of Cochin. Port View Lodge is a tip for
romantics, single rooms 10 Rs, double room 15 Rs. It is great when
you have rooms with a harbour view.
Bolghatty Island: Bolghatty Palace built in 1744 has been refurbished
into a Tourist Bungalow. Beautifully located but many mosquitoes. The
prices: single room 24 Rs, double room 35 Rs, extra bed 10 Rs. Has
rooms with A.C. which are about twice as expensive.

TRANSPORT

The best means of transport for moving from one city section to the
other is the boat. A whole network of motor boats and other boats
ensure a trouble-free connection. Fares range, depending on distance,
from 15 to 50 Ps. However, most lines stop running around 9.00 p.m.
This leaves the city bus for transport. Mattancherry, Willingdon Island
and Ernakulam are connected by a bridge.

SIGHTSEEING

Fort Cochin/Mattancherry: you'll find the most attractions in 'Old-
Cochin'. The northern tip of the peninsula is called Fort Cochin and
Mattancherry joins in the south. The main attraction in Fort Cochin
is the Chinese Fishing Nets, which you will encounter once again when
taking a trip along the 'backwaters'.

St. Francis Church, which is of quite humble appearance is also
interesting for sightseeing fans and historians. It is supposed to be the
first church built by Europeans in India. The famous explorer Vasco
da Gama was buried there in 1524 before he was exhumed and
transported to his native Portugal.

The Dutch Palace and Jewish Synagogue are in the neighbouring
Mattancherry. The Dutch Palace was however not built by the Dutch–as
the name might suggest, but by the Portuguese around 1520. However,
the Dutch as the next colonists carried out extensive renovations in
1663–hence the current name. The Jewish Synagogue stems from 1568.
A small Israeli-Jewish community resides in close proximity, having
settled there in 1661 just after the conquest by the Dutch. There are
two types of Jews in Cochin: the 'White Jews' (there are approx. 100
of them) which have retained their race pure and the numerous 'Black
Jews' which have mixed by marriage with the dark skinned population.

The Tourist Reception Centre in Ernakulam conducts a 3 1/2 hour
sightseeing tour for 10 Rs daily at 9.00 a.m. and 2.00 p.m. Departure
from the Boat Jetty opposite Sealord Hotel. You can however join at
the Tourist Office Jetty on Willingdon Island. The tour includes: Dutch
Palace, Jewish Synagogue, Chinese Fishing Nets, St. Francis Church,
Gundu Island and Bolghatty Island.

Kerala is the home of the famous Kathakali dance, a type of dance drama, performances and similar daily at 7.00 p.m.-8.30 p.m. at the Sea India Foundation, proximity of Ernakulam Railway Station. Entrance fee: 15 Rs.

MISCELLANEOUS

Tourist Offices: Kerala Tourist Reception Centre, Shanmugham (Shunmuham) Road, Ernakulam Tel. 33 234, open daily from 8.30 a.m.-5.30 p.m.

Govt. of India Tourist Office, close to Malabar Hotel, Willingdon Island, Tel. 6045, open Monday-Friday 9.00 a.m.-5.00 p.m., Saturday 9.00 a.m.-1.00 p.m. Closed every Sunday and second Saturday of the month. Here you can obtain extensive brochures on India.

The 'Map of Cochin' (2.50 Rs) can be obtained from the Malabar Hotel, Willingdon Island.

Pai and Company, Broadway, Ernakulam, offers a good selection of paperbacks and newspapers.

Mail: mail marked as 'hold mail' (Poste Restante) Ernakulam, does not land at the GPO in Ernakulam in General Hospital Road but must be collected from the GPO Fort Cochin, close to the Chinese Fisher Nets.

Indian Airlines Office Address: Luiz Hall, Broadway, Ernakulam, Tel. 32065

FURTHER TRAVEL FROM COCHIN

to Ootacamund (Ooty)
Bus departing from bus station Ernakulam to Palghat; there change to connecting bus to Ooty (5 direct connections). The whole stretch costs 21.50Rs by bus. Other variation: Do the whole stretch by bus, or take the bus from Palghat to Mettupalaiyam and then the Nilgiri Railway (departing at 7.15 a.m. and 8.00 p.m.) to Ooty.

to Mysore/Bangalore
Approx. twice daily a direct bus from the bus station in Ernakulam to Mysore (397 km) and Bangalore (537 km). It is more complicated by train.
Plane: daily one connection to Bangalore, 244Rs.

to Mangalore and Goa
With train or bus to Mangalore (approx. 450 km). Then travel with the local bus (two changes) or direct bus (see also Goa/'Further Travel to Mangalore').

to Bombay
Daily one direct train connection with the 82 Jayanti Janata Express; departs Ernakulam railway station at 1.50 p.m. (in the summer at 1.45

p.m.) arriving Bombay V.T. on the second next morning at 4.55 a.m., 1841 track kilometres.
Plane: two connections daily to Bombay, 640Rs.

to Madras
There are two train connections in the winter with the 42 Cochin Express, departing Cochin Harbour Terminal at 7.25 p.m. and Ernakulam Railway Station at 8.00 p.m., arrival at Madras Central on the next day at 11.05 a.m. and 20 Trivandrum Mail, departing Ernakulam at 5.05 p.m., arriving Madras Central at 6.10 a.m. In the summer only with 42 Cochin Express, departing 4.50 p.m. Cochin main terminal and 5.20 p.m. Ernakulam railway station, arriving at Madras Central at 7.30 a.m., 714 km route.
Plane: Only possible with change in Bangalore.

to Delhi
Departing Ernakulam Railway Station on Monday and Thursday at 7.00 p.m. (6.00 p.m. in the summer) with the 125 Karnataka-Kerala Express, arriving in New Delhi on the second next day at 1.30 p.m. (summer 1.35 p.m.) or with 131 Jayanti Janata Express, Cochin main terminal, departing at 10.05 a.m., Ernakulam railway station departing at 10.35 a.m. (summer 10.30 a.m.), daily except Monday and Thursday, arriving Delhi-Hazrat Nizamuddin on the second next day at 2.10 p.m. (summer 2.40 p.m.). It's approx. 2830 km to Delhi.

to Periyat National Park
Daily two direct buses at 6.30 a.m. and 2.45 p.m. to Thekkadi, main park town (depart in Kumily when looking for a cheap hotel); 185 km, approx. 7 hr. trip, 14.70Rs, reservation (50Ps) recommended. Other variation: train or bus to Kottayam and then join connecting bus there.

to South Kerala
There are excellent bus connections from Ernakulam to Alleppey-Quilon-Trivandrum. Buses drive day and night to Trivandrum (223 km). There is also a rail connection via Kottayam and Quilon to Trivandrum.

THE ISLAND WORLD OF THE LACCADIVES

The Laccadive Islands which belong to India lie 200 km east of Kerala's coast. Nine of the 23 islands are inhabited and the population is around 30,000, most of them moslems. Only the main island of Bangara (Bingaram) is somewhat developed for tourists. The Laccadives belong to the 'restricted area', i.e. foreigners need a special permit from the Ministry of Home Affairs in Delhi to visit the Laccadives. However, permits are only granted for Bangara (see Delhi/'Permits for restricted areas').

ARRIVAL

A ship leaves from Cochin to Bangara approx. every two weeks and the trip takes about 20 hours. However, should the ship dock at other islands first, the trip takes longer. No tourists are transported during the monsoon season. Tickets (one way): first class 432 Rs, 2nd class 367.50 Rs, bunk class 232.50 Rs, deck class 182.50 Rs; meals are not included in the price.

ACCOMMODATION

There are 16 bungalows with room for 32 tourists on Bangara; calculate about US$50 per person (excluding meals). Apparently no cheaper accommodation is available for tourists.

INFORMATION CENTRES

Cochin: Lakshadweep Office, Harbour Road, Willingdon Island, Tel. 6405/6374 and Travel Corporation of India (the official agent) Karuna Buildings, M.G. Road, Ernakulam, Tel. 31646.

Calicut: Lakshadweep Head Office, Beach Rd., Tel. 72873.

Bombay: Travel Corporation of India, Chandermukhi, Nariman Point.

Delhi: Ministry of Home Affairs and Travel Corporation of India (see Delhi/'permits for restricted areas').

PERIYAR

Periyar (777 sq. km) is in the Western Ghats betwen 914 and 1828 metres above sea level and is the best known national park in India. The biggest attraction is the 26 sq km large, heavily nooked dam sea which can partially be traversed by boat. The best time for a visit is during the dry season when the animals, on search for water, can be seen particularly often at the sea.

ARRIVAL/ACCOMMODATION

Get off in Kumily, approx. 4 km from the Park Sea if you're looking for cheap hotels. If you prefer accommodation in the park area, continue to Hotel Periyar House or Hotel Aranya Nivas.

In Kumily: numerous cheap Lodges (e.g. Mini Lodge), average price for single rooms 4 Rs, double rooms 8 Rs. The Woodlands Hotel is at the exit of the village, in the direction of the park (double room 10 Rs, triple room 15 Rs). Accommodation is also available with private persons. There are two choices available in Thekkady (just about on the park area): Periyar House, Tel. 26, (single room 15 Rs, double room 30 Rs, extra bed 8 Rs, dormitory-for 10 persons 3 Rs per head; 10 % tax extra) and the Aranya Nivas Hotel, Tel. 23 (double room 80 Rs, 60 Rs for single occupancey).

See 'Sightseeing' for accommodation within the park.

SIGHTSEEING

Ship

The park management owns five boats, which they however only partially lend for tourist purposes. Hotel Aranya Nivas supplies a further four boats (it is advisable to book early at the Hotel Reception). The number of boats available also depends on demand. The first boat leaves at about 7.00 a.m. (hotel boat) from the sea entrance at the Information Centre. There are various sized boats available; with full occupancy that cost 3Rs per person (excluding park entrance fee and camera charges). Duration of the trip (circular course) approx. 2 hours.

Elephant rides/Jeep

The park has one young riding elephant. A one hour trip costs 10 Rs for two persons. It is not worthwile: unexciting ride. The park does not have its jeeps available for tourist purposes.

With a guide/on your own

Officially, walking tours around the park are only permitted in the presence of a guide. The guide is available free of charge but does expect bakshish. Usually, a tour will start in the mornings from the

Information Centre. This is worthwhile! Unfortunately, guides are rare so that walking around on your own has become rather common and is more or less tolerated. A walk to the Mangala Devi Temple (1466 m) can be recommended. It is 13 km from Thekkady Check post; take drinking water (soda). You can also use a jeep taxi to the temple from Kumily. This will cost you more than 100 Rs; and it's more of a motorcross–less nature experience. Strictly speaking, the trip to the Mangala Devi Temple is also 'guide required'. The park and state border of Kerala/Tamil Nadu runs along the temple and with a bit of luck you might see the Nilgiri-Tahr, a rare 'mountain goat'.

The most beautiful experience of nature is however a stay in the centre of the park. Apart from the luxurious Lake Palace (double room 80 Rs, 60 Rs for single occupancy) which is located a few boat-minutes from the Information Centre, you will find four simple Rest Houses which all sport an observation post in close proximity and can be reached by boat; transport costs depend on distance. The round trip to the remote Thannikudy Rest House costs, for example, 225 Rs. All four rest houses have two rental rooms each for the standard price of 5 Rs for the first person and 3 Rs for the following persons. Each rest house has a hut warden who cooks for his guests. Groceries must however be brought along. Reservations can be made at the Information Centre at the sea.

MISCELLANEOUS

The information centre at the sea (Tel. 28) is responsible for boat trips (if they're not already being conducted by the Hotel Aranya Nivas) and for the reservations for the two room Rest Houses within the park. Report to the Wildlife Preservation Officer (Tel. 27) for park trekking. The Assistant Wildlife Preservation Officer is responsible for the Magala Devi Temple (see 'Sightseeing'). Both officers have their headquarters along the road to Kumily.

There is no resident limitation for the three large hotels within the park area. The residency granted to you in the two room Rest Houses is regulated according to demand.

Entry to the park is forbidden under threat of prosecution between 6.00 p.m. and 6.00 a.m. Of course the surroundings of the park hotels and the connecting road to Kumily are exempt from this regulation. Fees: Park entry 1 R, (students 50 Ps), cameras 3 Rs, movie cameras 10 Rs.

The choice of groceries and cheap meals is very limited in Thekkady. But you will be able to obtain everything in Kumily. You can cash travellers cheques at the State Bank of Travancore.

Periyar's wildlife corresponds to that of Mudumalai (see Mudumalai/'Wildlife'). The main attractions in Periyar are the elephants which you can see at the sea lake during a boat trip.

The closer and further surrounding district of Periyar is not only famous for its fauna; the famous Kerala grass grows in the mountains of Idikki.

FURTHER TRAVEL

Some departure times for Thekkady/Periyar House (you can board at
the Kumily House): buses to Kottayam, first connection at 4.30 a.m.,
last at 6.30 p.m., approx. 4 1/2 hours drive, 9.40 Rs; Quilon 5.15. a.m.;
Ernakulam 5.45 a.m., 2.30 p.m.; Madurai 7.30 a.m., 1.30 p.m., 6.30 p.m.;
Trivandrum 8.00 a.m., 1.30 p.m., 2.30 p.m.

BACKWATERS

The inland water routes of Kerala are called Backwaters. It is a net
of narrow or broader, palm lined channels which suddenly pass into
deep seas where fishermen cast their nets. The boat sails through
carpets of colourful flowering water plants, transparent jelly-fish glitter
in the water and bathing children wave from the shores. The palm frond
huts fit easily into the coconut palm forests and paradise conditions
seem to prevail for the passing boat passenger. The backwaters are also
an experience for the non-sightseeing fan.

Boat Trip on the Backwaters
Kottayam-Allepey-Quilon

Kottayam
Starting point for the Periyar National Park and for the Backwaters.
A stay-over in Kottayam is hardly advisable. It is better to continue
by boat straight to Allepey. Take a scooter from the arrival point to
the boat dock (2.50 Rs from bus station).

Kottayam-Allepey
The trip to Allepey takes about 2 1/2 hours and costs 1.60 Rs, which
is a gift. Not only because the comfort of the ride is better than most
Indian buses: drinks are available on board and what seems to be even
more important, the boats are well booked but not over full (as most
Indian buses are). There are more than a dozen boat connections daily
from Kottayam to Allepey. They also have night services, but that's
not advisable since you won't see anything.

Allepey
Many channels and quite pretty. The season's high point is the annual
Snake Boat Race which takes place in the second half of August. An
excursion to the white sand beach is also good; take a scooter to the
Beach Rest House, costs about 3 Rs from the city.

ACCOMMODATION

Small, cheap lodges are right next to the boat docks (e.g. Sri Krishna
Bhavan Lodge, single rooms 5 Rs, double rooms from 10 Rs). The
Dhanalekshmi Lodge, Mullakkal has developed into a proper
backpacker meeting point; Tel. 21387, single rooms 5 Rs, double rooms
(with bath) 12 Rs, approx 7 minutes from the boat dockyard, not very
clean.

Further Travel by Boat from Allepey to Quilon

The trip can of course be made by bus but the boat is far more exciting. There are only two boats, leaving at 7.30 a.m. and 10.30 p.m. The trip takes 8 hours and costs 3 Rs. There are two meal stops along the way and at both places attempts are made to cheat you.

Quilon

It has a population of about 150,000. Accommodation is available right next to the dock.

Continuation: day and night buses to Trivandrum (72 km), 5.20Rs, approx. 2 hours drive. There are two boats daily to Allepey, leaving at 10.00 a.m. and 8.30 p.m. Buses also run on this stretch.

TRIVANDRUM

500,000 inhabitants, capital of Kerala, little worth seeing but known as the starting point for the famous Kovalam Beach.

ARRIVAL/ACCOMMODATION

Numerous cheap hotels at the K.S.R.T.C. bus stand and at the (neighbouring) Central Railway Station, e.g. Sreevas Tourist Home, Station Road, Tel. 3385, single room 12/14 Rs, double room 16/18 Rs, triple room 25 Rs, rooms partly equipped with own bath. There are more hotels along the Mahatma Gandhi (M.G.) Road, the main business road in Trivandrum. Pretty noisy, like Station Road. The best cheap hotel area is on the 'rear' side of the bus station, approx. 5 minutes walk away-if you stand with your back to the station, follow the road to the left and turn left again at the big crossing. The hotels are then located on the right hand side:

Sree Kumar Lodge, Tel. 63705, single room 10 Rs, double room 15/17 Rs.
Sreevi Tourist Home, Tel. 63738, rooms between 10 and 30 Rs.
Aristo Lodge, Tel. 63622, single room 8 Rs, double room 15 Rs (with bath 20 Rs); they have some nice large and quiet rooms.
Grand Udipi Lodge, Tel. 63510, single room 6 Rs (with bath 10 Rs), double room 10 Rs (with bath 10/14 Rs).
Greenland Lodging, Tel. 63485, single room 12 Rs, double room 20 Rs all rooms with bath.
Shalimar, Tel. 67578, double room 35 Rs, triple room 45 Rs, very nice large rooms.

MISCELLANEOUS

Tourist Offices: Tourist Information Office, Park View (opposite the zoo), Tel. 61132. Further information centres at the Central Bus Station, Central Railway Station and at the airport; furthermore the Tourist Reception Centre of the Kerala Tourist Development Corporation (K.T.D.C.), Thampanoor, Tel. 2643.

Post office: The GPO is on M.G. Road, Tel. 3071. Poste Restante (held mail) is open from 8.00 a.m. to 4.00 p.m. Monday to Saturday-you can get parcels sewn up by the 'parcel man' at the GPO.

Indian Airlines Office, Air Centre Mascot Junction (at Hotel Mascot), Tel. 60181, open daily 10.00 a.m. to 1.00 p.m. and 1.40 p.m. to 5.00 p.m.

The city map 'Street Guide to Trivandrum' (3 Rs) is available from the bookshop Pai and Company on M.G. Road. Free city map available from Tour India, also on M.G. Road.-Further interesting publications: 'Kerala Tourist Guide' (4 Rs) and 'A Tourist's Companion in and around Trivandrum'.

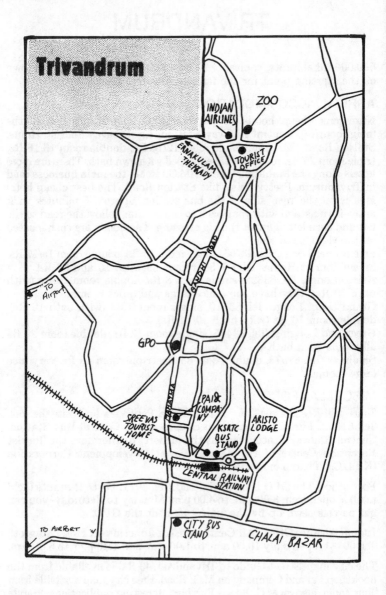

Sightseeing: There isn't much to see in Trivandrum. Exception: a beautiful zoo (entrance fee 50 Ps); the reptile house is particularly worth visiting.

Health: There are free-of-charge cholera injections available at the Corporation Office Building next to the Tourist Office, Park View. Report on the second floor (Health Department) Tel. 60821. Vaccination times are always on Monday, Wednesday and Saturday at 10.00 a.m.-12 noon.

FURTHER TRAVEL

Rail
(all connections from Trivandrum Central)

To Bangalore (via Ernakulam): departure daily at 10.15 a.m. (in summer 10.00 a.m.), also on Monday and Thursday at 2.40 p.m. (summer 1.45 p.m.), approx 20 hour trip for the 950 km.

To Bombay V.T. (2062 km): with the 82 Jayanti Janata Express, departure 8.10 a.m. (summer 8.20 a.m.), arriving in Bombay Victoria Terminal on the second next day at 4.55 a.m.

To Delhi (3054 km): Monday and Thursday at 2.40 p.m. (summer 1.45 p.m.), leaves Trivandrum and travels via Bangalore. Arrives in New Delhi on the second next day at 1.30 p.m. (summer 1.35 p.m.)

To Madras: daily with the 20 Trivandrum Mail, departure 12.15 p.m. (summer 1.05 p.m.), arriving Madras Central on the next morning at 6.10 a.m.

To Kannyakumari (87 km): two connections daily, the fastest with the 7.00 a.m. train (summer 6.50 a.m.), arriving in Kannyakumari at 9.50 a.m. (summer 9.30 a.m.).

Bus
Good bus connections to Cochin, Allepey, Quilon, Thekkady and other important places in Kerala. Buses to the 88 km distant southern tip of India, Cape Comorin, (Kannyakumari) which is in Tamil Nadu, leave between 4.30 a.m. and 9.45 p.m. for 6.10 Rs. There is also a bus connection to Madras (752 km): 2.30 p.m. A.C. bus, 97.80 Rs; 7.00 p.m. Super-Deluxe bus, 62.10 Rs. Travel time approx. 18 hours.

Plane
Domestic connections with Madras, Bombay and Cochin. Apart from that, there is at least one daily flight to Colombo (except on Monday and Sunday) for 411 Rs; to Male (capital of the Maledives), 508 Rs, each Monday, Thursday and Saturday.

EXCURSIONS FROM TRIVANDRUM

Kovalam Beach
Kovalam Beach is the undisputed No. 2 beach in India, after Goa's beach paradises with all sand and sun. Kovalam Beach, which from its length cannot compare with its rivals in Goa can be divided into three sections:

the 'Hotel Beach' with some luxury hotels and primarily Indian tourist, 'Lighthouse Beach' ('Freak Beach') and Vizhinjam Beach.

ARRIVAL

Buses leave between 6.20 a.m. and 9.20 p.m. approx. every 40 minutes from City Bus Stand (East Ford) to Kovalam (13 km), platform 15, route no. H4, price 1 R.

ACCOMMODATION

Lighthouse Beach: several simple beach hotels; Sea Rock Lodge, 20 Rs per room, Sreevas House, all two-bed rooms, 10/12 Rs, Jee Van House, directly on the ocean, double room 12 Rs. There is further accommodation available with families, similar prices to Goa, starting with about 4 Rs.

Vizhinjam Beach: on the other side of the lighthouse is the Hotel Rockholm, Tel. 57. Very nice, but expensive: single room 90 Rs, double room 110 Rs, 35 per cent tax extra; warm water available.

Far more exclusive is the Kovalam Hotel (Tel. 3031), at the beginning of 'Hotel Beach', single room 220 Rs, double room 275 Rs, 25 per cent tax extra. The associated Ashok Beach Resort where you can rent motor boats (100 Rs per hour), has similar prices; water skiing for 5 minutes ('per round') 12 Rs. The Kovalam Hotel also maintains a Yoga and Massage Centre.

Further hotels are located in proximity of the Kovalam Beach bus station.

MISCELLANEOUS

Meals: in the simple restaurants along the beaches and at the bus stop, where you will also find some grocery shops.

Money: you can exchange cheques at Kovalam Junction (30 Ps with the bus).

CAPE COMORIN (KANNYAKUMARI)

Cape Comorin is the Land's End of India. There is nothing between here and the Antartic but open sea. Cape Comorin is at the junction of three seas, the Arabian Sea, The Bay of Bengal and the Indian Ocean. It is a popular place for Indian Tourists and for pilgrims.

ACCOMMODATION

Many new lodges and hotels have been built here which are definitely recommended because they are such an improvement on the older type accommodation, which often afforded a view only of the next property. Some examples: Kaveri Lodge, Kovalam Road, Tel. 88, Single 10 Rs, Double 20 Rs, all rooms with bath and shower.
Sree Bhagavathi Lodge, Tel. 98, East Car Street, Single 10 Rs, Double 15 Rs, all rooms have baths.
Tri-Sea Lodge, Sannathi Street, Tel. 67, Double 25 Rs (with bath 50 Rs) 4-bed room 30 Rs, 10-bed dormitory 8 Rs/Person.

SIGHTSEEING

On an island south-east of the Cape lies the main attraction, the Vivekananda Rock Memorial. This was built in 1970 to honour Swami Vivekananda. Open 7.00-11.00 a.m. and 2.00-5.00 p.m. (1 R). You are now allowed to take photographs on the island.

The Gandhi Memorial. It was here the ashes of Mahatma Gandhi were stored until they were scattered over the sea. It was built here because on October 2 (Gandhi's birthday) the sun shone directly on the casket containing the ashes.

Other places of interest are the Kannyakumari Temple built in honour of the goddess Bhagavathi, and the Roman Catholic Church built in the middle of a small fishing village.

It is also fascinating to watch the fishermen in their small boats travelling over the rough sea.

MISCELLANEOUS

The Information Centre is right opposite the Bus Station. Tel. 51. The Govt Tourist Information Centre is in the Hotel Tamil Nadu, Tel. 76, open daily 10.30 a.m.-5.00 p.m., closed Sunday and the second Saturday of the month.

Food: Fish is unexpectedly rare. Try some dates–7 Rs/Kg.

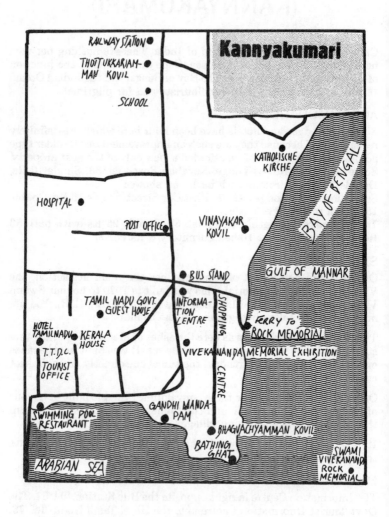

Kannyakumari

RAILWAY STATION

THOTTUKKARIAM-MAN KOVIL

SCHOOL

KATHOLISCHE KIRCHE

BAY OF BENGAL

HOSPITAL

POST OFFICE

VINAYAKAR KOVIL

GULF OF MANNAR

BUS STAND

TAMIL NADU GOVT. GUEST HOUSE

INFORMA-TION CENTRE

SHOPPING CENTRE

FERRY to ROCK MEMORIAL

HOTEL TAMILNADU

KERALA HOUSE

VIVEKANANDA MEMORIAL EXHIBITION

T.T.D.C. TOURIST OFFICE

SWIMMING POOL RESTAURANT

GANDHI MANDA-PAM

BHAGVACHYAMMAN KOVIL

BATHING GHAT

ARABIAN SEA

SWAMI VIVEKANANDA ROCK MEMORIAL

Souvenirs: in the centre of Cape Comorin there is one souvenir shop next to the other. They sell shell necklaces, shells of all sizes, dried sea urchins and material for bamboo mats with pictures of God and the landscape, etc. woven into them.

FURTHER TRAVEL

To Sri-Lanka: take the bus which leaves Cape Comorin at 3.45, 7.15, 10.15 a.m., 4.45 and 9.00 p.m. Fare with reservation 18.90 Rs, travelling time 8 hours for the 300 km journey in (for India) a relatively comfortable bus.

From Mandapam take the train to Rameswaram, 18 km away–8 trains daily.

From Rameswaram the ferry goes directly to Talaimannar (Sri Lanka). From Cape Comorin buses run to Trivandrum, Coimbatore, Madurai, Madras and Pondicherry, or take the train to Trivandrum.

SRI LANKA

You may think that Sri Lanka is a southern appendage of India, an island heavily influenced by its large neighbour, albeit with a principally Buddhist rather than Hindu population. In fact, you'll discover that Sri Lanka is very different from India, and not only because of its different religion.

POPULATION

Sri Lanka has a population of 20 million. That is an average of about 200 per square kilometre. The population density in the dry North of the island is relatively low (around 30 per square kilometre). On the other hand, the humid southwestern region, which accounts for a fifth of the total area, contains over 60 per cent of the total population.

The Buddhist Singhalese, who lived originally in the North of India and colonised the island in the 6th century BC, not only form the majority of the population (accounting for 70%) but also dominate the whole of Sri Lankan public life. Their language is Singhalese, which after the country gained independence they made the official language.

Being only 20% of the total population, the Hindu Tamils are very much in the minority. About half of them, the 'Ceylon Tamils', have lived for centuries in the North and East of the island and hold Sri Lankan citizenship. They are living proof of the warlike arguments that for more than 2000 years have dominated relations between the South Indian Tamils and the Singhalese. The Tamils invaded Sri Lanka again and again, and in the 11th century AD even ruled the whole island. Later, however, they had to withdraw to the north-but it was not possible to drive them out of there. The 'Indian Tamils', on the other hand, came to the country during the British colonial period. At the beginning of this century the European masters of the time required large numbers of labourers to work their tea plantations in the highlands.

Because of their caste, which forbade any agricultural work, the Singhalese would not do the work. So foreign workers were imported from densely populated South India and they settled around the plantations. The independence of India and Sri Lanka from Great Britain forced the 'Indian Tamils' into statelessness-because they didn't live on Indian soil they weren't entitled to Indian citizenship and as they were Indians they were denied the island's citizenship.

The Tamils' language is Tamil, which bears no resemblance at all to Singhalese. Since 1956, when Singhalese replaced English as the official language, Tamil has effectively been 'ignored'. In 1964 an arrangement was agreed to between India and Sri Lanka in an attempt to solve the conflict between Tamils and Sri Lankans: more than half a million

'Indian Tamils' were to be 'taken back' to South India and at the same time be given Indian citizenship. Under the settlement, some 300,000 'Indian Tamils' were also to be made citizens of Sri Lanka. To this day, the arrangement worked to only a minimal extent. The reason: there is hardly any work or living space for the returning Tamils in poor and overpopulated South India, so the repatriation incentives offered by the Indian Government did not produce the expected result. In addition, Singhalese plantation owners have had to recognise that as workers the Tamils are irreplaceable and that where large numbers of them have left, estates can no longer be worked. Although in recent times there has been increasing violence related to the Tamil-Sri Lankan problem, everything remains much the same. The Tamils will continue to struggle for the establishment of their own State in the North of the island–an inflammatory cause that may soon change our image of a peaceful, buddhist Sri Lanka.

The remaining 10 per cent of the population is composed of the following: principally descendants of the Moorish traders who settled mainly in the towns during the middle ages; the so-called 'burghers', who are descendants of Portuguese, Dutch and British colonials; a few Malays from Java who arrived in the wake of Dutch colonialism; and the Veddhas. These last are the island's true original inhabitants, who were pushed back to remote areas by the Singhalese. They once wandered as nomadic hunter-gatherers through the jungle. Only during this century have most of them settled, today hiring themselves out as day-labourers for the most menial agricultural work. There are only estimates of the number of 'pure-blood' Veddhas still living their traditional 'primitive' ways, as they have retreated to parts of the most inaccessible jungle. About 6000 are believed to live there still. Ethnologists rank their race as being amongst the oldest in the whole of Asia.

RELIGION

Just as it comprises various races, so also is the Sri Lankan population represented by the various world religions: Buddhism, Hinduism, Islam and Christianity. The last two are quite well represented with about 7% of the whole population. It is remarkable that the Tamils, with 20% of the population, account for only about 17% of the population being Hindus. The reason: many Tamils have been converted from Hinduism to Christianity as Christianity recognises no caste system, so Hindus from the lower castes can escape the narrow, restricted lives that the rules of their castes demand.

Buddhism dominates life in Sri Lanka.

The Four Holy Truths Of Buddhism

1. To live is also to suffer.
2. The cause of suffering is desire.
3. To lose desire means freedom.

4. The eight-fold way to freedom from desire is: correct thought, correct perception, correct effort, correct style of living, correct deed, correct speech, correct memory, meditation.

An explanation.

Gautama Buddha lived in the fifth century BC, the son of a powerful ruler in North India. He renounced his wealth in order to search for truth. After 49 days' fasting he recognised the Divine in all beings and came back to the world to teach the 'wisdom of the middle path'. Gautama developed the scheme of the 'four holy truths', which he proclaimed for the first time at Benares after his enlightenment.

Meditation on the four holy truths stands at the centre of the life of a practising Buddhist. According to Buddha, one should follow the 'middle path of reconciling moderation'. Man is a pilgrim on this path to a sensible life.

The Buddhist teachings of Karma say that one is reincarnated after every death until one follows the eight-fold path and so attains salvation, the way to Nirvana. Until this time one is reincarnated in the next life according to how one has behaved in one's present life (Karma).

Buddha is a Sanskrit word meaning 'The Enlightened One'. Gautama is not seen as the first Enlightened One; he is considered to be the fourth Buddha, and Buddhists expect a new one at any time.

Gautama Buddha travelled throughout India for 24 years proclaiming his teachings, and founded a monastic order, the 'Sangha'. Buddha never wrote down his teachings (Dhamma). Eighty years after his death a schism developed in Kushinagara between two schools of thought: the Southern school, 'Hinayana' - belittled as the 'Lesser Vehicle' by its neighbours–in which one attains personal redemption through intensive study and by avoiding sensation. The other principal school, the northern 'Mahayana' (to which Tibetan and Zen Buddhism belong) rejects the goal of individual salvation as being selfish. The true goal is to attain the nature of Buddha, i.e. to become enlightened oneself. This is supposed to occur through complete isolation from the world, through prayer and selfless service to all forms of life; the principles of 'Vuvei', of non-action, serve as the basic rules.

In the second century before Christ, Hinayana Buddhism came to Sri Lanka, brought by Mahinda, son of the great Indian ruler Ashoka. Sri Lanka's King Tissa was converted and he established monasteries and temples. Ever since then, Hinayana Buddhism has, in a highly developed form, influenced the life of the Singhalese and their island. Statues, temples and monasteries cover the whole island, and in Kandy a tooth of Buddha is preserved as a relic.

Buddhism is not a religion that worships a god; it is, rather, a system of rules of conduct and a system of philosophical insights. Many Europeans find it hard to understand its non-theistic nature, i.e. the worship of Buddha not as God, but as a person, who has revealed the true path. But it nevertheless appears to fascinate many Europeans for various reasons, for example its tolerance towards other religions, and even towards variations within its own teachings. It demonstrates its ability to integrate with other religions in the way it tolerates combining the pure teachings of the monks with elements from the god- and demon-world of folk religion.

FESTIVALS AND HOLIDAYS

Official life stops on Saturday afternoons, Sundays and days of the full moon, which are Buddhist holidays. For this reason, in many places where the Buddhist Singhalese call the tune, no alcoholic drinks are sold on days of the full moon. Likewise the day before the full moon is often observed as a half-holiday.

As many of the holidays are determined according to the lunar calendar one often cannot establish exactly which dates they occur on in the Western calendar. We have therefore listed the most important festivals only according to the month they occur. Consult the brochures available in tourist offices for their exact dates as well as for an extensive listing of all holidays.

January
At the full moon, Duruthu Perahera in Colombo's Kelaniya temple. One of Buddha's three supposed visits to the island is celebrated in Kandy. 1 January is the national day of heroes.

February
On 4 February the Independence of the State of Sri Lanka is celebrated with parades, processions and presentations. The Hindus fete Shiva.

March
Easter Passion Play on Duva Island off Negombo (situated North of Colombo).

April
The New Year begins both for Buddhists and for Hindus. April is also the harvest month. The Southwest monsoon begins. April is truly Sri Lanka's festival month.

May
Labour Day on the first of the month. As in every country, the dominant (middle-class) parties show their social views and use the occasion to display their support for workers' interests to representative groups, or to initiate their campaigns for the next elections. Processions and show of strength, and the same again on 2 May. 22 May is Republic Day. These 'gazetted' holidays are, of course, overshadowed by the two-day Vesak, which celebrates the birth, enlightenment and death of Buddha. A carpet of flowers, presents, coloured paper lanterns, and oil lamps cover the island. Human and doll figures portray the life of Buddha, the temples are overwhelmed with fruit, flowers and other gifts made in honour of Buddha.

June

At the June full moon Mahindas, whose father Ashoka, the ruler of India, sent him to the island to spread the teachings of Buddha, is remembered. Lots of pilgrims go to Anuradhapura and Mihintale, where Mahinda converted King Tissa.

July

The pilgrimage from Batticaloa to Kataragama begins. Several events in Kandy from the end of July to the beginning of August.

August

The largest and most spectacular festival on the island; in honour of Buddha's tooth, which is preserved in the Temple of the Tooth in Kandy. For ten days in Kandy thousands of dancers and musicians celebrate 'Perahera' (procession), part of which is the famous parade of sumptuously decorated elephants. There are smaller peraheras in many of the island's Singhalese towns and villages.

Esala Perahera in Kataragama. A pilgrim festival lasting nine days, during which pilgrims are released from vows they have made in hard times to the god Skanda. Men and women walk along a road covered in glowing coals. Many people transfix their tongues, cheeks and thighs with small spears called 'vel', which are both the symbol of the god and the weapon he uses to drive out demons. Also, lemons, a symbol of purity, are attached to the skin on small hooks. The fire-walking usually takes place on the last day of the perahera.

October

At the end of October/beginning of November the Hindu festival of Deepavali. Countless oil lamps proclaim the triumph of good over evil, the return of Rama from his exile.

December

For Buddhists, Hindus and Muslims the time to make a pilgrimage to Adams Peak begins.

At the full moon Sangamitta is honoured. She was Ashoka's daughter and accompanied her brother Mahinda to Sri Lanka, bringing with her a sapling from the holy bo tree under which Buddha attained enlightenment. The tree was planted in the old royal city of Anuradhapura about 250 years BC.

LANGUAGE

Although Sinhala is the official language of Sri Lanka, you can get by with English everywhere.

Singhalese is an independent language that developed originally in the North of India, but in the course of time adopted many elements of the written language Sanskrit and especially of English. So nearly everything that came to the island during British colonial times is 'anglicised'.

Some examples:
bar
bill
conductor
hotel
eschtree (ashtray)
pahsport (passport)
plettform (platform)
pohst kard (post card)
telifohn (telephone)

A few bits of Sinhala

ou	yes
naa	no
honday	all right
mee mokadda	what's there?
mage nama	my name is
bohoma rahay	I like that
baseka kiiyata da?	when does the bus leave
meeka kiiya da?	how much does it cost?
hootale koheda?	where is the hotel?

GEOGRAPHY/CLIMATE

The island of Sri Lanka is fringed by vast coral reefs. In places where this natural protection is absent, there are strong tides and sometimes dangerous currents. The whole island has a one kilometre-wide coastal plain that is in some parts sandy and in others rocky. The dry north is principally a plain. Without the irrigation system of reservoirs (called wewas or tanks) built by the Singhalese kings this area would be barren.

Southwards the land climbs over the high country of Kandy to the mountainous highlands (about 2000 metres high) of the southern half of the island. In this region many mountains are over 2000 metres high. All the larger rivers rise in this central highland and keep the southern part of the island extremely fertile. Here are found terraces with the large tea plantations that are economically very important to Sri Lanka.

Sri Lanka has a typical tropical climate. From May to July the southwest monsoon brings moisture to the south, west, and the central highlands, resulting in the evergreen tropical rainforests of those areas. The northeast monsoon brings rain to the north and east in December and January-the scrub that covers this dry area regularly dries out later during the dry season. In October and November, between the monsoons, there is rain and storms in all parts of the island (except the north). The only region of Sri Lanka where you must expect rain regularly is on the east coast around Batticaloa. So you can in fact escape rain in Sri Lanka simply by moving from one side of the island to another.

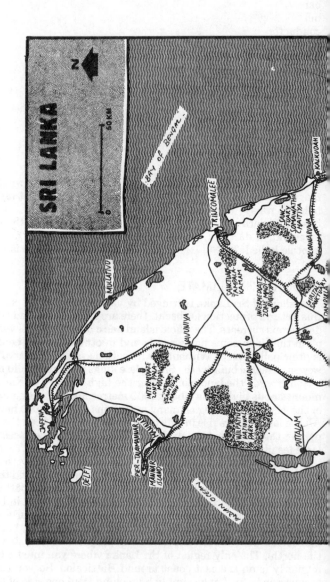

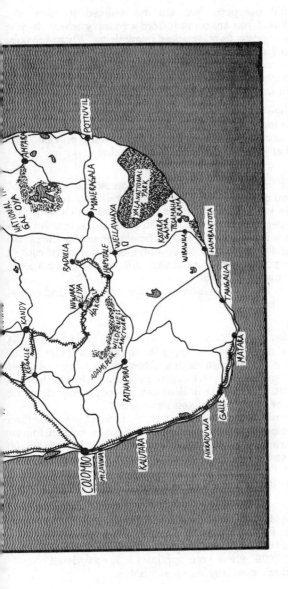

ENTRY REQUIREMENTS

You need a valid passport. You are not obliged to have any immunisations, but if you are coming from a country where there is smallpox, cholera or yellow fever, you need immunising. Wherever you're coming from, a cholera immunisation is recommended because recently there have been some deaths from cholera in Sri Lanka. Although no cases of malaria have been registered for three years, you should in any case take malaria tablets as a precaution.

Currency Exchange

Local currency cannot be taken into the country. When you leave, you can change back as many Ceylonese rupees as you want, provided that you can prove that you bought them in Sri Lanka.

Visa

On arrival you will be given the normal 30-day tourist visa. If you want to stay longer, you can apply at a Sri Lankan consulate in your own country for a visa valid for a maximum of six months (it's very hard to get one for longer than three months). To get this you usually have to produce a return flight booking and sufficient money for the period you are applying for (a healthy bank statement or a certificate of employment from your employer is usually sufficient for this purpose). Dress neatly as this is appreciated.

For consulates in your own country see 'Before travelling' 'Indian and Sri Lankan consulates'.

Visa Extensions

If you want to stay longer than 30 days and didn't get a longer visa before entering Sri Lanka, you can apply for an extension of up to four weeks before your 30-day visa expires. How much longer you get depends on how much money you can prove you have and whether you have a return ticket. Often they will also examine your money-changing receipts to see how much money you have spent.

As a rule of thumb: without a return ticket you won't get more than two weeks. The same is true if you don't look like a normal tourist (whatever that means). You must be able to produce at least $150-200 for one month's stay.

Only in Colombo is it possible to extend your visa. It usually takes no more than one day.

Procedure:

1. Go to the Aliens Building, 4th floor, New Secretariat Building (Fort). There you have to fill out a form.
2. Go to the Department of Immigration and Emigration, Galle Buck Road, tel. 29851/21509, where your application is considered.

Presently you don't need any passport photos.

TRANSPORT

C.T.B. Buses (Ceylon Transport Board)

The State C.T.B. buses must be the cheapest in the world, at about 9 cents per kilometre. In fact the bus network was established well but the number of passengers carried has not grown. Also, departure times are subject to a great deal of change.

Private buses

These are the ideal means of transport in Sri Lanka. Although a bit more expensive, they are more comfortable and quicker than the C.T.B. buses. Since 1980 a fleet of private buses, mostly new Japanese minibuses, has crisscrossed the island. They have reduced the income of the C.T.B. so officials have become more cautious in issuing licenses.

However, the private buses work according to the profit principle, so on minor routes or at certain times of the day or night you will be directed to C.T.B. buses. It is difficult to foresee how the private bus business will develop further.

Rail

Trains are slower but more comfortable than C.T.B. buses, insofar as you have a seat. Although the Sri Lankan rail network is small, it appears incapable of publishing a timetable showing connections. Departure times vary enormously.

There are three classes, of which 1st class exists only on certain trains. Fares are calculated as follows: 2nd class is twice as expensive as 3rd class and 3rd class fares are 1/3 of 1st class fares. 3rd class costs 9 cents per km, 2nd class 18 cents and 1st class 27 cents. The minimum fare is 70 cents. Seat reservations are possible only on certain trains: charges are 7.50 Rs for 3rd class, 10Rs for 2nd class.
Sleeper carriage charges: 40 Rs for 1st class, 25 Rs for 2nd class. There are no sleeper carriages in 3rd class, but for 7.50 Rs you can get a sleeperette (a sort of sleeper seat). A 2nd class sleeperette costs 10 Rs extra. It's possible to make reservations 10 days in advance.

On many routes 3rd class is hopelessly packed. It's worth making a reservation well in advance or travelling by 2nd class. In other respects 2nd class is no more comfortable than 3rd class.

'It's not unusual for 2nd class passengers to sit in the much emptier 1st class. There's often no ticket inspection on the train. But if a ticket inspector appears, you have to pay the difference between the two fares. Still, from time to time, it is the only way to travel in any dignity. On heavily used routes (e.g. Hikkaduwa-Colombo or Kandy-Colombo) it's worth going 3rd class as it's not possible to make a reservation and most of the trains have only one 2nd class carriage, which is so hopelessly crowded that you have to stand–which you can do just as well in 3rd class.'

N.B.: Some trains don't run at weekends.

Taxis

You can normally recognise taxis by their yellow roofs and the number on the white licence-plate. Hardly any taxi travels for less than 4Rs per kilometre. Make sure that the taxi meter is turned on at the start of the journey.

If you don't want to take a taxi, you have to go by public transport as rickshaws are almost completely unknown and scooters are seen only in Colombo.

Campers

Only a few car travellers take their cars to Sri Lanka, so the infrastructure for such tourists is bad. There are no actual camping places. Particularly in Colombo it's difficult to find a place to park your car, though it's easy in the bungalow districts of the resort towns. If you sleep in the vehicle you often have to pay only the parking fee for the car, about 10-20 Rs.

Drive on the left in Sri Lanka. Petrol is expensive and standard petrol is not available.

The address of the automobile club: The Automobile Association of Ceylon, 40 Sir Macan Marker Mawatha, Galle Face, Colombo 3, tel. 215 28/9.

Internal flights

No airport tax is charged for internal flights.

Tips for round-travellers

If you are doing a classic round-trip from Colombo (beginning and ending in Colombo), it is possible to leave any luggage you don't require at Colombo Fort railway station (5 Rs per day per piece of luggage) or in the Hotel Sri Lanka Ex-Servicemen's Institute (see 'Colombo'/'Accommodation') for 2.50 Rs per day.

POST

Airmail

5 Rs for letters up to 10 g, 2.50 Rs extra for each additional 10 g. 4 Rs for printed matter up to 20 g, 2 Rs for additional weight. Maximum weight for printed matter is 10 kg. Postcards cost 4 Rs. Aerogrammes 3.50 Rs.

Small parcels (seamail)

3.50 Rs up to 100g, 6 Rs for 100-250g, 12 Rs for 250-500g, 18 Rs for 500-1000g.

Parcels (seamail)

Maximum weight is 10kg. Approximate prices to Europe: 80 Rs for 1kg, 100 Rs for 1-3kg, 130 Rs for 3-5kg, 180 Rs for 5-10kg. It is not necessary to sew up parcels in Sri Lanka.

A letter to Europe takes about one week, a parcel about 2 1/2 months.

Telephone and telegrams

The Central Telegraph Office, Duke Street, Colombo, is always open.

MONEY

Sri Lanka's unit of currency is the Ceylonese rupee, the CR or, simply, R (rupee). One rupee is 100 cents. There are 2, 5, 10, 50, 100, 500 and 1000 Rs notes.

An average worker earns about 400 Rs a month, a teacher about 800 Rs.

Exchange rates (approx.)

1US$	= 26 Rs
1A$	= 18 Rs
£	= 45 Rs
1Can$	= 20 Rs
1NZ$	= 16 Rs

Banks

Opening hours: Monday 9.00 a.m.-1.00 p.m., Tuesday-Friday 9.00 a.m.-1.30 p.m., closed on Saturday, Sunday, and holidays. The Bank of Ceylon in the Hotel Ceylon Intercontinental in the Fort is open every day from 8.00 a.m. to 8.00 p.m. If you need money urgently and all the banks are closed, you can change travellers cheques in the many luxury hotels, but you'll usually get a bad exchange rate.

Money remittances

These are quickest by telex and should be possible in two days.

Make the remittance via the Bank of Ceylon, Foreign Branch, Prince Street, Colombo 1, via American Express, International Banking Corporation, 11 York Street, Colombo 1, tel. 312 88/89, or via a bank that has a good business relationship with a bank in your own country. You can have the remittance paid to you in travellers cheques.

If you have the remittance paid in cash, you'll get Ceylonese rupees for the full value. But if you want it paid in foreign currency, you'll lose money as the remittance is converted first into Ceylonese rupees and then into the currency you want.

When you enter Sri Lanka you will be given at Customs a form 'for customs clearance', on which you must enter all your exchange transactions. You must keep this card and surrender it on departure. Some banks don't enter the transaction on the card and give you a receipt instead. This is sufficient; but you should keep it in case you apply for a visa extension and have to produce it to prove how much money you have already changed, and also in case you want to change back any left-over rupees.

HOTELS

You will find hotels in all price categories. At the moment, a double in a cheap hotel costs about 35 Rs. In more expensive and better hotels there is a 10% service charge. Check-out time is normally 12 noon.

You will find an (incomplete) list of hotels in 'Welcome to Sri Lanka', a free brochure put out by the Ceylon Tourist Board. For hotels in the cheaper categories, see under the heading 'Economy Accommodation'.

In the 'Big John' booklet, which is given away free in some hotels and is often distributed on arrival of the ship from Rameswaram, you will find further cheap accommodation.

Paying guest accommodation (paid accommodation in private homes) is very widespread in Sri Lanka. For railway passengers there are Railway Retiring Rooms in the stations at Kandy, Jaffna, Galle, Anuradhapura and Trincomalee. Prices: around 30 Rs for a single, 50 Rs for a double.

Warning: many areas of Sri Lanka are mosquito-ridden. Check that mosquito nets don't have any holes.

FOOD AND DRINK

The main drink is tea, drunk in the English manner with milk and sugar. In Sri Lanka they say 'tea' and not 'chai' as elsewhere in Asia. Steer clear of the coffee. Milk coffee is atrocious and costs 1.50 Rs.

To the great joy of tourists coming from India, Coca-Cola is available in Sri Lanka (about 4 Rs), as are countless cheaper soft drinks. Elephant House soft drinks are widespread, costing on average 2.50 Rs; soda is available for about 2 Rs; and you will even find bottled milk at about 2.40 Rs a litre.

Alcohol

Local and foreign alcoholic drinks are available everywhere. Ceylonese beer is good but expensive compared with other living expenses. Try 'Three Coins' for about 24 Rs. The local schnapps, called arrack, is good value. One 750-ml bottle of pol arrack, which is made from the sap of the coconut palm or the palmyra palm, costs 37 Rs in shops. Gal arrack, distilled from sugar cane, costs only 29 Rs per bottle. The cheap spirit from illicit distilleries is called 'kasippu'. Steer clear of it; it can lead to serious poisoning.

Food

Western cuisine arrived with colonialism and tourism. Menus are international, especially in the tourist centres.

Unlike the Hindu, the Buddhist Singhalese eats meat. The local cuisine includes many delicious fish dishes and seafood such as mussels, crabs, oysters, prawns and lobster. 'Fish curry' is a standard Ceylonese dish. A Ceylonese curry consists of a minimum of 10-12 dishes plus rice. There are various types of meat and fish, and also fruit, vegetable and egg curries.

One speciality is hoppers, or egg hoppers. These are hot butter-dough cakes, sometimes served with a fried egg on top. They are flavoured with salt and pepper, with butter or with curry. String hoppers are served as side-dishes. There are small noodle cakes made from rice flour.

The choice of fruit is overwhelming: you will find mangoes, papaya, various bananas, pineapple, passionfruit, avocados and coconuts.

Tips
In small shops and in restaurants for locals no tips are usually expected.
But in the 'better' restaurants for tourists, allow 10 per cent for a tip,
if it hasn't already been included in the bill.

HEALTH

Most medicines are imported from India and Europe, so they are rather
more expensive than in other Asian countries, but are still much cheaper
than in Europe.

Treatment in the State hospitals is free even for foreigners (according
to the Tourist Board in Colombo).

N.B.: in Sri Lanka also you should drink only boiled water and take
malaria-prevention tablets.

Snakes
In Sri Lanka there are 83 types of snakes, of which seven are dangerous
to humans. The best-known are the cobra and the krait, but some species
that live in the sea are even more poisonous–though bites from sea-
snakes are practically unknown.

Sri Lanka has the third highest mortality rate from snake bites in
the world. About four people in 100,000 die every year from snake bites.
The reason is that people who have been bitten usually don't go, or go
too late, to be treated for them.

MASS MEDIA

Radio/television
Radio transmissions from 5.30 a.m. to 11.00 p.m. in six languages:
Singhalese, Tamil, English, Hindi, Urdu and Arabic.

Television was introduced at the end of 1979. But only the wealthy
can afford TV sets. Transmitted daily from about 6.00-11.00 p.m.

Press
Freedom of the press is guaranteed under the constitution. The most
important English-language newspapers are the Sun, Ceylon Daily
Mirror and the Ceylon Daily News. International news is covered well
in the daily press; much better than in the Indian press.

The Ceylon Daily News (1.50 Rs) is Sri Lanka's most comprehensive
and largest-circulation English-language daily paper. The Sunday
edition is called the Sunday Observer (1.75 Rs). The Daily News also
publishes an evening edition, the Ceylon Observer (60c, available only
in towns).

The Ceylon Daily Mirror (75c) has a Sunday edition, 'The Sunday Times'
(1.25 Rs).

The Sun (1 R) has a Sunday edition, 'Weekend' (1.50 Rs). Easily
digestible and with a hint of the gutter press, the Sun carries comics,
flight information (about all planes arriving in and departing from
Colombo), exchange rates and news about politics and showbusiness.

Chic (1.75 Rs) appears twice weekly with a flashy title page and often superficial reporting.

Tribune (3 Rs) appears weekly. A magazine with terrible print quality but interesting film reviews and, under the heading 'Sri Lanka Chronicle', a summary of reports from the Ceylon press for the week just past.

Newsweek, Time, Asiaweek, India Today and Illustrated Weekly of India are available in Colombo and some other towns. In Colombo you will also find some foreign newspapers such as the Herald Tribune or the Guardian Weekly, but they are usually old editions.

SHOPPING

Tea

There are various very different qualities. The Tea Promotion Board has a retail outlet at 574 Galle Road, Colombo 3, or at the airport. You can take out 2.7kg (6 lb) duty-free, and pay 6.45 Rs duty for every extra lb (453g).

Gemstones

Cheap gemstones are on sale everywhere in Ceylon. Anyone who is not an expert should buy from the State Gem Corporation, 24 York Street, Colombo 1, or from one of its agencies. The brochure 'Gem Buying Hints', which costs 25 Rs, is recommended; it is available in, for example, the Hotel Queens in Kandy.

Craft work

Prices are fair and fixed in the State-run Laksala Warehouses. You will find them in:

Colombo, York Street, Fort

Galle, 154 Maha Vidiya

Kandy, 4 Deva Vidiya

Matara, Broadway Street

Hikkaduwa, Coral Gardens

Jaffna, 100 & 104 Kankesanthuarai Road

Protected Areas and National Parks

With the exception of crows, hares, and wild pigs nearly all mammals are strictly protected. A network of more than 50 protected areas and 4 national parks should guarantee the survival of flora and fauna. In this way about 10 per cent of the island is safe from human intervention.

Sri Lanka's fauna is comparable to India's. But it lacks the big game of tigers, wild dogs, gaurs, hyenas, Indian lions and rhinoceroses.

Addresses

Wildlife & Nature Protection Society of Sri Lanka, Chaithiya Road, Fort, Colombo 1, tel. 25 248 (opposite the light-house)

Department of Wildlife Conservation, Zoological Gardens, Anagarika

Dharmapala Mawatha, Dehiwala, tel. 071-4146. With jurisdiction over the national parks, it takes reservations for bungalows in the parks.

Publications
The Nature Protection Society of Sri Lanka publishes twice yearly the newspaper 'Loris' (12.50 Rs). It is highly recommended but is only seldom available in bookshops. Apply direct to the Nature Protection Office.

Unfortunately it is really expensive to visit a national park in Sri Lanka and the most important and most beautiful parks can only be visited in organised groups.

NATIONAL PARKS

Before you intend visiting a national park, you should enquire at the Department of Wildlife Conservation about exactly how you can gain admittance to it. You also have to deal with the Department about bungalow reservations.

MISCELLANEOUS

Opening hours
Normal business hours are Monday-Friday from 8.30 a.m.-4.30 p.m. or 5.00 p.m. Official places are often open only in the mornings. The Fort in Colombo is like a morgue on Sunday.
   Bazaars and village shops are mostly open until evening.

Photography
It's best if you take film with you, as it's very expensive in Sri Lanka. Otherwise there is film and photographic supplies mainly in the European-style Fort in Colombo, e.g. Photo Technica, 28 Upper Chatham Street.

Photography permit
Anyone who wants to photograph in historical places needs a photo permit which can be obtained in the Archaeological Department of the place.

Cigarettes
The cheapest are the filtered Four Aces (4 Rs for 10). The best-known and perhaps the only filterless cigarettes are Three Roses (5 Rs). All brands of cigarettes, including foreign ones, are sold on street stalls in the Fort in Colombo. Example of prices: unfiltered blue Gauloise (45 Rs).
Noticeably few people smoke in Sri Lanka.

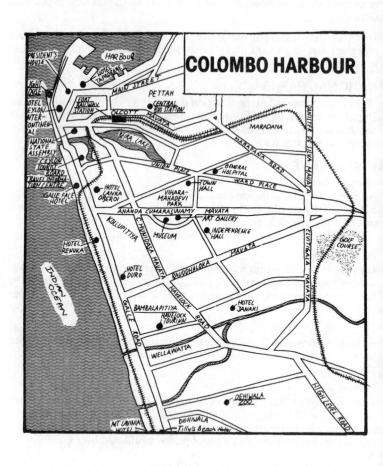

COLOMBO HARBOUR

Gulmarg, Himalayas

Srinagar

A Hindu funeral pyre

COLOMBO

Population 950,000, Sri Lanka's capital, business and administrative metropolis. Formerly an insignificant fishing village where the Portuguese built a fort in the sixteenth century and which the English later built up into a large fortification. Under their colonial rule Colombo developed into one of the most important ports and business centres in Asia.

Today all that is left of the fort, except for its striking tower that later found use as a light house, is its name: the Fort is the district of Colombo where the banks, department stores, official buildings, the GPO and the police are situated. It is the modern centre of Colombo.

The old city of Pettah with its bazaar is oriental in appearance. The railway station and the central bus station are located here.

The affluence of the villa district of Cinnamon Gardens, which the Dutch laid out in the South of Colombo around 1700, and the nearby shanties and corrugated-iron huts of the slums of Slave Island also demonstrate clearly that this is a third world metropolis.

Colombo doesn't offer very much to foreigners but as all important lines of transport leave from here you cannot really avoid it.

ARRIVAL

In Colombo you'll find that many streets have both a Singhalese and an English name. So don't be confused if you get two different addresses for the same place.

Rail and bus

Both stations are in the old city of Pettah, close to one another, and are about 10 minutes' walk from the hotel district in the Fort. So it's usually not worth taking a scooter or taxi. (Take care: pickpockets.)

All trains start and finish in the Fort Railway Station, Olcott Mawatha. The information office of the railway company is outside the station. Pettah Central Bus Station is on the same street. All overland and city buses leave from here. Information from the Ceylon Transport Board, Central Bus Station, Olcott Mawatha, tel.28081.

Private buses depart from the Fort Railway Station.

Air

The airport is situated 31 km north of Colombo. Between 5.00 a.m. and 9.00 p.m. bus 187 travels from the airport to the Central Bus Station in Pettah. Or ask about the Hotel Taprobane airport bus (55 Rs). The train takes 80 minutes to get to the Fort Railway Station. It travels four times daily between 8.00 a.m. and 5.20 p.m. See 'Colombo'/'Further travel' for the train timetable.

A taxi to the city costs about 200 Rs which, if you don't want to wait for public transport and are willing to share the cost of the taxi with three other people, is bearable.

ACCOMMODATION

There are too few simple hotel rooms and the prices of those that do exist are relatively high. So one cannot actually speak of cheap hotels. Many people therefore go straight to Dehiwala or Mount Lavinia, which are both one hour's bus ride from Colombo and generally have cheaper accommodation.

In Colombo itself most hotels are concentrated in the Fort:
YMCA, 39 Bristol Street, tel. 25252. Single 31 Rs without ventilator, 61 Rs with ventilator; double 96 Rs, 150 Rs with bath. Spending the night in a two-bed room with anyone who also happens to be allotted to it costs 31 Rs, and in a three-bed room 21 Rs. Has its own restaurant and library. For men and women. Recommended.
Sri Lanka Ex-Servicemen's Institute, 29 Bristol Street, next door to the YMCA, tel. 22650. Single 30 Rs, double 50 Rs, dormitory 20 Rs. Additional charge of 1 R for temporary membership. Good cheap restaurant in the building. Recommended.
British India Hotel, 13 Baillie Street, tel. 26501. Double 75 Rs. Acceptable.
Globe Hotel, Baillie Street, tel. 20304. Double 100 Rs.
Hotel Metropole, 30 Queen Street, tel. 21066. Single 110 Rs, double 132 Rs; all rooms have bath.
Hotel Dominion, 23 Upper Chatham Street, tel. 23876. Single 125 Rs, double 150 Rs; all rooms have bath.

Opposite the Fort Railway Station:
Ajantha Hotels Ltd. Single 45 Rs, double 90 Rs. Really dismal.

In Colombo as in most places in Sri Lanka there is a lot of private accommodation. This is often cheaper than the 'cheap' hotels. Breakfast is available in most places if requested. You can find addresses in the official brochure 'Welcome to Sri Lanka'. Even on the street you'll often be offered private accommodation.

Hotels in Dehiwala
YMCA, 31 Fair Line Road (in the direction of Mount Lavinia). Double (with communal bath) 50 Rs, 75 Rs with own toilet.
Tourist Rest, 7 Park Avenue, tel. 071-4521; near the Zoo. Double from 60 Rs.
Big John, 22 Albert Place, tel. 071-3321. Single from 20 Rs, double from 50 Rs. Self-catering possible. Big John also publishes a free brochure of the same name which has useful tips about Sri Lanka; it is distributed in some places.

FOOD AND DRINK

The YMCA restaurant and The Fort Restaurant (in the same building as the Ex-Servicemen's Institute) are cheap and okay. The Hotel Nanking (Chinese food) and the Peony Restaurant (good seafood and even a jukebox) are more expensive; both are in Chatham Street.

Meals can be obtained on request in most private accommodation.

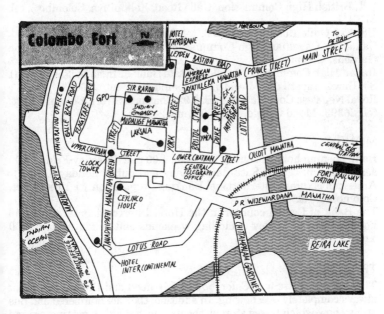

POST

Telephone–telegrams: GPO, Janadhipath Mawatha, Colombo 1, tel. 26203; near the Fort light-house.

Poste restaurant 7.00 a.m.-9.00 p.m. every day.

You can have your parcels packed (in cardboard boxes) from about 20 Rs in the Parcel Office. Even better: ask in Cargills or Millers department stores–they make wooden boxes to size and sew up the whole package.

All information about postal charges is available from the Superintendent of Foreign Mails, Duke Street, tel. 28301 ext. 21. Or see 'Sri Lanka General'/'Post'.

American Express Clients' Mail (around the corner in the office of the American Travel Service), in a side-alley off York Street, Monday-Friday 9.00 a.m.-1.30 p.m.

Central Telegraph Office, Duke Street: always open for telegrams and telephone. Minimum length of phone call is three minutes. You should reckon on a wait of at least 1 to 2 hours for your connection.

EMBASSIES

Australian, Australian High Commission, 3 Cambridge Place, Colombo 7, tel. 59 87 67/8/9.

NZ–The embassy in Singapore is accredited to Sri Lanka.

UK, British High Commission, Galle Road, Kollupitiya, Colombo 3, tel. 27 61 1.

US, 210 Galle Road, Colombo 3, tel. 54 80 07.

Canadian, Canadian High Commission, 6 Gregory's Road, Cinnamon Gardens, Colombo.

Indian High Commission, 3rd floor, State Bank of India building, 18-3/1 Sir Baron Jayatilaka Mawatha, Colombo Fort, tel. 21604.

Royal Nepalese Consulate General, 92 Chatham Street, Colombo Fort, tel. 26393. Monday-Friday 10.00 a.m.-12 noon.

MONEY

Bank opening hours: Monday 9.00 a.m.-1.00 p.m., Tuesday-Friday 9.00 a.m.-1.30 p.m. Closed Saturday, Sunday and public holidays.

American Express International Banking Corporation, 11 York Street, Colombo 1, tel. 31288/89.

The Bank of Ceylon counter in the Hotel Intercontinental (Colombo Fort) is open every day (including weekends and holidays) from 8.00 a.m. to 8.00 p.m.

TRANSPORT

The city bus system in Colombo is fairly good and the buses are not always completely overflowing. In addition, they are numbered and bus stops show which buses stop at them. Another aid to getting around is the 'Bus Services Colombo and Suburbs' map (10 Rs). More comfortable and, of course, more expensive are scooters and taxis. Unfortunately the cheap cycle-rickshaws so common in India do not exist here.

SIGHTSEEING

There's not much to see in Colombo itself. The Fort light-house in the middle of the town is worth mentioning–but it's not in operation any more.

The Zoo in Dehiwala is worth seeing. Several buses leave from the station in front of the Central Bank of Ceylon, no. 132 amongst others; about a 1-hour journey. 30 Rs admission. Opening hours 8.00 a.m.-6.00 p.m. The famous elephant circus takes place every day at 5.15 p.m. The Zoo is one of the most beautiful in the world, with a minimum of bars and fences; rather, it really is a 'park with animals'.

For important addresses in Colombo and for information about visiting national parks in Sri Lanka, see 'Sri Lanka'/'General'.

EXCURSIONS

To Negombo, a well-known swimming resort in the North of Colombo, a destination for package tourists, and one of the island's fishing centres. Get there by bus from Pettah. Frequency is about every 10 minutes, by minibus (5 Rs) or by train from the Fort Railway Station. Regular services, 3rd class 3.60 Rs.

'Instead of taking a taxi from the airport to Colombo, many people go direct to Negombo, which is cheaper (around 90 Rs, instead of 150-200 Rs).'

SHOPPING

Gemstones
State Gem Corporation, 24 York Street, tel. 23377. Here you can have your gemstones examined, even those bought elsewhere, at no charge for value and authenticity.

Craft work
Sri Lankan craft work is sold at fixed prices in the State-run Laksala in the Fort. These prices are useful as general guidelines and for comparing prices in other shops. Everywhere outside the State shops haggle about prices!

Pettah
The bazaar district. Similar selection of goods in each street, allowing price comparisons.
A tip: good mass-produced sandals.

Bookshops
Lake House Bookshop, Sir Chittampalam Gardiner Mawatha (near the Regal cinema). Carries among other publications, India Today, Illustrated Weekly of India, Daily Telegraph, Time, Newsweek, books on Buddhism. Has its own record department.

International Bookstores, 20 Queen Street. You can buy and sell second-hand books here.

Book department of Cargills department store in the Fort.

Photography
Photographic supplies and camera repairs: Photo Technica, 28 Upper Chatham Street, Fort. Also makes photocopies (1.25 Rs). Don't have any film developed in Sri Lanka as the quality is mediocre.

MISCELLANEOUS

Travel Information Centre, Galle Face Centre Road, tel. 32178. Open Monday-Friday 8.30 a.m.-5.00 p.m., Saturday and holidays 8.00 a.m.-12.30 p.m.
    The Tourist Office at Colombo's Katunayake airport is open day and night, tel. 0315-411.

The Colombo General Hospital (with outpatients' department), Regent Street, Colombo 8, tel. 91 111.
    Private doctors: you'd do well to ask at your embassy about doctors they have confidence in.

Reading rooms: German Kulturinstitut, 92 Rosmead Place, Colombo 7, tel. 93351.
British Council Library, 154 Galle Road, American Center, 39 Flower Road.

The selection of English-language films available is meagre. Cinemas are hopelessly packed. Programmes are given in the daily papers.

You'll find useful information and addresses in the free brochure 'Welcome to Sri Lanka', which is available at the Tourist Office. The information in the monthly publication 'This month in Sri Lanka' is more up to date; you can buy it for 25 Rs in the Lake House bookshop or in the Taprobane Hotel.

You can get maps at the Survey Department, Kirula Road and some from street sellers, e.g. 'Road Map of Sri Lanka' (25 Rs) and 'Tourist Map of Colombo' (15 Rs).

FURTHER TRAVEL (within Sri Lanka)

Colombo is the hub of Sri Lanka's transport network. Trains, buses and internal flights go from here to all the larger villages on the island. Warning: fares and departure times are always being changed. For accurate information phone 35838 (rail), 28081 (bus) and 20465 (Upali Travels–for air travel).

Bus
No. 01: Colombo-Kandy; 24-hour service, every 15 minutes; express bus every half hour; 9.60 Rs.
No. 02: Colombo-Galle; 24-hour service, every 15 minutes; 9.20 Rs.
No. 03: Colombo-Ratnapura; 4.30 a.m.-10.30 p.m., every 30 minutes; 3-hour journey; 7.60 Rs.
No. 04: Colombo-Anuradhapura; 12 midnight-6.00 p.m., every 2 hours; 7-hour journey; 15.80 Rs.
No. 48: Colombo-Batticaloa; departs 10.15 a.m. and 11.45 a.m.; approx. 8-hour journey; 26.20 Rs.
No. 49: Colombo-Trincomalee; departs 11.00 a.m., 1.30 p.m., 4.30 p.m. and 10.00 p.m.; approx 7 hours; 22.80 Rs.
No. 178: Colombo-Airport; 4.30 a.m.-9.00 p.m.; every 30 minutes; 3.20 Rs.
As well as these State C.T.B. buses, there are also private bus services to everywhere on the island.
For bus services to Talaimannar see 'From Sri Lanka to South India'.

Air
There are internal flights only on the following routes: Colombo-Jaffna, Colombo-Trincomalee and Colombo-Anuradhapura. All the flights travel

in both directions every day. Fares: Colombo-Jaffna 635 Rs, Colombo-Trincomalee 550 Rs, Colombo-Anuradhapura 485 Rs. No airport tax! You can make bookings at Upali Travels, tel. 20465 (Colombo); Mackinnon's, tel. 8154 (Jaffna); Jeganathan's, tel. 282 (Trincomalee); and Miridiya Hotel, tel. 212 (Anuradhapura).

FURTHER TRAVEL (from Sri Lanka)

To the Maldives
Air
Air Lanka and Maldive Airways each fly once a day from Colombo to Male. The return fare is US$80; the flight takes 50 minutes.

Ship
No passenger ships or ferries operate between Sri Lanka and the Maldives. However, Pioneer Shipping Agencies take passengers on their cargo ships. There is a service about every fortnight. The crossing takes 3-4 days, depending on the weather. The fare (which is paid to the captain) is US$35 one-way, plus 25Rs embarkation tax. Meals are included in the fare. As it is a cargo ship, there are no cabins and you have to sleep on deck. Also, you are not insured – you make the trip at your own risk.

Arriving in the Maldives by ship isn't legal but is tolerated.

Bookings in Colombo: Pioneer Shipping Agencies Ltd, 676 Galle Road, Kollupitiya, Colombo 3, tel. 87746. Open Monday-Friday 8.30 a.m.-12.30 p.m., 1.30-5.30 p.m.; Saturday and Sunday 8.30 a.m.-12 noon.

If you're lucky, you may find a yacht in Galle harbour that's going to the Maldives and will take you there.

Direct from Colombo to Nepal
If you don't want to make the long, tiring journey overland through India to Nepal, you can cover the distance in comfort (and in only 3 1/2 hours) by plane. The flight by RNAC costs US$190. Don't forget: before departure you have to pay 100 Rs International Airport Tax.

Direct from Colombo to Bangkok
Colombo is a good departure point for further travels in Southeast Asia. Many tourists fly on from here to Thailand. Allow around US$150 for the flight to Bangkok. Also you have to pay another 100 Rs in International Airport Tax.

HIKKADUWA

Hikkaduwa is situated on the heavily used main road between Colombo and Galle. Boutiques and luxury hotels abound so accommodation and restaurant prices are high.

ARRIVAL/ACCOMMODATION

By bus or train; the stations are next to each other. There's one hotel after another all the way southwards by the sea along Galle Road to Narigama.

In the countless hotels prices for a single range from 15 Rs to 750 Rs (Coral Gardens). As elsewhere in Sri Lanka, you can also get private accommodation, from about 15 Rs.

Hotel Seagulls, after the railway crossing near the railway station. Double 50 Rs (without bath) or 75 Rs with bath, mosquito net and fan.

Coral Front Inn, 279 Galle Road, opposite Mamas Restaurant. No singles. Doubles cost between 30 Rs and 150 Rs depending on degree of comfort. The hotel also has a small camping site; 5 Rs per person per day. Clean. Own restaurant.

Surfing Beach Guest House (about 1.2 km from the railway station), at the beginning of Narigama village. Double 60 Rs, 250 Rs facing the sea and with private bath.

'About 15 minutes from the railway station as you're going towards Galle on Waulagoda Road there is the Tourist Rest White House. A single costs 15 Rs. You can get excellent food if you request it in advance.'

There's lots of stagnant water in and around Hikkaduwa, so there's a plague of mosquitoes. If you stay right on the beach, you don't need to worry as mosquitoes don't like wind. But if your hotel room is inland and your mosquito net has holes you can buy mosquito ointment or mosquito coils.

BEACHES

The tourist beaches are by the Coral Reef, Coral Sands and Blue Coral hotels. The surf is broken by the coral reef, so the water is very calm here. Beware! You can hurt yourself on the sharp-edged coral.

The beach at Narigama is much wider and is fringed with palms rather than with luxury hotels. This beach is a surfer's paradise, with huge waves.

Coral gardens: various hotels (for example Coral Gardens Hotel. Coral Reef Hotel and Dragon Restaurant) organise trips in glass-bottomed boats to the protected coral gardens. Coral Gardens 30 Rs per person; the others 25 Rs. Minimum of four people. 30-60 minute trip. Beautiful but not overwhelming. Also, people diving for souvenirs are damaging the coral gardens. And the quality of the water has deteriorated in recent years with the increased sewage being released into the sea. Around the coral you can also see brightly coloured fish and, with any luck, sea-turtles. But you'll get the best view of this world if you have a look for yourself with a snorkel, flippers and goggles.

Watersports: hotels and shops hire out snorkels, goggles and flippers. A complete set costs about 10Rs per hour or 40-50 Rs per day.

Mamas Restaurant and Coral Gardens Hotel, among others, hire out complete diving equipment with oxygen tanks; 225 Rs per day. An additional 50 Rs per hour for the boat that takes you and other divers out.

Surfboards: 50 Rs per day. Coral Gardens Hotel hires out underwater cameras. Deposits are not included in all these prices.

Fauna: the coast of Hikkaduwa is full of sharks, swordfish, sawfish and rays, as a visit to the fish market (near the railway station) will prove. Sharks have a good name throughout Sri Lanka–there are no known cases of them attacking humans. The water monitor (a large lizard over 1 m long) lives in stagnant water.

MISCELLANEOUS

The post office is inland, between the railway station and the bus station.

The People's Bank (opposite the fish market) changes travellers cheques. The office is usually completely packed. You can also change money, although for a slightly worse rate, in the expensive hotels.

There's no map of Hikkaduwa itself, only the one-inch map of Ambalangoda, which includes the whole coastal area and hinterland as well as Hikkaduwa. It is published by the Survey Dept and can be bought for 60Rs in the shop next to Sigma Radio Works (near the turn-off to the post office).

Hikkaduwa has no public transport. It costs 15 Rs per day (2 Rs per hour) to hire a bicycle. There are also various places that hire out motorbikes. Minibuses travel when needed to the airport at Colombo (if they can get together eight passengers); cost is 100 Rs per person.

Souvenirs: batik, sharks' teeth and masks from Ambalangoda. There are comic masks, masks to drive away demons and devil masks. Bargain when buying.

In Hikkaduwa bad spirits are driven out with the aid of the devil dance. Datura (thorn-apple), which produces a drugged condition and is also used by 'witches', can be used in the performance. Until two years ago hardly any foreigners had seen these rituals, but now suddenly devil dances are put on for tourists: for 40 Rs you watch a two-hour long farce.

FURTHER TRAVEL

To Colombo

Trains travel between 4.00 a.m. and 5.00 p.m.; see also the timetable under 'Colombo'/'Further travel'.

C.T.B. buses depart day and night from Hikkaduwa bus station. There are also minibuses continuously.

To Galle

Trains depart regularly from 6.00 a.m. to 9.30 p.m. The State buses have a 24-hour service. Continuous minibus service from early in the morning until the evening: 2.90 Rs; 20 minutes' travelling time.

GALLE

120 km South of Colombo. Population 85,000. Fourth-largest town in
Sri Lanka. A colonial town: the Arabs came first, and then in 1587 the
Portuguese, who began building the fort. They were driven out in 1640
by the Dutch with 12 ships and 2000 men. Then the English arrived
in 1796. The Dutch fort is almost completely intact. The old town is
dominated by the fort, the town walls and eleven bastions. Until this
century Galle was Sri Lanka's major port. Its importance declined as
it is too shallow for modern ships and its approach is too dangerous
during the Southwest monsoon. There are many Muslims. By the way,
Galle is pronounced 'gawl'.

ARRIVAL/ACCOMMODATION

The bus and train stations are a few minutes' walk from the town's main
gate.

You'll find cheap hotels near the bus station. But you can also stay
at one of the colonial-style hotels in the Fort, which are nicer and just
as cheap. You can walk to the Fort in about 15 minutes, but you can
also go there on an ox cart.

There are only a few hotels in the old town (Fort), but you won't have
any difficulty getting a place, as there's always room.

Hassen's Roof Garden, 63 Pedlar Street. Most of the rooms have two
beds, but singles are also let. Single-occupancy about 15 Rs, double
about 25 Rs. Mosquito nets available.

YMCA, Pedlar Street, a few doors further on. Single 30 Rs. Only for
men. No mosquito nets!

Aquamarine, 31 Rampart Street, two minutes from the YMCA. Single
33 Rs, 44 Rs with bath; double 66 Rs, 88 Rs with bath. Mosquito nets
available. Large rooms. The front of the hotel is in the town walls.

FOOD AND DRINK

Palitha Restaurant, 1 Front Cross Street. 15 Rs for a Ceylonese fish
curry (hot) with eight side-dishes.

SIGHTSEEING

Walking through the narrow streets and along the walls of the Fort
you get a feeling of the fifteenth century.

Light-house. You can go up it for 5 Rs. The keeper has lots of time and
will tell you about his work. His working hours: 5.00 p.m.-6.00 a.m.
Beautiful panoramic view of the harbour.

Post fishermen. As their name says, these fishermen squat or stand
on posts in the water. You can watch them–preferably early in the

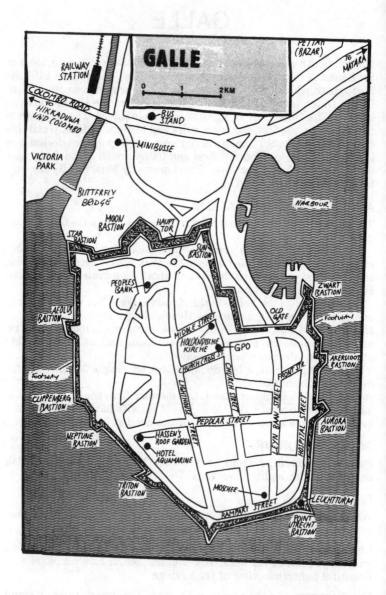

morning–from the walls of the Fort.

Pettah, the bazaar district, is about one kilometre north of the Fort.

SHOPPING

Gemstones (which are supposed to be cheaper here than in Ratnapura, where they come from). Don't let touts talk you into going to their 'father's' factory. If you want to buy without risk visit the State-run shop Laksala. Famous lace-work introduced by the Portuguese in the sixteenth century is also available.

Shells and shell-jewellery. Lots of places to buy it near the light-house.

FURTHER TRAVEL

to Colombo
For the railway timetable see under 'Colombo'/'Further travel'.
C.T.B. buses run 24 hours a day; 9.20 Rs. Minibuses run every 10 minutes from 4.30 a.m. to 7.30 p.m.; 15 Rs.

to Matara
11 trains between 5.00 a.m. and 6.30 p.m.; 3.90 Rs (3rd class). Matara is the terminus of the West coast railway line.
C.T.B. buses regularly between 12.30 a.m. and 9.45 p.m.; 4.20 Rs. A total of 20 minibus services between 6.30 a.m. and 7.30 p.m., 6 Rs.
The trip between Galle and Matara covers one of the most beautiful coastal areas in the world–palm forests and sea. You can get out at three resorts: Koggala, Weligama and, of course, Unawattuna.

Other Destinations
By train to Alutgama; six services between 3.00 a.m. and 6.00 p.m.; 5 Rs.
By C.T.B. bus via Matara to Tissamaharama; nine buses from 6.00 a.m. until nearly midnight; 14 Rs.

TRIP FROM MATARA VIA TISSAMAHARAMA TO KATARAGAMA

Several C.T.B. buses to Tissamaharama; 10Rs; about a three-hour journey. Minibuses only go in the morning from Matara to Tissa. In Tissa, get out at the main station; wait there for a jeep that will take you to family accommodation. You get to Kataragama from Tissa in 30 minutes by bus (2.60 Rs).

Matara
Population 35,000. 160 km South of Colombo. Also has a fort built by the Portuguese. The town is known for 'Matara diamonds', which are semi-precious zircons.
Worth seeing: Werahena Temple (7 km outside the town), which has Sri Lanka's largest statue of Buddha and underground passages. Matara is also the batik centre of the south coast.
   Polhena Beach, 2 kilometres outside the town, is quite polluted and is hardly worth the effort.

Hambantota

Fishing village with many Muslims, descendents of men who came as soldiers of the Dutch in the seventeenth century.

'The Government Rest House is too expensive. The Blue Guest House, which is near the sea, is better.'

Tissamaharama

Locals call it 'Tissa'. Old royal Singhalese town. When the royal towns in the North were occupied by Tamils, the kings retreated to here. So there are lots of ruined dagobas and palaces to explore in and around the town. Tissa is today the departure point for Buddhist pilgrimages to Kataragama, 18 km to the North. From Tissa you can go to Yala National Park.

There are some Rest Houses near the Wewa, a reservoir with pelicans and sanctuary; for example the Anupama Guest House, double 50 Rs (no singles).

Kataragama

With extensive temple buildings, the destination of pilgrimages from Tissa. A famous festival takes place every year around the end of July/beginning of August. See 'Sri Lanka–General'/'Festivals and holidays'.

Accommodation in the Mahajana Hotel, near the bus station; single 25 Rs, double 35 Rs, fans but no mosquito nets. The Kataragama Guest House, tel. 299, is better and more expensive; single 100 Rs, double 200 Rs; all rooms have two beds, so there are no real singles.

YALA NATIONAL PARK

Its area amounts to about 1100 square kilometres. The only entrance to the park is 28 km east of Tissa.

Jeep trips
On arrival in Tissa you will usually be asked immediately by a jeep-driver if you want to go to the park the next morning. If you say yes, you'll be taken to your accommodation for free, as the driver is often the proprietor or, if not, he gets a commission. If there are no jeep-drivers when you arrive, which is unlikely, ask at your hotel. The jeep costs 200 Rs and can take up to six people. If you cannot find anyone to share it with, you have to pay the whole fare yourself.

The Tissamaharama Rest House on Wewa Tank even has its own jeep service, so the tariff there is higher.

Bus trips
There are no bus services to the park entrance. You can simply take the bus going to Kirinda, get out at the turn-off to Yala and wait for a lift to the park, which is difficult.

PARK CHARGES

Admission to the park is 50 Rs. A seat in the minibus costs 70 Rs. During the wait that results from all the red-tape, you can visit the park museum.

PARK VISITS

Minibus trips take place daily at about 6.30 a.m. and 3.30 p.m. Reservations are not necessary. You have to make a reservation only if you want to take a trip round the park in a jeep. This has to be booked 14 days in advance at the Department of Wildlife Conservation in Colombo (see 'Sri Lanka–General'/'Sanctuaries and National Parks'. Cost for five people: 375 Rs.

The minibus journey takes about 2 1/2 hours. The park exhibits open pasture on which the animals are easy to see. Yala is suffering from an invasion of domesticated water buffalo that have left their owners and congregated in herds. In addition, you will see spotted deer, wild pigs, crocodiles, many birds, possibly also elephants and, with a lot of luck, leopards. Near the end of the trip you have a short break by the sea (not for swimming!). Fishermen lived here until a few years ago. Now they have been moved outside the park area.

ACCOMMODATION IN THE PARK

There are a few bungalows in the park where you can stay overnight.

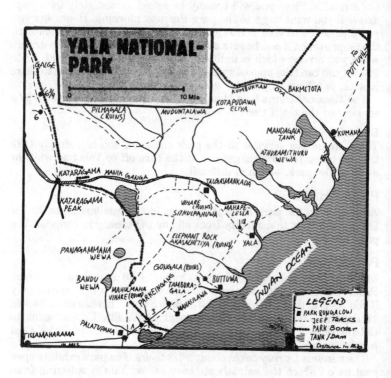

Minimum rent per bungalow: 500 Rs–five people at 100 Rs each or one person at 500 Rs. Every additional person pays 100 Rs (maximum of eight people). Additional 50 Rs per person per day for park admission. The bungalows can be rented for a maximum of five days (however, the length of stay you'll be allowed depends on the demand for bungalows). A cook is provided for every bungalow. Provisions have to be taken.

Accommodation close to the Park

Yala Safari Beach Hotel (single 410 Rs, double 450 Rs) and Browns Safari Beach Hotel (single 225 Rs, double 290 Rs) are situated on the sea right next to the park boundary. They can be reached only by jeep.

FURTHER TRAVEL FROM TISSAMAHARAMA

C.T.B. buses:

Colombo (via Matara/Galle) 4.50 a.m.-9.50 p.m.; about eight buses; the 9.15 a.m. bus goes via Ratnapura; about 22 Rs.

Several buses that only go as far as Matara or Galle.

Monaragala: the village to change at for Pottuvil (Arugam Bay); 4.30 p.m.

Nuwara Eliya/Kandy: only one direct bus to Kandy; 8.45 a.m.; 24.50 Rs to Kandy.

Nuwara Eliya/Kandy: change in Wellawaya or Bandarawela.

If you want to get to Kandy the same day, you have to catch a bus to Wellawaya before 10.00 a.m. at the latest. Get out at the school at Buduruagala Junction, about 6 km before Wellawaya (the bus will stop if you ask). A path leads from there to some 10th century stone statues (Buddha, with three figures on either side). You need about 3/4 hours for the walk. The trip can also be made by boat. Watch for the sign 'By boat to the Buduruagala ruins'.

The Journey from Wellawaya to Bandarawela and Haputale

After Wellawaya, a hill trip through the tea plantations begins. In Ella, the first pass (1050 m), you can change to a train.

Countless buses go to Haputale (1528 m) from Bandarawela, which is a favourite holiday and spa resort with a mild climate. At Haputale Pass there is an overwhelming view of the lowlands of southern Sri Lanka.

NUWARA ELIYA

Situated at 1890 m above sea-level in the hill country. It has a cool climate, and it often rains. An umbrella and warm clothes are an advantage. A mountain resort with tennis and other sporting facilities. Remnants of English colonialism dominate; one sees, for example, typically British lawns and golf courses. Nuwara Eliya (pronounced 'Nurelia') is also a tea centre.

ARRIVAL
Bus
If you arrive in the evening, you'll have difficulty finding cheap accommodation. Nuwara Eliya goes to sleep at 9.00 p.m. and no guides will be waiting for you after that. Hotels near the bus station are usually fully booked.

Rail
The train stops 7 km away in Nanu Oya. There are buses from there to Nuwara Eliya.

ACCOMMODATION
Woodlands, opposite the bus station. Single 30 Rs, double 50 Rs. Restaurant on the ground floor.
Windsor Hotel (keeping Woodlands on your left, go to the first cross-roads). Single 20 Rs, double 40 Rs. Restaurant on the ground floor.
Nuwara Eliya Inn. No singles; double 40 Rs, 50 Rs, 75 Rs; triple 75 Rs, 125 Rs; 4-bed room 100 Rs. Prices depend on degree of comfort. Hot and cold water. Colonial-style house.
Molesworth, not far from Grand Hotel. Single 20 Rs, double 40-100 Rs. No fixed check-out time. Colonial-style house.
You'll find other, mostly expensive, hotels near the racetrack (Dharmapala Circus). Most of the hotels in this area have their own restaurants, but you'll eat more cheaply in the town.

SIGHTSEEING
Horton Plains: Great and Little World's End
You can reach this from Ohiya railway station. You'll find a map in the Highcliffe Hotel in Haputale.
   Horton Plains, 2133 m above sea level, is Sri Lanka's highest plateau and has a landscape of subtropical and tropical vegetation and fauna. Little World's End is a 600-metre deep precipice, and Great World's End a 1500-metre precipice. The view is very impressive. The rainforest is famous.
   The Department of Wildlife Conservation (situated in Colombo) runs

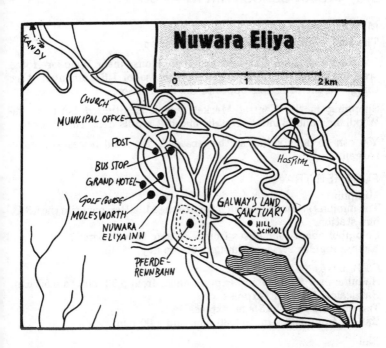

Anderson Lodge (100 Rs per person) in Horton Plains Nature Reserve. Accommodation there is possible generally only by booking ahead in Colombo. Exceptions to this depend on the demand for the lodge.

The Farr Inn, Horton Plains, tel. 23501/23504 has singles for 270 Rs and double for 365 Rs.

Safari Travels, 92/3 Queen Elisabeth Drive, Nuwara Eliya, runs a jeep service to Horton Plains (and also to other places on request). Apart from the driver there is room for six passengers. The day trip costs 600 Rs.

Hakgala Botanic Gardens
Hakgala, 10 km from Nuwara Eliya, is easily reached by bus from the Main Bus Stand.

Tea factory
Visit a tea factory, e.g. The Pedrew Tea Factory. Can be reached on foot, about 4 km; everyone knows the way. Visitors are welcome all day long. No-one will ask for an admission fee. You will see how tea is dried and packe, but much of the work is done at night.

Pidurutalagala Mountain (2524 m)
Situated just outside Nuwara Eliya, this mountain can easily be climbed by non-mountain climbers.

MISCELLANEOUS

The Post Office is opposite the bus station.

For food, the Hotel Dalewest and Bake House (near Windsor Hotel) are good and cheap. You can get 100g cheese for 7 Rs, amongst other things, in the Milk Bar opposite the bus station.

Shopping in the Central Market, which is situated between the Woodlands and Windsor Hotels, and in Cargills department store.

You can go pony riding at the racetrack. No fixed prices–you must bargain.

FURTHER TRAVEL

Minibus
The minibus station is situated next to the Milk Bar, opposite the C.T.B. bus station.
Colombo: about four buses from 8.30 a.m. to 5.00 p.m.; 35 Rs.
Kandy: regular services throughout the day; 17 Rs.

C.T.B. buses
Badulla: over 20 local and express buses from 5.30 a.m. to 5.50 p.m.
Batticaloa: 7.15 a.m. express.
Tissamaharama: 11.15 a.m. express.
Kandy: from 5.00 a.m. to 6.30 p.m. and 1.00 p.m.

Rail
From Nanu Oya to Colombo: 9.38 a.m., 2.05 p.m. and 10.35 p.m.

KANDY

Population 110,000. 305 m above sea-level. Kandy is the Buddhist centre of Sri Lanka and an important place of pilgrimage. The tooth of Buddha, is preserved here. An artificial lake was built in the middle of the town at the beginning of the nineteenth century.

The area around Kandy was settled late by the Singhalese. For centuries Kandy was a royal city. The surrounding mountains and jungle made the place a natural fortress; this was one of the reasons why Kandy was able to hold out the longest of any Sri Lankan towns against European conquerors. Only in 1815 did the English succeed in occupying it and capturing the king, thus ending the rule of the Singhalese kings.

Thanks to the town's long protection from foreign cultural influences, traditions, rites and dances have remained more alive and more intact in Kandy.

Of course, Kandy has to-day become one of the most important centres of mass tourism in Sri Lanka.

ACCOMMODATION

Muslim Hotel, right by the Clocktower, easy to find from the bus stand and the railway station. All rooms have 2-3 beds, but are also let as singles. Single 30 Rs, double 40 Rs, triple 45 Rs. Simple Ceylonese restaurant on the ground floor.

YMCA: there are two in Kandy. One is situated on the opposite side of the lake from the Temple of the Tooth-on Sangarata Mawatha, at the beginning of the lake as you come from the Clocktower: single 12 Rs, double 18.50 Rs, hall (i.e. mattress) 4.85 Rs; partitioned rooms-not soundproof; only for men. The other is on Kotugodella Vidiya, tel. 3529; single 10 Rs, double 15 Rs, dormitory (4-bed room) 6 Rs, hall (i.e. on the floor) 3.50 Rs; only for men.

Constellation Hotel, tel. 3513, up the path to the right of the Temple of the Tooth; follow the sign. Various prices, depending on position and degree of comfort: single 25 Rs, 35 Rs and 40 Rs; double 60 Rs, 80 Rs, 100 Rs, 120 Rs and 140 Rs; triple 125 Rs and 175 Rs.

Woodstock, a bit further along the path to the Constellation Hotel. No singles, doubles from 35 Rs to 75 Rs, 4-bed dormitory 15 Rs. The hotel has a marvellous position on the edge of the jungle (Udawattekele Sanctuary), with views of the lake.

Rosewood Tourist Lodge, 27/5 Sumangala Mawatha. Double 50 Rs, dinner 15 Rs. Run by a nice teacher's family. Very quiet, and beautifully situated.

The Sunray Inn, Travellers Nest and Traveller's Home are all situated close to one another. The three lodges compete strongly. All three are

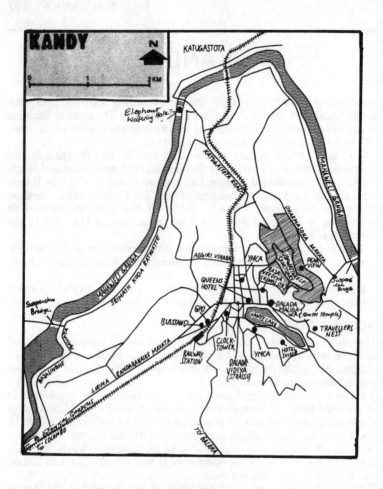

equipped with their own kitchens, but you can eat more cheaply in one of the places nearby. Take bus 655/2 or 654 from the city bus stand for 50 cents and get out at the petrol station.

Sunray Inn, 117/5 Dharmapala Mawatha (formerly Malabar Street), tel. 3322. No singles (but single guests get a 25% reduction), double from 50 Rs to 200 Rs, depending on degree of comfort. 10% additional service charge.

Traveller's Home, 117/3 Anagarika Dharmapala Mawatha, tel. 2800. Only doubles (10 rooms), but there's a reduction for single guests; double 30 Rs to 200 Rs, depending on degree of comfort. Warm water available.

Travellers Nest, 117/4 Anagarika Dharmapala Mawatha, tel. 2633.

Single from 20 Rs, double from 30 Rs, 'special rooms' from 100 Rs. Warm and cold water. The proprietress promises to pay the taxi fare from the bus stand or railway station for anyone who comes to her. Backpackers' experiences reveal that this appears to be only for people taking the expensive rooms.

In addition, there is a great deal of private accommodation available in Kandy.

SIGHTSEEING

Dalada Maligawa (Temple of the Tooth)

It is situated in the district around the old royal palace, right on the main street next to the lake. The Temple complex consists of innumerable buildings. The whole thing is surrounded by a moat in which there are fishes. Entry is via a bridge flanked by two stone elephants.

The basic fee for a guide is 5 Rs. If there are more than five people, each additional person pays 1 R. The fee for photography amounts to 15 Rs. In the middle of the Temple is the Sanctuary, where the relic, one of Buddha's teeth, rests on a gold lotus blossom under seven concentric gold pagodas.

In one of the Temple outbuildings you will find a library in which are housed rare palm-leaf manuscripts with carved wooden bindings.

The History of the Tooth

The Tooth is supposed to have been smuggled from India to Sri Lanka in the hair of a princess. Once in Sri Lanka, it fell into the hands of the kings of Anuradhapura in the 4th century. During the wars and Tamil invasions in the 10th century, the Tooth was rescued by monks from Ruhuna, in the South. A war is believed to have taken place, because of this relic, against the king of Ruhuna, during which the Tooth was won back and taken to Polonnaruwa, the new capital in the North. The legitimate power of the king thenceforth depended on possession of the Tooth. In the 13th century the Tooth is supposed to have been carried off to India and later to China. When it was back on the island again, the Portuguese ceremonially destroyed the relic as a heathen god. But Buddhists claim that only an imitation and not the real Tooth was destroyed.

Museum

It is on the right near the Temple of the Tooth. The collections of jewellery and weapons once belonged to the royal palace.

Kandy Lake

A boat trip of approximately 10 minutes costs at least 10 Rs per person. If you are the only passenger, you have to pay 25 Rs. It's better to take a walk around the lake. In the evenings especially, you'll see turtles and water snakes. Fishing and swimming are forbidden (or you'll end up in gaol).

Elephant bathing places

Katugastota lies a short way from Kandy on the Mahaweli Ganga. 'Performances' take place daily here from 2.00 p.m. to 4.00 p.m. The locals are used to being paid for being photographed. A real tourist spot.

Another bathing place: take bus no. 655 (in the direction of Travellers Nest) to its terminus. You can watch the elephants bathing from the suspension bridge. Less touristy.

Kandy dances

You can see the old ritual dances of the Kandy Dancers in the Hotel Suisse, Dharmaraja College (opposite the Temple of the Tooth) or at Dance Lanka (Surathura Hall). The Kandy Dancers used not to be allowed to leave the island so that the dances couldn't be copied anywhere else.

The performances last from 7.30 p.m. to 8.30 p.m. and everywhere cost about 50 Rs. You can get further details in the Queens Hotel bookshop.

Udawattakele Sanctuary

This protected area begins right behind the Temple of the Tooth. It's ideal for a jungle walk. You'll see monkeys, birds and magnificent butterflies.

Peradeniya Botanic Garden

This is situated about 7 km outside Kandy. Buses leave from the city bus stand. Take e.g. bus no. 652. The park is open from 8.00 a.m. to 6.00 p.m. Admission costs 15 Rs or half that with an international student card.

The park has existed on the horseshoe-shaped peninsula since the 14th century. It was part of the royal gardens and today is the largest botanical garden in Sri Lanka. There are over 5000 different plants to see. Specialities are the orchid house, the herb garden, the palm avenue and, for some travellers, the coca shrub.

MISCELLANEOUS

The Tourist Office is situated in Queens Hotel, 1st floor, tel. 2121. Open Monday to Friday 8.30 a.m.-4.45 p.m.

The GPO is opposite the railway station. Poste restante is open daily from 8.00 a.m. to 9.00 p.m. The 'parcel man' charges about 10 Rs for a 2.5 kg package, including box and string.

Reading rooms: the British Council Library is opposite the Clocktower and has a fairly extensive library. You'll find amongst other things The Times. Open Tuesday-Saturday 8.30 a.m.-6.00 p.m.

German Library, Wilhelm Geiger Society, Queens Hotel, 1st floor. Limited selection.

Alliance Francaise, 106 Yatinuwara Vidiya.

American Center, side-street opposite Cargills. Open Monday to Friday.

Motorbike hire: enquire at Meewatura Tours, 5 Deva Vidiya, opposite Laksala, tel. 2422.

Shopping: Laksala (not far from Queens Hotel) and Walkers and Cargills department stores are on the main shopping street, Dalada Vidiya. In Walkers, which is crammed full, you'll find many lovely handcrafts and souvenirs near the tourist knick-knacks. You'll find Newsweek, India Today and Asiaweek to read. Kandy is full of antique (real and imitation) shops. You can have disposable lighters refilled in the market quarter for 3 Rs.

On Dalada Vidiya you will find the East China Restaurant and the Devon Restaurant, in which you can have Chinese or Western food.

There's cheap fruit at the market by the bus stand; you can get e.g. a pineapple for from 2 Rs.

Perahera Festival

Every year at the time of the full moon in July/August a large-scale procession takes place over 10 days. During it the Sacred Tooth is carried through the town every night on an elephant. It is accompanied by innumerable decorated elephants, dignitaries and representatives, masked dancers, musicians, drummers, people cracking whips and torchbearers. Buddhists from all over Asia take part in the festival. The Kandy Perahera is Sri Lanka's largest festival and one of the most important Buddhist events.

Warning: at festival time hotel prices sky-rocket. Reserving accommodation is therefore recommended.

FURTHER TRAVEL

C.T.B. buses (from the bus station by the GPO)
Sigiriya: take the 8.05 a.m. direct bus or ordinary bus to Dambulla and change buses there.
Badulla: 7.40 a.m. and 1.45 p.m.
Colombo: 24-hour service; 9.60 Rs; it's possible to make a reservation for 2 Rs.
Trincomalee: 4 buses; the first leaves at 6.30 a.m., the last at 3.15 p.m.
Batticaloa: 4.30 a.m. and 10.15 a.m.; 19.60 Rs.
Polonnaruwa: 8 buses from 4.00 a.m. to 4.30 p.m.
Anuradhapura: 12 buses from 5.00 a.m. to 6.25 p.m.

C.T.B. buses (from the bus stand in Kings Street)
Nuwara Eliya: 13 buses from 4.30 a.m. to 6.00 p.m.
Hatton (for Adams Peak): 10 buses from 5.30 a.m. to 6.30 p.m.
Badulla: some buses between 6.30 a.m. and 1.30 p.m.
Tissamaharama: 8.00 a.m.

Minibuses
There are two minibus stands, one near Kings Street and the other in the GPO district. Minibuses go to Nuwara Eliya, Badulla, Colombo, Trincomalee, Polonnaruwa etc.

Rail

There are services to, amongst other places, Colombo, Hatton, Haputale, Badulla, Bandarawela.

Colombo: 2.10 a.m., 6.45 a.m., 9.35 a.m., 2.57 p.m., 5.00 p.m., 6.25 p.m.; 3rd class costs 10.90 Rs.

Badulla: direct trains at 5.00 a.m. and 9.45 a.m.; indirect service at 10.55 p.m.; 3rd class 16.60 Rs

From Kandy to Kalkudah

Instead of travelling all the way to Batticaloa, get out at Eravur and wait for the bus to Kalkudah. If one doesn't come for some time, take the bus to Vallachchenai. Change buses there or take a taxi for 20 Rs. There is a considerable chance that other backpackers will be waiting at the bus station and could share taxi costs with you to Kalkudah.

Adams Peak-2242 m. above sea-level

This mountain is venerated as much by Buddhists and Hindus as by Muslims and Christians. At its summit is an indentation in the stone (1.60 m x 75 cm) that is believed by the four religions to be the footprint of Buddha, Shiva, St Thomas and Adam respectively. The summit is surrounded by Adams Peak Wilderness Sanctuary, an almost impenetrable mountain jungle. There's an information office on the Peak.

The Ascent from Maskeliya/Arrival

By train or bus to Hatton, then change for Maskeliya or take a direct bus from Kandy (a five-hour journey). Accommodation is available in Maskeliya.

The ascent

To reach the top of the mountain you have to climb steps for about three hours. This is really strenuous. At night the pilgrimage path is lit by electric lights. The way is bordered by countless tea shops and resting places, so it's not necessary to take food with you.

If you don't want to do the whole climb in one day, you can spend a night on the way up. If you want to experience sunrise on the summit you have to get up really early. The shadow of the mountain at sunrise is impressive and famous.

You can even sleep at the summit, on the cement floor of one of the pilgrim rooms (take a sleeping bag!).

Thousands of pilgrims climb the mountain at pilgrimage time (December to April), especially on religious festivals. At those times the path is often hopelessly crowded.

The ascent from Ratnapura

This route is older, less well-used and more arduous, but therefore more adventurous.

Take the bus from Ratnapura to Carnay Estate, a latex plantation.

It goes about 20 km along the Kalu Ganga. The steep path starts at the plantation and climbs through the jungle.

'8 hours and never again. Very tiring, although there are few steps on this side. The way is also lit here.'

RATNAPURA

90 km from Colombo. It's THE gemstone town. The sapphires, tourmalines, amethysts, rubies and tigers' eyes that are taken from the alluvial soil here have been famous since olden times. Traditional methods of digging and washing the gemstones and jewels are used in the pits and mines. The gemstone business is dominated by Muslims. The area around Ratnapura is hilly and full of latex plantations.

It's possible to get accommodation in a family home. As many of the breadwinners are involved in some way with the gemstone trade, they usually want to do business with you immediately. Since many tourists come here simply because of the stones, the prices in Ratnapura are often higher than in other places.

'Travellers Halt, 30 Outer Circular Road. Double 20 Rs. Recommended.'

The Gemstone Museum is 2 km beyond Gentangama; go by bus from the station in the direction of Gentangama. Admission is about 40 Rs. At the museum you can find out for yourself about prices and qualities of stones.

You can have stones tested for free in the laboratory office.

BADULLA

680 m. Terminus of the Colombo-Kandy-Nanu Oya train line.

Badulla is situated on the Eastern edge of the hill country, in a hill landscape where the tea plantations end and the rice-fields begin. Badulla is a market town with merchants, magicians and doctors.

ACCOMMODATION

YMCA, Bandarawela Road. Only 5 beds. About 12 Rs per person.
Uva Hotel, for years a favourite meeting-place. Double 25 Rs.

SIGHTSEEING

The rail journey through the hills past all the tea plantations is very attractive.

Surrounding rice plantations.

Waterfall: Duhinda Falls (60 m high). Travel about 5 km in the direction of Mahiyagana. After following a 1 km path through the bush you come to the waterfall. There are rock pools which are good to swim in. At weekends the waterfall is overrun with picnicking locals and tourists.

POTTUVIL AND ARUGAM BAY

This is the end of the East coast road. This area with its beaches has

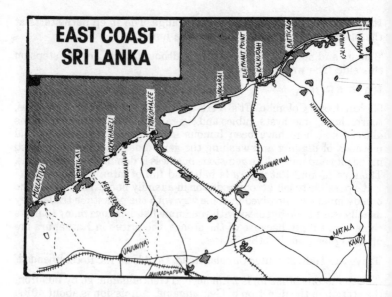

EAST COAST SRI LANKA

not yet been opened up to mass tourism. Many things are still cheap and the choice of hotels and restaurants is small.

Arugam Bay is south (2-3 km) of Pottuvil. Take the bus to Ulla (about 10 minutes, 1.25 Rs). You can get accommodation with fishing families or in the Beach Hut. You have to pay about 10 Rs for the hut.

Ulla beach is rather dirty, but a bit further south, just outside the village, there are beautiful deserted bays. The waves are ideal for surfing. As in Hikkaduwa, you'll meet lots of Australian surfers. As it hardly ever rains here, the tourist season lasts all year.

The area between Pottuvil and Hambantota is a dry, sparsely populated savannah.

'The best place to stay in Arugam Bay is called the Beach Hut. The proprietor is a good guy and has about 12 huts, which he lets for 10 Rs to 15 Rs, irrespective of how many people stay in each. The place is not right on the beach but is nevertheless very pretty.'

SIDE TRIPS
Lahugala
A small wildlife sanctuary 16 km from Arugam Bay in the direction of Wellawaya/Kandy. It's not rare to see herds of up to 50 elephants. There's a Bungalow near the park. Enquire in Colombo at the Department of Wildlife Conservation or at the Nature Protection Society.

Gal Oya National Park

Situated 289 km from Colombo. Size: 260 sq. km. The region around Senanayake Sumadra Lake was declared a protected area in 1954. The main attraction is the herds of elephants which can be watched from a boat. But jeep trips around the park are also possible (ask at the Safari Inn in Inginiyagala).

ACCOMMODATION

Safari Inn, Inginiyagala, tel. 26. Expensive unfortunately. Single about 150 Rs, double about 200 Rs.

In Ekgal Oya, also outside the Park, the Nature Protection Society of Ceylon has a Bungalow; 100 s per person. You can also find cheaper accommodation in Inginiyagala.

BATTICALOA

There's not much to this town. In fact it is only a transport centre with good services to Trincomalee, Polonnaruwa, Kandy, Colombo and Badulla. It's the jumping-off point for Kalkudah. The Dutch landed in Ceylon here for the first time in 1602. Around Batti, as the town is also known, there are lagoons.

Batticaloa has a nice little Dutch fort, but it is famous for its 'singing fish'. With luck they can be heard in the lagoons from April to September, but only on nights of the full moon. The sound is similar to the noise you get by running a wet finger round the top of a wine glass. There are various theories on who or what makes the sounds.

FURTHER TRAVEL

Bus

Kalkudah: 6 buses between 6.30 a.m. and 5.45 p.m.; 3.20 Rs; about a 70-minute trip.

Kandy: 5.30 a.m. and 2.00 p.m.

Pottuvil (Arugam Bay): 6.50 a.m., 9.30 a.m., 1.30 p.m. and 3.00 p.m.

Nuwara Eliya: 8.30 a.m.

Badulla: 5.30 a.m., 7.15 a.m., 8.45 a.m. and 12.30 p.m.

Private bus to Jaffna

Neilanthi Travels, Sivavadavasa Stores, 12 Bazaar Street. Departs about 5.30 p.m. 50Rs fare. Even if you get on after Batticaloa (e.g. in Polonnaruwa), you still have to pay 50 Rs.

KALKUDAH

This small backwater lies 32 km north of Batticaloa. Few people would search out the place if it weren't for its wonderful sandy beach. Kalkudah has been spared the hurly-burly of tourism–except for a few bays on Passekudah Beach which have ostentatious luxury hotels. This is reflected in, for example, the low prices for accommodation.

At the end of 1978 Kalkaduh was destroyed by a powerful cyclone. 80 per cent of the coconut palms were knocked down by the storm. The scars are still clearly visible today.

ARRIVAL/ACCOMMODATION

The C.T.B. buses stop at the post office. There is no regular minibus service to or from Kalkudah.

A horde of touts will surround you as soon as you arrive, all offering to arrange accommodation. As there is a large selection, you can take your time and look at a few different places before choosing.

You can get accommodation in a palm bungalow on the sea from 5 Rs. By ordering in advance you can eat with many families. For example the family near the Government Rest House lets rooms in a fishing hut from 5 Rs. A meal costs about 10 Rs, which is the average price in Kalkudah.

Sandyland: a complex with 30 bungalows, on the beach. Dormitory 10 Rs. The charge for a bungalow for one person is between 17.50 Rs and 40 Rs, and for two people between 25 Rs and 50 Rs. Some bungalows have electric light. If you do without bedlinen, you get a discount of 2.50 Rs on all charges. A restaurant is available. Sandyland is an ideal place to meet other tourists.

Sundis Place. Simple bungalow accommodation. Single 5 Rs, double 10 Rs.

Mala Guest House, opposite Sundis Place. Single 20 Rs, double 25 Rs. Meals are available on request. There is a new building nearby: all rooms have their own bath and electricity. Charges are about 50 Rs.

Government Rest House. It was completely destroyed by the cyclone, but has now been rebuilt.

MISCELLANEOUS

You can hire motor bikes in the Safari Club on the road to Vallachchenai, and bicycles in Kalkudah itself.

Shopping facilities are very limited in Kalkudah. Go to Vallachchenai, where you can get everything.

Along the coast coral reefs are dynamited illegally and exploited. Behind the huts you can watch coral being burnt to chalk.

FURTHER TRAVEL

Bus

From Vallachchenai, 6 km before Kalkudah

Colombo: 7.00 a.m., 10.55 a.m. and 12.20 p.m.

Jaffna: 8.00 a.m. and 7.15 p.m.

Talaimannar: 6.10 a.m.

Anuradhapura: 6.10 a.m. and 8.00 a.m.

Trincomalee: 9.15 a.m.

Polonnaruwa: on the hour at 6.00 a.m., 7.00 a.m., 8.00 a.m., 9.00 a.m., 10.00 a.m. Fare: 4.80 Rs. About a 2-hour journey.

Kalkudah: 9 buses from 5.45 a.m. to 8.50 p.m. About a 15-minute journey.

TRINCOMALEE

This town is supposed to have existed for over 2500 years. Its natural harbour made Trincomalee important. Europeans fought again and again for the bay. After the Dutch, who built Fort Frederick, Trincomalee fell to the English, to the French, then again to the Dutch, and in 1800 it went back to the British. It remained under their rule until Sri Lanka became independent in 1948. Sri Lanka's navy is stationed here. The Mahaweli Ganga flows into the sea in two main estuaries south of Trincomalee.

ACCOMMODATION

Mehila Beach Place, 224 Dyke Street, on the beach. Double 15 Rs to 30 Rs. Has its own restaurant.

Travellers' Halt, 300 Dyke Street. Double from 10 Rs per person. On the beach.

Chinese Rest House, Dyke Street. Double from 25 Rs. Cheap meals on request. On the beach.

Beach Paradise, Dockyard Road, not far from the Chinese Rest House, on Dutch Bay. Double from 20 Rs. Clean and simple.

BEACHES

Kilometre-long sandy beaches stretch from Uppuveli to Irrakkakandi. The tourist season is from May to September, which is the time of the Southwest monsoon, when bad weather dominates the Southwest coast. It's hardly worth spending any time here–or anywhere on the East coast–from November to January, during the winter monsoon.

SIGHTSEEING

Fort Frederick and the harbour.

Swami Rock; a 130-metre high rock in the sea. On the top is a temple. It's worth diving around Swami Rock as there are lots of wrecks on the seabed in the area.

Pigeon Island, so called after the Blue Rock Pigeon that breeds there.

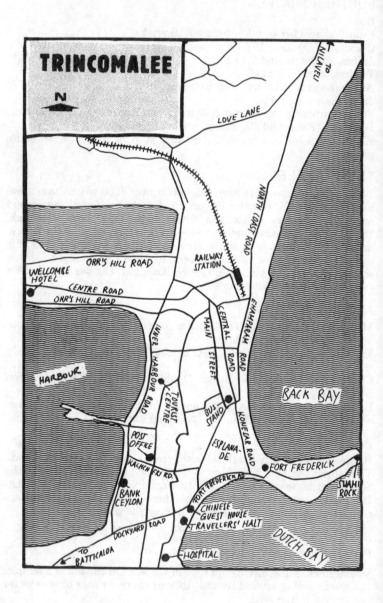

Numerous hotels and restaurants organise boat trips to the island.

Kanniyai Hot Springs. They are situated 10 km North of Trincomalee.

FURTHER TRAVEL

There are direct services to all of the larger places in Sri Lanka. The trip along the coast road to Kalkudah is beautiful; take the boat to Mutur and then a bus to Vallachchenai.

POLONNARUWA

A village with a market, a lake for swimming in, and a large area of ruins. A tip: anyone who isn't interested in ruins shouldn't stop in Polonnaruwa (Polo for short).

The old royal city of Anuradhapura was abandoned in the 8th century because of frequent attacks by Tamils. Polonnaruwa, further to the South, then became the capital. In the eleventh century South Indians occupied the city, so there are Hindu buildings to see, principally a temple to Shiva. A bit later the Singhalese won back the city. Parakramabahu the First (12th century) erected huge buildings, planted parks and constructed Parakrame Samudra reservoir, which is so large that it is called the Sea of Parakrama.

Some time later Polo again fell into Tamil hands. The Singhalese often won the town back until they finally abandoned it in 1314 and it was given over to the jungle for 600 years.

ARRIVAL

By bus from Dambulla, Kandy or Trincomalee. Or by train from Colombo or Batticaloa.

The direct bus from Batticaloa and Vallachchenai to Polonnaruwa goes only as far as the main bus station (Kaduruwala). To reach the old town, where the ruins and hotels are, you have to change buses. There are lots of buses between 4.00 a.m. and 9.30 p.m. The railway station is also in Kaduruwala. If you come from the opposite direction, you must make it clear to the bus driver that you want to get out at the ruins ('ancient sites').

ACCOMMODATION

There are some lodges in the old town, for example:

Wijaya Hotel, right by the 'old town' bus stop. Single 20 Rs, double 30-40 Rs. Good Ceylonese restaurant in the building.

Chinese Tourist Guest House, Circular Road, tel. 027-2011. Single 35 Rs, double 40 Rs, 50 Rs, 60 Rs, 75 Rs and 125 Rs. 10% service charge on all rooms. Own kitchen. Hires out bicycles for 2.50 Rs per hour.

You can also stay in Giritale and make a day trip to Polo whenever you want. Giritale is 15 km outside Polonnaruwa by a bird sanctuary. A bus goes every hour from here to the ruins at Polonnaruwa.

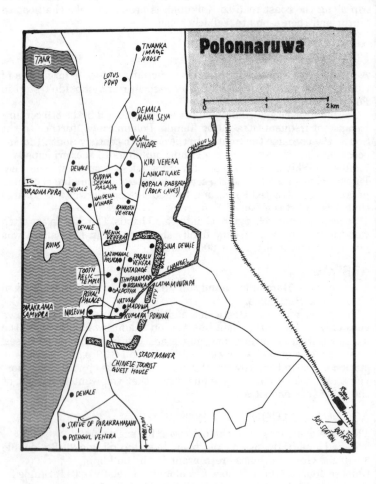

Polonnaruwa

0   1   2 km

TANK

TIVANKA IMAGE HOUSE

LOTUS POND

DEMALA MAHA SEYA

GAL VIHARE

KIRI VEHERA

DEVALE

BUDDHA SEEMA PASADA

LANKATILAKE

GOPALA PABBATA (ROCK CAVES)

CHANNEL

TO ANURADHAPURA

DEVALE

NAIPENA VIHARE

RANKOTH VEHERA

DEVALE

MENIK VEHERA

RUINS

SATHMAHAL PASADA

PABALU VEHERA

SIVA DEVALE

VATADAGE

CHANNEL

TOOTH RELIC TEMPLE

THUPARAMAYA

HISSANKA LATHA MANDAPA

CITY

ROYAL PALACE

GALPOTHA

VATUAS MADUNA

PARAKRAMA SAMUDRA

MUSEUM

KUMARA POKUNA

STADTMAVER

CHINESE TOURIST GUEST HOUSE

DEVALE

STATUE OF PARAKRAMABAHU

POTHGUL VEHERA

RAILWAY
CU.

BUS STATION

SOUTH ROAD

SIGHTSEEING

The temple district lies a few minutes from the old town, near the reservoir. Admission 30 Rs. A photography permit, which is valid also for Sigiriya and Anuradhapura, costs 45 Rs. Charges are paid at the entrance. As a visit is so expensive, many people don't pay the official admission fee any more, but climb over the fence.

FURTHER TRAVEL

C.T.B. bus
Anuradhapura: 5 buses from 5.00 a.m. to 4.30 p.m.
Batticaloa: 8 buses between 5.40 a.m. and 6.20 p.m.
Colombo: 7 buses from 6.15 a.m. to 5.00 p.m.
Jaffna: 10.15 a.m. and 9.00 p.m.
Kandy: 9 buses between 5.15 a.m. and 4.30 p.m.
Talaimannar: 8.40 a.m.
Trincomalee: 11.45 a.m.
Sigiriya: no direct service.

Private buses
To Kandy, Batticaloa, Colombo and Jaffna. The bus stop is, as usual, near the C.T.B. station (Kaduruwala).
Travellers to Jaffna: a luxury bus run by the private company Neilanthi Travels stops by the bus station at about 8.45 p.m. The fare to Jaffna is 50 Rs. The trip takes about 7 hours.

Rail
Batticaloa: 3.00 a.m., 8.00 a.m., 11.46 a.m., 3.45 p.m. and 7.05 p.m.
Colombo: 6.51 a.m., 3.51 p.m. and 10.15 p.m.
Maho: 9.15 a.m. and 5.45 p.m.

DAMBULLA

Can be reached from Polonnaruwa, Trincomalee, Kandy and Anuradhapura. 19 km from Sigiriya.
The five caves of the Cave Temple are in a hill above the village of Dambulla. A staircase leads up to them. They were known even before Christian times. The largest cave is about 50 m long and 6 m high. The caves are full of richly decorated Buddhas in various poses. On the walls you will see frescoes of scenes from the life of Buddha and from Singhalese history.
Monks show visitors around but they don't live in the caves any more. The temple is closed at 7.00 in the evening.

SIGIRIYA

Arrival: no problem by direct bus. Otherwise get out at the Sigiriya turn-off and wait for a connecting bus.
On a rock platform there are lions paws chiselled in the rock. Between them a staircase leads up to the palace ruins and to a plateau with a

wonderful panoramic view. At the foot of the hill is a royal park with ponds.

Tip: do the trip in the morning so that you can watch the shadow of the rock move around.

A 200-metre high rock, the Lion Rock, towers up out of the jungle. On it you can see the remains of the castle of King Kassapa from the 5th century. In those times the rock was a fortress and surrounded by a rampart.

Kassapa succeeded illegally to the throne. He left the royal city of Anuradhapura and barricaded himself in Sigiriya against his brother, whom he had driven out. But a fight between the brothers soon ensued. Kassapa committed suicide. Anuradhapura became the capital again and Sigiriya was forgotten.

The famous frescoes are halfway up the steep ascent. 19 of the original 500 figures remain. It's not clear whether they depict heavenly beings or wives of King Kassapa with their servant women.

ANURADHAPURA

Around 400 BC Anuradhapura was the capital of the Singhalese princes, and since 250 BC, when King Tissa was converted to Buddhism, it has been a holy city for Ceylonese Buddhists. The shoot of the sacred bo tree that was given to King Tissa grew here, cared for by many 'guardians'. It is said to be the oldest living tree in the world, having been planted in 250 BC.

Anuradhapura was for a long time the commercial and administrative centre of the island. From the foundation of the city onwards, the rulers ensured the survival of rice cultivation around the city with an irrigation system of reservoirs and an extensive canal network. These water installations still dominate the character of this pilgrim town today, even if the enormous scale of the old city (it covers an area of over 600 sq. km) sometimes makes one forget them.

The new town on the Nuwarawewa lies outside the sacred area and is today the capital of the province. The railway station, both bus stations (the newer is a little outside in the direction of Colombo), post office and most hotels are situated here.

ACCOMMODATION

The hotel district is in two locations–by Jaffna Junction and the New Bus Stand. Both places can be reached by bus (80 cents) from the railway station and the Old Bus Stand respectively.

Jaffna Junction district

Travellers' Halt Youth Hostel, 15 Jaffna Junction, tel. 290. Single 20 Rs with mosquito net; double 25 Rs without, 35 Rs with mosquito net, 50 Rs with mosquito net and fan; 5-bed dormitory 10 Rs/bed. Has its own restaurant. Bicycles: 2.50 Rs per hour or 20 Rs per day.

Kings Dale, 520 Mihintale Road, tel. 575. Single 30 Rs, double 40 Rs

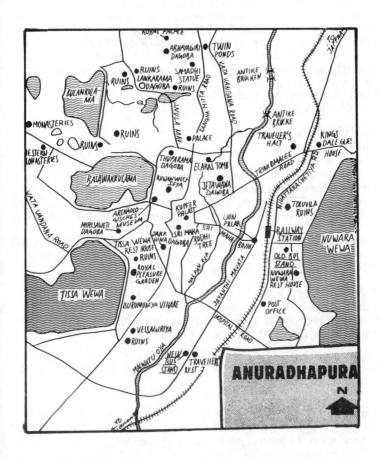

with mosquito net and bath, 60 Rs with mosquito net, bath and fan; 5-bed dormitory 10 Rs/bed. Has its own restaurant. Hires out bicycles and arranges jeep tours to Wilpattu National Park. The return fare for four people costs 650 Rs.

Near the New Bus Stand
Travellers' Rest (Jayawardena Hotel), opposite the bus station, tel. 611. Single 30 Rs, double 40 Rs. All rooms have mosquito nets. Ceylonese restaurant on the ground floor. Hires out bicycles.
Hotel Monara, 63 Freeman Mawatha; walk about 200 m from the New Bus Stand towards the town centre, and then take the first street on the right; tel. 210. Single 100 Rs, double 130 Rs. 10% service charge. Restaurant and bar available.
Little Paradise, 622/18 Godage Mawatha, near the Hotel Monara. Single and double from 30 Rs to 100 Rs.

SIGHTSEEING

The ruined city, which is extensive, is worth seeing. Because of the city's size, it's a good idea to hire a bicycle. There are no admission charges, but you have to pay 45 Rs per camera. This permit is then valid also for Polonnaruwa and Sigiriya. The permit will be checked in only a few places, e.g. at the Samadhi statue. You can buy the permit in the Archaeological Department of the Museum. Open from 9.00 a.m. to 5.00 p.m.

The free brochure 'Anuradhapura' put out by the Tourist Board is recommended. The Tourist's Guide Sketch Map of Anuradhapura is rather clearer; it is available in some hotels for 15 Rs.

FURTHER TRAVEL

Bus (from the Old Bus Stand)
Colombo: between 12.15 a.m. and 10.00 p.m.; 15.80 Rs.
Jaffna: 6.30 a.m., 11.30 a.m. and 2.10 p.m.; 16 Rs.

Bus (from the New Bus Stand)
Trincomalee: about 8 buses between 4.30 a.m. and 4.30 p.m.; 12 Rs.
Batticaloa: 11.20 a.m.
Talaimannar: 5.00 a.m., 7.00 a.m., 8.20 a.m. and 6.45 p.m.; 12 Rs.

Minibuses
They leave from the Old Bus Stand, but pass by the New Bus Stand to pick up extra passengers if the bus is not full.
Colombo: about 10 buses from 6.30 a.m. to 7.00 p.m.; 25 Rs.
Dambulla: about 8 buses daily; 10 Rs.
Kandy: about 8 buses daily; 15 Rs.

Rail
Jaffna: 12.25 a.m., 2.15 a.m., 3.45 a.m., 9.48 a.m., 1.05 p.m., 4.17 p.m. and 9.32 p.m.; 3rd class 17.20 Rs.
Colombo: 12.20 a.m., 2.07 a.m. (not on Tuesday, Thursday or Saturday),

2.55 a.m. (Tuesday, Thursday, and Saturday only), 5.23 a.m., 10.22 a.m., 12.56 p.m. (slow; not recommended), 4.15 p.m. and 10.40 p.m.; 3rd class 18.50 Rs.

Talaimannar Pier: 1.03 a.m. and 1.24 p.m.; 3rd class 12 Rs.

PS: The trains that leave Colombo at 6.50 p.m. and 7.25 p.m (Monday, Wednesday and Friday only) both leave Anuradhapura at about 1.03 a.m. It's difficult to get a reservation in Anuradhapura for these night trains as most of the sleepers and sleeperettes are already booked up from Colombo.

WILPATTU NATIONAL PARK

Established in 1938, Wilpattu National Park has an area of 1050 sq. km and, together with Yala National Park, is an important sanctuary in Sri Lanka.

ARRIVAL

Anuradhapura is the departure point for a visit to the park. The park entrance is 40 km away.

a) Take a C.T.B. bus (3 Rs) from either the Old or the New Bus Stand or a minibus (5 Rs) in the direction of Pattalam. After 30-45 minutes' travelling time, get out at Wilpattu Junction, which is 8 km from the park entrance. Up to 20 hire-jeeps will be waiting there.

b) You can make the trip in a jeep hired in Anuradhapura. Enquire in the Hotel Kings Dale (see 'Accommodation') or in one of the tourist hotels on the Nuwarawewa.

What does it cost to visit the Park?

Admission to the park costs 50 Rs per person. Fixed charges: a jeep trip from Wilpattu Junction is 450 Rs, from Anuradhapura 650 Rs; vehicle charge 25 Rs; driver's fee 5 Rs. If you take the trip on your own, the whole thing will cost you 530 Rs from Wilpattu Junction. If you can share the costs with three other people–there's room for four paying passengers apart from the driver and look out–you have to pay 210 Rs for the section from Wilpattu Junction.

Where can you find people to share the costs?

Ask in the hotels given in the chapter on Anuradhapura under 'Accommodation'. If you don't have any luck, go to Wilpattu Junction on the off-chance and try to get a group together there (see also 'Accommodation near the Park').

If you can't find anyone to go with you and still want to visit the Park, ask for a discount tariff (you get a reduction of about 100 Rs) or ask the jeep-owner if he's prepared to make a shorter trip for a reduced price.

PARK VISIT

It's preferable to make the trip early in the morning or late in the afternoon. The round trip takes 3-4 hours. The look-out takes pains to

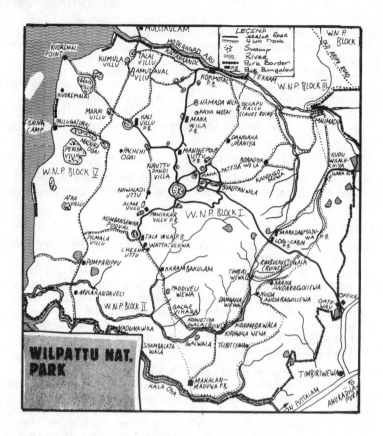

WILPATTU NAT. PARK

show you the numerous leopards that the Park is famous for. In 1979 the Park suffered badly from drought, so extra artificial water-holes were constructed.

There's a charming museum by the Park entrance. There you can get the 'Map of Wilpattu National Park' for 3.50 Rs.

ACCOMMODATION

In the Park
Eight bungalows are let in the Park area by the Department of Wildlife Conservation (see 'Colombo'). Charges and conditions are the same as for Yala Park.

Near the Park
Preshamel Tourist Hotel, at Wilpattu Junction. Only has doubles, for 150 Rs. 10% service charge. Runs a jeep service to the Park.

Hotel Wilpattu, Kala Oya, 10 minutes by bus from Wilpattu Junction, by the bridge over the Kala-Oya River. Single 145 Rs to 180 Rs, double 180 Rs to 250 Rs. With a bit of luck you can see crocodiles in the river. Runs a jeep service.

Campers

In contrast to Yala National Park, Wilpattu is not forbidden to private vehicles. The Park can be toured during opening hours from about 6.00 a.m. to 6.00 p.m. It's compulsory to take a guide, who nevertheless costs nothing, with you. Charges are therefore only the 50Rs for admission and 25 Rs for the vehicle.

Attempts are under way to establish a Park coach service and to forbid private traffic in the Park.

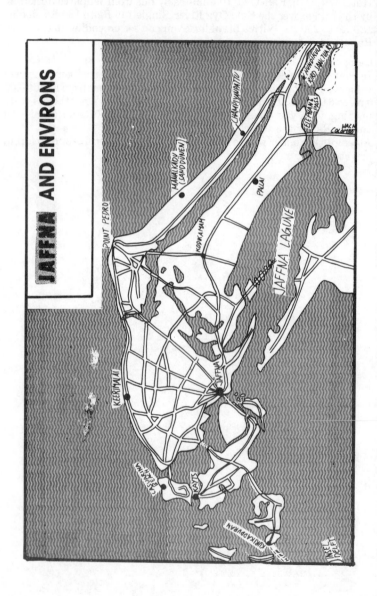

JAFFNA AND ENVIRONS

JAFFNA

Population 125,000. Situated on the northernmost tip of the island, it's the least visited region of Sri Lanka. You'll meet Tamils all over the island, but here their culture and religion dominate. The contrasts with the South–whether of climate or religion–are great and obvious.

Jaffna was formerly the capital of an independent Tamil kingdom. It was also the last Portuguese foothold on Ceylon before the Dutch arrived.

Today Jaffna is a market centre for fruit (grapes, mangoes and pomegranates), cotton and tobacco. Salt is extracted by evaporation from sea-water along the coast.

Depending on the state of the civil war it is unlikely that tourists will be able to visit the city or region.

ARRIVAL

By rail
The railway station lies a little outside the centre. Buses go from there to the centre.

By bus
Buses arrive at the bus station in the centre. There is only one bus station in Jaffna.

ACCOMMODATION

Grand Hotel, 37 Beach Road, tel. 544. Single 15 Rs, double 30 Rs. The front rooms have a clear view over the lagoon. Has its own bar with, e.g., Becks' Beer at 19 Rs a bottle.
YMCA, opposite Kancheri, bus 793 for 80 cents from the bus station; tel. 7151. The YMCA isn't within walking distance of the rail or bus stations for a fully laden backpacker. Single 17.50 Rs without a fan, 20 Rs with a fan; double 25 Rs and 30 Rs respectively. Only for men.
Subhas Tourist Hotel, 15 Victoria Road, near the bus station, tel. 7228. Actually a 'better' hotel (150-300 Rs for a single, 200-350 Rs for a double), but it has some 'economy class' 2-bed rooms. Single occupancy 75 Rs, double 100 Rs. 10% extra service charge. Bar available.

SIGHTSEEING

Nallur Temple
This Hindu temple is on Point Pedro Road. Its facade is covered with statues of various Hindu gods. A large Hindu temple festival with richly colourful processions takes place every year in July/August.

Old Fort
Built by the Dutch in 1680 and well preserved.

Lagoon
You'll find a fishing settlement on the lagoon, near the Customs House on Reclamation Road.

Nearly all Hindu culture, and most evidence of it, was completely destroyed under Portuguese rule, so there's not very much to see. As a result, excursions to Delft and the 'Mini-Sahara' at Manalkadu are all the more fascinating and worthwhile.

Excursions

Delft, the island of ponies
Take bus 776 from the Central Bus Station to its terminus Kurikadduvan; 32 km; about an hour's journey; 5 Rs. To connect with the first boat you have to take the 7.30 a.m. bus. Boats leave at about 9.00 a.m., 11.00 a.m. and 3.00 p.m. The fare is 50 Ps. You may see lots of flying fishes during the crossing.

When you arrive on Delft, take the local bus to Welawa Junction. You have to walk about 3 km from there to get to the ponies. These are about 100 descendents of the 'wild ponies' that were brought here from Arabia by the Portuguese in the sixteenth century. They are not particularly timid, so you can get quite close to them. The number of ponies is continually declining, so there have been many calls to declare their pasture-land a sanctuary.

The last boat returns to Kurikadduvan at about 3.00 p.m. If you want to stay overnight on Delft, you should organise accommodation early in the day. There are no hotels but it's possible to spend the night at the Delft police station or in the school.

Mini-Sahara of Manalkadu
Take bus 750, 751 or 752 (or a minibus) from the Central Bus Station to Point Pedro (about 34 km). Change there to a local bus (625), going towards Champiyanpattu. You must get out at Manalkadu Junction. It's not far to the fishing village of Manalkadu, but it's boiling hot. There are only Palmyra palms and sand to be seen. It's hard to believe one's still in Sri Lanka. A lot of trucks travel the sand track to Manalkadu, because of the sandmining for building purposes. It's possible to hitch a ride on a truck.

Beaches
Casuarina Beach, 24 km from Jaffna by bus 782; 2.60 Rs. Sandy beach and calm sea.
Keerimalai, 21 km from Jaffna by bus 769. The sea is quite rough and the beach is rocky.

Chundikulam Bird Sanctuary–This bird sanctuary lies about 80 km Southeast of Jaffna.

MISCELLANEOUS
The GPO is near the Clocktower. Poste restante Monday-Saturday

24-hour service, Sunday 8.00 a.m.-10.00 a.m. and 3.00 p.m.-midnight.

Newspapers and magazines: you can get Sri Lankan daily papers, Newsweek and Asiaweek in the Poobala Singham Book Depot (first crossroads by the bus station).

Maps: the Hotel Subhas publishes two advertising pamphlets in which are printed a town map of Jaffna and a general map of Jaffna and district.

Souvenirs: Jaffna gold filigree work and basketwork of Palmyra palm leaves are well-known craftworks.

FURTHER TRAVEL
C.T.B. long-distance bus service
Leaves from the Central Bus Station. Reservations are possible for 5 Rs.
Batticaloa: 7.30 a.m. and 5.45 p.m.; 30.80 Rs.
Trincomalee: 5.30 a.m., 8.00 a.m. and 2.00 p.m.; 21.60 Rs.
Mannar: 5.15 a.m., 10.00 a.m. (19.60Rs to Talaimannar), 12.30 p.m. and 3.00 p.m.
Anuradhapura: 3 buses; 16 Rs.
Colombo: no direct C.T.B. services.

Private bus service–large, comfortable buses.
To Colombo:
a) K.G. Express Bus Service, opposite Wellington Theatre, tel. 559. Daily departures at 7.30 p.m. and 8.00 p.m. 65 Rs. Warning: even if you travel only part of the way, you still have to pay the full fare!
b) Sri Mahal Traders, near the bus station. Daily at 8.00 p.m. 60 Rs. Same conditions as K.G. Express.
c) Ajantha Travel Service (AC bus), Hotel Brinthavanam, Hospital Road. Daily at 8.00 p.m. It costs 50 Rs to Colombo. Same conditions as a) and b).
d) Jaffna Cooperative Stores Ltd, 420 Hospital Road, tel. 438. Departs daily at 8.00 p.m. 35 Rs to Anuradhapura, 55 Rs to Colombo.
To Batticaloa and Kalmunai:
Neilanthi Travels, 274 Sivankovilady Road, tel. 7348. Departs daily at 5.30 p.m. It costs 50 Rs to Batticaloa, 55 Rs to Kalmunai.

Minibuses
Two buses daily to Trincomalee and to Batticaloa. Leave from the Central Bus Station.

Rail
Colombo: 6.20 a.m., 7.55 a.m., 12.25 p.m., 6.25 p.m. and 7.05 p.m. 3rd class costs 35.70 Rs.

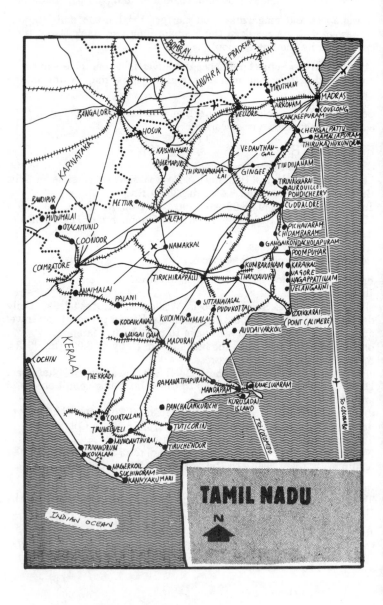

TAMIL NADU

N

INDIAN OCEAN

FROM SRI LANKA
TO SOUTH INDIA

To Talaimannar and by ferry to Rameswaram

Two trains travel every day from Colombo to Talaimannar. To catch the ferry, which according to the timetable leaves for India at 9.00 a.m. on Tuesday, Thursday and Saturday, you have to take a train from Colombo Fort the evening before (at 6.50 p.m. or 7.25 p.m., depending on which day of the week it is). This should arrive at Talaimannar at about 5.00 a.m.–but, in fact, it is usually a good hour late. You'll probably also experience a delay of 30-60 minutes in the departure time of the ferry. The train fare in third class is 26.40 Rs. As all trains going directly to the ferry are always hopelessly full, you can indulge yourself by travelling in the less crowded 2nd class for twice the price, instead of spending a 'heavy' night in 3rd class. The investment is worth it.

'Important: It's best to book ferry tickets 10 days in advance in Colombo, as no tickets are sold in Talaimannar any more. They send back to Colombo for them, so you could be waiting for days.'

Theoretically you can make ferry bookings in Talaimannar, but only if there are seats still available. However, as they are mostly booked up from Colombo, you'll be in trouble, as has been described. Book in Colombo at Asha Agencies, 72 New Buller's Road, Colombo 4, tel. 87892-4. Upper deck costs 175 Rs, lower deck 125 Rs. Usually only upper-deck tickets are sold to tourists.

In Colombo you can also buy Indian train tickets (for example to Madras and Madurai). A second-class train ticket to Madurai, including an upper-deck ferry ticket, costs 241 Rs. Book at Colombo Fort railway station, platform 4, 7.30 a.m.-6.00 p.m. on Monday, Wednesday and Friday, and between 7.30 a.m. and 2.00 p.m. on other days. You have to produce a passport with an Indian visa in it. It's not possible to book more than 10 days in advance.

DEPARTURE/CUSTOMS

In Talaimannar you should change back any Sri Lankan rupees you still have left. The bank on the railway platform gives dollars (cash) for them, but no Indian rupees. If asked, you must be able to produce your currency exchange form–if you have lost it, have your money changed by a fellow-traveller. In fact, you can change your Sri Lankan rupees on the streets in Rameswaram, but the rate of exchange there is worse. In addition, Sri Lankan rupees are not accepted in the restaurant on the ship.

You should allow about an hour for all the Customs formalities in Talaimannar–amongst other things, you have to surrender your currency exchange form. You'll get an exit stamp in your passport once you are on board the ship.

The ferry
The ferry service is suspended during the monsoon period in November/December until January. Depending on weather conditions, the journey takes about three hours. You can eat for a reasonable price in the ship's restaurant, but you have to pay in dollars, pounds sterling or Indian rupees (only notes of small-denomination are accepted).

ARRIVING IN INDIA

On the ferry you'll be given two forms to fill in; an Embarkation/Disembarkation Card and a Government of India Disembarkation Card; they should be handed in at Rameswaram.

As an upper-deck passenger you'll have the advantage of disembarking first. European travellers are dealt with separately. If the ship anchors at 12.30 p.m., you'll be on Rameswaram station at 2.30 p.m. at the earliest.

There's a branch of K.O. Nagoormera & Sons in the clearance hall, where you can change cash and travellers cheques. You should be aware that American Express travellers cheques only up to the value of 10 dollars will be accepted. The reason for this is that too many travellers cheques that have been lost or reported stolen have been changed here.

FURTHER INFORMATION FOR TOURISTS TRAVELLING FROM SRI LANKA

For detailed information about taking a vehicle from Talaimannar to Rameswaram see 'By ferry to Sri Lanka'/'General' in the Indian section of this book.

To take your car anywhere by boat you should buy the Daily Shipping List for 30c from any shipping company in Colombo. In it you'll find all shipping information for the following week, including destinations and ports of call. With it you can work out what you want to do and then make contact with the appropriate agent.

An example of shipping to Australia: you can book at three companies–Aitken Spence Shipping Ltd, Nedlloyd and Mackinnon. Transport to Fremantle costs $500 one-way, with or without a container. The maximum height for a container is 2.40 metres. The only catch is that you cannot travel on the ship too.

AIR SERVICES TO INDIA

By Indian Airlines (five flights a week) or Air Lanka (three flights a week) to Trivandrum, four services a week to Bombay, and about two flights a day to Madras. You can also fly from Colombo to Tiruchirapalli. Airfares: US $132.90 to Bombay, US $91.20 to Trivandrum, US $61.50 to Madras.

MADURAI

Population about 700,000. 100 m above sea-level. About 2000 years old, Madurai is one of the oldest cities in India.

ARRIVAL/ACCOMMODATION

Madurai Junction Railway Station and the Express Bus Stand are about 10 minutes' walk from one another. You can get to the cheap lodges situated between the rail and bus stations on foot or by rickshaw.

The 24-hour system of checkout times is usual in Madurai.

Cheap hotels between the railway station and Sree Meenakshi Temple
Saraswathi Lodge, Town Hall Road, tel. 25873. Single 15 Rs, double 25 Rs.
Uma Lodge, West Perumal Maistry Street (a side-street off Town Hall Road), tel. 26621. Single 8 Rs, double 15 Rs.

Hotels with a view of Sree Meenakshi Temple:
Lodge Senthil, 8-9 North Chitrai Street, tel. 32384. Single 8 Rs, double 15 Rs.
Lodge Saravana, 16/17 North Chitrai Street, tel. 27293. Single 8 Rs, double 15 Rs (25 Rs with bath), triple with bath 35 Rs.
Ambika Lodge, East Chitrai Street. Single 7-10 Rs, double 12 Rs.

Middle-class hotels
Tourist Bungalow, West Veli Street (opposite the Express Bus Stand), tel. 31455. Single 30 Rs (60 Rs with AC), double 40/45 Rs (90 Rs with AC), 4-bed room 60 Rs, extra bed 10 Rs (20 Rs in a room with AC).

SIGHTSEEING

Sree Meenakshi Sundareswarar Temple
The Sree (Sri) Meenakshi Temple, situated 1 km from the Railway Junction, is one of the most beautiful temple complexes in India. Built in the seventeenth century, it covers an area of 254 x 237 m, according to official information. The temple on the South side is devoted to Sree Meenakshi, the consort of Shiva, and the other to Shiva (Lord Sundareswarar). The tallest of the five towers is on the South side and is decorated with over 1000 statues.

In April/May the marriage of Meenakshi and Sundareswarar is celebrated with the Chithirai festival.

Non-Hindus are allowed to visit almost every part of the temple. Open 5.00 a.m.-1.00 p.m. and 4.00-10.00 p.m. For a fee of 5 Rs you can also visit the temple between 1.00 p.m. and 4.00 p.m.; you can photograph the interior of the temple only during this time–the photography fee is included in the 5 Rs (take a flash with you!).

You can climb the 55-metre high South Tower for 50 Ps between 6.00

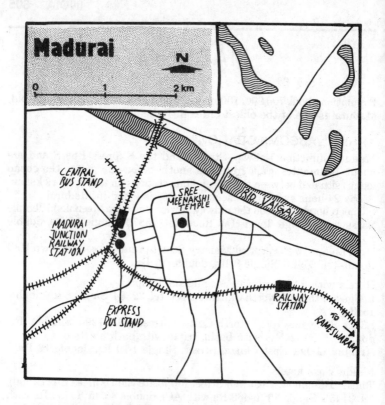

a.m. and 5.30 p.m. Marvellous view of the whole temple complex and of Madurai. Don't miss it!

The Temple Art Museum (admission 50 Ps, camera 5 Rs extra) is interesting for temple enthusiasts. It's situated in the '1000-pillared hall' (in fact almost 1000 pillars–it's three short of the full 1000).

MISCELLANEOUS

Government of Tamil Nadu Tourist Office, Wet Veli Street, opposite the bus station, tel. 22957. Open 10.30 a.m.-5.00 p.m. Closed Sunday and every second Saturday in the month. Tourist Information Counter at the railway station, tel. 24535. Open 7.00 a.m.-8.00 p.m.; Saturday, Sunday and public holidays 7.00-10.30 a.m. and 5.00-8.00 p.m.

The GPO is situated on Scott Road, near the railway station. Poste Restante is open from Monday to Saturday 7.00 a.m.-6.00 p.m., Sunday 10.00 a.m.-6.00 p.m. The State Bank of India and Indian Airlines are both also on the road from the railway station to the GPO.

You can get Time and Newsweek in the Carter Book House (named after the American ex-President) at 15 West Veli Street.

Sightseeing trips are organised by, e.g., A-1 Travels, 84 West Perumal Maistry Street. Daily at 9.30 a.m. For 7.50 Rs you can take in, amongst others, the following attractions: Thirupparankundram Temple, Perumal Temple, Sree Meenakshi Temple, Thirumalai Nayak Palace, the Gandhi Museum and the Vishnu temple Alagar Koil, 21 km Northeast of Madurai.

Food: the AC restaurant Aradana, near Uma Lodge, is good. Close by are numerous cheaper restaurants. You can also eat at any time of the day or night at the street stalls in the side-streets off Town Hall Road.

FURTHER TRAVEL

Rail

To Madras: 6 or 7 services daily to Madras Egmore.
To Pondicherry: by rail in the direction of Madras. Change in Tiruchchirappalli and Villupuram if the train takes the main line. Stay on the train on all services on the (shorter) 'chord line' to Villupuram. However, it's better to take a bus as some rail services to Pondicherry take up to 16 hours.
To Rameswaram (and Sri Lanka): 5.35 a.m., 1.40 p.m., 5.40 p.m. and 10.45 p.m. every day; 164 km. The night train (which arrives at Rameswaram at 5.00 a.m.) gives a direct connection to the ferry which only travels, however, on Monday, Wednesday and Friday. In Madurai you can buy a ticket all the way to your destination in Sri Lanka (e.g. Colombo). Usually tickets for the more expensive upper deck only are sold to tourists.
To Coimbatore: 12.25 p.m. and 10.10 p.m. every day.
To Quilon: 6.15 a.m. and 8.35 p.m. every day.

Bus

Below is an extract from timetable of services from the Express Bus Stand:
Madras (483 km): 24-hour service; about 30 buses; 28.20 Rs.
Kottayam: 5.00 a.m., 9.00 a.m., 12.30 p.m., 7.15 p.m.; 22 Rs.
Calicut: 9.30 a.m., 8.30 p.m.; 24 Rs.
Bangalore (400 km): 12.19 a.m., 6.30 a.m., 7.00 p.m., 8.00 p.m., 9.00 p.m.; 28.20 Rs.
Trivandrum (267 km): 2.30 a.m., 7.30 a.m.; about 27 Rs.
Coimbatore: 12.06 a.m.-11.00 p.m., about hourly; 14.50 Rs.
Kannyakumari (Cape Comorin): 12.44 a.m.-11.30 p.m., almost hourly; 17.70 Rs.
Pondicherry: 2.44 a.m., 9.15 p.m., 10.00 p.m., 11.30 p.m.; 22.40 Rs.
Another possibility: take the Madras bus and change in Villupuram. Apart from these State buses, private companies also operate on some routes (e.g. to Bangalore).

Air

There's one direct flight daily to Madras and three times weekly to Bangalore.

KODAIKANAL

Kodaikanal, 2125 m above sea-level, was once a favourite resort of English colonials, rather like Ootacamund. Today it is a favourite holiday place during the hot season for rich Indians escaping the sweltering heat of the lowlands. During the Kodaikanal season hotel prices increase enormously.

ARRIVAL

By bus from Madurai Central Bus Stand: services between 4.45 a.m. and 4.00 p.m.; 8.45 Rs. By bus from Kodaikanal railway station at 6.10 a.m., 7.00 a.m., 8.20 a.m., 10.45 a.m. and 4.00 p.m., or by bus from Coimbatore via Palani.

ACCOMMODATION

The best thing to do is to get a tout to take you, as soon as you arrive at the bus station, to the MNS Lodge, which is by far the best lodge in Kodaikanal but is not very easy to find. Lovely rooms from about 5 Rs to 15 Rs. If it's fully booked, try the Paradise Lodge nearby. Warning: even in these two lodges prices soar during the season.

MISCELLANEOUS

The Tourist Office is situated in the Town Ship Office by the lake.

After Pokhara/Nepal, Kodaikanal is the second most famous place for 'magic mushrooms'. These mushrooms are found almost only after it has rained and they prefer to grow in cow dung. To test whether they are the real thing: cut them–if they're real, the place where you've cut them will immediately turn blue.

Food: the Muslim Restaurant is good, and will even prepare 'magic omelettes' on request, but you have to bring the mushrooms with you. For gourmets a visit to the bakeries, shops and the market is worthwhile: black bread, apples (expensive), honey, cheese and tasty cheap tomatoes are available.

The reservoir, built in 1853, is in fact quite clean, but is rather too cold to swim in.

FURTHER TRAVEL

By bus to Madurai or Coimbatore.

PONDICHERRY

The Ashram and Beach are (in alphabetical order) the special features of Pondicherry, which is called Pondi by the locals.

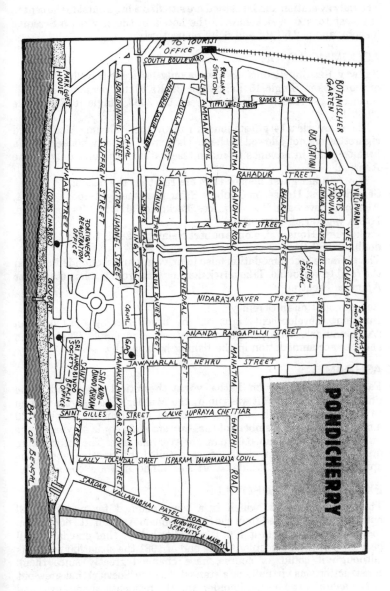

ARRIVAL

The railway station and bus stand are situated a little outside the centre. It's best to take a rickshaw to the hotels in the city or to Serenity (beach); about 2.50 Rs and 6 Rs respectively.

ACCOMMODATION

Railway Retiring Rooms, as always only for train travellers with an onward ticket. Single 15 Rs, double 30 Rs. Extra person: 3 Rs.
Shanti Guest House, 6 Saffren Street, tel. 2983. Single 10 Rs, double 20-30 Rs.

There are also 14 guest houses run by the Ashram. Alcohol and cigarettes are not allowed in them. They are often fully booked, so it's best to write in advance to make reservations. Enquire only at the Ashram.

Two Ashram guest houses that are right on the beach:
Seaside Guest House, on Goubert Salai, near the light-house, tel. 494. All rooms have bath. Various prices. Reckon on about 30 Rs per person. Has a vegetarian restaurant.
Park Guest House, also on Goubert Salai, tel. 2971. Single 10-80 Rs, double 20-80 Rs.
There's more accommodation (also in private houses) outside Pondi on the road to Auroville. Take a rickshaw or bus (from the bus station or Ajantha Theatre).

Accommodation in Serenity
Bungalow development right on the beach run by a Frenchman ('Aurobindian'). 6 Rs per person. Restaurant available. There's even cheaper accommodation in the fishing huts nearby.

ASHRAM

Famous for courses on hatha yoga, theoretical yoga and Vedic philosophy. Until 1973 it was run by the 'Mother'. The Ashram is open to everyone, although at different times for different people: 4.30 a.m.-11.00 p.m. for members of the Ashram and people staying in the guest houses; 8.00 a.m.-6.00 p.m. for everyone else. The information office at the Ashram gladly gives detailed information about the spiritual 'menu'. The 'Guide to Sri Aurobindo Ashram' costs 75 Ps.

EXCURSION TO AUROVILLE

This famous project, which is a town planned for people of all nationalities, developed from the Sri Aurobindo Ashram. Its population today is a fairly constant 400. It's hard to believe that one day it will be a town of 50,000 people. At the end of 1981 the situation was thus (although it could, of course, have changed greatly since then): construction was virtually at a standstill as the 'Society' that grew out of the ashram, the actual founder and the residents of the town had fallen out, and were fighting a legal battle. The case came to the

Supreme Court in Delhi. Until it is decided, all Auroville businesses are being run by a court-appointed administrator. So the 'new city for spiritual co-existence' is, like (almost) every dream of an ideal society that people try to put into practice, struggling under conflicts of interest that surely no court decision will solve.

Arrival from Pondi
Take a bus in the direction of Madras, get out after about 10 km at the turn-off to Auroville, and continue on foot. This option is cheap but tiring as it's quite a long walk.

It's better to hire a bicycle or go by scooter for a fixed price.

There's a sightseeing trip every Tuesday and Friday at midday, organised by the Ashram travel bureau, Aurotravels.

MISCELLANEOUS

The Tourist Office is on Uppalam Road, near the railway station. Open 9.00 a.m.-12.30 p.m., 2.00-5.15 p.m., and Saturday 9.00 a.m.-12.45 p.m.

Auroville Information Centre and Reception Centre: Monday-Saturday 9.00 a.m.-12.00 noon and 3.00-5.00 p.m. Closed on Sunday. It is situated a few metres from the Seaside Guest House. Amongst other things, it sells a combined Pondi-Auroville map.

Food: India Coffee House, right on the beach. Also vegetarian food in Bliss, 15 Gingee Street; this is the meeting place for 'Aurobindians', so it's a good place to get word-of-mouth information.

FURTHER TRAVEL

Rail
Only the 162 Pondicherry Express goes directly to Madras. Arrives Madras Egmore at 10.40 a.m.

Bus
To Madras: about 20 buses from 2.00 a.m. to 10.15 p.m.; 9.80/13.95 Rs.
To Nagapattinam: 7 buses from 2.22 a.m. to 11.52 p.m.; 10.50 Rs.
To Coimbatore: 8.00 a.m., 8.00 p.m.; 22.50 Rs.
To Bangalore: 7.25 a.m.; 21.30 Rs.
To Tuticorin: 6.15 p.m.; 30.80 Rs.
To Nagercoil via Madurai: 8.00 a.m., 6.00 p.m., 9.00 p.m.; 37 Rs.
To Madurai: see Nagercoil. Also at 2.45 p.m. and 6.00 p.m.; 23 Rs.

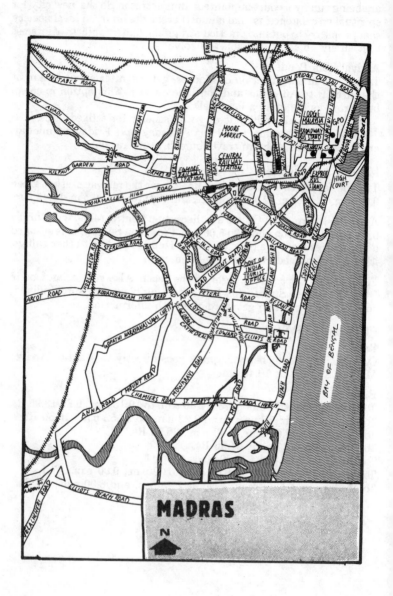

MADRAS

N

MADRAS

The capital of Tamil Nadu. With a population of over 4,000,000, it is India's fourth-largest city. In recent years it has become the most important film industry centre after Bombay and Calcutta. Has one of the longest beaches in the world.

ARRIVAL
By train usually at Central Station, by bus at the Express Bus Stand. There's no distinct cheap-hotel district; cheap hotels are scattered all over the city and to get to them you have to choose between scooters, rickshaws and city buses.

ACCOMMODATION
The 24-hour system operates in most lodges in Madras.
Lodge Malaysia, 44 Armenian Street, tel. 27053. Single 10 Rs, 12 Rs with bath. Double 15 Rs, 20 Rs with bath. Dormitory 5 Rs. Take a bus to Parrys Corner. Two of the proprietor's daughters are practising doctors so he offers his guests free medical advice. Medicines are, of course, not free.
Moorthys' Mansion, same proprietor as Malaysia Lodge, 24 Subramania Mudali Street, tel. 665949. 72 rooms. Single 8 Rs, double 15 Rs, dormitory 4 Rs. Same medical service as at the Malaysia.
YMCA, Esplanade 223, tel. 23941. Single 25 Rs, double 35 Rs. Only for men.
YWCA Guest House, 530 Poonamallee High Road, tel. 39920. Double 48 Rs including breakfast. Car parking: 5 Rs. For 10 Rs you can put up your tent on the camping ground. For men and women.

FOOD
There are lots of restaurants and snack-bars (even with European food) on Mount Road. Also recommended: Ganga, 57 Armenian Street; e.g. tomato spaghetti for 3.25 Rs.

POST
Poste restante in the GPO, First Line Beach, tel. 24289. Open Monday-Saturday 7.00 a.m.-6.00 p.m. Closed Sunday. Right behind the GPO is the Overseas Communication Centre.
   Sending parcels: Spencer's department store has a parcel service. To have a parcel made up there will cost you between 6 Rs and 10 Rs. It's worth it because you won't be able to do it much better or more cheaply yourself.

SIGHTSEEING

Marina Beach: over 7 km long.

Elliots Beach: take e.g. bus 19S, 23C or 4G from Broadway bus stand. Good swimming.

High Court: open from about 10.30 a.m. to 4.30 p.m.

Aquarium: open daily 8.00 a.m.-8.00 p.m.

Light-house on Marina Beach: a lift takes you to the top (1 R). Unfortunately photography is not allowed. Open 2.30-4.30 p.m.; Sunday: 10.00 a.m.-12.00 noon.

Deer Sanctuary: the only national park within a city in India.

Snake Park: about 9.00 a.m.-6.00 p.m.

MISCELLANEOUS

Government of India Tourist Office, 154 Anna Salai (this road is also called Mount Road), tel. 86240/86249. Monday-Saturday 10.00 a.m.-5.00 p.m. Closed 9.00 a.m.-1.00 p.m. on every second Saturday of the month.

Government of Tamil Nadu Tourist Office, tel. 88805/06. Monday-Saturday 10.00 a.m.-1.00 p.m., 2.00-5.00 p.m. Closed on every second Saturday and on Sunday.

Money: you'll find the banks on Anna Salai. The State Bank of India usually has the best rates of exchange.

Health: The 24 Hours Drug House, 225 Royapettah High Road, tel. 847734, is a chemist that's open round the clock. The chemist at Central Railway station is open till 9.30 p.m. Government General Hospital, Park Town, tel. 39181.

Information: 'Hello Madras' (2 Rs) is a very informative and always up to date monthly brochure; has a town map. Also has a good summary of city bus services and lots of important addresses.

Transport: rickshaw and scooter drivers won't take passengers to destinations that are less than 5 Rs away.

English films e.g. in the Casino, 4 Blackers Road.

Visa extensions: Foreigners' Regional Reg. Office, 13 Victoria Crescent Road, tel. 88864.

FURTHER TRAVEL
Rail

Trains leave from Central Station, but some go from Madras Beach. Reservations can take a really long time at Central Stations; queuing for 3 hours isn't unusual. You can also buy 2nd class (not 1st class) tickets in the Southern Railway Booking Office on Anna Salai, tel.

85642; 10.00 a.m.-5.00 p.m.; closed Sunday. Make reservations there two days in advance at the latest.

Departure times (all from Central Station):
To New Delhi: 7.10 a.m.(Monday, Thursday, Saturday only), 10.10 a.m., 2.20 p.m. (2.40 p.m. in summer), 7.20 p.m. (summer: 7.30 p.m.); 2188 km.
To Bombay Victoria Terminus: direct trains at 3.35 p.m. and 10.15 p.m. Arrive 10.55 p.m. and 5.10 a.m. 1279 km.
To Calcutta: it's best to leave at 8.15 a.m. by Coromandel Express, which arrives at Howrah at 9.00 a.m. the next day; 1662 km.
To Trivandrum (via Cochin): one service daily; it's 921 km to Trivandrum.
To Pondi: direct train at 3.55 p.m., arrives 8.55 p.m. There are several trains to Villupuram, where you have to change for Pondi.

Bus
Leave from the Express Bus Stand. Practically all departure times are given correctly in 'Hello Madras', which is THE exception to the general standard of Indian information publications, so get all you need to know there. A reservation costs 50 Ps, and 75 Ps for Super and AC buses.

Air
Several bus services to the airport, e.g. 18A and 52B. Flights to all major Indian towns (see also under 'India-General'/'Flights'). Also flights to Colombo (Sri Lanka).

Ship
To the Andamans and to Penang/Singapore: tickets and information from The Shipping Corporation of India Ltd, K.P.V. Shaik Mohamed Rowther & Co., 202 Linghi Chetty Street, tel. 25756. Open Monday-Saturday 10.00 a.m.-5.30 p.m. The passenger department is closed for lunch from 1.15 p.m. to 2.00 p.m. The 'Shipping Times', in which are listed all ship arrivals and departures, appears every day except Saturday and Sunday. Shipping agents are all in the Armenian Street district. Shipping information arranged according to destination:

ANDAMANS

Shipping Corporation of India ships go every fortnight. Ask the agent in Madras (see above) about exact dates and conditions. The trip from Madras takes about 3-4 days. Fares range from 69 Rs (bunk) to 558 Rs (deluxe). Meals are not included in the fare–you must reckon on another 13 Rs per day in bunk class.

Penang/Singapore
A rough example of fares to Penang: from 1072 Rs (tourist II) to 2450 Rs (deluxe). To Singapore: from 1283 Rs (tourist II) to 2762 Rs (deluxe). Tourists are not allowed to book bunk class. The ship leaves every three weeks. Detailed information from the agent (see above). Route: Madras, Nagapattinam (you can get embark here too), Penang, Singapore. Nagapattinam is not visited from October to January.

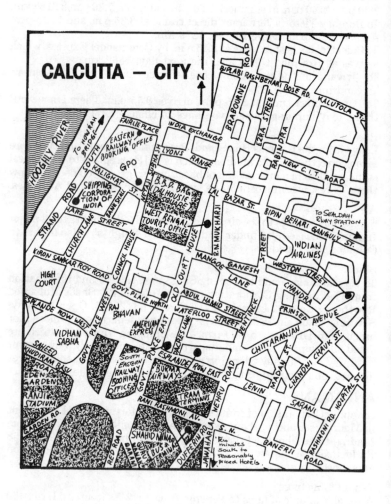

CALCUTTA

The politically restless capital of West Bengal, Calcutta, with some 10 million inhabitants, is the largest city in India. An Indian saying has it that: 'What Calcutta thinks today, India thinks tomorrow'. Outsiders tend to think of overpopulated Calcutta as merely the alms-house of India. This view is not entirely correct, although the slums of Howrah and other parts of the city number among the worst in Asia.

ARRIVAL

Train
Take a No. 5, 6, 12 or 30 tram from Howrah Station, then go on foot to the cheap hotel area on Sudder Street. Otherwise, take one of the numerous city buses (30Ps)–ask for Esplanade or Indian Museum. A taxi direct from Howrah to Sudder Street costs approx. 9 Rs per person. It is also possible to take a tram, bus or taxi (at more or less the same prices) from Sealdah Station to the Sudder Street area.

Bus
Get off at Esplanade and walk from there to Sudder Street.
Plane: Take a city bus (S10 or 30B) for 50 Ps from Dum Dum Airport to Esplanade. Other possibilities are the Indian Airlines Bus (10 Rs) or the coach of another airline to the city. A taxi to Sudder Street costs approx. 30 Rs per person.

ACCOMMODATION

There is a large selection of cheap hotels in the central area of Sudder Street, or nearby.
YMCA, 25 Jawaharlal Nehru Road (Chowringhee Road), Tel. 233504; single with bath and breakfast 45 Rs, double 60 Rs (incl. bath and breakfast). Temporary membership a couple of Rs extra. Women also admitted.

'The YMCA is home to many people who work with Mother Therese and who will gladly take you with them.'

Shilton Hotel, 5A Sudder Street, Tel. 243613; single 25 Rs (30 Rs with bath), double 50 Rs.
Tourist Inn, 4/1 Sudder Street, Tel. 243732; single 25 Rs, double 50 Rs. Total 14 beds, very clean and friendly. Good manager who offers guests 'free yoga advice'.
The Salvation Army Red Shield Guest House, 2 Sudder Street, Tel. 242895; dormitory-style beds (separate for men and women) 12-14 Rs, double also available, 5% tax extra. Check-out time–10.00 a.m.
Hotel White Hall, 5/1 Sudder Street, Tel. 243311; single 10/15 Rs, double 20/25/30 Rs.

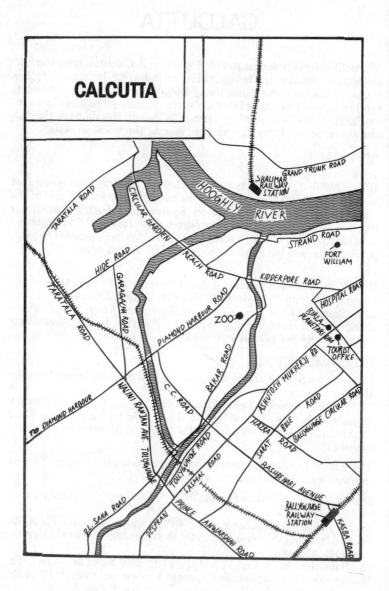

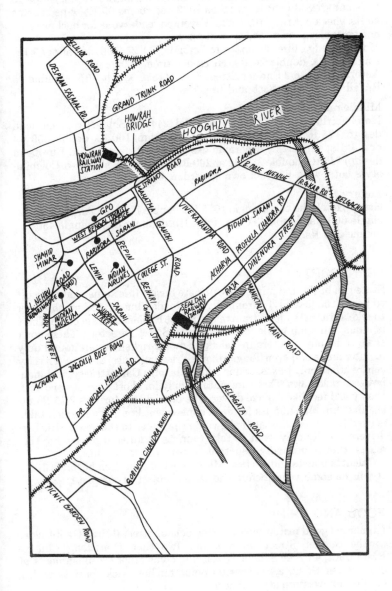

Hotel Paragon, 2 Stuart Lane, Tel. 213115; dormitory 10 Rs, single 15 Rs, double 25 Rs (40 Rs with bath), 3-bed rooms 35 Rs, 4-bed rooms 40 Rs, check-out time 10.00 a.m. Favoured rendezvous for backpackers, not very clean, own modest restaurant.
Modern Lodge, directly opposite Paragon, Tel. 244960; dormitory 7 Rs, single 15 Rs, double 20 Rs, check-out time 10.00 a.m.
Astoria Hotel, 6/2 Sudder Street, Tel. 241359; single 40Rs, double 65 Rs, all rooms with bath and breakfast.

Middle-range Hotels
Hotel Fairlawn, 13A Sudder Street, Tel. 244460. Single (AC, American design) 175 Rs, single (AC, Continental design) 160 Rs, double 250 Rs or 230 Rs; single DC, American design) 155 Rs, single (DC European design) 145 Rs, double 230 Rs or 200 Rs. 25% tax on all prices. Colonial-style hotel with English owner, garden, clean.

Luxury Hotels
Grand Hotel (the best), single 1075 Rs, double 1175 Rs; Airport Ashok, single 660 Rs, double 760 Rs; Park Hotel (inner city), single 450 Rs, double 550 Rs.

TRANSPORT

State-run buses and minibuses, private buses. It is somewhat difficult to board the (usually) chronically overloaded buses, and much easier to take a tram. Ask for a tram map (free) at Esplanade tram office. There is a bus and tram guide in the Calcutta Street Directory. There don't seem to be any scooters in Calcutta, motor-rickshaws are found only in outer areas and even Tongas (horse-drawn vehicles) are rare. The city centre offers only buses, trams and taxis, plus Calcutta's typical man-powered rickshaws. These are suitable only for short journeys and even then you'll feel like a slave-driver. The official taxi tariff is 2.75 Rs for the first km and 1.35 Rs for each subsequent km. A conversion table is used to convert the tariff shown on the meter to the new tariff. Taxi drivers usually only want to take tourists at inflated prices. For this reason they're normally reluctant to turn the meter on.
    Calcutta boasts India's first Metro. Partial operation began in 1982. It will be some years before the whole project is complete.

FOOD AND DRINK

Numerous good restaurants on Free School Street (Mirza Galib), close to the Sudder Street intersection. Two tips: Hongkong Chinese Restaurant, 44 Free School Street, and some other establishments at 55A; Super Snax, a rendezvous point for homesick tourists with a craving for western-style snacks.
    Also recommended: the Chinese restaurants on Bentinck Street (extension of Jawaharlal Nehru Road.)

SIGHTSEEING

The Howrah Bridge is Calcutta's main landmark. From the Bridge (457 m long) you can watch freshwater dolphins playing in the muddy-brown waters of the Hooghly River, a lesser tributary of the Ganges. It will cost you 25 Ps to take the ferry across to the other side.

If you obtain a permit, which is cost and hassle-free from the Commisssioner of Police, Lal Bazar Street, you can climb the 50 m high Shaheed Minnaret (still referred to occasionally as the Ochterlony Monument). It is forbidden, according to a sign, to take along cameras and umbrellas(!).

Also worth seeing: Indian Museum (Sudder Street), Victoria Memorial, Jain Temple and the Zoo, with its white tigers.

POST

The Poste Restante office of the GPO in Dalhousie Square (Tel. 236899/221451) is open from Monday-Saturday, 7.00 a.m.-8.30 p.m. Closed Sunday and public holidays.

New Market Post Office (Free School Street) is located close to the cheap hotel area.

American Express Office, 21 Old Court House Street, Tel. 236281; 'clients mail' can be collected from Monday-Friday, 10.00 a.m.-1.00 p.m. and 3.00-4.00 p.m., and Saturday 10.00 a.m.-12.00 noon.

VISAS

Nepalese Consulate, Woodlands, 19 Sterndale Road, Tel. 45293; open Monday-Friday, 10.00 a.m.-1.00 p.m. and 2.00-5.00 p.m., and Saturday 10.00 a.m.-1.00 p.m. A 30-day visa costs 90 Rs. Three application forms and three passport photos required. You're not usually asked about onward tickets and funds. Visa available same day upon request.
Bangladesh Consulate, 9 Circus Avenue, Tel. 445208; open Monday-Thursday, 7.30 a.m.-2.00 p.m., Friday 7.30 a.m.-12.00 noon, and Saturday 7.30 a.m.-1.00 p.m. Three passport photos and a 24-hour wait for a 30-day visa. Costs: varies according to nationality.
Thai Consulate, 18-B Mandeville Gardens.
NB: No Burmese Consulate in Calcutta. Visas are available only from New Delhi. If you're going to Kathmandu or Dacca (Bangladesh), you can get a visa there.

MISCELLANEOUS

West Bengal Govt Tourist Bureau, Dalhousie Square, Tel. 238271; open Monday-Saturday 7.00 a.m.-1.30 p.m. and 2.15-6.00 p.m., Sunday 7.00 a.m.-1.00 p.m.

Indian Govt. Tourist Office, 4 Shakespeare Sarani, Tel. 443521/441402; open Monday-Saturday 9.00 a.m.-6.00 p.m., public holidays 9.00 a.m.-1.00 p.m., closed Sunday. There is also a Tourist Counter at Howrah Railway Station and Dum Dum Airport, plus tourist offices of some other Indian States (e.g. Jammu & Kasjmir Tourist Office, 12 Jawaharlal Nehru Road).

Money: Cash and cheques can be changed (at less than favourable rates) from 8.00 a.m.-8.00 p.m., 365 days of the year, at Manick Lal Sen & Son, New Market (Hogg Market).

Entertainment: Wide range of western films (see daily papers). Some nightclubs on fashionable Park Street. Ask at Tourist Office for the latest edition of Calcutta This Fortnight.

Visa extensions: Foreigners' Registration Office, 237 Lower Circular Road.

Camera Repairs: Photo Mart, 26 Jawaharlal Nehru Road (near Sudder Street intersection). Passport photos can be obtained from Foto Shops on Jawaharlal Nehru Road. If needed urgently, try Harico, 3 Jawaharlal Nehru Road. Three photos cost 25 Rs, minimum 1 hour wait.

Daily power failures of several hours duration are common in Calcutta.

Reading rooms: Max Mueller Bhavan, 8 Ballygunge Circular Road, Tel. 479398. British Council Library, 5 Shakespeare Sarani (near Govt India Tourist Office), Tel. 445379, open Tuesday-Friday 10.00 a.m.-6.30 p.m., Saturday 10.00 a.m.-1.00 p.m.

Good bookshops (e.g. Oxford Book Shop and Stationery) on Park Street. Also recommended: Singh Book Stall, Hogg Market (current English dailies available). Newsweek and most Indian papers can be obtained along Jawaharlal Nehru Road. Best local papers are the dailies Amrita Bazar Patrika (45 Ps) and the Hindustan Standard (evening paper, 20 Ps). Two normally available publications on Calcutta: Map of Calcutta & Howrah (3 Rs) and Calcutta Municipal General Guide with Street Directory (also 3 Rs), containing information on city and overland buses, important addresses and an index of alternate street names.

FURTHER TRAVEL

General Notes
Train
Departure point is usually Howrah Railway Station, sometimes Sealdah Station (e.g. for trains to the Bangladesh border). These station can be reached from the Sudder Street area by bus, tram or taxi. For details, see 'Arrival'.

The quota for foreigners (seats held specially for tourists) can be booked from the Eastern Railway Booking Office, 6 Fairlie Place (for trains to Delhi) and from the Suth Eastern Railway Booking Office, Esplanade (for connections with Madras, Bombay etc.).

'You must use the City Booking Office for sleeper reservations. There don't seem to be any sleepers available for tourists at Howrah Station.'

Bus
Reasonable rates for long-distance buses. Departure from Esplanade, within walking distance of Sudder Street.

Plane
Both internal and international flights from Dum Dum Airport, north of Calcutta (for airport connections, see Arrival).

Airlines offer 25% Youth Fare (also known as Student Discount although no Student Card required) to neighbouring countries. The age limit for this discount varies from airline to airline. Argue because they won't want you to go to the opposition. It becomes more difficult if you're over 30: try Thai Airways, which has been known to offer Youth Fares up to 32 years, or Bangladesh Biman, where you're still young up to 35.

Notes: If you're under the age limit and have a Student Card, don't think you're going to get the Youth Fare plus the Student Discount (i.e. 50% off).

If you're looking for a cheap plane ticket, try individual airlines (some addresses below) or Pan Asian Tours, 20 Free School Street (Mirza Galib Street), near the Sudder Street intersection (Tel. 20814).

Don't Forget: There is a departure tax of 50 Rs for flights to neighbouring countries and 100 Rs for other countries. Any remaining Rs can be exchanged for dollars at the airport. The export of Rs is forbidden by law.

Airline addresses:
Indian Airlines, 39 Chittaranjan Avenue, Tel. 260730.
Bangladesh Biman, 1 Park Street, Tel. 212864.
Royal Nepal Airlines, 41 Jawaharlal Nehru Road, Tel. 244434
Union of Burma Airways (UBA), Esplanade East, Tel. 231624.
Thai Airways, 18 Park Street, Tel. 249696

Car Shipping
If you want to ship a car to South-east Asia, consult Everett Private Ltd, 4 Govt Place North, Tel. 236295. Note: No passenger transport, even for the car owner.

From Calcutta to Darjeeling

Note: Overland to Darjeeling (like Calcutta, part of West Bengal) is possible only if you have a permit, obtainable cost and hassle-free from the Foreigners' Registration Office in Delhi, Madras or Calcutta (237 Lower Circular Road). The permit is valid for 7 days and can be extended in Darjeeling for an extra 8 days. No permit is needed if you fly direct to Bagdogra. You can get a 15-day permit at the airport.

Train
Best connection by 43 Darjeeling Mail, departing Sealdah Railway Station at 7.00 pm, arriving New Jalgaiguri at 6.45 am the next morning. Another good connection: depart Howrah 6.55 pm, arriving

New Jalpaiguri 7.25 am (7.30 am in summer). The 165 Janata Express, leaving Howrah at 12.30 pm, is very slow. Jalpaiguri is 566 km by rail from Sealdah.

From New Jalpaiguri to Darjeeling by branch-line (beautiful trip). Departures (according to timetable) 7.10 am (7.25 am in summer) and 9.35 am (9.00 am in summer).

Return: The Darjeeling Mail leaves New Jalpaiguri at 7.15 pm (7.45 pm in summer).

Bus

A bus leaves Esplanade for Siliguri at 8.00 pm, continuing on to Jalpaiguri: 60Rs to Siliguri, reservation (50 Ps) recommended. Arrival in Siliguri, 7.30 am. Return: depart New Jalpaiguri at 7.00 pm.

Plane

Daily flights on Indian Airlines from Calcutta to Bagdogra, approx. 1 hour flying time, 293 Rs.

From Calcutta to Nepal

Train

For the best trip, take the train to Muzaffarpur and then continue to Raxaul and Kathmandu as described under 'From Delhi to Kathmandu'. Two good connections from Howrah: 4.25 pm departure by 21 North Bihar Express, arriving Muzaffarpur the next day at 6.40 am; or by 19 Mithila Express, departing Howrah at 10.00 pm, arriving Muzaffarpur at 12.45 pm (1.15 pm in summer). Muzaffarpur is 587 km by rail.

Plane

The Nepalese capital of Kathmandu can be reached by Thai Airways (3 flights per week), Indian Airlines (at least 1 flight daily except Saturday) and Royal Nepal Airlines (3 flights per week). A Youth Fare (see above) to Kathmandu costs approx. 750 Rs.

Route variations

You can also get from Calcutta to Kathmandu via Darjeeling. There are direct bus connections to Kathmandu from the Nepalese border station at Kakarvitta (pron. -bitta). Bad road.

From Calcutta to the Andaman Islands

A permit is needed for the Andaman Islands and can be obtained from the Ministry of Home Affairs in Delhi. Count on a delay of about 4 weeks. The permit is free and requires you to stay in Port Blair or nearby.

The Nicobar Islands neighbouring the Andamans are completely out-of-bounds to tourists.

Ship

On average they sail fortnightly from Calcutta to Port Blair, capital of the Andamans. Four ships per month in exceptional cases. Fares: Between approx. 100 Rs and 560 Rs.

Plane

Indian Airways flies twice weekly from Calcutta to Port Blair.

From Calcutta to Burma and South-East Asia

Since it is not permitted to enter Burma by road, the farthest east you can go is the Burmese border.

Plane

Including the 25% Youth Fare discount, the flight to Bangkok costs about 1200 Rs. A stopover in Rangoon (Burma) is possible with UBA. At the time of writing Thai Airways no longer flies from Calcutta to Rangoon.

Almost every traveller to Burma makes a bit on the side by purchasing whiskey and cigarettes at the duty free shop before taking off for Rangoon. Both can be sold easily and for a profit soon after arrival. You can take in 200 cigarettes and a quart bottle (1.136 litres) of spirits. Preferred are Benson & Hedges and Johnny Walker, Red Label.

Car Shipping

Approx. once per month to Bangkok. Total costs are based on $40.1/cubic metre, plus 78.9% of the overall cubic metre cost.

Penang or Singapore: No price difference between the two cities: $31.2/cubic metre, plus 78.9% of the overall cubic metre cost. The Everett Line (see above) offers tourists a discount of 10-15%.

Other Connections from Calcutta

See also the information given under 'Calcutta/Further Travel–General Information'.

Train

To Delhi: Depart Howrah at 9.50 a.m. (10.10 a.m. in summer) by 7 Toofan Express, arriving New Delhi the next day at 6.10 p.m. (7.25 p.m. in summer), and in Old Delhi at 6.40 p.m. (7.55 p.m. in summer). This train goes via Agra.

Daily except Monday and Friday by A.C. Express from Howrah at 9.55 a.m., arriving New Delhi the next morning at 9.35 a.m..

Depart Howrah at 5.00 p.m. by 101 Rajdhani Express (Monday and Friday only), arriving New Delhi at 9.30 a.m. (10.40 a.m. in summer).

Depart Howrah at 9.00 p.m. by 11 Delhi Express, arriving Old Delhi two days later at 5.05 a.m.

Depart Howrah at 9.10 p.m. by 39 Delhi Janata Express, arriving Old Delhi (according to the timetable) at 8.35 a.m. (8.40 a.m. in summer) two days later.

Depart Sealdah Station at 8.45 p.m. (8.20 p.m. in summer), arriving Old Delhi at 10.40 a.m. (10.30 a.m. in summer) two days later. Some trains go via Benares (Varanasi). New Delhi is 1445 km away by rail.

To Jammu Tawi or Amritsar (both via Benares): Depart Howrah at 5.45

a.m. by 173 Himagari Express (Wednesday and Sunday only), arriving Jammu Tawi at 11.10 a.m. the next day. Depart Sealdah at 11.45 a.m. by 51 Jammu Tawi Express, arriving the next day at 7.45 a.m.. Depart Howrah at 8 pm by 5 Amritsar Mail, arriving Amritsar at 8.55 a.m. two days later. Depart Howrah at 1.30 p.m. (2.20 p.m. in summer) by Amritsar Express, arriving in Amritsar at 10.45 a.m. two days later. The journey to Amritsar covers 1829 km and to Jammu, 1967.

To Bombay: Depart Howrah at 8.55 p.m. (2 Bombay Mail), 1.00 p.m. (30 Bombay Express) and 4.15 p.m. (60 Gitanjali Express, Monday, Wednesday, Friday and Saturday only). Departure approx. 10-15 minutes earlier in summer. Bombay's Victoria Terminus is 1968 km away; minimum travelling time approx. 30 hours (60 Gitjali Express). Two further connections over a somewhat longer route (via Allahabad): Depart Howrah at 10.55 a.m. (64/72 Janata Express, Monday, Wednesday and Friday only) and 7.30 p.m. (3 Bombay Mail). Arrive Bombay Victoria Terminus two days later at 1.40 p.m. or 11.20 a.m. (3 Bombay Mail), 2178 km away. If you want to visit Varanasi, get off before Varanasi at Mughalsarai.

To Madras: best connection by 141 Coromandel Express, departing Howrah at 5.40 p.m., arriving Madras Central the next day at 6.50 p.m.

Bus
Attractive fares from Calcutta only on overland buses. As well as Siliguri (see 'From Calcutta to Darjeeling') there are connections to Cuttack, Puri and Ranchi.

Plane
For information on internal flights, see 'India General/Flights'.

Excursions from Calcutta to Bangladesh
Overland
Train from Calcutta-Sealdah to Bangaon, 2.5 hours, approx. 3.5 Rs 2nd class. Connections between 4.35 a.m. and 11.55 p.m. From Bangaon by rickshaw (approx. 30 mins, 7 Rs) to the Bangladesh border (visa must be obtained before trip). Border formalities are mostly uncomplicated. Then on by bus (approx. 3 Takas) or by communal taxi to Jessore, where you can stay the night.

From Jessore by plane to Dacca, the capital of Bangladesh. The bus trip lasts one whole day with boat crossings of branches of the Ganges at several points. Most impressive spectacle: the crossing of the joining of the main arm of the Ganges with the Brahmaputra, another huge river. You may see Ganges dolphins during the crossing. A connecting bus waits on the other side to take you to Dacca.

Plane
The flight from Calcutta to Dacca by Bangladesh Biman costs 302 Rs, or 25% cheaper with Youth Fare.

DACCA

Capital city of Bangladesh, 2 million inhabitants.

ARRIVAL/ACCOMMODATION

Bus
There are some cheap hotels within walking distance of the bus terminus. The YMCA is not among them.

Plane
12 Takas from Dacca Airport to the city by Biman bus, city bus 3 T, scooter 15 T, taxi 50 T; don't go into the city if you want the YMCA—get out halfway.

YMCA, New Eskaton Road, the best-known backpacker rendezvous in Dacca; dormitory 25 T, doubles also available.

BANGLADESH AND DACCA—GENERAL

The currency unit is the Taka. One dollar equals approx. 17 T (approx. 20 T for cash on the blackmarket).

Tourist Offices are located at Dacca Airport and at the Intercontinental Hotel.

Bangladesh is virgin country for tourists and opinions on the country vary enormously. Whereas some say 'never again', others find it the most pleasant country of their trip. At the very least, it is, and will remain, an experiment.

Anyone who wants to get to know Bangladesh should of course not restrict themselves to Dacca. Also worth a look are the Bhawal National Park to the north of Dacca and Cox's Bazar, the world's longest beach (75 miles).

Food: similar to India but with more meat (the population are Moslems). Hard times for vegetarians . . . The YMCA cafeteria is not particularly good. Instead, try one of the nearby restaurants.

SIGHTSEEING

Most of Dacca is modern; not much to see there.

Beautiful and rewarding: a wander in the old city at Buriganga, swarming with antiquated barges and steamers. You can go by motor rickshaw to the harbour at Buriganga, where innumerable oarsmen wait with their boats for customers, offering 1-hour sightseeing trips on the Buriganga itself. As with rickshaw drivers, haggle over the price.

Other attractions: Lalbagh Fort, Chowk Bazaar, Star Mosque and Baitul Mukarram Mosque.

Remember: It is impossible to reach South-east Asia overland from India or Bangladesh. Burma, which can only be entered by plane, is the spanner in the works.

Bus
Back to India: see 'Arrival/Overland' (just reverse everything).

Ship
Some places in Sunderbans (the Ganges delta and kingdom of the Bengal tiger) can be reached by ship. Enquire at the Tourist Office in Dacca.

Plane
For journeys to India and transport to the airport, see 'Arrival/Plane'. Don't forget to pay the 50 T departure tax for neighbouring countries. If you're flying on to Rangoon: buy cigarettes and whiskey in the duty free shop. Unfortunately the duty free shop at Dacca Airport is only poorly stocked and is regularly closed for inexplicable reasons.

INDEX